Anonymous

A Complete History of the Origin and Progress of the Late War

from its commencement, to the exchange of the ratifications of peace, between

Great-Britain, France, and Spain on the 10th of February, 1763 - Vol. 2

Anonymous

A Complete History of the Origin and Progress of the Late War
from its commencement, to the exchange of the ratifications of peace, between Great-Britain, France, and Spain on the 10th of February, 1763 - Vol. 2

ISBN/EAN: 9783337224769

Printed in Europe, USA, Canada, Australia, Japan

Cover: Foto ©ninafisch / pixelio.de

More available books at **www.hansebooks.com**

A COMPLETE
HISTORY
OF THE
ORIGIN and PROGRESS
OF THE
LATE WAR,
From its Commencement,
TO THE
Exchange of the Ratifications of Peace,
BETWEEN
GREAT-BRITAIN, FRANCE, and SPAIN:
On the 10th of FEBRUARY, 1763.
AND TO THE
Signing of the Treaty at HUBERTSBERG,
BETWEEN
The King of PRUSSIA, the EMPRESS-QUEEN, and the Elector of SAXONY,
On the 15th of the fame Month.
IN WHICH,
All the BATTLES, SIEGES, SEA-ENGAGEMENTS, and every other Transaction worthy of public Attention, are faithfully recorded; with political and military Observations.

VOL. II.

LONDON:
Printed for J. KNOX, near Southampton Street, in the Strand.
MDCCLXIV.

A HISTORY OF THE WAR.

CHAP. XIX.

Duke Ferdinand opens the campaign. D'Arberg driven out of the landgraviate. Battle of Bergen. Gottingen, Munden, Lipstadt, Ritberg, Munster, and Minden, surrender to the french. Affairs of the king of Prussia. Woberfnow's expedition into Poland. Russian magazines destroyed. Prince Henry's irruption into Bohemia. Austrian magazines destroyed. General Maguire defeated.

I Before mentioned the formidable chain, which the winter quarters of the french, imperial, and austrian armies, composed at the end of the last campaign. The possession of Frankfort, which the french had seized last year, in open violation of the liberties of the empire, gave them the command of the Rhine and Main; by which they might receive reinforcements and supplies. Prince Ferdinand, therefore, resolved to dislodge them. The latter end of february, the army of the empire having extended themselves into Heffe, his serene highnefs detached general Urff towards Vacha, with four battalions, and about 1000 dragoons, huffars, &c. This detachment falling unexpectedly, in the night between the 1ft and 2d, upon the enemy's quarters, fome of them were taken, and the reft retired in the utmoft confufion. Hirfchfeld, Vacha, and all the heffian bailiwicks, which the enemy poffeffed, were immediately evacuated; but the hanoverians were obliged in their turn to retire. The hereditary prince leading a large body of troops thro' ways deemed impaffable, on the 31ft of march, furprifed a regiment of curiaffiers, and a battalion of Wurtemburgers, moft of whom he killed or made prifoners. The next day he marched, with fome light troops, and two battalions of grenadiers, to Meinungen, where he found a confiderable magazine, and took two battalions prifoners of war. Another battalion pofted at Wafungen alfo furrendered to him, after he had defeated d'Arberg, who was coming to its relief. The 2d, the duke of Holftein alfo diflodged the french from Freyenfteinau, making a captain with his company prifoners of war. All the enemy's parties on this fide retired, on thefe fucceffes, towards Bamberg. The duke de Broglio, who commanded the french army on the Maine, alarmed at them, took an advantageous poft near Bergen, a little town between Franckfort and Hannau, which it was neceffary that the allies fhould pafs, before they could penetrate to his line.

Duke Ferdinand, to poffefs himfelf of Franckfort, drew his troops together from their quarters in Weftphalia, on the Lippe, and in Heffe; he left 10 or 12,000 men to guard the electorate, and the bifhopric of Munfter; and having collected about 30,000 more at Fulde, he marched from thence the 10th of march, and on the 12th arrived at Windeken, by Freyenfteinau and Budingen, and the next morning early, he marched towards Bergen, refolving to attack the duke of Broglio, who was ftrongly pofted there. He had
the

the right of his army towards Bergen; and had secured his flanks and center in such a manner, that the prince was obliged to make his attack by that village. The allied army arrived opposite to that of the french, at nine o'clock in the morning, of the 13th of april; and the grenadiers of prince Ferdinand's advanced guards immediately began the attack upon Bergen with great intrepidity, and were received with a very severe fire, which the enemy had prepared for them; and though they were supported by a reinforcement of several battalions, under prince Isenburg's command, they were yet repulsed; they rallied again, upon being supported by the hessian horse, but were forced to retreat in some disorder; a third attack was made with the like bad success. Duke Ferdinand then finding that the enemy were too numerous, and too strongly posted to be attacked any more with success, began to think of a retreat, whilst his loss was yet inconsiderable, and the disorder of his men easily to be repaired. But to retreat in the face of a victorious enemy, is always very hazardous; and the day was not as yet above half spent. In this exigence, he separated his infantry into two bodies, one on the right and the other on the left, forming his cavalry in the center, and a small column of infantry before it; bringing up, at the same time, his artillery, to play against Bergen, on the enemy's right, and the wood on their left. These dispositions convinced the duke of Broglio, that he designed, at the same time, to attack both the village and the wood; and, if one of these attacks should succeed, afterwards to fall on the center of the french; this being the expectation of the french general, he returned the furious cannonade of the prince, as briskly as he could. But he was much deceived in his opinion; and, as he expected a lively attack every moment, he kept close to his post; and in this posture things continued until night came on, when the prince made an easy retreat, without disorder or molestation, and halted at Windeken. He did not lose above 2000 men in the action; that of the french was by no means less considerable. Had he gained the victory, his reputation could not have been greater; the retreat he made, which was planned and executed with equal skill, did him great honour; nor was his conduct during the action less conspicuous. But in its consequences, this battle was very different; the prince missed the blow he intended; and Broglio still kept Franckfort, receiving all the reinforcements that were sent him without molestation, besides the many other advantages which he drew from the possession of that city.

Duke Ferdinand left Windekin the 15th, and retreated to Fulde; finding that he should not be able to maintain his ground in Hesse, he resolved to make his retreat by the Weser, well knowing the great consequence of the communication by that river. About the middle of may the french armies, on the Upper and Lower Rhine assembled, and began to move towards one another; and the 3d of june, they joined near Marpourg, from whence they marched northward, and on the 10th arrived at Corbach, where marshal Contades took up his head quarters; and the next day, some of their light troops took possession of Cassel, without opposition; general Inhoff, with the troops under his command, who were there, having retired towards Paderborn.

During this uninterrupted progress of the french, duke Ferdinand continued to retreat along the Weser; the principal design of the french seemed to be to cut off his retreat to that river, but they were not able to effect it; he threw garrisons into Lipstadt, Ritberg, Munster, and Minden, in order to retard their progress; but all his precautions proved ineffectual: marshal Contades encamped the 12th, at Stadtberg; and the duke of Broglio, who commanded his right wing, marched from Cassel into the territories of Hanover,

nover, where he took poffeffion of Munden and Gottingen. During thefe marches of the french, the allied army only moved to Lipftadt, and encamped near Soeft and Werle. The 17th of June, the head quarters were at Erdberenberg, the army occupying the heights of Buren, as the french did thofe of Effen and Meerhoff. From Buren, duke Ferdinand retreated to Ritberg, and from thence to Marienfeld, the 30th. And Contades encamped between Lipfpring and Oeftlangen. The 3d of July, the allies were at Driefen, between Ofnabrug and Minden; where they were joined by general Wangenheim, with a body of hanoverians, under his command, that had been left in the ftrong camp at Dulmen, from whence he retreated under the cannon of Munfter, and then joined the army. Duke Ferdinand continued his retreat, by Bromte, Baden, Stoltznau, Nyenburg, and at laft fixed his quarters in an advantageous camp at Peterfhagen.

In the mean time, the french continued their progrefs. Ritberg was furprifed, Lipftadt continued blockaded. The duke de Broglio took Minden by affault, with a garrifon of 1500 men, where he found immenfe magazines. Monf. d'Armentiers advanced againft Munfter, and attempted to take it by a coup de main; but was difappointed. But getting a train of artillery from Wefel, after a fhort fiege made himfelf mafter of the city; the garrifon of 4000 men becoming prifoners of war. After this rapid fuccefs, the main body of their army took an advantageous camp near Minden, where they remained fome time, and where I fhall leave them for the prefent. It is now time to fee what were the events of war in other quarters.

His pruffian majefty's affairs at the beginning of the campaign, wore a very promifing appearance; but yet his numerous enemies were all preparing to renew their attacks on him. He had formed a fcheme to keep the ruffians back, by burning their magazines in Poland. This plan was executed with great spirit by general Woberfnow, who marched the 23d of february, from Glogau in Silesia, with 46 squadrons and 26 battalions, entering Poland, by the way of Lissa, he marched directly to Posna; where he defeated a body of 2000 cossacks, who guarded a magazine there, which contained such an immense quantity of flour, that it was sufficient to have maintained 50,000 men for three months. He carried off and destroyed several other vast magazines of the russians; and having fully executed his commission, returned without loss into Silesia, on the 18th of april.

His prussian majesty finding that general Woberfnow had met with success, formed a second plan still more important. He was in hopes that the russians would not be able to attack his dominions, till late in the campaign, nor act in concert with marshal Daun. As he imagined he had cut the austrians off from that assistance, he wanted to do the same in regard to the army of the empire and the french, as the austrians, by being separated from their allies, would be obliged to act against the king under great disadvantages. Pursuant to this admirable scheme, about the latter end of february, general Knobloch was detached from the prussian army in Saxony, to drive some corps of the army of the empire from Erfurth, Gotha, and Eisenach, who, if they remained there, would be able from their situation, to take advantage of the absence of those troops that were to be employed in executing this plan. The three cities were taken without opposition, the imperialists were drove from all that part of the country, and heavy contributions raised in the neighbourhood.

During these operations, the king himself with the grand army, which was posted in Lusatia, made several movements, with design to draw marshal Daun's army towards Silesia, and by that means to uncover the frontiers of Bohemia towards Saxony; the

the auſtrians acted juſt as he expected. Prince Henry, who commanded the pruſſian army in Saxony, of about 36,000 men, immediately laid hold of the opportunity, as he had before concerted with the king, and dividing his army into two columns, marched towards Bohemia, entering that kingdom himſelf at Peterſwalde, the 15th of april; the column under general Hulſen doing the ſame by Paſsberg and Commota. Prince Henry found an eminence beyond Peterſwalde, fortified with a redoubt, and a ſtrong barricade before it, guarded by 600 croats, and ſome hungarian foot. This paſs was forced; and the vanguard dividing into two bodies, one proceeded to Auſſig, and the other to Toplitz: the enemy fled precipitately every where. The magazine of Auſſig was deſtroyed, and the boats of the Elbe burnt. The vanguard returned on the 16th to the main body at Welmina. The magazines at Lowoſitz and Leitmeritz were ſeized, and the new bridge that was built there, burnt. Prince Henry from thence marched to Budin, where he deſtroyed another magazine; and the flames ſpreading by accident, ſet the town on fire, and did ſome damage.

In the mean time, general Hulſen found the paſs of Paſsberg ſtrongly guarded by two regiments of foot, and a large body of croats. The general conducted his cavalry another way, ſo as to fall directly on the rear of the auſtrians, while he attacked them with his infantry in front; which was executed ſo ſuccefsfully, that the auſtrians were driven from all their intrenchments, and a general, 51 officers, and 2000 men were taken priſoners, together with three colours, two ſtandards, and three pieces of cannon. General Hulſen marched directly to Saatz; but the auſtrians had burnt their magazines there, before he arrived; but he took and deſtroyed ſeveral others.

others*. Prince Henry, with both the divisions of the army returned to Saxony, the middle of april.

The prince gave his troops but a few days rest about Dresden; for on the 26th he marched them to Obel-Geburgen; from thence he continued his march through Voightland, towards the army of the empire; and on the 7th of may entered Franconia, by the way of Hoff. Next day a detachment from his army attacked general Macguire, who commanded a body of austrians and imperialists at Aseh; which bravely withstood all their efforts the whole day; but as he was in danger of being overpowered by numbers, and having no prospect of relief, he retired in the night through Hassau towards Egra. During this time, general Haddick, who commanded a body of austrians in Franconia, that acted in conjunction with the army of the empire, quitted the camp which he

* Magazines taken and destroyed by the prussians in this expedition.

	Tons of meal.	Loaves of bread, each four pound.	Berlin measures of oats.	Rations of hay, eight pound each.
Auffig,	700		200	1000
Toplitz,	60		2000	
Lowositz,	450			
Leitmeritz			3000	2000
Luckowitz,		36000		
Liboschowitz,			10000	
Worwitzaw,	1000	30000		
Budin,	1000		100000	20000
Saatz,	32000		20000	60000
Postleburg,	50			
Commotau,	205	4000	700	1375
Brix	21	3400	920	192
	35486	34700	136820	863000

All these magazines were valued at upwards of 880,000 rixdollars. The contributions were divided amongst the troops; every field officer received an hundred rixdollars; every subaltern fifty; every serjeant twenty; and all the private men a rixdollar a-piece; exclusive of all they had helped themselves to before.

held

held near Menchfberg, and marched in the night between the 8th and 9th to Culmbach, where he arrived the 10th in the morning; his troops were hardly encamped, when he again filed off towards Bamberg. The prince purfued him very expeditioufly; he was at Murichberg the 10th, and the next day in the neighbourhood of Bareith Cronach; and Rotenburg furrendered after a fhort bombardment. On his approach near Bamberg, that city furrendered on terms; but fome confufion happening before the capitulation was completely finifhed, a party of croats fired upon a party of pruffians, who had approached near one of the gates; this was refented by the prince, as a breach of the capitulation; and under that pretence gave up the city to be plundered by his troops; they pillaged during the fpace of two days, in a very unrelenting and licentious manner; loud complaints were made all over Europe againft the pruffians, with great juftice, on account of this affair; and afterwards produced a fevere retaliation. The army of the empire, unable to ftop the progrefs of the prince, retired to Nuremberg, and left the greateft part of the circle of Franconia to the contributions inflicted by the pruffians; they would have been followed, had not the prince been informed, that a large body of auftrians, under general Gemmingen had entered Saxony; this intelligence obliged him to return into that country, and accordingly he began his march from Bamberg the 21ft of june.

On his retreat, the imperialifts fent a detachment under count Palfy, to harrafs his rear, who came up with it on the 30th, near Hoff; a fmart engagement enfued, in which the imperialifts were intirely defeated, with the lofs of a general, and a good number of men, either killed or taken prifoners. On the return of prince Henry to his old poft in Saxony, Gemmingen retired into Bohemia.

CHAP.

CHAP. XX.

Motions of the russians. Count Dohna takes the command of the prussian troops against them. Advances into Poland. Retires. Is disgraced. General Wedel succeeds him in the command. Battle of Zullichau. Motions of the king of Prussia and marshal Daun. General Laudohn joins count Soltikoff. King of Prussia joins general Wedel. Battle of Cunnersdorf. Austrian and russian armies join. Admirable conduct of the king of Prussia.

Although general Wobersnow had been so successful in destroying the magazines which the russians had amassed in Poland, yet his prussian majesty found he should have that enemy to deal with sooner than he expected. Having left their camp at Posna, and quitting the Vistula, they drew near to the banks of the Oder. General Manteuffel had been some time posted at Grypswalden, in Pomerania, and general Schlaberndorf at Koninswalde, to oppose them: the king also sent orders to count Dohna, who had been employed in reducing and levying contributions and levies in Mecklingberg, to march, and take the command of his troops who were destined to act against them; and he accordingly encamped with them near Custrin. The enemy began the campaign in their usual manner, by ravaging without pity the frontiers of Pomerania, Brandenburg and Silesia. As it was impossible to cover every part of such an extensive tract of country, the cossacks made inroads in different parts, where they were sure of meeting with no resistance. A body of prussian troops

under

under general Hulfen, and another under general Woberfnow, joined count Dohna's army the 26th, at Meferitz, in Poland. During his ſtay at this place, that general publiſhed a declaration, ſetting forth the reaſons that induced his maſter to cauſe his troops to enter Poland; alſo requiring the neighbouring country to furniſh proviſions and forage for an army of 40,000 men, promiſing that every thing ſhould be paid for with ready money. He encamped the ſame day at Scheverin; but as he was obliged to march with caution, and having many ſkirmiſhes with the enemy's irregulars, he did not reach Poſna till the 3d inſtant, when he arrived in ſight of it and the ruſſian army. But the count found their numbers were too conſiderable, and their poſts too ſtrong to be attacked with any proſpect of advantage, ſo that he contented himſelf with obſerving their motions; and, as they ſoon continued their march towards Sileſia, he conſtantly endeavoured to harraſs their rear; but finding that his proviſions failed, he was obliged to retreat towards the Oder, encamping near Zullichau in Sileſia, and the ruſſians doing the ſame between Langemeil and Schmellan.

In the mean time, the king of Pruſſia was far from being contented with the conduct of count Dohna: it was more dilatory and timid than the inclinations of his majeſty could bear; and he is ſaid to have reproached that general in ſo ſevere a manner for his conduct, (which many have thought was very juſtifiable) that he took the firſt opportunity to reſign his command, and under a pretence of recovering his health, retired to Berlin. The king immediately appointed lieutenant general Wedel to ſucceed him, and detached to his army ſome conſiderable reinforcements, giving him poſitive orders to engage the ruſſians at all events.

The new general arrived at the pruſſian camp at Zullichau, on the 22d; and finding the next day, that the

the enemy were directing their march towards Crossen in Silesia, with design to get before his army, and by that means secure the passage of the Oder; he resolved in consequence of his master's orders, to attack them on their march. Nothing could be more advantageous than their situation; they were posted on high and almost inaccessible eminences, defended by a vast artillery, and were 70,000 strong. Wedel's army did not amount to 30,000 men; and the disadvantages they had to struggle with were excessive. They had a bridge to pass, and such a narrow defile to go through, that scarce a third of a battalion could march in front; the ground was such, that their cavalry could not support the infantry, nor their artillery be of any great service to them. All these difficulties proved but spurs to the ardor of the prussians, the attack was resolutely made, but after the greatest efforts numbers at last prevailed. General Wedel was obliged to retreat, which he did unpursued, leaving upwards of 4000 men killed or prisoners; his wounded amounting to 3000. General Wobersnow was killed, and general Manteuffel wounded. Wedel passed the Oder without opposition, and the russians made themselves masters of Francfort on the Oder, and Crossen.

In the mean time, his majesty the king of Prussia had, about the middle of april marched his army from Rhonstock, near Strigau, to Bolchenhayn, a small town in the mountains near Landshut, where he entrenched it. Marshal Daun had collected the austrian troops in a camp a Schurtz, in the circle of Konigsgratz; about the middle of may, he detached a considerable body of troops into Lusatia, which by forced marches arrived at Spremberg, within 15 miles of Berlin, with design to surprise that city; but some prussian battalions, supported by a large body of cavalry, followed them with the greatest secrecy. The austrians perceiving their design to be discovered, changed their rout, and fell back on Liebau, the small garrison
having

having retired on their approach towards the pruſſian camp. On the firſt notice which the king had of the affair, he immediately ordered his troops to march, and went himſelf to the place of the attack. The auſtrians ſeeing the good countenance of the pruſſian troops, thought proper to retire after a ſlight ſkirmiſh, and were purſued by the pruſſians, till the darkneſs of the night and the danger of the defiles obliged them to deſiſt.

General Fouquet, who commanded a large body of pruſſian troops, in the ſouth part of Sileſia, and the auſtrian general de Ville, who commanded on the frontiers of Moravia, made ſeveral marches and countermarches, each endeavouring to catch ſome advantage of the other. About the middle of april, Fouquet made himſelf maſter of Sacorndorff and Troppau; and endeavoured to do the ſame with the auſtrian magazine, at Hoff in Moravia; but finding it impracticable, he retired to his former poſt at Lobſchutz, in order to cover Neiſs. The king left his camp at Landſhut the 29th, and arrived at Neiſs the ſame day. General de la Ville was poſted on the heights behind Neuſtadt, and decamped that evening, placing himſelf behind Ziegennals and Zugmantel. The king having joined general Fouquet, marched againſt de Ville; but as he retired, nothing further was done in Moravia, ſo his majeſty returned to Landſhut. Marſhal Daun's quarters were changed from time to time to Gitſchin, Konigſhoff, and Jaromirs.

That general having remained inactive in his camp at Schurtz ſo long, on account of the ſlow progreſs of the ruſſians; formed a deſign to march round by Luſatia, and the moſt northern part of Sileſia, and join them as ſoon as they had advanced far enough. It was in conſequence of this plan, that he left his camp the 28th of june, and marched by Neudorf, Lomnitz, Turnau, and Reichenburg, from whence

whence he turned off to the Queiss, which separates Lusatia from Silesia. His prussian majesty, as soon as he had notice of this march, left his camp at Landshut, and entered Bohemia, making himself master of Schatzlar, without much resistance. On the 30th, he detached general Rebentish to occupy Trautenau; and general Seidlitz towards Hirschberg, to secure the passes, in case the austrians should attempt to enter Silesia that way. These precautions had the desired effect, for on the 16th of july general Laudohn entered Grieffenberg, with a large body of pandours and croats, and would have pushed to Hirschberg; but finding general Seidlitz there before him, with the van-guard of the prussian army, he was obliged to return back with all expedition. The king marched the same day by that place to Lahne; on the 10th, his army was at Geppersdorff; and soon after chose a strong camp on the heights before the village of Schmotfieffen: the situation of this camp was very advantageous, both the flanks being well covered; its left was towards Liebenthal, and behind its right stood Loewenberg. Marshal Daun's head quarters were at Gorlitz-Heim in Lusatia, and his army was posted on the heights behind the Queiss, his right extending towards Grieffenberg, and the left towards Lauban. The two armies were in this situation, when his prussian majesty was informed of the defeat of his troops under general Wedel.

Marshal Daun being acquainted with the success of that action, immediately foresaw, that the king would march himself against count Soltikoff; and considering that the great want of the russian army, was a good body of cavalry; a want that had been so fatal to the common cause, last year at Zorndorff: he determined to detach a numerous corps to reinforce them. With this view, he selected about 12,000 of his horse and 8000 foot, which he divided into two columns, placing one under general Laudohn, who com-

commanded in chief, and the other under general Haddick; the firſt marched through Sileſia, and the other through Luſatia. General Wedel, for ſome time found means to prevent the deſigned junction by marching to Plauen, oppoſite to Croſſen. The king, informed of this march, had, in the mean time, ordered a part of the troops which were under the command of prince Henry, to advance; and having appointed his royal highneſs to the command of the army oppoſed to marſhal Daun, his majeſty put himſelf at the head of the abovementioned reinforcement, amounting to 10,000 men; and marched on the 1ſt of auguſt from Chriſtianſtadt to Sommerfeldt, from whence the corps under general Haddick retired on his approach. The pruſſians however came up, on the ſame day, with the rear guard of the auſtrians, and attacked it, making a conſiderable booty. Several other ſkirmiſhes happened, in which the pruſſians made near 2000 priſoners. On the 3d, general Wedel's army was at Croſſen, which place he had retaken from the ruſſians; and the king arrived the ſame day at Beſko, and on the 4th joined Wedel at Muhlroſe; but he was not able to hinder the two auſtrian generals from joining the ruſſians, which they effected about the ſame time. His majeſty ſtill finding himſelf too weak to hazard an engagement with the enemy, recalled the corps of of 9000 men under general Finck, which had been detached to cover Saxony; and it joined his army at Lebus on the 8th.

The reinforcement of auſtrians, under general Laudohn, increaſed Soltikoff's army to 90,000 men. That of the pruſſians, after general Finck had joined it, did not amount to 50,000. The ruſſians had moreover intrenched themſelves in the ſtrongeſt manner, between Francfort and Cunnerſdorff; and were defended with ſuch an immenſe artillery, that an attack on them was exceſſively difficult. Yet ſeveral reaſons concurred, which made it abſolutely neceſſary that the king should fight them. They were encamped in Silesia, the best and richest part of his dominions, which would very soon be over-run, if he deferred an action. Marshal Daun had detached several considerable parties that threatened Berlin itself. Saxony undefended, was become a prey to the imperialists, who made great progress. In short, all his dominions were in danger, and nothing could rescue them but a victory.

His majesty passed the Oder on the 11th, a mile to the north of Custrin. The passage being completed, the army formed in order of battle, near the village of Escher, and pursued its march to Bischoffsee. The reserve, under lieut. gen. Finck, took post on the eminences, between that place and Trettin. The van-guard occupied the first of those villages, behind which, the army pitched its camp. On the 12th, at two in the morning, it began its march towards Reppin, but halted in a wood, and there formed, and afterwards advanced to the russians, keeping back the left wing. As soon as the van-guard arrived at the eminence, which was opposite to the enemy's left, the king ordered several batteries to be erected, which, as well as some others raised by general Finck, poured destruction on the russians for some time; the fire began about eleven in the morning. The king designed to make his greatest efforts against the left wing of the enemy; the cannonade no sooner ceased, than he attacked it with several detachments of infantry, disposed in columns. Never did any troops exert themselves with more bravery, than the prussians on this occasion. In spite of the formidable artillery of the russians, which lined their almost impenetrable intrenchments, they attacked them, and forced them one after another, taking eighty pieces of cannon. They then passed a defile, and attacked several redoubts, which covered the village of Cunnersdorff, and mastered

stered them all. The russians made a stand at that village, by bringing on several fresh battalions to defend it; but nothing could withstand the resolution of the prussians, they every where drove the enemy before them, with the greatest firmness, and as terrible a slaughter; they no longer occupied the same ground, as when they began the action. In short, for upwards of six hours, the advantage of the day was entirely on the side of the prussians, who had slain upwards of 10,000 of the enemy. The king then wrote a billet to the queen, to this effect, "Madam, "We have drove the russians from their intrenchments, "and have taken a vast artillery. You may soon "expect to hear of a glorious victory." This news arrived at Berlin just as the post was going out, so that the friends of the king of Prussia throughout Europe, exulted in the certain and decisive victory which they made not the least doubt of his having gained.

Count Soltikoff, in the mean time, finding himself defeated in almost every quarter, resolved to make his last stand on his left wing, which, though much shattered, was more entire than any other part of his army. He accordingly assembled the remains of his right wing, and drawing off the whole second line of his center, divided them both into small corps, or large battalions, formed in long squares or columns; and with these supported the flank of his left. He had before erected a redoubt on that wing, on an advantageous eminence, called, the Jew's burying ground; round this redoubt, the count drew up a great body of his troops, his forlorn hope. Had the king of Prussia desisted, without attempting any thing further against the enemy, he would in all probability have had every advantage of a complete victory; but he resolved to drive them from this post; difficult as the attack must be, to troops who had fought for six hours, in an excessive hot day.

The prussian infantry, ever resolute, was easily brought on to this fresh attack. But here they met with obstacles of the severest kind. The unevenness of the ground rendered it impossible for them to bring up any other artillery than a few small pieces; whereas the enemy had still a great train mounted on their intrenchments; in a situation really impregnable. Under these great disadvantages, the king's infantry were repulsed with a considerable loss; a second attack was made, with the like bad success, and a still greater loss. At last the cavalry were brought against the russians; they redoubled their furious attacks; but all was unsuccessful. Count Soltikoff seeing the prussian horse in some confusion, seized the critical moment, and let loose part of the russian, and all the austrian cavalry, which had not yet been engaged, on the weakened squadrons of the prussians. This fresh body, which was commanded by general Laudohn, met with little resistance, they broke their enemy's horse to pieces, forced them back upon their foot, threw the whole into an irreparable disorder, and a most dreadful slaughter ensued. This miserable misfortune was greatly owing to general Seidlitz's being wounded, who commanded the prussian horse, so that he was disabled from giving any orders. The king made every effort to restore the field, that skill, courage, or despair could dictate; hazarding his own person in the thickest of the fire, and prodigal of life, he thrice led on his troops to the charge; two horses were killed under him; and several balls were in his cloaths; but all was unsuccessful. Scarce an officer in his army escaped unwounded. It is very probable that the destruction of the whole prussian army would have followed, had not night came on; which enabled the king to take possession of some eminences which were easily defended, and by that

that means, to cover the retreat of his troops. As it was, his lofs in this battle was much greater, than any he had fuftained fince the beginning of the war. The killed, wounded, prifoners, and deferters amounting to 20,000. General Putkammur was amongft the flain. The generals Seidlitz, Wedel, Finck, Hulfen, and Itzenplitz, the prince of Wurtenberg, and five major generals, were all wounded. The lofs of the ruffians was generally calculated at about 12,000 men killed and wounded.

Such was the fatal reverfe of the king of Pruffia's fortune; from being almoft fure of the victory, to have it fnatched from him, through his own imprudence. Ever fince the beginning of the war, he had never committed fo fatal a miftake. Had he defifted, when he had driven the ruffians from their intrenchments, without throwing all into the hands of fortune a fecond time, he would have had all the advantages of a victory; his troops had fuffered but little, whereas the enemy had fuftained a great lofs, both in the number of the flain, and in that of half their artillery; little doubt was made, but that they would retire immediately into Poland, leaving him the fruits of the victory, whilft they would be filling their gazettes with frivolous difputes about the field of battle, as was the cafe at Zorndorff. Inftead of acting thus, the king led on his brave troops, who had been fighting fo long a time in one of the fevereft actions, perhaps ever known, and in one of the hotteft days ever felt, againft a poft of fuch immenfe ftrength, lined with a numerous artillery, and defended by an army ftill fo much fuperior in numbers to his own, when his troops were too much exhaufted for a new attempt. All the pruffian generals were unanimous in their advice to the king, not to engage a fecond time; the above reafons, which they gave him, for a few moments had fome effect; but the rapidity and vehemence of his difpofition, would

not

not suffer him to bear the thoughts of being a conqueror by halves: he determined to risk one effort more, which, if successful, would, in all probability, free him for ever from this dreadful adversary. He tried it, and was defeated.

He no sooner quitted the field, than he wrote a second note to the queen, " I have hazarded another attempt, in which I have failed; remove from Berlin, with the royal family. Let the archives be carried to Potzdam. The city may make conditions with the enemy." I leave the reader to judge the effect this news had on the court and city, which was received in the midst of the joy and diversions, occasioned by that which came but a few hours before. And what heightened the terror was, the confused accounts they continued to receive, which made no mention of the king; but informed them, that an army of russians, the most dreadful of all enemies, was on the point of taking possession of their city. It was directly concluded, that the king was either dead or taken prisoner.

The day after the battle, his majesty repassed the Oder, and encamped at Retwein; from whence he marched to Fustenwalde; placing his troops in such a manner, as to protect Berlin from any incursions of the russians. Here he received supplies of provisions, ammunition, and cannon, from his stores at that city; and was reinforced by general Kleist, whom he recalled from Pomerania, with 5000 men. In short, every thing was soon in the greatest order in his camp.

In the mean time the russian general, count Soltikoff, instead of marching into Brandenburg, as was expected, moved further into Silesia, and joined a large body of the austrian army, under marshal Daun. The two generals at this meeting, consulted about the most proper measure for insuring their late success; by their motions, the king was convinced, that their design was to besiege great Glogau. Never did
the

the greatness of this monarch's genius appear with clearer advantage, than in his exquisite management, by which he prevented the victorious army of the russians, united with the austrians, from making use of the victory they had so lately gained. The superior and victorious army, by the manœvres of his prussian majesty, was obliged to act upon the defensive. Perceiving their intention of besieging Glogau, he, by a daring and masterly movement, threw himself between their army and the city; by which he effectually defeated their design. It is true, this march cut off all communication between himself and his brother Henry; but that was remedied by the admirable conduct of his royal highness; which, together with the successes of the imperialists in Saxony, and their being drove from thence by general Wunsch, I shall reserve for the subject of another chapter.

CHAP. XXI.

Campaign in north America. General Amherst commander in chief. Plan of operations. Expedition under general Amherst to the northward. Ticonderoga and Crown Point abandoned. Their importance. Expedition against Niagara. General Prideaux killed. Sir William Johnson succeeds him in the command. Defeats the french. Takes Niagara. Its importance. Affairs in England. Preparations in France for an invasion. Measures of the british ministry. Several squadrons sail. Havre de Grace bombarded by admiral Rodney. Toulon fleet sails. Battle of Lagos-bay. Boscawen defeats de la Clue, the french admiral. Message to the Commons. Grants.

FOUR campaigns had passed in north America, without having obtained those advantages which might reasonably have been expected, from the great force employed. But as the ministry in England seemed determined to prosecute the war in that part of the world, with all possible vigor, more sanguine hopes were now conceived from the operations there; and especially as the chief command was conferred on a young officer of distinguished merit, who had exerted himself so greatly at the taking of Louisburg: General Amherst now commanded in America.

It had been determined in England, that the face of the war there should be new modelled; instead of making but one real attack on the enemy, and several false ones, it was now resolved, at the same time, to attempt Quebeck, by the river St. Lawrence,

Lawrence, whilst a great force attacked Crown Point, and a third expedition was undertaken against Niagara. By acting in so vigorous a manner, it was expected that the enemy would prove much weaker than hitherto, when they were enabled to collect their force to defend a single place.

General Amherst himself commanded the army, that was destined to act against Ticonderoga and Crown Point, which amounted to about 12,000 men, regulars and provincials. He was in motion very early; having employed the latter end of the winter and the beginning of the spring in preparing for the expedition. So early as the first of may, many of his troops were in motion, and he arrived himself at Albany the 12th; he set out from fort Edward the 3d of june, having posted all the regular regiments on the road thither, to assist in bringing up the provisions in the battoes. General Gage was left at Albany to bring up the rear. They arrived at the fort the 12th. The greatest care was taken by the general in his march through the woods to prevent a surprise; considerable parties were continually dispatched every way to scour the country, and inure the provincials and new raised troops to marching, and the other parts of the service. It was with great difficulty that the battoes, and other boats, in which the army was to cross the lake, were brought up. On the 21st, general Amherst, with brigadier general Gage, and a large part of the army left fort Edward; it was the end of the month before they reached lake George, on which, by degrees, the battoes and other vessels were embarked. This lake, which the french call lake Sacrament, is a water near 40 miles long, but narrow in proportion; enclosed on every side with marshy grounds, it communicates with lake Champlain, by another long and very narrow streight: and this streight is defended on each side by a fort, that towards lake George is called Ticonderoga, that next

lake

lake Champlain is called by the french fort Frederick, and by us Crown Point, both of them being extremely strong by their situation, and having many considerable works built about them. It took general Amherst a considerable time to get up his artillery, ammunition, stores, and provisions, and to embark them on the lake; however, in spite of a thousand difficulties, the whole army embarked the 21st of July, and arrived with very little difficulty before Ticonderoga; at first the french made some appearance, as if they meant to defend the place. But they found in general Amherst, an enemy of much greater abilities, than any they had before opposed in this part of the world; they saw, that every operation was conducted with a prudence equal to the force employed, and having little hopes of resisting the english army long, they abandoned their lines at Ticonderoga the 23d of July; general Amherst marched into them with his grenadiers with bayonets fixed. This drew the fire of the fort on them, with cannon and mortars, but they did no execution. Having succeeded thus far, the general set about fortifying it, as its situation rendered it a post of infinite consequence, either for the prosecution of his further operations, or for covering a retreat, in case bad success made one necessary. The only loss we sustained in this acquisition was that of colonel Townshend, a young officer of great hopes, who was killed by a cannon ball.

General Amherst waited a few days, before he attacked Crown Point, for his artillery; but his troops in the mean time were thoroughly employed, in carrying on the approaches necessary, and making ready the batteries to receive their guns: although he had great reason to believe, that the french would abandon this fort, as they had done the other; yet he resolved to trust nothing to fortune, but take his measures exactly the same, as if he was sure to meet with a desperate

perate defence. His artillery came up by degrees, and when he was just on the point of attacking the fort, the french general, M. Bourlemaque abandoned it, retiring with about 3500 men and 100 cannon to the bottom of lake Champlain; and posted himself at the island called, Isle du Noix. Before he evacuated the fortress, he charged all the mortars, guns, muskets, &c. up to the very muzzles, with powder and shot, fixing port-fusees to their vents, and then setting fire to the buildings of the fort, left it; which made it impossible to approach it, without great danger; but a serjeant of regulars desired the general's permission to cut down the colours, which were then flying amongst the flames, and being permitted, he brought them off safe, for which he was rewarded with ten guineas. Mr. Amherst marched into the fort, the 4th of august; and directly set about repairing it, as he had done at Ticonderoga, where col. Montresor was left to finish the fort, and command all the troops posted from thence to Albany. The artillery, &c. taken at these two fortresses was very considerable, together with a large quantity of ammunition of all sorts.

The importance of this conquest, was, till lately, very little known. It results entirely from its situation; standing at the head of lake Champlain, by which there is a navigation to it from all parts of Canada. A small point of land, surrounded by this lake on every side, and secured by a moat towards the land, with the fortifications raised there by the french, is what was called by them, fort Frederick, and by us Crown Point. It lies mid-way, between Albany and Montreal, the two chief places on our frontiers, and those of the french. While it was in their possession, it effectually covered Canada, by blockading up our passage in that country; while it lead the french directly into New England, and New York, as was severely found by those colonies, in the

beginning,

beginning of this war, when the french let loose their indians from it, to scour, plunder, and burn the english frontiers. Without this post, the french would not have begun the war in America, they saw its importance so clearly, that they immediately set about strengthening it, and collecting a great force about it; but its most material strength consisted in the difficulty of getting at it; before this war, there were no roads through those extensive woods, which are between it and the settled parts of our colonies; but still they were passable enough for their indians, whose whole life is spent in hunting in them. I should lastly observe, that this fort was built in 1730, in the very middle of our colonies of New England, and New York, a clear proof how much the celebrated minister, who then governed Great Britain, knew his country's interest, or knowing it, how much he neglected it. It is to him, we owe in a great part, the existence of this war, and all that immense train of debts and expences occasioned by it.

During these operations of the commander in chief, those in other parts of America were no less advantageous. I have before hinted, that one part of the general plan of the campaign, was to attack the french fort at Niagara. General Prideaux commanded in this expedition; the provincials and indians under him were commanded by Sir William Johnson. The siege was but just formed, when brigadier general Prideaux was killed by the bursting of a cohorn, which happened the 20th of july. On his death, the command of the army devolved on general Johnson, who continued to pursue the deceased general's vigorous measures, with the greatest alacrity; he was enabled to do this, in a country where the provincials and indians are of such great service, not only by his own abilities, but by the great interest he has amongst them. He pushed the siege

siege with so much ardor, that in a few days he had erected his third battery within an hundred yards of the flag bastion. The french alarmed at these vigorous operations, began to be in pain for the place; they therefore collected all their regular troops and provincials, which they had about the lakes, amounting to near 2000 men, and joining to these a large body of indians, they advanced to give the english battle.

General Johnson having intelligence from his indians of their approach, made a disposition to prevent their throwing succours into the fort. The 23d in the evening, he ordered the light infantry, and piquets of the line, to lie near the road on his left, leading from the country where the french army was assembled to the fort. These he reinforced the next morning, with the grenadiers, and part of the 46th regiment, all under the command of lieutenant colonel Massey. Lieutenant colonel Farquhar, with the 44th battalion, was ordered to the tail of the trenches, to support the guard commanded by major Beckwith, in case the garrison should make a sally. The action soon after began, with that horrid scream of the indians, which had before been one of the principal causes of general Braddock's defeat, by striking a terror into those troops, who were unaccustomed to this kind of fighting; but now the english army was so well disposed to receive them in front, and their indians on the flank, that, in less than an hour's time, the whole french army was ruined. The number of the slain was not ascertained, as the pursuit was continued for five miles. Seventeen officers were made prisoners, among whom were M. d'Aubry, chief, and M. de Lignery, second in command. After this defeat, which was in sight of the garrison, sir William sent major Harvey into the fort, with a list of the officers taken, recommending it to the governor to surrender, before more blood was shed, and while he had

had it in his power to restrain the indians. The governor, to be certain of such a defeat, sent an officer of his to see the prisoners; they were shewn to him; which had such an effect, that he capitulated that very night. The garrison, consisting of about 600 men, surrendered prisoners of war, and were conducted to New York. The fort and the stores, which were considerable, was given up to the english troops.

The conquest of this fort was of infinite consequence to the security of the english colonies; it is without exception the most important pass in America; and by its situation, secures a greater number of communications, through a more extensive country, than perhaps any other pass in the world. It is in the middle of the country of the six nations, between their chief settlements and their many dependants and confederates, and in a manner entirely commands them all; having on one side the mountains, which abound in game; and on the other, the great lakes, and being surrounded every way, by one or the other, with the whole continent open to it on the west, and our colonies on the east; so that none can pass that away, or have any access to the interior parts of north America, without crossing endless mountains on one hand, or broad seas on the other, but by the narrow pass of Niagara, and an unfrequented path at the heads of the Ohio, which lead up that river. The only communication between Canada and Louisiana, and the country on the banks of the Ohio is by Niagara; all the other encroachments, except Crown Point, quite to the mouth of the Missippi are supplied from Canada, and consequently by this pass. By the advantage of its situation, it also gives its possessors the benefit of the fur trade, with a multitude of indian nations, spread far and near over the whole continent of north America; and also the navigation of all the great seas of fresh water, called the five lakes

lakes of Canada, to the extent of 1300 miles. In short, it prevents or secures the junction of the two french colonies in Canada and Louisiana; laid our colonies open to the incursions both of the french and their indians, whilst it was in their hands; and secures them from both, if in our possession.

As to those immense lakes, which are all in a manner commanded by this fort, the reader need only cast his eyes on a map of north America, to be convinced of their importance. They afford by far the most noble and extensive inland navigation in the world. Whoever is the master of them must, sooner or later, command that whole continent They are all surrounded by a fine and fruitful country, in a temperate and pleasant climate. The day may possibly come, when this noble country, which one would think is calculated for universal empire, will sufficiently display its own importance.

The affairs of Great Britain in Europe, were equally glorious; the spirit of the nation was now accustomed to success, which diffused a general joy over the whole kingdom, the more just, as it was well founded. The parliament, the ministry, and every order of the people, vied with each other in promoting the interest of their country. What proved a great spur to this unanimity, was the vast preparations that were making in all the ports of France, with design to invade Great Britain. Three different embarkations were to be undertaken. M. Thurot, who had been so active in the command of a french privateer, the marshal de Belleisle, in destroying the english trade, was to command a small squadron of royal ships, and several transports, from Dunkirk, which were intended against Scotland. Great preparations were making in the ports of Normandy, for a second embarkation against England, in flat bottomed boats of a new construction, many of which, had been built for that purpose. The third expedition, which was imagined to be against Ireland, was preparing in the ports of Britanny, the embarkation to be made from Vannes and Nants; and covered by a formidable fleet preparing in Brest, under the command of M. de Conflans; a great body of troops* was assembled in that province, under the duke d'Aguillon. Had all these expeditions succeeded as I have here represented them, so far as to land their troops, there is no doubt but it would have thrown Great Britain into terrible confusion; and it is impossible to say what would have been the consequence.

But the most vigorous measures were taken by the ministry in England, to counteract these preparations. A squadron under commodore Boys was stationed before Dunkirk. Admiral Rodney, with a second was sent to bombard Havre de Grace. Admiral sir Edward Hawke blocked up the harbour of Brest, with a very strong squadron; and a smaller kept a watch upon that of Vannes. The first advices that were received from these several fleets were from admiral Rodney. The squadron under his command, consisting of four ships of the line, two frigates, two sloops, and six bomb vessels, sailed from St. Hellen's the 2d of July, and anchored the next day in the great road of Havre, the admiral placed the bombs in

* By an account which the french court published of their armaments, it appeared, that the number of troops to be employed on the invasion amounted to 53,000 men, consisting of 63 battalions of infantry: and the following cavalry, viz. 200 mousquetaires, 400 life guards, 150 horse grenadiers, 200 gen d'armes and light horse, 2500 horse, making eight regiments, 2400 dragoons, 2600 legion-royale, artillerie, &c. The prince of Conti commander in chief,

Prince de Soubise, } Field marshals.
Count de Thomond,

Eight lieutenant generals, 12 major generals, 18 brigadier generals, 26 ships of the line, 12 frigates, 8 fireships, 6 chebecs, 8 armed gallies, 500 transports, 20 physicians, 100 surgeons, 50 apothecaries, 2 chaplains in each ship.

the

the narrow channel of the river, leading to Harfleur, it being the most proper and only place to do execution from. About seven in the evening, two of the bombs were stationed, as were all the rest early the next morning, and continued to bombard for 52 hours without intermission, with such success, that the town was several times in flames; and their magazine of stores for the flat bottomed boats, burnt with very great fury for upwards of six hours, notwithstanding the continual efforts of several hundred men to extinguish it; and many of the boats were overturned and damaged by the explosion of the shells. During the attack, the french troops appeared very numerous, were continually erecting new batteries, and throwing up intrenchments; their consternation was so great, that all the inhabitants left the town. This service was performed with very inconsiderable loss in the squadron.

Part of the french plan of an invasion consisted in being able to bring round a strong squadron of ships which they had equipped at Toulon, from thence to Brest, to unite all their strength at that port. To prevent this, admiral Boscawen * had been stationed before the harbour of Toulon to block it up. But some unfavourable weather, and the foulness of his ships, obliged him to retire to Gibraltar to refit: the french took this opportunity to slip out, and they proceeded with great diligence to the streights. Mr. Boscawen, in the mean time had very near got

* With the following ships under his command,

Ships.	Guns.	Ships.	Guns.
Namur	90	Intrepid	64
Prince	90	Edgar	64
Newark	80	America	64
Culloden	74	St. Albans	60
Warspite	74	Jersey	60
Conqueror	74	Portland	60
Swiftsure	70	Guernsey	50

Besides fireships and frigates.

his ships ready to sail; and that the french fleet might not escape him, he ordered the Lime and Gibraltar, (the only frigaties ready) the first to cruise off Malaga, and the last from Estepona to Ceuta Point, to give him notice of their approach. On the 17th of august, at eight in the evening, the Gibraltar made the signal of their appearance; the admiral was so very expeditious, that he got under sail out of the bay, by ten, with his whole squadron, of fourteen sail of the line, and two fireships. At day-light, he saw the Gibraltar, and seven sail of large ships lying to; but on his not answering their signal, they made sail from him. As there was a fresh gale, the english fleet came up with them fast, till about noon, when it fell little wind. About half an hour past two, some of the headmost ships began to engage; but Mr. Boscawen could not get up to the french admiral's ship, the Ocean, till near four, when he began to engage her. In about half an hour his own ship, the Namure's mizen mast, and both top-sail yards were shot away; the Ocean then made all the sail she could. The english admiral shifted his flag to the Newark, and soon after the Centaur, of 74 guns, struck. He pursued all night; and in the morning of the 19th, saw only four sail standing in for land, (two of their best sailors having altered their course in the night). About nine, the Ocean ran on shore amongst the breakers, and the three others anchored. Admiral Boscawen sent the Intrepid and America to burn the Ocean; the former could not get in, but the latter performed the service alone: On his first firing at the Ocean, she struck; the english captain sent his officers on board; but M. de la Clue, the french admiral, having lost one leg, and the other being much wounded, had been landed about half an hour, and died soon after. Captain Kirk, of the America, finding it impossible to bring the Ocean off, set her on fire. Captain Bentley, of the Warspite, was ordered against

the

the Temeraire, of 74 guns, and brought her off with little damage, the officers and men all on board. At the same time, vice-admiral Broderick, with his division of the english fleet, burnt the Redoubtable, her officers and men having quitted her, being bulged; and brought the Modeste of 64 guns off, with very little damage. The scattered remains of their fleet *, with difficulty got into the harbour of Cadiz, where they remained a considerable time blocked up.

This victory, so advantageous to Great Britain, was purchased at a very cheap rate. Amongst the english ships were no more than 56 killed, 196 wounded; 13 of the former, and 44 of the latter were on board Mr. Boscawen's ship, which had more of each, than any other in the fleet. It is difficult to say, which was greatest, the cowardice of the french, or the bravery of the english. Had de la Clue formed a line, and fought Boscawen regularly, it is thought by many he would have escaped much better than he did. The english fleet had the superiority only of two ships of the line, but the

* Which at first consisted of the following ships:

Ships.	Guns.	
Ocean	80	} burnt.
Redoubtable	74	
Centaur	74	taken.
Souveraine	74	} escaped.
Guerrier	74	
Temeraire	74	taken.
Fantasque	64	lost company.
Modeste	64	taken
Lion	64	
Triton	64	
Fier	50	} lost company coming through the Streights.
Oriflamme	50	
Chimere	26	
Minerve	24	
Gracieuse	24	

Besides two ships more of the line, unknown.

french ships were much larger in bulk, and had a superiority in number of men; so that on the whole, the two fleets were pretty near of equal force. The cowardice or incapacity of M. de Clue was manifest, had his fleet been rather inferior, it is the duty of every admiral to form his line and fight, instead of separating his ships and running away; but this blow was as glorious to Britain, as it was disgraceful to France. It weakened the force with which they intended to execute the invasion; and, what was of more consequence, considerably sunk the spirits of the french sailors, who found how unequal they were in action to the english.

In the mean time, nothing was omitted in England to render abortive the designs of the french. For this purpose, his majesty sent the following message to the house of commons, on the 21st of may, by Mr. secretary Pitt.

" GEORGE, R.

His majesty, relying on the experienced zeal and affection of his faithful commons, and considering that, in this critical juncture, emergencies may arise, which may be of the utmost importance, and be attended with the most pernicious consequences, if proper means should not immediately be applied to prevent or defeat them, is desirous, that this house will enable him to defray any extraordinary expences of the war, incurred, or to be incurred for the service of the year 1759, and to take all such measures as may be necessary to disappoint or defeat any enterprizes or designs of his enemies, and as the exigencies of affairs may require."

The house of commons took this message into consideration directly; and on the 24th, resolved that there should be granted to his majesty, for the purposes

poses mentioned therein, one million upon account *. So large a sum voted unanimously was an unquestionable

	l.
* Grants for the year 1759.	
For 60,000 seamen, including 14,845 marines, and ordnance for sea service,	3120000
For 52,343 men, for guards and garrisons, and other land forces in Great Britain, Guernsey, and Jersey,	1256131
For the pay of the general and staff-officers, and officers of the hospital,	52484
For the forces and garrisons in the plantations, and Gibraltar, and for provisions for the garrisons in Nova Scotia, Newfoundland, Providence, Cape Breton, and Senegal,	742531
For four regiments of foot and one battalion, on the irish establishment, serving in North America, and Africa,	40879
For the office of the ordnance of the land forces,	220700
For the extra-expence of the ordnance in 1758, not provided for,	323988
For the ordinary of the navy, including half-pay to sea-officers,	238491
For the support of Greenwich hospital	10000
For 38,000 of the troops of Hanover, Wolfenbuttle, Saxe-Gotha, Buckeburg, with the general and staff-officers,	398698
For 19,012 hessians, with the general and staff-officers of the hospital, and train of artillery, pursuant to treaty,	339480
Towards defraying the charges of forage, &c. for the army under prince Ferdinand,	500000
Towards paying off the debt of the navy,	1000000
For allowance to the officers and private men of the horse guards, and regiments of horse reduced, and the superannuated men of the horse guards,	2909
To the reduced officers of the land forces and marines,	34368
For the pensions of the widows of ditto, married before december 25, 1716,	2128
To the king of Prussia, pursuant to the convention,	670000
To the landgrave of Hesse Cassel, pursuant to treaty,	60000
To defray the like sum raised last session, and charged upon the first aids,	800000
For building, re-building, and repairing his majesty's ships,	200000
For the out pensioners of Chelsea hospital,	26000

For

able proof what great harmony reigned in every part of the constitution and administration; so much the contrast of what was to be seen in France, where the ministry

	l.
For widening and enlarging the passage over London bridge,	15000
To the foundling hospital,	50000
For transport service and victualling the land forces for 1758,	667772
For supporting the colony of Nova Scotia, for 1759,	9902
For defraying the charges of supporting ditto, in 1757,	11279
For the civil establishment of Georgia, from june 1758, to ditto, 1759,	4058
To make good the deficiency of the additional duty on licences for retailing wine, the duty on coals exported, &c. july, 1758,	24371
To make good the deficiency of the duty on glass and spirituous liquors,	8882
For supporting the british forts on the coasts of Africa,	10000
To Roger Long D. D.	1280
For paying and cloathing the militia, to March 25, 1760,	90000
For the extra expences of land forces, &c. in 1758, not provided for,	466786
For fortifying Chatham dock,	708
For fortifying Portsmouth town,	6937
For fortifying Plymouth citadel,	25159
For fortifying Milford haven,	10000
For paying the debts upon the estate, forfeited to the crown upon the attainder of lord John Drummond,	69911
To the East-india company, for defending their settlements,	20000
To the provinces in north America, for the expences of troops raised by them,	200000
To the innholders on which the hessian troops were billetted in 1758,	2500
For augmenting the salaries of the judges in Great Britain,	11450
To the widows of Nicholas Hardinge, esq. for the ballance of an account, for printing the journals of the house of commons,	779
For interest of money laid out, to purchase land about Chatham, Portsmouth, and Plymouth,	1716
For purchasing lands about ditto,	2443
To defray any expence of the war, in 1759,	1000000
Total	12749860

ministry found it a matter of the greatest difficulty to raise money, even when they tried the most opprefive methods; The exhausted state of that kingdom became every day more manifest, owing to the vast losses their trade had sustained.

It is now time to take a view of the operations of the two armies on the Weser, where we shall find Britain attended with the same success, where it was least expected.

CHAP.

CHAP. XXII.

Motions of the two armies on the Weser. Hereditary prince detached towards Paderborn. Battle of Minden. Great bravery of the english infantry, &c. The french army defeated. Hereditary prince defeats the duke of Brisac. Fine conduct of duke Ferdinand. He enters Minden. His orders after the battle. Lord G—— S——'s letter to col. Fitzroy, and answer. Captain Smith's declaration. Remarks on the conduct of lord G—— S——. He obtains leave to return to England. Duke Ferdinand pursues the french. Munster blockaded. Investiture of duke Ferdinand with the order of the Garter.

I Left the hanoverian army under duke Ferdinand of Brunswick, just arrived in the camp at Petershagen, and that of France, under marshal de Contades, in their camp near Minden. This position of the french, was chose with great judgment, and the advantages resulting from it, were of such importance, that nothing could be attempted against them. The strength of their camp prevented its being attacked; their right extended near Minden, their left was defended by a steep mountain; their rear was guarded by a rivulet, and several ridges of hills, and in their front was a marsh, inaccessible only in a narrow passage, which led into the plain of Minden. The situation of this camp, rendered it impossible for the duke to attack it; and, at the same time, nothing but a battle could possibly prevent the french army from taking up their winter quarters in the electorate of Hanover. Contades had it in his power to stay in

the

the camp at Minden as long as he pleafed, as all the country in his rear was in his poffeffion, and from whence he could draw his forage and provifions, during the remainder of the campaign; whereas duke Ferdinand being fo much inferior in force to the french, would be obliged to retreat, whenever marfhal Contades fhould think proper to advance. This was the opinion of the french generals, and it was feared in England, that their fchemes would prove but too fuccefsful. The greateft gloom fpread over the electorate; the archieves, and every thing valuable was removed from Hanover to Stade; and the inhabitants once more expected and dreaded a french army being quartered on them.

In the mean time duke Ferdinand, attentive to every motion of the french, and every advantage of their prefent fituation, faw that it was impoffible to attack them in their camp; but as a battle alone could retrieve the affairs of the allies, the point he endeavoured to compafs, was to draw them out of it into the plain, as he might there fight them on more equal terms; but the movements which were neceffary to effect this, were extremely hazardous and difficult to an army fo much inferior as his ferene highnefs's; but dangerous as they were, he refolved to execute them.

The 27th of july, he detached the hereditary prince of Brunfwick, with 6000 men, to make a compafs towards the enemy's left flank, and to poft himfelf in fuch a manner, as to cut off the communication of their convoys from Paderborn. The duke's army did not amount to 40,000 men, when he fent off the detachment, whereas the french army was near 90,000 ftrong; the weakening his force, before fo much inferior to his enemy, convinced the french generals that his ferene highnefs did not intend to fight.

The

The 29th, duke Ferdinand left his camp at Petershagen, and marched toward Hillen, a village considerably to his right, with the greatest part of his army, leaving general Wagenheim behind him at Thornhausen, on the brink of the Weser, with a considerable body of troops under his command, strongly intrenched, and defended by a numerous artillery. The duke, as soon as he arrived in his camp at Hillen, gave orders that the generals should take particular notice of the nine debouchês, by which the army might advance to form in the plain of Minden, that they might be well acquainted with them, in case they should be ordered to advance in front. And at the same time lord George Sackville, the commander in chief of the british forces in Germany, was appointed lieutenant general of the day. The 31st in the evening, the prince further ordered, that at one o'clock the next morning, the army should be ready to march; that the cavalry must be saddled; the artillery horses harnessed, and the infantry gatered; but the tents were not to be struck, nor the troops put under arms till further orders.

The french, in the mean time, were very attentive to the motions and designs of prince Ferdinand. On the 31st, at six in the evening, a grand council of war was held at marshal de Contades's quarters, consisting of all the generals in the french army; and the result of it was, that they should march to the enemy that very night, and attack them at day-break. The marshal gave the generals the order of the march, and the disposition of the attack. The army was to move in eight columns to the ground, where it was to be formed in battle array, which was the plain before Thornhausen, where general Wangenheim was intrenched. Marshal Contades formed the whole plan of the action, upon a supposition, that duke Ferdinand having removed the greatest part of his army so far to the right of Hillen, was at too great a distance from Wangenheim, to succour him; and as that general's corps was but weak, it was not doubted, but it would prove a very easy task to defeat it; the consequences of which would be, that prince Ferdinand's communication with the Weser would absolutely be cut off, which was the very thing that the french aimed at, ever since the battle of Bergen, without being able to effect it.

It was under these notions that marshal Contades left his advantageous camp on the 1st of august, crossed the marsh, and moved into the plain of Minden, to attack general Wangenheim. The duke of Broglio was charged with that attack, and his order bore, that after routing and overwhelming it, he should fall on the left flank of duke Ferdinand's army, and thereby facilitate the attack and victory of the marshal's grand corps.

The whole french army was marching into the plain of Minden, by five o'clock in the morning. The duke of Broglio's first line consisted of nine battalions, his second of nine, and his reserve of three. His cavalry was posted in two columns, behind the left of his infantry, that it might form in battle array to support it in case of need. This corps came close to the Weser. Their cavalry formed the center of the french army, and occupied a heath; and the infantry of their left extended to the marsh near the village of Hahlen. The duke of Broglio's corps was the first that arrived at its post; but before he had occupied his ground, he was obliged to wait some time, till the other divisions of the french army came up, when he advanced to cross an eminence, which was between him and the plain, whereon the french army was to be drawn up in order of battle. He had no sooner arrived at the top of this eminence, than he was struck with the utmost amazement, when instead of Wangenheim's intrenchments weakly guarded, he beheld the whole hanoverian army, drawn up in excellent order, on the plain before him, and extending from the banks of the Weser, quite to the morass, in the front of the late french camp. This was a stroke of generalship entirely unexpected. But let us return to the motions of duke Ferdinand, who had been able to deceive his enemy in such an exquisite manner.

I before mentioned that the duke gave orders in the evening of the 31st of july, for the army to be ready to march at one o'clock the next morning; and he also recommended it to all the advanced posts to be very attentive, and to inform him of the least motion they should observe during the night. By some mistake the order was not brought to lord George Sackville, so that, instead of the horses being saddled at one o'clock, as had been directed, they were not saddled before four. The night passed without the duke's receiving any intelligence of the enemy. But about three in the morning, M. de Redan, adjutant general, informed him of the arrival of two deserters, with the news, that the enemy's army was marching to attack him, and that they had passed the marsh at midnight. Although this information was a little exaggerated, yet how important soever was the news they brought, it did not reach the duke till near three in the morning, whereas the deserters arrived at Hactim at ten o'clock the preceding evening. He immediately sent every aid de camp he had about him, in order to make the army strike their tents, form, and march without the least delay. His order was speedily put in execution, although it was not brought to lord George Sackville, by another mistake, so that the army was drawn up in lines before he knew any thing of the matter; but the french having raised a battery at Lickhorst, which played early in the morning, on some out posts on the right of the hanoverian army, with intent to draw the attention of the prince that way, the firing waked his lordship, and being informed, that the army was drawn up, he immediately repaired to the head of the line, and the whole army marched in eight columns from the camp at Hille, a little before five o'clock. The cavalry of the right wing formed the first; the heavy artillery the second; the infantry of the right, the third and fourth; the heavy artillery of the center, the fifth; the infantry of the left wing the sixth and seventh; and the eighth column consisted of the cavalry of the left wing. General Wangenheim's corps having moved out of its camp, much about the same time, through the openings already made in the dyke of Landwehr, was formed in order of battle, at the same time with the rest of the army. The grenadiers of his corps were posted upon the right of the batteries at Thornhausen; the eight battalions of infantry in the hedges of Kutenhausen, upon the right of the grenadiers; and the 18 squadrons of cavalry, in the open fields upon the right of the infantry. Between six and seven, the whole allied army drew up in order of battle, having its right, consisting of cavalry, under lord George Sackville, extended towards the village of Hartum; its center was composed of infantry; and its left of general Wangenheim's corps, and some german cavalry. The right wing had on its left a wood, which though thin and open, prevented that wing from seeing the infantry of the center; the country in the front of it was corn fields, for some distance, and then an open plain, where the picquets of the army under the prince of Anhalt, as lieutenant general of the day were drawn up, near the village of Hahlen; and from thence were dispatched the picquets of the infantry, with two howitzers, to get possession of Hahlen, wherein the enemy had thrown two battalions.

This was the position of the allied army, when the duke of Broglio beheld it from the eminence abovementioned. He directly acquainted marshal Contades of this unexpected appearance; but it was then too late to recede. Indeed their situation was at that time very disadvantageous; they were cooped up between the hanoverian army, the morass and the Weser. About seven o'clock the french began to fire upon a battery in the front of the right wing of the allied army, from one in the front of their left wing; but as soon as the english artillery was prepared, (of which that battery consisted) it returned their fire, and in less than ten minutes silenced the enemy's guns.

In the mean time, duke Ferdinand finding the french slower than he expected, ordered the infantry of his center to advance against the center of the french, which consisted of the flower of their cavalry, and who anticipated the shock of the allies, by attacking their infantry. The whole brunt of the battle was sustained by a few regiments of english and hanoverian foot, who repulsed the reiterated and fierce attacks of the french cavalry, with a firmness hardly ever equalled; and having been exposed, as they marched about 1500 paces to meet the enemy, to an extreme smart cannonade from two french batteries (posted at some distance from each other) which played on them obliquely; but notwithstanding the loss they sustained by this cannonade, before they could get up to the enemy, notwithstanding the furious and repeated attacks of all the french cavalry, notwithstanding the efforts, and a fire of musketry, well kept up by the enemy's infantry, notwithstanding their being exposed in front and flank, such was the unshaken firmness of these troops, such their resolution, steadiness, and expertness in their maneuvre, never exceeded, perhaps, never equalled, that nothing could stop them; they cut to pieces several bodies of the enemy's cavalry, and entirely routed the whole of it. The saxon foot, which were on the left of the french horse, made a show of coming down upon those conquering regiments, and attempted to support their broken cavalry;

but

but they vanished before the english infantry. Never did troops behave in a more intrepid manner; the english regiments, Kingsley's, Napier's, Stuart's, Huske's and Brudenel's; but especially the three former; the hanoverian guards, and Hardenberg's regiment, all behaved to admiration. At the same time, the attack which the french made on the left of the hanoverian army, and on the corps under general Wangenheim, was attended with the like bad success. The latter maintained pretty near the same position, during the whole action. The batteries erected under the care of the count la Lippe Buckeburg, grand master of the artillery, in the front of Thornhausen, contributed greatly to decide the fortune of the day, as he soon silenced two batteries of the enemy's, and made, at the same time, great havock among the Swifs, and the grenadiers de France.

Just at the time, when the center of the french army began to give way, which was between eight and nine o'clock, his serene highness duke Ferdinand sent his aid du camp, captain Wintzingerode, to lord George Sackville, with orders for him to move with the cavalry under his command, through the thin wood on his left, then to form on the heath, in the rear of the infantry, and advance to support it. Lord George misunderstood that particular of his order, which required him to march through the trees on the left; and the dispositions he made to execute this order, were such, as if the cavalry were to move streight forward. He ordered captain Hugo, one of his aid du camps, to clear his front of the Saxe-Gotha regiment of foot, which had been posted there; he ordered captain Broome, another of them, to go forward, to reconnoitre the position of the enemy; and sent captain Lloyd, another aid du camp, to find out the hanoverian infantry, and report to him their situation. In about seven or eight minutes after Wintzingerode left lord George, captain Ligonier, another aid du camp to prince Ferdinand arrived with a second order, for the cavalry to advance, in order to profit from the disorder which appeared in the enemy's cavalry. His lordship then, on receiving this, drew his sword, and gave the word to march; on which the cavalry moved a few paces forward: captain Ligonier then told him, it was to the left he was to march. At that minute, lieutenant colonel Fitzroy, third aid du camp to duke Ferdinand, came up and delivered an order to lord George Sackville, for the british cavalry only to advance to the left, upon which his lordship turned to captain Ligonier, and said, their orders were contradictory; he answered, they differed only in numbers, the destination of his march was the same, to the left. Colonel Fitzroy offered to lead the column himself, through the wood on the left, where he imagined they might pass two squadrons in front; but his lordship was not satisfied with the order, and again observed, that it was different from captain Ligonier's, and that he could not imagine the prince would break the line; and the two aids de camp persisted, that the order each brought was right; his lordship then desired lieutenant colonel Fitzroy to lead him to the prince, that he might have an explanation of the orders; which was accordingly done; but as he passed through the wood, observing that it was not so thick as he before imagined, he sent back captain Smith, one of his aids de camp, to bring up the british cavalry. Just before his lordship came up, the duke a second time dispatched lieut. colonel Fitzroy, with orders for the cavalry to advance as fast as possible, and directed him to carry this order to lord Granby, who commanded the second line of cavalry. It was immediately executed, and lord George, while he was taking the prince's orders shewed him that line of cavalry coming through the wood. The prince gave him his own orders, to form the cavalry on the heath, and sustain the infantry. This order

lord

lord George Sackville, proceeded to put in execution, and placing himself at the head of the line, marched it (after it had got through the wood) to the rear of a body of infantry. These were all the movements which the cavalry of the right wing made that day, and when his lordship arrived at the rear of the infantry, the battle was over.

About nine o'clock in the morning, the french army gave way: a general confusion soon followed; and about ten the whole of it fled in disorder: part took shelter under cover of the cannon of Minden, and the rest made the best of their way over that part of the marsh, which they had before crossed, and broke down the bridges to prevent their being pursued. The duke of Broglio covered the retreat: he occupied with his infantry, the gardens near Minden; soon after which, his cavalry followed the main body of their army. Towards the end of the battle, the artillery of the right of the allied army was marched forward till it arrived close to the marsh, and then played upon the french army, which had retreated into its old camp, when they left it, and retired further back behind some high grounds near Dutzen, with their right extending towards the Weser.

The battle of Minden was now over, but the consequences hitherto, were far from being fatal to the french; they had lost a great number of men, it is true, and had all the disgrace of a total defeat; but then their advantageous situation was still of the same consequence to them, and from which they would not have been drove, had not prince Ferdinand detached the hereditary prince to cut off their convoys, which came by the way of Paderborn; this young hero completed the defeat.

The duke de Brissac commanded a body of seven or eight thousand men, which marshal Contades had posted near Coveldt, to guard his convoys, and keep possession of the passes in his rear: the hereditary prince attacked him on the 1st of august; after making the following dispositions: the position of the french was inaccessible in front, and there was no other way to come at them, but by surrounding their left; for which purpose three attacks were formed, all of which were to depend on the success of that on the right: the troops destined for which, consisted of three battalions, four squadrons and 200 volunteers. Four battalions, one squadron, and all the heavy artillery, composed the center: the left was formed of three battalions and four squadrons. The troops of the center were designed to keep the enemy at bay, whilst those of the right should surround their left; those of the prince's left were to march to a bridge near a place called the Salt Pitts, in order to prevent the enemy's retreat to Minden. The hereditary prince himself marched with the right; count Kilmansegge was in the center; and M. de Dreves and M. de Bock brought the left. As soon as count Kilmansegge had come out of a defile in his way, the french presented themselves before him; and a cannonade began on both sides. The right was to pass the Weser, in order to turn the enemy's left, upon a very narrow bridge. This difficulty was in an instant removed by the gallantry of the prince, who setting himself the example, the infantry forded the river, partly behind the horsemen, and partly in peasants waggons. By this passage, the position of the french was entirely changed; the fire of the artillery was brisk on both sides, and lasted two hours. At last, on the hanoverians shewing themselves on the rear of the french, the latter immediately gave way, and, in filing off, came upon the skirts of M. de Bock, who received them with a discharge of artillery, which was well supported. At last, finding themselves entirely surrounded, they had no other resource but in flight. The hereditary prince took five pieces of cannon, and all the baggage of the french.

By

By this stroke, which does such infinite honour to the genius of duke Ferdinand, all the passes through which the french could draw succour or provision were seized. That victory, which was before so inconclusive, now was decisive. Marshal Contades received the news of the duke of Brissac's defeat, just as the english infantry was marching up to attack the french cavalry, he admired the judicious boldness of the duke, in detaching so large a number of men, at the very time, when he was on the point of engaging an enemy so much superior. The marshal immediately abandoned his strong post, and passing the Weser, retreated on the eastward of that river; losing in this manner all the advantages he had gained during the whole campaign, and forced to retreat through a country different from that through which he had advanced, and in which he had taken no measures for subsistence.

The french lost in this battle about 8000 men, killed, wounded, and prisoners; among the latter of whom were the comte de Hutzelbourg, and the marquis de Monti, marechaux de camp, and M. de Vogué, colonel; and many other persons of distinction. Thirty pieces of cannon, twelve colours, and eight standards were taken.

The admirable conduct of prince Ferdinand in those maneuvres, which brought on the battle, is perhaps one of the most perfect and finished pieces of generalship, that ever was executed; the masterly motions that he made, to draw the french out of their impenetrable camp; his detaching the hereditary prince with 6000 men from his army, just when he was endeavouring to bring the enemy to an engagement, who had a superiority of 50,000 men; in short, the whole conduct of his serene highness displayed such a sagacity and penetration, such guarded and judicious boldness, that never any action spoke a more exalted genius.

The 2d of august, duke Ferdinand issued the following orders from his head quarters at Suderhemmeren, viz. " His serene highness orders his greatest thanks to be given to the whole army for their good behaviour yesterday, particularly to the british infantry, and the two battalions of hanoverian guards; to all the cavalry of the left wing; and to general Wangenheim's corps, particularly to the regiment of Holstein, the hessian cavalry, the hanoverian regiment of du corps, and Hamerstin's; the same to all the brigades of heavy artillery. His serene highness declares publicly, that, next to God, he attributes the glory of the day to the intrepidity and extraordinary good behaviour of these troops, which he assures them he shall retain the strongest sense of as long as he lives; and if ever, upon any occasion, he shall be able to serve these brave troops, or any one of them in particular, it will give him the greatest pleasure. His serene highness orders his particular thanks to be likewise given to general Sporcken, the duke of Holstein, lieutenant generals Inhoff and Urff. His serene highness is extremely obliged to the count de Buckeburg, for all his care and trouble in the management of the artillery, which was served with great effect; likewise to the commanding officers of the several brigades of artillery, viz. colonel Bowne, lieutenant colonel Hutte, major Hasse, and the three english captains Philips, Drummond, and Foy. His serene highness thinks himself infinitely obliged to major generals Waldegrave, and Kingsley*, for the great courage and good order in which they conducted their brigades. His serene highness further orders it

---

* Kingsley was wounded at the head of his brave regiment, and fell off his horse, a squadron of french cavalry rode over him without his receiving any hurt from them; as he was lying on the ground a french soldier was going to run him through with his bayonet; but he discovered himself, was taken prisoner, and afterwards retaken by his own men.

to be declared, to lieutenant general the marquis of Granby, that he is perfuaded, that if he had had the good fortune to have had him at the head of the cavalry of the right wing, his prefence would have greatly contributed to make the decifion of that day more complete and more brilliant. In fhort, his ferene highnefs orders, that thofe of his SUITE, whofe behaviour he moft admired, be named, as the duke of Richmond, colonel Fitzroy, captain Ligonier, colonel Watfon, captain Wilfon, aid de camp to major general Waldegrave; adjutant generals Erfthoff, Bulow, Derendolle, the counts Tobe and Malherti; his ferene highnefs having much reafon to be fatisfied with their conduct. And his ferene highnefs defires and orders the generals of the army, that, upon all occafions, when orders are brought to them by his aids de camp, that they be obeyed punctually, and without delay."

The duke, on difcovering a miftake in the preceding order of thanks, to the officers of the britifh artillery, by which captain Macbean was omitted to be mentioned, his ferene highnefs was pleafed to write a letter with his own hand to him, which was delivered by his excellency count la Lippe Buckeburg, grand mafter of the artillery in the allied army, and of which the following is a tranflation:

" SIR,

It is from a fenfe of your merit, and a regard to juftice, that I do in this manner declare, I have reafon to be infinitely fatisfied, with your behaviour, activity, and zeal, which in fo confpicuous a manner you made appear, at the battle of Thornhaufen, on the firft of auguft. The talents which you poffefs in your profeffion, did not a little contribute to render our fire fuperior to that of the enemy; and

it

it is to you and your brigade that I am indebted for having silenced the fire of a battery of the enemy, which extremely galled the troops and particularly the british infantry.

Accept then, sir, from me, the just tribute of my most perfect acknowlegments, accompanied with my sincere thanks. I shall be happy in every opportunity of obliging you, desiring only occasions to prove it, being with the most distinguished esteem,

Your devoted, and
entirely affectionate servant,
FERDINAND,
Duke of Brunswick and Lunenburg."

And his serene highness again on the 3d, issued another order, viz.

" In the compliment his serene highness made to the troops yesterday, he forgot four regiments, that particularly distinguished themselves, viz. Hardenburg's, third battalion of hessian guards, prince William's, and Gillse's: it is not that his serene highness has reason to complain of any others, but as they had particular opportunities of distinguishing themselves, it is for that reason his serene highness mentions the attention he himself gives to their good conduct."

Soon after another order came out to the following effect: " His serene highness duke Ferdinand sent orders to monsieur Hedeman his treasurer, to pay the following officers of the british artillery, the undermentioned gratuities, as a testimony of his great satisfaction of their gallant behaviour in the late action of the first of this month:

To

To captain Philips	1000 crowns.
To captain Macbean	500
To captain Drummond	500
To captain Williams	500
To captain Foy	500

I hope the said gentlemen will accept of this present from his highness, as a mark of his particular esteem for them." This condescending and affectionate manner, in which the prince thanked the particular officers for their good behaviour, rendered him extremely dear to the whole army; and it was the greatest incentive to raise an emulation amongst them to endeavour at rendering themselves conspicuous by their conduct and courage when they found their general so quick-sighted in perceiving and rewarding merit.

In the mean time, the orders of the 2d of august, which shewed how much dissatisfied the duke was with the conduct of lord George Sackville, could not but touch that commander to the quick. There clearly appeared some very great fault in the cavalry of the right wing's not obeying the duke's orders to advance; owing, as we have great reason to believe, to his lordship's wasting that time in requiring an explanation of his highness's orders, which ought to have been spent in their execution. However, his lordship wrote the following letter to col. Fitzroy, the 3d of august, dated at Minden.

"DEAR SIR,

The orders of yesterday, you may believe, affect me very sensibly. His serene highness has been pleased to judge, condemn, and censure, without hearing me, in the most cruel and unprecedented manner; as he never asked me a single question in explanation of any thing he might disapprove, and as he must have formed his opinion on the report of others, it was still harder he would not give me an opportunity of first speaking to him, upon the subject; but you know, even in more trifling matters, that hard blows are sometimes unexpectedly given. If any body has a right to say, that I hesitated in obeying orders, it is you. I will relate what I know of that, and then appeal to you for the truth of it.

When you brought me orders to advance with the british cavalry, I was then very near the village of Hahlen, as I think it is called; I mean that place which the saxons burnt. I was there advanced by M. Malhorte's order, and no further, when you came to me. Ligonier followed almost instantly; he said the cavalry was to advance. I was puzzled what to do, and begged the favour of you to carry me to the duke, that I might ask an explanation of his orders. But that no time might be lost, I sent Smith with orders to bring on the british cavalry, as they had a wood before they could advance, as you directed; and I reckoned by the time I had seen his serene highness, I should find them forming beyond the wood. This proceeding of mine might possibly be wrong; but I am sure the service could not suffer, as no delay was occasioned by it. The duke then ordered me to leave some squadrons upon the right, which I did; and to advance the rest to support the infantry. This I declare I did, as fast as I imagined it was right for cavalry to march in line: I once halted by lord Granby, to complete my forming the whole. Upon his advancing the left before the right, I again sent to him to stop. He said, as the prince had ordered us to advance, he thought we should move forward; I then let him proceed at the rate he liked, and kept my right up with him, as regular as I could, till we got to the rear of the infantry and our batteries. We both halted together, and afterwards received no

order

order till that which was brought by colonel Webb and the duke of Richmond, to extend one line towards the morass. It was accordingly executed, and then, instead of finding the enemy's cavalry, to charge, the battle was declared to be gained, and we were told to dismount our men.

This I protest is all I know of the matter; and I was never so surprised, as when I heard the prince was dissatisfied, that the cavalry did not move sooner up to the infantry. It is not my business to ask, what the disposition originally was, or to find fault with any thing. All I insist upon, is, that I obeyed the orders I received, as punctually as I was able; and if it was to do over again, I do not think I should have executed them ten minutes sooner than I did; now I know the ground, and what was expected; but indeed we were above an hour too late, if it was the duke's intention to have made the cavalry passed before our infantry and artillery, and charge the enemy's line. I cannot think that was his meaning, as all the orders ran, to sustain our infantry: and it appears, that both lord Granby and I understood we were at our posts, by our halting when we got to the rear of our foot.

I hope I have stated impartially the part of this transaction, that comes within your knowledge. If I have, I must beg you would declare it, so as I may make use of it in your absence; for it is impossible to sit silent under such reproach, when I am conscious of having done the best that was in my power. For God's sake, let me see you before you go for England.

I am, dear sir,

Your faithful humble servant,

SACKVILLE."

To this letter colonel Fitzroy returned the following answer, dated the same day at Minden.

" My lord,

His serene highness, upon some report made to him by the duke of Richmond, of the situation of the enemy, sent captain Ligonier and myself with orders for the british cavalry to advance. His serene highness was, at this instant, one or two brigades beyond the english infantry, towards the left. Upon my arrival on the right of the cavalry, I found captain Ligonier with your lordship. Notwithstanding I declared his serene highness's orders to you: upon which, you desired I would not be in a hurry. I made answer, that galloping had put me out of breath, which made me speak very quick. I then repeated the order for the british cavalry to advance towards the left, and at the same time mentioning the circumstance that occasioned the orders, " That it was a glorious op-
" portunity for the english to distinguish themselves ;
" and that your lordship by leading them on would
" gain immortal honour."

You yet expressed your surprise at the order, saying, it was impossible that the duke could mean to break the line. My answer was, that I delivered his serene highness's orders, word for word, as he gave them. Upon which, you asked, which way the cavalry was to march, and who was to be their guide. I undertook to lead them towards the left, round the little wood on their left, as they were then drawn up, where they might be little exposed to the enemy's cannonade.

Your lordship continued to think my orders neither clear nor exactly delivered ; and expressing your desire to see prince Ferdinand, ordered me to lead you to him ; which order I was obeying, when you met his serene highness. During this time, I did not see

the

the cavalry advance. Captain Smith, one of your aids de camp, once or twice made me repeat the orders I had before delivered to your lordship; and I hope he will do me the justice to say they were clear and exact. He went up to you, whilst we were going to find the duke, as I imagine, being sensible of the clearness of my orders, and the necessity of their being immediately obeyed. I heard your lordship give him some orders. What they were, I cannot say; but he immediately rode back towards the cavalry.

Upon my joining the duke, I repeated to him the orders I had delivered to you, and appealing to his serene highness, to know whether they were the same he had honoured me with, I had the satisfaction to hear him declare, they were very exact. His serene highness immediately asked, where the cavalry was; and upon my making answer, that lord G—— did not understand the order; but was coming to speak to his serene highness, he expressed his surprise strongly.

I hope your lordship will think I did nothing but my duty, as aid de camp, in mentioning to his serene highness my orders being so much questioned by your lordship.

I am, &c."

" Minden, august 3.

Lord G—— S——, as he resolved to get his recall as soon as possible, endeavoured as much as he could, to get such letters and declarations tending to clear his conduct, to carry home with him; besides the above letter, he got his aid de camp, capt. Smith, to sign a declaration * of what he knew concerning

* What I have to say with regard to the orders colonel Fitzroy brought, and to their not being put in execution, is—I heard lord G—

cerning colonel Fitzroy's orders. It is no wonder his lordship was willing to throw off so deep a stain, as the implied censures in the orders of the 2d of august. Time was certainly lost—and the most precious time that could have been used. Had lord G—— S—— obeyed the first order brought to him from the duke, and made a regular and vigorous charge on the french cavalry, already in confusion, the consequences would, in all probability, have been fatal to the french army—and never victory would have been more complete. In a few days after the battle, he resigned his command, and obtained his majesty's permission to return to England. As soon as he arrived in London, he wrote to the * secretary of state, requesting

G—— S—— say, on his receiving them, as they differed from those he had just before received by captain Ligonier, he would speak to the prince himself; and accordingly put his horse in a gallop to go to him. I immediately went up to colonel Fitzroy, and made him repeat the orders to me twice.—I thought it so clear and positive, for the british cavalry only to advance where he should lead, that I took the liberty to say to his lordship, I did think they were so; and offered to go and fetch them, whilst he went to the prince, that no time might be lost. His answer was, he had also an order from the prince, from Mr. Ligonier, for the whole wing to come away; and he thought it impossible the prince could mean that. I replied, that if he would allow me to fetch the british, they were but a part, and if it was wrong, they could sooner remedy the fault.—He said, then do it as fast as you can.—Accordingly I went, as fast as my horse could go, to general Mostyn.—He knows the rest.—This is all that passed, as near as I can recollect.—It was spoke as we galloped, and could not be long about, as I have been on the ground since, and do not believe, when his lordship sent me back, I had above six hundred yards to go to general Mostyn."

" My lord,
* I have the honour of acquainting your lordship of my arrival in England, in pursuance of his majesty's permission, sent to me at my request, by your lordship.

I thought myself much injured abroad, by an implied censure of my conduct; I find I am still more unfortunate at home, by being

requesting a court martial, and was assured for answer, that his desire should be gratified, as soon as the officers, capable of giving evidence, could leave their posts. However, before his lordship received this answer, he was dismissed from all his posts. The marquis of Granby succeeded him in his command, and in the lieutenant generalship of the ordnance, and his regiment was given to general Waldegrave. As his lordship was afterwards tried by a court martial, I shall dismiss the subject at present, till I come to to speak further of it on that occasion.

In the mean time, duke Ferdinand followed his victory so close, that the french had not a moment allowed them to recover their order. The 4th the army marched to Coovelt, and the 5th to Hervorden. The same day, lieutenant general Urff, with seven battalions and 20 squadrons, was detached to Lemgow, and arriving at Detmold the 5th, he surrounded and took 800 prisoners, together with the heavy baggage of the french army, among which were found mar-

publicly represented as having neglected my duty in the strongest manner; by disobeying the positive orders of his serene highness prince Ferdinand. As I am conscious of neither neglect nor disobedience of orders; as I am certain I did my duty to the utmost of my abilities; and as I am persuaded that the prince himself would have found, that he had no just cause of complaint against me, had he condescended to have enquired into my conduct, before he had expressed his disapprobation of it, from the partial representation of others: I therefore most humbly request, that I may at last have a public opportunity given me of attempting to justify myself to his majesty, and to my country, by a court martial being appointed; that if I am guilty, I may suffer such punishment as I may have deserved; and, if innocent, that I may stand acquitted in the opinion of the world; but it is really too severe, to have been condemned before I was tried, and to have been informed neither of my crime, nor my accusers.

I am, my lord, &c. &c. &c.

G. SACKVILLE.

shal Contades's papers, with the original letters of the duke de Belleisle to the marshal, which were of so curious a nature, that the officer who took them was offered two millions of livres for their ransom, but refused it ; the ministry in England afterwards published some of them. The 6th, the army marched to Bielefield ; the 8th, to Stukenbroeck, and the next day to Paderborn. The hereditary prince of Brunswick, at the head of 15,000 men, passed the Weser at Hamelen the 4th, and pursued the flying enemy, with the greatest expedition. The french magazines at Osnabrug, Minden, Bielefield, Paderborn, Dulmen, and Warrendorff, were all either taken or destroyed.

Marshal de Contades was obliged by want of subsistence, to make his retreat towards Cassel ; the allied army pursued him, without intermission ; on the 11th it was at Deleimand, the next day encamped at Stalberg : on the 13th, it entered the county of Waldeck, and directed its march so as to gain the flank of the enemy, who was then posted in the neighbourhood of Cassel. But Contades abandoned that city, the 18th, and retired towards Marpourg. Major Fridricks of the hanoverian chasseurs summoned Cassel, and it surrendered after some cannon shot, with a garrison of 400 men, prisoners of war, together with 1500 wounded, which the french had been obliged to leave behind them ; a very considerable magazine was also taken there.

Munster was still in the hands of the french ; but duke Ferdinand detached general Inhoff with a strong corps to besiege it. He began to bombard and cannonade it the 3d of september ; marshal Contades however, knowing the importance of that place, also detached M. d'Armentiers, with a body of troops, which were encreased on their march to 14 or 15,000 men, to relieve it. Inhoff did not think it adviseable to continue the siege, while the enemy had so great a superiority ;

superiority; he raised it on the 6th, retiring with his corps between Nobisbruck and Tellight. Some days after he received a reinforcement of troops, which enabled him in his turn to drive M. d'Armentiers from under the cannon of Munster; on which he again reassumed the siege; the french general retired towards Wesel, a place which had been of the greatest service to the french during this campaign.

In the mean time, duke Ferdinand continued his pursuit: the 22d of august his army halted at Francenburg. The hereditary prince, with the corps under his command, was then at Haina, and being joined there by the prince of Holstein, and general Wangenheim, with their respective corps, he marched the 24th to Wohra, and arrived the next day at Schonstedt. On the 23d, lieutenant colonel Freitag attacked Ziegenhayn, the governor capitulated, after an hour's defence; and the garrison of 400 men were made prisoners of war. The hereditary prince, one of the most active officers in the world, marched with a very strong corps to dislodge the famous partizan Fischer, from the post of Wetter, where duke Ferdinand intended to encamp. The prince attacked him with the greatest bravery, and defeated him with great loss, besides 400 prisoners he took. Lieutenant colonel Harvey of the Inniskilling dragoons, meeting with Fischer, struck his head off at one blow with his broad sword. By this action, the allies became masters of all the Wetteraw. On hearing of their success, duke Ferdinand marched by the way of Monighausen, and encamped at Wetter.

In this swift pursuit, the hereditary prince was always foremost in harrassing the flying enemy. His highness commanded a detachment from the right of the allied army; and having passed the Lahne, he
pushed

pushed forward to Neider-Weimar, where he surprised a party of the enemy, took two pieces of cannon, and some prisoners. Marshal Contades, to put a stop to the progress of the allies, threw a garrison into Marpourg; but duke Ferdinand marching to Neider-Weimar became master of that town in a few days, making 800 men prisoners of war. He remained in that camp some time; and marshal Contades had his head quarters at Anroth; the river Lahne being between the two armies. The 18th of september, a detachment from the allied army made themselves masters of Wetzlar, but were soon after dislodged by the duke of Broglio. The next day, duke Ferdinand marched to Korsdorff, where he fixed his head quarters, his army encamping about two miles from Giessen, with their right to Rotheim, and their left to Weissmar; he also posted a body of troops opposite Wetzlar, under general Wangenheim and the prince of Bevern. In this situation, the duke remained for some time, employing his army in little detachments, which were continually beating up the enemy's quarters, and harrassing them even to the walls of Franckfort. Munster was still blockaded by general Inhoff; that he might be the more expeditious in reducing it, the duke sent him a reinforcement from his camp at Korsdorff, of four battalions and four squadrons.

In the month of october, duke Ferdinand was invested with the order of the garter; the marquis of Granby and S. Martin Leak, esq. being appointed by his majesty plenipotentiaries for that purpose. The ceremony was performed with all the magnificence that a camp would permit; and the marshal Contades was so extremely polite, as to order a general discharge of his artillery, during the investiture, in honour of his serene highness.

The battle of Minden, an event so unexpected *, threw the court of Versailles into the utmost confusion. The king was told of it just as he was going to hunt; but the ill news struck him so sensibly, that

---

* To shew how little the court of France thought of this event, I need only lay before the reader, a letter from the duke de Belleisle to marshal Contades, which was taken amongst the rest of the marshal's papers after the battle.

"Versailles, july 23, 1759.

SIR,

I am still afraid that Fischer set out too late: it is however very important and very essential, that we should raise large contributions. I see no other resource for our most urgent expences, and for refitting the troops, but in the money we may draw from the enemy's country; from whence we must likewise procure subsistence of all kinds, (independently of the money) that is to say, hay, straw, oats, for the winter, bread, corn, cattle, horses, and even men to recruit our foreign troops. The war must not be prolonged, and perhaps it may be necessary, according to the events which may happen, between this time and the end of september, to make a downright desert before the line of quarters, which it may be thought proper to keep during the winter, in order that the enemy may be under a real impossibility of approaching us: at the same time, reserving for ourselves a bare subsistence on the route, which may be the most convenient for us to take in the middle of the winter, to beat up, or sieze upon the enemy's quarters.

That this object may be fulfilled, I cause the greatest assiduity to be used in preparing what is necessary for having all your troops, without exception, well cloathed, well armed, well equipped, and well refitted, in every respect before the end of november, with new tents, in order that, if it be adviseable for the king's political and military affairs, you may be able to assemble the whole, or part of your army, to act offensively, and with vigor, from the beginning of january; and that you may have the satisfaction to shew our enemies, and all Europe, that the french know how to act and carry on war, in all seasons, when they have such a general as you are, and a minister of the department of war, that can foresee, and concert matters with the general.

You must be sensible, sir, what I say to you may become not only useful and honourable, but perhaps even necessary, with respect to what you know, and of which I shall say more in my private letter.

he retired to the apartment of madam de Pompadour, in a dejected manner, and for several days saw none of his ministers. The general opinion of the people laid all the blame on the marshal Contades, and he threw it on the duke of Broglio; the marshal duke de Belleisle lost much of his credit; but still preserved a considerable part of his influence with his sovereign.

But it is time to take a view of some military transactions in another quarter, no less glorious and advantageous than those of which we have been speaking.

CHAP.

CHAP. XXIII.

Expedition against Quebec. Armament sails from Louisburg. Occupies the isle of Orleans. Situation of the french army. Action at the falls of Montmorency. The army removes to Point Levi. It goes up the river. Lands at Sillery. Battle of Quebec. General Wolfe killed, and general Moncton wounded. General Townshend takes the command. M. de Montcalm killed. French defeated. Quebec surrenders. Motions of general Amherst on lake Champlain. Builds several vessels. Sails against M. de Bourlemaque. Returns. Fortifies Crown Point. His army goes into winter quarters. Reflections on the campaign in north America.

THE principal part of the plan for the campaign in north America, which I before mentioned, consisted in an attack on Quebec, the capital of all the french empire in those parts; at the same time that general Amherst advanced towards the river St. Lawrence, by the way of Crown Point. As this was to be the decisive stroke, so the greatest force was to have been employed against it. The armament destined for this service rendezvoused at Louisburg. The fleet consisted of 19 sail of the line * besides

Ships.	Guns.	Ships.	Guns.
* Neptune	90	Alcide	64
Royal William	80	Devonshire	64
Princess Amelia	80	Captain	64
Dublin	74	Sterling Castle	64
Shrewsbury	74	Pr. of Orange	60
Northumberland	70	Medway	60
Oxford	70	Pembroke	60
Somerset	70	Bedford	60
Vanguard	70	Centurion	54
Terrible	64	Sutherland	50
Trident	64		

frigates,

frigates, transports, &c. &c. &c.; commanded by admirals Saunders, Holmes, and Durel. The land forces amounted to 7000 regulars and provincials, commanded by major general Wolfe; brigadiers general Moncton and Townshend were second in command. The whole sailed from Louisburg the 5th of June; and anchored at isle Bic 70 leagues up the river, the 19th, where the fleet was divided into three divisions, in order to make the passage the easier. The 27th the fleet anchored between the island of Orleans, and the south shore, on which the army landed that evening. As this island extends quite up to the harbour of Quebec, it was necessary to possess it before any operations could be begun against the town; for the most westerly point of it (which is not above four miles from Quebec) advances towards another high point of land on the continent, called point Levi. It was absolutely necessary to possess these two points, and fortify them; because from either the one or the other, the enemy might make it impossible for any ship to lie in the bason of Quebec.

Quebec lies in lat. 40. 32. long. 60. 40. at 120 leagues distance from the sea, and is the only fresh water harbour in the world, which is so spacious as to contain an hundred sail of men of war of the line; and at such a great distance from the sea. From the mouth of the river St. Lawrence to the isle of Orleans is 112 leagues, and is no where less than from four to five leagues broad; but above that island it narrows, so that at Quebec, it is not above a mile broad.

This city, which was founded in 1608, consists of an upper and lower town; the latter is built at the foot of a high rock, on the top of which the upper town stands. It is the seat of the governor general, intendant, and the supreme tribunals of justice for all Canada. Many of its buildings, both public and private are elegant and grand. The whole city
is

built with stone; the merchants generally live in the lower town for the convenience of their trade; which, before the war was considerable. It contains about 7000 souls. The fortifications were not regular; but they had been long at work to render it capable of a siege: the town, as it is, is naturally strong, the port was flanked with two bastions, which at high tides were almost even with the water. A little above the bastion to the right, is a half bastion, cut out of the rock; a little higher was a large battery, and higher still is a square fort, called the citadel, which was the most regular of all the fortifications; and in which the governor resided. The ways which communicate between these works are extremely rugged. The rock which separates the upper from the lower town extends itself, and continues with a bold and steep front, westward along the river St. Lawrence, for a considerable way. Another river from the north west, called St. Charles, falls here into the former, washing the foot of the rock on which Quebec stands; the point on which the town stands thus becomes a sort of peninsula, by the junction of these rivers; so that, to attack the city, it is necessary to make the approaches above the town, and overcome the precipice which I have mentioned, or cross the river St. Charles, and attempt it upon that side. Both of these methods would be extremely difficult; as in the former the precipice would be in his way defended by all the enemy's force; and in the latter, the country from the river St. Charles to the northward for more than five miles is extremely rough, broken and difficult, full of rivulets, gullies, and ravines, and continues so, to the river Montmorenci, which flows by the foot of a steep and woody hill. On this side the river St. Lawrence is a bank of sand of great extent, which prevents any considerable vessel from approaching the shore.

It

It was in this advantageous situation that the french army commanded by M. de Montcalm, who had been so often successful against the english in north America, was posted, extending along from the river St. Charles to that of Montmorenci, intrenched at every accessible spot, with the river and sand bank abovementioned in their front: and thick impenetrable woods upon their rear: there never was a stronger post; it was impossible to attack them in it; and whilst they remained there, it was in their power to throw succours into Quebec every day. The marquis de Montcalm very wisely resolved to continue in this post, although his force amounted to near 12,000 men, besides indians.

When general Wolfe learned that succours of all kinds had been thrown into Quebec; and perceived the strength of the french army, and its advantageous situation; he despaired of being able to reduce the place. But he sought however an occasion to attack their army, knowing well, that with his troops he was able to fight, and hoping that a victory might disperse them.

I have before said, that as soon as the general landed on the isle of Orleans, he perceived the absolute necessity of possessing himself of the two points Levi, and Orleans; soon after his landing, he received advice from the admiral, that there was reason to think the enemy had artillery and a force on the former of these points; wherefore, he detached brigadier Moncton with four battalions, to drive them from thence. The brigadier passed the river the 29th at night, and marched the next day to the point; he obliged the enemy's irregulars to retire, and possessed himself of that post. The general also detached colonel Carleton to point Orleans, from whence his operations were likely to begin. Batteries of cannon and mortars were erected with great dispatch, on point Levi, to bombard the town and magazines, and to injure the works

and

and batteries: the french perceiving thefe works in fome forwardnefs, paffed the river with 1600 men to attack and deftroy them. Unluckily they fell into confufion, fired upon one another, and went back again, by which the englifh loft an opportunity of defeating this large detachment. The effect of the batteries on Levi point was very great, although they fired acrofs the river, the upper town was foon confiderably damaged, and the lower town entirely deftroyed.

On the 28th at midnight, the garrifon fent down from Quebec feven firefhips; and though the englifh fhips and tranfports were fo numerous, and neceffarily fpread fo great a part of the channel, yet they were all towed clear aground without fuffering the leaft damage. Admiral Saunders was ftationed below in the north channel of the ifle of Orleans, oppofite to Montmorenci; admiral Holmes was ftationed above the town, at once to diftract the enemy's attention, and to prevent any attempts from them againft the batteries that played upon the town.

The beginning of july, general Wolfe fent a flag of truce to the commandant, publifhing his defign of attacking the town, on the part of his britannic majefty; at the fame time fignifying that it was his majefty's exprefs command, to have the war conducted without practifing the inhuman method of fcalping, and that it was expected the french troops under his command to copy the example, as they fhould anfwer the contrary. The marquis de Vadreuil returned a very polite anfwer; intimating his furprife, that with fo few forces, he fhould attempt the conqueft of fo extenfive and populous a country as Canada.

The works for the fecurity of the hofpitals and ftores upon the ifland of Orleans being finifhed, on the 9th of july at night, general Wolfe caufed the troops to be tranfported over the north channel of the river St. Lawrence, to the north eaft of the river Montmorenci,

Montmorenci, with a view of passing that river, and forcing the enemy to an engagement. The ground on his side the river was higher than that on the enemy's side, and commanded it in such a manner, that the general was of opinion it might be made useful to him. There is besides, a ford below the falls in the river Montmorenci, which may be passed for some hours in the latter part of the ebb, and beginning of the flood tide; Wolfe had hopes that possible means might be found of passing the river above, so as to fight the marquis de Montcalm upon terms of less disadvantage, than directly attacking his intrenchments. In reconnoitring the river Montmorenci, he found it fordable at a place three miles up; but the opposite bank was intrenched, and so steep and woody, that it was to no purpose to attempt a passage there.

The 18th of July, two men of war, two armed sloops, and two transports with some troops on board passed by the town without any loss, and got into the upper river. This enabled the general to reconnoitre the country above: but he there found the same attention on the enemy's side, and the same disadvantages on his own, arising from the nature of the ground, and the obstacles to his communication with his fleet.

However, general Wolfe, to divide the enemy's force, and to draw their attention as high upon the river as possible, and to procure some intelligence, sent a detachment under colonel Carlton, to land at the point de Trempe, to attack whatever he might find there, bring off some prisoners, and all the useful papers he could get. The general had been informed, that a number of the inhabitants of Quebec, had retired to that place, and that probably he would find a magazine of provisions there. The colonel was fired upon by a body of indians the moment he landed; but they were soon dispersed, and driven into the wood: he searched for magazines, but to no purpose;

purpose; brought off some prisoners, and returned with little loss.

The latter end of the month, the marquis de Montcalm sent down the river above an hundred fire stages; but the admiral having advice thereof some hours before, the whole fleet was prepared for the alarm. Nothing could be more dreadful than these machines; each was about 18 feet square, composed of rafts of timber to a considerable height, filled with the most combustible materials, and armed with drags and grapplings, to lay hold of hawsers and cables; each separately representing a lofty pillar of solid fire, and numbers of them uniting, would frequently form a rank of fire a quarter of a mile long. Even these did the english fleet no harm, being dragged ashore by the boats.

The general found that no assaults on the city would prove of any service, whilst the fleet could only batter the lower town, and must suffer greatly by the cannon and bombs of the upper; for after the reduction of the lower town, the passages to the upper were so extremely steep, and moreover so well intrenched, that this advantage would prove little towards the conquest of the city. The only point left therefore, was, by every means to entice or force the enemy to an engagement. Nothing was ever finer contrived, than the maneuvres which general Wolfe made to bring that design to bear. But M. de Montcalm, in chusing his post was well apprised of its importance, he kept himself close in it, disposing his parties of savages, in which he was very strong, in such a manner as make any attempt upon him by surprise absolutely impossible. Nevertheless, in spite of every difficulty, the general resolved to take the first opportunity which presented itself, of attacking the enemy; though posted to such great advantage, and every where prepared to receive him.

As

As the men of war could not (for want of sufficient depth of water) come near enough the enemy's intrenchments, to annoy them in the least, the admiral prepared two transports (drawing but little water) which upon occasion, could be run aground, to favour a descent. With the help of these vessels, which the general understood would be carried close in shore; he proposed to make himself master of a detached redoubt near the water's edge, and whose situation appeared to be out of musket shot of the intrenchment upon the hill: If Montcalm supported this detached piece, it would necessarily bring on an engagement, what the general most wished for; and, if not, he would have it in his power to examine the enemy's situation, so as to be able to determine where he could best attack them.

Preparations were accordingly made for an engagement. The 21st of july in the forenoon, the boats of the fleet were filled with grenadiers, and a part of brigadier Monckton's brigade from point Levi: the two brigades, under brigadiers Townshend and Murray, were ordered to be in readiness to pass the ford, when it should be thought necessary. To facilitate the passage of this corps, the admiral had placed the Centurion in the channel, so that she might check the fire of the lower battery, which commanded the ford: this ship was of great use, as her fire was very judiciously directed. A great quantity of artillery was placed upon the eminence, so as to batter and enfilade the left of their intrenchments.

From the vessel which run aground nearest in, general Wolfe observed, that the redoubt was too much commanded to be kept without very great loss; and the more as the two armed ships could not be brought near enough to cover both with their artillery and musketry, which at first he conceived they might. But as the enemy seemed in some confusion, and his troops were prepared for an action, he thought it a

proper

proper time to make an attempt upon their intrenchments. Orders were sent to the brigadiers general to be ready, with the corps under their command; brigadier Monckton to land, and the brigadiers Townshend and Murray to pass the ford. At a proper time of the tide the signal was made; but in rowing towards the shore, many of the boats grounded upon a ledge, that runs off at a considerable distance. This accident put them into some disorder, lost a great deal of time, and obliged Mr. Wolfe to send an officer to stop brigadier general Townshend's march, whom he then observed to be in motion. While the seamen were getting the boats off, the enemy fired a number of shot and shells; but did no considerable damage. As soon as this disorder could be set a little to rights, and the boats ranged in a proper manner, some of the officers of the navy went in with the general to find a better place to land. They took one flat bottomed boat with them to make the experiment; and, as soon as they had found a fit part of the shore, the troops were ordered to disembark, as it was thought not yet too late to make the attempt.

Thirteen companies of grenadiers, and 200 of the second royal american battalion got first on shore. The grenadiers were ordered to form themselves into four distinct bodies, and to begin the attack, supported by brigadier Monckton's corps, as soon as the troops had passed the ford, and were at hand to assist. But whether from the noise and hurry at landing, or from some other cause, the grenadiers, instead of forming themselves, as they were directed, ran on impetuously towards the enemy's intrenchments in the utmost disorder and confusion, without waiting for the corps which was to sustain them, and join in the attack. Brigadier Monckton was not landed, and brigadier Townshend was still at a considerable distance, though upon his march to join them in very great order.

der. The grenadiers were checked by the enemy's firſt fire, and obliged to ſhelter themſelves in or about the redoubt, which the french abandoned upon their approach. In this ſituation they continued for ſome time, unable to form under ſo hot a fire; and having many gallant officers wounded, who (careleſs of their perſons) had been ſolely intent upon their duty. The general ſaw the neceſſity of calling them off, that they might form behind brigadier Monckton's corps, which was then landed, and drawn up on the beach in exceeding good order. By this new accident and this ſecond delay, it was near night, a ſudden ſtorm came on, and the tide began to make, ſo that general Wolfe very wiſely thought it not adviſeable to perſevere in ſo difficult an attack, leſt, in caſe of a repulſe, the retreat of brigadier Townſhend's corps might be hazardous and uncertain.

Nothing could be better choſen, than the place where Mr. Wolfe made this attack. It was the only ſpot wherein his artillery could be brought into uſe, and it had a good effect upon the left of the french. The greateſt part, or even the whole of the troops might act at once. And, a retreat (in caſe of a repulſe) was ſecure, at leaſt for a certain time of the tide. Neither one or other of theſe advantages were to be found in any other place. The french were indeed poſted upon a commanding eminence. The beach upon which the troops were drawn up, was of deep mud, with holes, and cut by ſeveral gullies. The hill to be aſcended very ſteep, and not every where practicable. The enemy numerous in their intrenchments, and their fire hot. If the attack had ſucceeded, the loſs of the engliſh muſt have been great, and that of the french inconſiderable, from the ſhelter which the neighbouring woods afforded them. The river St. Charles remained ſtill to be paſſed, before the town was inveſted. All theſe circumſtances the general conſidered; but the deſire to act, in conformity

formity to his sovereign's intentions, induced him to make this trial, persuaded, as he himself gallantly expresses it, that a victorious army finds no difficulties. General Wolfe made a noble retreat, exposing his person with that intrepidity, which distinguished him during the attack.

The loss sustained in this check was not inconsiderable; and the bad success discouraged the general from making any further attempts upon that side. But immediately after it, he sent brigadier Murray above the town with 1200 men, directing him to assist rear-admiral Holmes in the destruction of some french men of war (if they could be got at) in order to open a communication with general Amherst. The brigadier was to seek every favourable opportunity of fighting some of the enemy's detachments, provided he could do it upon tolerable terms; and to use all the means in his power to provoke them to attack him. The men of war sailed up the river for more than 12 leagues: the brigadier made two different attempts to land upon the north shore, without success; but in a third was more fortunate. He landed unexpectedly at de Chambaud, and burnt a magazine there, in which were some provisions, some ammunition, and all the spare stores, cloathing, arms, and baggage of the french army; but finding that their ships were not to be got at, and that there was little prospect of bringing the enemy to a battle, he reported his situation to the general, who thereupon ordered him to join the army. The prisoners he took, informed him of the success of sir William Johnson against Niagara; they learned likewise, that the french had abandoned Crown Point and Ticonderoga. But this intelligence, otherwise so pleasing, brought them no prospect of the approach of any assistance from that quarter. The season wasted a-pace; and what was equally of bad consequence, the general fell violently ill of a fever, consumed by care, watching, and fatigue, too great to be supported by so delicate a body, which was so unequal to the greatness of the soul which it lodged. It was death to him to think of returning home, without being victorious : and and although he knew every thing was executed to ensure success, which his enterprising genius could suggest; yet he also knew how partial the world is to success, and that no military conduct can shine unless guilded with it. In short, the fear of not being successful, the hopes of his country, and great success of other generals turned inward upon him, and converted disappointment into disease *. As soon as he was a little recovered, he dispatched an express, with an account of his proceedings, to England; we may trace throughout it several marks of his despair of taking the town; but, although his letter is wrote in the stile of despondency, yet, he has expressed himself with such perspicuous elegance, that we may fairly say, he fought and wrote with the same spirit.

It was determined in a consultation which he held with his general officers, a little before he sent away his dispatches, that, (as more ships and provisions were then got above the town) they should try, by conveying up a corps of 4 or 5000 men (which was nearly the whole strength of the army, after the points of Levi and Orleans were left in a proper state of defence) to draw the enemy from their advantageous situation, and bring them to an action.

This determination was accordingly put in execution. General Wolfe drew off all his artillery, stores, baggage, &c. from his camp at Montmorency, which was broke up, and the troops, &c. conveyed to the south east of the river, and encamped at point Levi. The squadron under admiral Holmes made movements up the river, for several days successively, in order to draw the enemy's attention as far from the

* Campbell.

town

town as possible. But nothing could induce M. de Montcalm to quit his post; indeed these feints succeeded in some measure, as it induced him to detach M. de Bougainville with 1500 men to watch their motions, and to proceed along the western shore of the river, while the english army directed its march the same way on the eastern bank.

On the 5th and 6th of september, the general marched from point Levi, and embarked the forces in transports, which had passed the town for that purpose. And as soon as he saw that matters were ripe for action, he ordered the ships under admiral Saunders to make a feint, as if they proposed to attack the french in their intrenchments, on the Beauport shore below the town, and by their motions to give this feint all the appearance of a reality which it possibly could have. This disposition being made below the town, general Wolfe ordered the light infantry, commanded by colonel Howe, the regiments of Bragg, Kennedy, Lascelles, and Anstruther, with a detachment of highlanders, and the american grenadiers, the whole under the command of brigadier Monckton and Murray, to be put into the flat bottomed boats, about one in the morning of the 13th. To amuse the enemy, and conceal his real design, they went with admiral Holmes's division three leagues further up the river than the intended place of his landing; then the boats fell down silently with the tide, unobserved by the french centinels posted along the shore. The rapidity of the current carried them a little below the intended place of attack; the ships followed, and, by the greatest good management in the world, arrived just at the time which had been concerted to cover their landing. Never was moment more critical; never any conduct more admirable, both on the part of the land and sea service, than what was displayed on this occasion, amidst the continual danger of losing the communication in a dark night, and on such a rapid current.

The troops not being able to land at the place proposed; they were put on shore at another spot; where, as soon as they had landed, an hill appeared before them, extremely high and steep in its ascent; a little path winded up this ascent, so narrow, that two men could not go a-breast. Even this path was intrenched, and a captain's guard defended it. Such great difficulties did not abate the hopes of the general, or the ardor of the troops. Colonel Howe's light infantry scrambled up this path, by laying hold of boughs and stumps of trees, and, after a little firing, dislodged the guard, and cleared the path; by which means, with a very little loss from a few canadians and indians in the wood, they got up, and were immediately formed. The boats, as they emptied, were immediately sent back for the second embarkation, which brigadier Townshend made. Brigadier Murray, who had been detached, with Anstruther's battalion to attack a four gun battery upon the left, was recalled by the general, who formed his little army in order of battle, having his right covered by the Louisburg grenadiers; on the right of these were Otway's; to the left of the grenadiers were Bragg's, Kennedy's, Lascelle's, highlanders, and Anstruther's; the right of this body was commanded by brigadier Monckton, and the left by brigadier Murray; his rear and left were protected by colonel Howe's light infantry. The whole army was in order of battle at break of day.

The marquis de Montcalm, when he heard that the english had ascended the hill, and were formed on the high ground at the back of the town, scarcely credited the intelligence, and still believed it to be a feint, to induce him to abandon that strong post which had been the object of all the real attempts that had been made since the beginning of the campaign.

But

But he was soon fatally undeceived. He clearly saw that the englifh fleet and army were in fuch an advantageous fituation, that the upper and lower town might be attacked in concert, and that nothing but a battle could poffibly fave it. He accordingly determined to fight, and quitting his camp, croffed the river St. Charles, and formed his troops oppofite to the englifh army. His center was a column, and formed by the battalions of Bearne and Guienne; his right was compofed of half of the troops of the colony, the battalions of la Saure, Languedoc, and the remainder of the canadians and indians; his left confifted of the remainder of the troops of the colony, and the battalion of royal Roufillon. General Wolfe perceiving that Montcalm defigned to flank his left, ordered brigadier general Townfhend, with Amherft's battalion, and two battalions of the royal americans, to protect it: and alfo drew Webb's up, as his corps de referve, in eight fub-divifions, with large intervals. The french lined the bufhes in their front, with 1500 indians and canadians, where they alfo placed their beft markmen, who kept up a very galling, though irregular fire upon the whole englifh line, who bore it with the greateft patience and good order, referving their fire for the main body of the french, now advancing. This fire of the enemy was however checked, by the pofts in Mr. Wolfe's front. The french brought up two pieces of cannon; the englifh were able to get up but one gun, which being admirably well ferved, galled their column exceedingly. The general exhorted his troops to referve their fire; and at forty yards diftance they gave it, which took place in its full extent, and made terrible havock among the french; it was fupported, with as much vivacity as it was begun, and the enemy every where yielded to it; but juft in the moment, when the fortune of the field began to declare itfelf, general Wolfe (in whofe life the fuccefs of all was included)

included) fell; general Monckton, the next to him in command, fell immediately after, and both were conveyed out of the field; the command now devolved on general Townshend, at a very critical time; for, although the enemy began to fall back, and were much broken, the loss of the two generals was a very discouraging circumstance to the men, whose spirits are generally damped at the loss of their commanders; but this was not the case here. Part of the enemy soon after made a second feint attack. Part took to some thick coppice wood, and seemed to make a stand. It was at this moment that each corps seemed in a manner to exert itself, with a view to its own peculiar character. The grenadiers, Bragg's, and Lascelle's pressed on with their bayonet's. Brigadier Murray advancing with the troops under his command, briskly completed the rout on that side; when the highlanders, supported by Anstruther's took to their broad swords, and drove part of the enemy into the town, and part to their works at the bridge, on the river St. Charles. The action on the left and rear of the english was not so severe. The houses into which the light infantry were thrown, were well defended, being supported by colonel Howe, who, taking post with two companies behind a small coppice, and frequently sallying upon the flanks of the enemy, during their attack, drove them often into heaps; against the front of this body of the enemy, general Townshend advanced, platoons of Amherst's regiment, which totally prevented their right wing from executing their first intention. Mr. Townshend was no sooner told that he commanded, than he immediately repaired to the center of the army, and finding the pursuit had put part of the troops in disorder, he formed them as soon as possible. Scarce was this effected, than M. Bougainville, with his corps, which had retired to cape Rouge, of 2000 men, appeared in his rear. The general advanced

two

two pieces of artillery, and two battalions towards him; upon which he retired. But he could not be pursued, as his corps occupied ground which was almost impenetrable, by the woods and swamps. A great number of french officers were taken on the field of battle; and one piece of cannon; 1500 of their men fell; most of them regulars. The loss of the english did not exceed 500; but in the death of their commander they sustained a loss much more considerable. A retentive memory, a deep judgment, a comprehension amazingly quick and clear; a constitutional courage, not only uniform, but daring, perhaps sometimes even to excess, all conspired to form an accomplished hero. He possessed a strength, steadiness, and activity of mind, which no difficulties could obstruct, nor danger deter; and which enabled him when very young to signalize himself in his profession. Even so early as the battle of La-feldt, when scarce 20 years of age, he exerted himself in so masterly a manner, at a very critical juncture, that it drew the highest encomiums from the great officer, then at the head of our army. Even after the peace he spent great part of his time in forming the military character: he introduced such regularity and exactness of discipline into his corps, that, as long as the six british battalions on the plain of Minden are recorded in the annals of Europe, so long will Kingsley's stand amongst the foremost in the glory of that day. He was early in the most secret consultations for the attack of Rochfort; where he afterwards offered to make good a landing: his conduct at Louisburg, I have already given an account of. And at Quebec, having completed his character, and answered the expectations of his country, he fell at the head of his conquering troops, and, like the great Gustavus, expired in the arms of victory. There were a few circumstances attending his death, that deserve to be remembered. He first received a wound in his head;

but that he might not discourage his troops, he wrapped it up in his handkerchief, and encouraged his men to advance; soon after he received another ball in his belly; this also he dissembled, and exerted himself as before; when he received a third in his breast, under which he at last sunk, and suffered himself unwillingly to be carried behind the ranks. As he was struggling under three such wounds, he begged one who attended him, to support him to view the field; but finding, that the approach of death had dimmed his sight, he desired an officer near him, to give him an account of what he saw. He was answered, that the enemy seemed broken; repeating his question soon after, with much anxiety; he was told that the enemy was totally defeated, and that they fled in all parts. Then said he, " I am satisfied;" and immediately he expired. It is very remarkable, that the first in command on both sides should be killed, and second dangerously wounded; the french officer died of his wounds; but general Moncton happily recovered. In the marquis de Montcalm, the french lost an able and experienced general, who had supported his high reputation during the whole war in north America: his conduct in the command of that army, at the head of which he fell, was very great; he omitted nothing that human prudence could suggest, during the whole campaign; but it was his fate to be conquered by superior abilities.

General Townshend employed himself after the action in strengthening his camp beyond insult; in making a road up the precipice for his cannon; in getting up the artillery, preparing the batteries; and cutting off the enemy's communication with the country. The 17th at noon, before he had any battery erected, or could have any for two or three days, a flag of truce came out of the town, with proposals of capitulation, which the general sent back again, allowing the governor four hours to capitulate,

tulate, or no further treaty. The admiral had at this time brought up his large ships, as intending to attack the town; but the french officer returned at night, with terms of capitulation *, which the admiral and general

---

* Article I. M. de Ramefay demands the honours of war for his garrison; and that it shall be conducted back to the army in safety, by the shortest road, with their arms, baggage, six pieces of brass cannon, two mortars or howitzers, and twelve rounds. " The " garrison of the town, composed of land forces, marines, and " sailors, shall march out with their arms and baggage, drums " beating, lighted matches, with two pieces of cannon, and 12 " rounds; and shall be embarked as conveniently as possible, in " order to be landed at the first port of France."

Art. II. That the inhabitants shall be maintained in the possession of their houses, goods, effects, and privileges.——" Granted, " provided they lay down their arms."

Art. III. That the said inhabitants shall not be molested on account of their having borne arms for the defence of the town, as they were forced to it, and as it is customary for the inhabitants of the colonies of both crowns to serve as militia.——" Granted."

Art. IV. That the effects belonging to the absent officers or inhabitants, shall not be touched.——" Granted."

Art. V. That the said inhabitants shall not be removed, nor obliged to quit their houses, until their condition shall be settled by a definitive treaty between their most christian and britannic majesties.——" Ganted."

Art. VI. That the exercise of the catholic, apostolic, and roman religion shall be preserved; and that safeguards shall be granted to the houses of the clergy, and to the monasteries, particularly to the bishop of Quebec, who, animated with zeal for religion, and charity for the people of his diocese, desires to reside constantly in it, to exercise freely, and with that decency, which his character, and the sacred mysteries of the catholic, apostolic, and roman religion require, his episcopal authority in the town of Quebec, wherever he shall think it proper, until the possession of Canada shall have been decided by a treaty, between their most christian and britannic majesties. — " The free exercise of the roman religion. " Safeguards granted to all religious persons, as well as to the bi- " shop, who shall be at liberty to come and exercise freely, and " with decency, the functions of his office, whenever he shall think " proper, until the possession of Canada shall have been decided, " between their britannic and most christian majesties."

Art. VII. That the artillery and warlike stores shall be delivered up, bonâ fide, and an inventory taken thereof.——" Granted."

Art. VIII.

general considered, agreed to, and signed at eight in the morning of the 18th. The terms were more advantageous than would have been granted, had not several circumstances concurred to induce the admiral and general to consent to them. The enemy were assembling in the rear of the english army, and, what was more formidable, the very wet and cold season,

Art. VIII. That the sick, wounded, commissaries, chaplains, physicians, surgeons, apothecaries, and other persons emyloyed in hospitals, shall be treated agreeable to the cartel settled between their most christian and britannic majesties, on the 6th of february, 1759.——" Granted."

Art. IX. That before delivering up the gate, and the entrance of the town to the english forces, their general will be pleased to send some soldiers to be placed as safeguards at the churches, convents, and chief habitations.——" Granted."

Art. X. That the commander of the city of Quebec shall be permitted to send advice to the marquis de Vaudreuil, governor general, of the reduction of the town; as also, that this general shall be allowed to write to the french ministry, to inform them thereof.——" Granted."

Art. XI. That the present capitulation shall be executed accordding to its form and tenor, without being liable to non-execution, under pretence of reprisals, or the non-execution of any preceding capitulation.——" Granted."

The present treaty has been made and settled between us, and duplicates signed at the camp before Quebec, the 18th of september, 1759.

CHARLES SAUNDERS,
GEORGE TOWNSHEND,
DE RAMESAY.

Return of the killed, wounded, and missing, at the battle of Quebec, september 13, 1759.

Killed—1 general, 1 captain, 6 lieutenants, 1 ensign, 3 serjeants, 45 rank and file.——Wounded—1 brigadier general, 4 staff officers, 12 captains, 26 lieutenants, 10 ensigns, 25 serjeants, 4 drummers, 506 rank and file.——Missing—3 rank and file.

Guns, mortars, ammunition, &c. found in the city of Quebec.

Brass ordnance, { 6 pounders 1
                { 4   3
                { 2   2
                              Iron

(443)

feafon, which threatened the troops with ficknefs, and the fleet with accidents; it had made the road fo bad that general Townfhend could not get a gun up for fome time; add to this, the advantage of entering the town, with the walls in a defenfible ftate, and the being able to put a garrifon in it ftrong enough to prevent all furprife. Thefe were fufficient confiderations for granting the governor the terms that were agreed to. A garrifon of 5000 men was left in the city under brigadier general Murray, with a plenty of provifions and ammunition for the winter. The fleet failed to England foon after, fearing leaft the fetting in of the frofts fhould lock them up in the river St. Lawrence.

In this glorious and fuccefsful manner was finifhed as difficult and fevere a campaign as ever was conducted. How could it reafonably have been expected, that an army of 7000 men fhould take a city, extremely

Iron ordnance,	{	36 pounders	10
		24	45
		18	18
		12	13
		8	43
		6	66
		4	30
		3	7
		2	3
Brafs mortars,		13 inch	1
Ditto howitzers,		8	3
Iron mortars,	{	13 inch	9
		10	1
		8	5
		7	2
Brafs petards,			2
Shells,	{	13 inch	770
		10	150
		8	} 90
		6	

With a confiderable quantity of powder, ball, fmall arms, and intrenching tools, &c. Befides 37 cannon and one mortar, found between the river St. Charles and Beauport.

ftrong

strong by its situation, defended by a numerous garrison, and having an army, superior to that of the besiegers, intrenched under its walls, in one of the most advantageous posts, perhaps, in the world; and when that army was to be forced to an engagement, against the inclinations of an able and cautious commander? There never possibly was an enterprise of such extreme difficulty, conducted with so such wisdom and success as this expedition. The impediments which the nature of the country, and the strength of the enemy threw in the commander's way, were such difficult obstacles, that nothing but the genius of genius Wolfe could ever have surmounted them. Those movements, so daring, judicious, and admirably well concerted, which at last drew Montcalm from his impregnable intrenchments, were hardly ever equalled: they were masterpieces in the art of war. Nor was unanimity, diligence or skill, wanting on the part of the marine: Without them, even the genius of the general could not have succeeded. It does honour to the several commanders in this expedition, both in the sea and land service, to find what a perfect harmony subsisted between them, during all the operations that were performed; wherein they used the most zealous endeavours to second each other's efforts. The joy which overspread the whole kingdom, on receiving the news of the conquest of Quebec, would have been general and complete, had there not been a mixture of grief for the loss of the general. Mr. Pitt, in a most elegant speech set off the great services performed at Quebec, in the house of commons, which had such an effect, that a magnificent monument was voted for the deceased general in Westminster abbey; the living generals and admirals received that great honour, the thanks of their country by their representatives *.

After

* A little circumstance was talked off at that time, and it deserves to be recorded, as it shews a firmness of sentiment, and justness

After Quebec surrendered, the french army under M. de Levy retired to Montreal and Trois Rivieres, the only places of any consequence they had left in Canada: and in order to deprive them of subsistence in any attempt they might be induced to make towards the recovery of Quebec in the winter, that country along the river was laid waste for a considerable extent. A measure which would not have been executed, had it not been found necessary *.

In the mean time, general Amherst was prosecuting the war on lake Champlain with great diligence; but the nature of the country all over America, makes it very difficult to carry on any military expedition. M. de Bourlemaque, the commander of the french troops against him, after having abandoned Ticonderoga and Crown Point, retired to the isle au Noix, with 3500 men, and 100 cannon; he had four vessels on the lake, viz. la Vigilante, a schooner of 10 guns, six and four pounders, a sloop called Masque Longuy, of two brass 12 pounders, and six iron six pounders; la Brochette, of eight guns, six and four pounders; and l'Esturgeon of eight guns, six and four pounders,

---

ness of thinking, in the lower kind of people, that is rarely met with, even amongst persons of education. The mother of general Wolfe was an object marked out for pity, by great and peculiar distress; the public wound pierced her mind with a particular affliction, who had experienced the dutiful son, the amiable domestic character, whilst the world admired the accomplished officer. Within a few months she had lost her husband; she now lost this son, her only child. The populace of the village where she lived, unanimously agreed to admit no illuminations or firings, or any other signs of rejoycing whatsoever, near her house, least they should seem by an ill-timed triumph, to insult over her distress. There was a justness in this, and whosoever knows the people, knows that they made no small sacrifice on this occasion.

CAMPBELL.

* But I cannot here help taking notice how, similar this behaviour towards Canada, was to that which the duke de Belleisle directed marshal Contades to use towards Hanover, &c.; both were for exactly the same reason; but yet we did not scruple to cry out loudly against the inhumanity of the french.

besides

besides swivels mounted in all. General Amherst no sooner understood, that the french had this naval force, than he sent for captain Loring, who was building a brigantine at Ticonderoga; and having informed him of it, the captain thought the brigantine would not be of sufficient force, and concluded on building a Radeaux, to use its guns on the lake, as well as to transport them over the same.

On the 1st of september, the general learnt further, that M. de Bourlemaque had launched a new vessel, pierced for 16 Guns; he therefore again sent for captain Loring, that a second vessel might be built, if it could be done, without retarding the other, as it appeared that the enemy were trying all they could to have a superior force by water; the captain came on the 3d, and in conclusion a sloop of 16 guns was built. The utmost diligence being used in building these vessels, so that, by the 29th of september, the Radeaux, 84 feet in length, and 20 in breadth, to carry six 24 pounders, was launched. On the 10th of october, the brigantine arrived at Crown Point, carrying six 6 pounders, twelve 4 pounders, and twenty swivels, 70 seamen, and 60 marines, detached from the troops. The next day, the sloop arrived, she had four 6 pounders, twelve 4 pounders and 22 swivels, 60 seamen, and 50 marines. The same day, general Amherst, with the troops under his command, embarked in the battoes; the sloop and brigantine sailed with a fair wind, and the troops followed in four columns, with a light hoisted in the night aboard the Radeaux. The 12th, major Reid returning with some battoes of the royal highland regiment, lost the columns in the night, following the light of the brigantine, instead of that of the Radeaux, and at day break, found himself among the enemy's sloops, at les isles aux quatre vents; they fired several guns at him, and took one battoe, with a lieutenant, a serjeant, corporal, and 28 men. The general soon after

saw

saw the french sloops make all the sail they could; but bad weather coming on, general Amherst ordered the troops into a bay on the western shore, to be covered from the wind, which begun to blow hard. The 13th, it blew a storm, and quite contrary wind. During this necessary delay, the general received advice from captain Loring, who commanded the brigantine, that on the 12th, at day break, when they judged they were 45 miles down the lake, they saw the schooner, gave chace, and unfortunately run the brigantine and sloop aground, but got them off again; and then saw the enemy's sloops, which they had passed in the night, between them and the english army, and chaced to bring them to action, drove them into a bay on the western shore, and anchored so as to prevent their getting away. The next day they sent into the bay, in search of them, and found they had sunk two of them in five fathom water, and ran the third on ground, when the crews escaped.

The general, in the mean time, was forced to remain in the bay; as it blew a storm the 15th all night, and the continuance of it that day, made the lake impassable for boats, the waves running like the sea in a gale of wind. The 16th it froze in the night; and in the morning no change of weather. At last, on the 18th, the wind came to the southward; general Amherst proceeded immediately down the lake, as far as the place where the french sloops were; he repaired one of them, so that she sailed that day, with the brigantine and sloops: finding the wind changed to the northward, and an appearance of winter being set in, the general determined to lose no more time on the lake, by striving to get to the isle aux Noix, when, if he should arrive there, it would be too late in the season to force Bourlemaque from his intrenchments; he therefore determined to return to Crown Point, to complete the works there, as

much

much as possible, before he destributed his troops into their winter quarters. He accordingly arrived there the 21st. He found the repairs at Ticonderoga finished; and for the better defence of Crown Point, and to make that fortress as formidable as he could, he ordered, with the advice of the engineer, three forts to be erected, which he named the Grenadier fort, Light Infantry fort, and Gage's Light Infantry fort, ordering those corps to build each their own as fast as possible. The situation of these fortresses was the best the general had seen in America, as it was no where commanded, and had all the advantages of the lake, and strength of ground, that could be desired. These several works were not completely finished by the end of november; but they were put in such a posture of defence, as to make it impossible for the enemy to be successful in any attempts which they might make on them. After this laborious campaign, the general distributed his men in such quarters, that they effectually protected the country from any inroads of the french or their indians.

In this difficult expedition, general Amherst exerted all his abilities, which before had been employed so successfully in the service of his country, to surmount a thousand obstacles, arising from the nature of the country, in which the war was carried on. The tediousness of building a naval force, superior to that of the enemy, is hardly to be conceived. And having every operation that was carried on, depend so entirely on the wind and weather, necessarily protracted the campaign excessively. If these causes had not concurred, to delay general Amherst's crossing lake Champlain, he would very probably have taken up his winter quarters at Montreal, instead of Crown Point. I cannot help observing here, how finely the general conducted this whole expedition, how much caution and prudence was used in every operation,

ration, so necessary in such a country as America. His building several vessels on the lake in so short a space of time; and directing their order of sailing in so judicious a manner; his pursuing his advantages no further than was consistent with prudence; and afterwards employing the remainder of the campaign in securing his conquests, in such an effectual manner, are so many distinguishing marks of wisdom and abilities, as the american colonies had not experienced, in any of Mr. Amherst's predecessors, in his important command.

In this glorious and succesful manner, ended the campaign in America. The conquests gained there, were of such infinite importance to Great Britain, that they could not fail of raising the most perfect satisfaction throughout the whole kingdom. As the american colonies are the great sources of our trade and naval power, so these advantages, as they tend so much to secure the former, cannot but support and encrease the latter.

It was a pleasing contrast, to compare the state of north America, at the end of this campaign, with its state soon after the breaking out of the war. The french encroachments then, extended into the very heart of the english colonies; and they had formed such a connected chain of forts along the frontiers, as threatened to confine us within such bounds as they should please to dictate; but at the end of this campaign, the case was very different. The forts du Quesne, Frontinac, Niagara, Ticonderoga, and Crown Point, which before had been so formidable, were no longer in the hands of the french: whole nations of indians changed their masters, and instead of burning and destroying the english settlements, turned their arms against those of the french. Quebec, the capital of the dominions of France in America, was in the hands of the english; and the only remains of so many thousand miles of territority, which the french possessed, at the beginning of the war, was the tract between Trois Rivieres and lake Ontario; and their possessions in Louisiana. To what can we attribute such a surprising change, but to the happy influence of a firm and vigorous ministry, who exerted the strength of the nation they governed, in the most natural and advantageous manner.

CHAP.

CHAP. XXIV.

Situation of the king of Prussia. The army of the empire takes Dresden, and makes great progress in Saxony. King of Prussia detaches general Wunsch into Saxony. General Wunsch defeats the army of the empire, and joins general Finck. General Haddick defeated at Corbitz. Prince Henry's fine march into Saxony. Motions of marshal Daun. General Wunsch defeats the duke d'Aremberg. King of Prussia marches into Saxony, and joins prince Henry. General Finck surrenders at Maxen. General Diercke defeated at Meissen. Marshal Daun occupies the camp of Pirna. Remarks on his conduct. Munster capitulates. Hereditary prince of Brunswick defeats the duke of Wurtemberg at Fulda. Marches into Saxony, and joins the king of Prussia. Remarks on the campaign.

I Left the king of Prussia after the battle of Cunnersdorf, guarding his dominions against the united efforts of the austrians and russians; and rising superior to that formidable train of difficulties, which always follow a defeat. As he had been obliged to draw the greatest part of his troops out of Saxony; the army of the empire, under the duke of Deux Ponts, took advantage of their absence, and having no army in the field to oppose it, made itself master of Hall, Naumburg, and Zeitz; and on the 3d of august, summoned general Haufs, the prussian commandant at Leipsick, to surrender that city, and he agreed to a capitulation on the fifth, the garrison marching out with the honours of war. After making themselves masters of Leipsick, they attacked Torgau, which was evacuated by the prussian garrison on the 19th, who left behind them a magazine, valued at 1,060,000 florins; and 170,000 florins in specie in the military cheſt; their heavy artillery, all the hoſtages, priſoners of war, and deſerters that were in the town; burning the ſuburbs before they evacuated it. The duke of Deux Ponts, next marched againſt Wittenburg where there was a ſtrong garriſon of pruſſians, who after a feeble defence, ſurrendered upon honourable terms; but as they might have held out much longer, their commander, general de Horn, was put under an arreſt, as ſoon as he arrived at Berlin. From Wittenburg, the imperial army drew near to Dreſden, and on the 27th of auguſt ſummoned count Schmettau, the commandant, to ſurrender, who anſwered, that he would hold it out to the laſt extremity, for which purpoſe he left the new town, and retired into the old; upon this the duke of Deux Ponts gave orders for a regular attack; but before the batteries began to fire, Schmettau deſired to capitulate; and the city was ſurrendered the 4th of ſeptember, upon honourable terms.

Such was the rapid progreſs which the imperial army made in Saxony; to ſtop it, and, if poſſible to remedy the blows already received, his pruſſian majeſty detached general Wunſch from his own army, with 6000 men to march into Saxony, and endeavour to retake the towns, which the army of the empire had conquered. That general with his little army croſſed the Elbe at Torgau, the 3d of ſeptember. He made ſome priſoners at Groſſenhayn the 4th, and the ſame evening puſhed on towards Dreſden; and, at the diſtance of a mile from thence, met with a conſiderable body of huſſars, croats, and hungarian infantry, that were poſted at Drachenberg, and immediately attacked them. He drove the enemy from one thicket and height to another, till he came within ſight of Dreſden. The cannonade and fire of ſmall arms continued the whole day, without its being poſſible for general Wunſch to diſcover, if that city was ſtill in the poſſeſſion of the pruſſians or not. He was

was however of opinion, that it had capitulated; and therefore retreated that night to Groſſenhayn, and next day, the 7th, to Korſdorff. While he was on his march, he received advice, that the army of the empire, under the baron de St. André, was near Torgau. The general directly detached three battalions, and all his cavalry to attack him. On the 8th, after reconnoitring, the attack was reſolved. The infantry which had been left behind, arrived by degrees, and filed off, as they came up, by the town, into the gardens in the neighbourhood, where they had an hour's reſt. The baron de St. André, in the mean time, cannonaded general Wunſch's army as it formed, but without any ſucceſs; ſo that he did not anſwer it till his heavy artillery and ſome battalions and ſquadrons were poſted on his flanks. At one o'clock in the afternoon, he entered a plain in his front, with his lines formed, and began the attack, with ſuch ſucceſs upon the enemy's left, which was poſted in ſome vineyards, that it was broke intirely, after they had rallied four times. The baron de St. André loſt his whole camp, tents, camp equipage, and ſeven pieces of cannon. The purſuit continued above an hour, towards Eulenburg.

After obtaining this victory, general Wunſch marched to Leipſick, which ſurrendered to him, on the 1th of ſeptember. Wittenburg, Zeitz, and all the other places, except Dreſden, which the imperial army had made themſelves maſters of, were retaken. The king of Pruſſia to puſh this ſucceſs ſtill further, detached general Finck with another ſtrong corps into Saxony. Wunſch, after ſcouring the whole electorate with his little army in amazing ſecurity, joined general Finck at Eulenburg. The united corps then, as it ſhould ſeem with deſign to make itſelf maſter of Dreſden, marched ſtraight towards that city. At Noſſen, Finck learnt that general Haddick with a large body of austrians had joined the imperial army; and was encamped with all his forces at Roth-Schimberg. But he retired on the approach of the prussians, who cannonaded his rear. General Finck advanced and encamped at Teutschen Lohra, and from thence marched to Corbitz near Meissen. General Haddick having, in the mean, received some reinforcements, attacked general Finck the 21st. The cannonade in the action, which was very hot, began at nine in the morning, and lasted till dark in the evening; but notwithstanding the goodness of general Haddick's dispositions, and the great superiority of his numbers, yet he was forced to yield the field of battle to the prussians, and to retire towards Dresden. The loss of the austrians in this action was considerable, but that of the prussians did not exceed 800 men killed and wounded. The victory enabled general Finck to maintain his ground in Saxony, till he was relieved by his royal highness prince Henry, who was upon his march to join him.

I before mentioned the march which the king of Prussia made, by which he got between the russian army and great Glogau, and thereby baffled their design upon that important place. This movement, which many circumstances rendered necessary, prevented the russians from taking winter quarters in his dominions; but at the same time, it unavoidably cut off all communication with the army of prince Henry.

His royal highness, seeing, that all attempts to second the operations of the king his brother, on the side of Silesia, would be ineffectual, formed another plan of co-operating with him, which was immediately to direct his march towards Saxony; a scheme as daring, as it was judicious. Nothing was more desirous than the possession of that electorate; and the prince's march must have another good effect; for it would certainly draw the attention of marshal Daun from the side of Silesia, and disable him from assisting

ing the ruffians againſt Głogau. Indeed the difficulties which lay in the prince's way were very great: the whole country of Luſatia, through which this projected march lay, was in a manner overſpread with the enemy. M. Daun with the main army of the auſtrians, was poſted at Sorau, oppoſite to the prince's camp. Five bodies of ruffians occupied as many advantageous poſts, between the Bober and the Neiſs. General Laudohn poſſeſſed the whole country along the Spree, with ſeveral auſtrian corps. To get round marſhal Daun, it was neceſſary to make a vaſt circuit, and to march between the auſtrian and ruſſian armies, for more than 60 engliſh miles.

After the prince had ſecured the paſſes of the mountains of Sileſia, his royal highneſs quitted his camp of Schmotzſeiffen, and made a haſty march to Sagan, which prevented marſhal Daun, either from coming nearer the ruſſian army, or detaching any more troops to reinforce it. His royal highneſs next turned the auſtrian camp at Sorau, by marching by Buntzlau and Sprottau towards Laubahn; which not only obliged the marſhal to retire as far as Gorlitz, but alſo general de Ville, to abandon the advatageous poſt of Laubahn, and join marſhal Daun's army. His royal highneſs ordered the poſt of Laubahn to be immediately occupied; and took that opportunity of detaching major general Stutterheim (who had till then, been obſerving general de Ville) towards Friedland and Zittau. The general took at Friedland, two lieutenant colonels, four captains, and 669 grenadiers priſoners; brought away two pieces of cannon, and deſtroyed a magazine conſiſting of 1600 quintals of flour, 4000 buſhels of oats, and 10,000 rations of bread, for want of carriages to bring it off. He then marched to Zittau; but the auſtrians having taken the reſolution to reinforce the garriſon there, and remove the magazine from thence to Gabel, M. Stutterheim went in purſuit of it came up with it, and burned and destroyed 5000 casks of flour, 10,000 quintals of oats, with the carriages, and a number of chests of arms. Not being able to force the town of Zittau, for want of heavy artillery, was obliged to content himself with the advantages he had gained, having lost no more in this whole expedition than 15 men killed, wounded, or deserted. However, these circumstances obliged marshal Daun to retire from Gorlitz, beyond Bautzen; whereupon, prince Henry possessed himself of the camp of Hermsdorff, near Gorlitz.

It was now the prince found, how difficult an enterprise it was, which he had undertaken; the five bodies of russians, I mentioned before, occupied the posts of Christianstadt, Guben, Pforten, Sommerfeldt, and Gassen: the austrians under general Laudohn were in possession of Tribel and Sorau; and another corps of austrians, under general Palfi, occupied Spremberg, Cotbus, Peitz, and other places upon the Spree; so that, in order to get round Daun's army, it was necessary to make a very great detour between the austrian and russian armies. In spight of all these obstacles, his royal highness pursued his march. Having recalled general Zeithen from Seydenburg, and general Stutterheim from his post at Schouwald near Zittau, in order to form his rear guard, gave orders for the march of his whole army, which was accordingly begun the 23d of september, at seven o'clock at night; and in the morning of the 24th, they crossed the river Neiss, near Rothenberg, (four german miles distant from Hermsdorf) and after halting two hours, continued on to Klitten, where the van-guard arrived about eleven that night, and the rear at eight the next morning.

On the 25th in the morning, the prince's van-guard marched from Klitten towards Hoyerswerda; major general Lentulus having been sent before to take possession of it. That general having advanced within half

half a german mile of Hoyerfwerda, had the good fortune to difcover, that the auftrian general Vehla, with a corps of 4 or 5000 auftrians, chiefly irregulars, was encamped behind the town, in perfect fecurity; notice of this was immediately fent to his royal highnefs, who ordered Vehla to be attacked, and foon drove him from the town, and his camp to the neighbouring woods, where he made a very brave defence, and was himfelf taken prifoner in the rear of his corps, which was foon afterwards entirely difperfed. After halting two days at Hoyerfwerda, the pruffians marched the 28th in the morning to Ruland, and the next day to Elfterwerda.

On the 1ft of october, the prince received advice that marfhal Daun had thrown 3 bridges over the Elbe at Drefden, he therefore detached general Ozttritz to crofs that river, with five battalions, and two regiments of dragoons, at Torgau, and approach general Finck's corps, in cafe of a probability of its being attacked. His royal highnefs marched himfelf, and arrived at Torgau the 2d, where he alfo croffed the Elbe, and proceeded on to Belgern, and there joined general Finck on the 4th. In this manner the miferable country Saxony, was again made the grand theatre of war, and was now to fuffer all its hardfhips and diftreffes once more. Since the beginning of the war, there never has been made a more difficult, or a finer conducted march, than this of prince Henry. To lead an army over fo extenfive a tract of country, every where occupied by the enemy, in fuch a rapid manner, equally difplays the genius of the commander, and the goodnefs of the pruffian troops.

Soon after his royal highnefs arrived in Saxony, his pruffian majefty received advice of another piece of good news, the ruffians began to retreat from the neighbourhood of the king's camp, and by their march feemed to have a defign on Breflaw; but they afterwards

afterwards turned off towards Poland, and left the prussian dominions free for the remainder of that campaign.

Prince Henry finding it necessary to leave his strong camp at Strachla, near Belgern, marched on the 16th of october to Torgau, and posted himself in a well placed and strong camp, the left extending itself to the town, with a large morass before part of it, the left flank of it covered by the Elbe, as the right was by a wood, at two english miles distance from the town. Marshal Daun posted himself at Belgern, and detached a large corps to his left, to cut off the prince's communication with Leipsick.

Prince Henry, to prevent the marshal from executing this scheme, detached general Rebentish to Duben, as well to observe his motions towards Leipsick, as to watch the rear of his own camp, in case the enemy should attempt to get behind, and cut off his communication with Wittenburg. On the 25th, the prince received intelligence, that the austrians had pushed a strong party through the woods, behind his right, and got possession of Voglesang, some other villages, and the small town of Dommitsch, by which means, his camp was entirely surrounded, having the Elbe on the left, and the austrian posts on the other three sides at Belgern, Schuldau, Rochwitz, and Dommitsch, at which last place, the duke d'Aremberg commanded a body of about 16,000 men. His royal highness, thereupon ordered general Finck's corps, which was in the rear of his camp, to march towards Voglesang, from whence the austrians were drove, and general Finck remained in possession of the post. The next day the prince (who found it impracticable to dislodge the enemy from Dommitsch, without great loss of men) detached general Wunsch with six battalions and some cavalry across the Elbe at Wittenburg, where he was to be joined by general Rebentish's corps, which had retired to that place

from

from Duben, upon the approach of the auſtrians. On the 29th, the duke d'Aremberg decamped from Dommitſch, in order to occupy the heights near Pretſch; upon perceiving the van of general Wunſch's corps, which was marching that way, he immediately formed into order of battle. General Wunſch (whoſe whole force joined to that of general Rebentiſh, did not exceed 5000 men) poſted himſelf with ſome dragoons and huſſars, on two riſing grounds, and waited till the arrival of his infantry with the artillery. He then began to cannonade the auſtrian corps, which never attacked, or attempted to diſlodge him; but it ſuffered ſeverely in the action; 1200 priſoners were taken, amongſt whom was lieutenant general Gemmingen; they likewiſe loſt ſeveral pieces of cannon, a great part of their tents, and a very large quantity of baggage. Marſhal Daun, finding by the prince's vigorous operations, that he ſhould not be able to make any progreſs againſt him, decamped on the 4th of november in the moſt private manner, directing his march towards Strehla. As ſoon as the prince perceived it, he detached lieutenant general Ziethen after him, to harraſs his rear, who made ſome priſoners. General Wunſch alſo marched from Duben, and took poſſeſſion of Eulenburg, which the auſtrian detachment abandoned in the night of the 3d, and general Warſſeſleben occupied Belgern on the 4th.

To enable prince Henry to puſh theſe advantages as far as poſſible, his pruſſian majeſty detached general Hulſen from his own army, with 18 battalions and 30 ſquadrons, the end of october, acroſs Luſatia, to reinforce his royal highneſs. Hulſen arrived at Spremberg, by the way of Moſka, on the 3d of november, with his van-guard at Hoyerſwerda; and joined the prince's army the 8th, at Lommatſch; having croſſed the Elbe on a bridge of boats. The king finding that the ruſſians continued to retreat into Poland, marched at the head of near 20,000 men, from his camp in Sileſia,

Silesia, on the 7th of november, leaving general Itzenplitz, with a part of his army, to keep the russians from availing themselves of his absence, and joined prince Henry at Meissen the 12th, who had before under his command 44,000 men, so that his prussian majesty, notwithstanding the losses he had met with in this campaign, found himself at the head of a gallant army of above 60,000 men, in high spirits, and ready to execute the most desperate of his orders, notwithstanding the advanced season, and the great extremity of the cold. Marshal Daun, it is true, was superior to him, both in numbers and situation. He had it in his power at any time, to take possession of the famous camp at Pirna, where it was impossible to attack him. But several circumstances made this post as dangerous in some respects, as it was desirable in others; the freezing of the Elbe, and the snow on the mountains, which divided Bohemia from Saxony, made it very difficult to procure the necessary provisions and forage. Add to this, the being continually molested by the prussian parties, as there was great reason to suppose he would.

Had the king of Prussia, in this situation, contented himself with only pursuing the advantages he had already gained, by joining his forces so successfully, marshal Daun would in all probability have abandoned Dresden, and retired into Bohemia. But that monarch imagining, that he might oblige the marshal to come to a battle, by possessing himself of some strong posts, which command the passes that lead into Bohemia, as the austrians retreat into that kingdom, would then, in a manner, be cut off, determined to attempt executing this plan.

His majesty, by a movement he made, obliged marshal Daun to retreat as far as Plauen; and advanced his own army to Kesseldorf; from whence he detached general Finck, with 19 battalions and 35 squadrons, to take possession of the defiles of Maxen and

and Ottendorf, through which alone it seemed possible for the austrians to communicate with Bohemia. General Finck accordingly turned the left flank of the austrian army, and posted himself at Maxen, placing on a hill to the right of a village, three battalions, and a battery of ten pieces of cannon. In the mean time, marshal Daun, who was aware of the king's design, had occupied all the eminences about this rough and dangerous place, and made his dispositions for attaking the prussians on the 20th. General Finck had got too far amongst the defiles without having secured a retreat, when he saw a large body of austrians moving to attack him, he made a very brisk fire from his artillery, but with little effect, on account of the elevation. The austrian cannon played with more success, and protected their grenadiers, who marched against the prussian left, and attacked it with great intrepidity, making themselves masters of the battery of ten pieces of cannon. General Finck made during the whole day the most intrepid efforts to disengage his army from the enemy, but he was defeated in every attempt, with a considerable loss of men, and great part of his artillery. The engagement lasted with great fury till night; during which, marshal Daun took every precaution possible to entangle the prussians, by guarding with double strength and vigilance, every avenue through which it was possible for them to escape. When morning appeared, Finck saw all the hills covered upon every side with great bodies of austrians, and every defile presented a wall of bayonets, through which it was impossible to penetrate. The prussian troops almost exhausted with the preceding day's fighting, wherein they had used almost all their ammunition, seeing so formidable an enemy on all sides, and without the least prospect of relief, lost all spirit. In this condition, general Finck thought it would be needless to throw away the lives of so many
brave

brave men, to so little purpose, in any more attacks upon an invincible enemy; he therefore, notwithstanding the known severity of his master, and the stain which he was sensible the world would fix on his character, came to a resolution of demanding a capitulation. Marshal Daun granted it in one article, whereby general Finck, and nine other prussian generals were received prisoners of war, with 19 battalions and 35 squadrons, composing near 20,000 men, by the austrian account; above 12,000 by the prussian confession; 64 pieces of cannon, 50 flags, and 25 standards were also taken on this occasion.

With the most trifling loss did marshal Daun execute this service. It was without exception the most severe blow, which the prussians had felt since the beginning of the war; it happened in the most critical time, and brought a great disreputation on their arms, from the manner in which this numerous corps was taken: so that we cannot be suprised, that the friends of the house of Austria should have exulted so much, especially as the stroke which his prussian majesty now received, was of much worse consequences to his cause, than the capture of the saxon army, in the year 1756, was to that of his enemies.

The king had not recovered this stroke before he received another severe one. General Dierke had been posted on the right bank of the Elbe, occupying a strong camp opposite to Meissen, with seven battalions of infantry and a thousand horse. This post was so advantageous, that he thought his retreat to Meissen absolutely secure, especially as he had been assured by the pontoneers, that they could lay a bridge over the Elbe in a few hours, (for they had been obliged during the hard frost, to withdraw the bridge of boats they had over that river, and the wooden bridge at Meissen had been broken down by the austrians) but when they attempted to lay a bridge of pontons, it was found impracticable, because of the

quantity

quantity of ice, floating in the river. General Diercke was therefore reduced to the necessity of making use of boats, to carry over his cavalry, and part of his infantry, on the 3d of december, which took up a great deal of time, whilst he himself with three or four battalions formed the rear guard. The next day, in the morning, he was attacked by the austrians, and after a very brave defence, the battalions that formed the rear guard, were either killed or made prisoners, to the number of near 3000 men. The general himself was wounded, and a prisoner.

Marshal Daun, by his inactivity, after these two blows, so fatal to the prussian cause, surprised all Europe; a few vigorous efforts, were now only wanting to crush the king of Prussia. But Daun, instead of advancing, retired, as if he had been defeated, and took refuge in the impregnable camp of Pirna, having secured all the defiles in such a manner, that his prussian majesty, now too weak to send out any great detachment, could not cut off his communication with Bohemia. Surely marshal Daun's measures after these two defeats were by far too feeble. He had now the fairest opportunity which had presented itself since the beginning of the war, of totally ruining his enemy, before the defeat at Maxen he had a superiority of above 20,000 men, and consequently after it, by his own account, of 40,000, if he could not improve this success, with such a vastly superior force, how could he expect to be able to do it, when he had given his enemy time to recruit his shattered army. This was a critical moment, which count Daun should have seized, and for once have carried on the war offensively; and have attacked the king, while his army was so diminished in its numbers, and the remainder of it dispirited under its late loss? Had marshal Daun, even after he took possession of the camp at Pirna, where it was impossible he should be attacked, sent out some very strong
detachments,

detachments, to push the war in Silesia, and even in Brandenburg itself, the king of Prussia would have found it impracticable to defend so many parts of his dominions. The cold, which was then indeed very severe, would not have prevented some strong corps being detached. In short, it was impossible to unravel this part of Daun's conduct; for, although he was so well known to be an excessive cautious commander, yet, under such strong circumstances as these of which I have been speaking, we must suppose he would throw something into the hands of fortune, who had so lately befriended him, in such a signal manner. But if his genius, which leads him so directly to defensive operations, would not permit him to hazard a battle, still there are a thousand different methods, which an able commander knows how to use, to follow such a blow as his prussian majesty had just received, and reap from it its greatest consequences.

In the mean time, while the two armies in Saxony carried on the campaign, through all the rigor of the severest winter, for many years felt in Europe; duke Ferdinand did the same, but with much better success than his prussian majesty. Indeed the french army having received considerable reinforcements, and the obstinate defence of the city of Munster, together with the great extremity of the cold had prevented his serene highness from forcing his enemy to a decisive action. At length, after a tedious siege and blockade, Munster capitulated, whereby general Inhoff with the corps under his command, was enabled to join the army under duke Ferdinand.

Soon after this, the hereditary prince of Brunswick, whose activity, I have so often had occasion to celebrate, performed a piece of service of much more prejudice to the french, than even the loss of Munster. The duke of Wurtemburg had this year renewed his treaty of subsidy with France, and having recruited,

and

and augmented his troops, to the number of near 10,000 men, was posted at Fulda, a great way to the right of the french army; as there were no great bodies of troops posted near Fulda to preserve a free communication between that town and the rest of their army, the prince formed a design of attacking the duke of Wurtemburg.

On the 28th of november, he, with prince Charles of Bevern, taking two regiments of dragoons, two of cavalry, four battalions of foot, two regiments of grenadiers, 100 hunters, and two squadrons of hussars, and disengaging them from their baggage, marched the same day to Kisdorff, and Heimershausen, and the following, being the 29th, seperating into two corps, the hereditary prince with one, lay that night at Angersbach, and prince Charles with the other at Lauterbach. At one o'clock in the morning of the 30th, the whole corps was again put in motion, and marched directly towards Fulda. As the enemy did not in the least expect this visit, no troops were met on the road. At a little distance from Fulda, having ordered the whole corps to be drawn together, behind the nearest height, and the hussars to march forward, his serene highness went to reconnoitre, almost to the gates of the town. The country about Fulda forms a plain of tolerable even ground, the right of which is watered by a river of the same name; the fields on this side being divided by a long hollow way. On one side of it the Wurtemburg troops had ranged themselves, in small bodies, on separate spots of ground, very irregularly posted. The duke was himself in the town, and had ordered a feu de joye for that day; his troops were all in their best cloaths; and he had invited all the ladies in the town to his table, and to a ball which he intended to have given; but the hereditary prince overturned all his measures, both of war and diversion. His highness having reconnoitred their situation, attacked

tacked them unawares in their front and flank, and drove them into the town; they shut the gates after them, but they were soon forced open with the cannon, and the hereditary prince pursued them through it. On the other side of the town, they were met by prince Charles of Bevern, who had made a compass about the place, and attacked them vigorously, as soon as they had got out of it; three battalions and a regiment had formed again in order of battle, as if with an intention of defending themselves; but they were instantly attacked, and all either cut in pieces, or taken prisoners, together with all their officers, two pieces of cannon, two pair of colours, and their baggage. The duke himself, with the rest of his troops, made a shift to escape, under cover of the defence made by those battalions. The prince took above 1000 prisoners; and having rested his troops a day at Fulda, retired to the army of the allies, having disabled the Wurtemburghers from performing any thing considerable.

This stroke had more good consequences than one, as it not only prevented the french from forming a communication with the army of the empire, for the mutual extension and security of their winter quarters, as they did the last campaign; but it also was in part the occasion of their abandoning their camp at Giessen, which they did on the 5th of december, and fell back towards Butzbach, on the direct road to Franckfort, leaving a garrison of 2000 men in Giessen.

Duke Ferdinand finding the season grown too severe to push further the advantages he had gained over the french, and that their army was going into winter quarters, determined to send a reinforcement to the king of Prussia. He considered the distressed condition of that monarch's affairs, which were at so low a pitch, and his army so weak, that he had no hopes of dislodging marshal Daun, or preventing him from taking his winter quarters in Saxony. His serene

rene highness accordingly placed the hereditary prince at the head of 12,000 men, and detached him to succour his prussian majesty. They marched from Korsdorff, the 11th of december, and in the depth of so severe a winter, without losing a man by sickness or desertion, in 15 days marched near 300 miles, and joined the king of Prussia at Freyburg in Saxony. For a moment this junction raised the spirits of the prussians; but it did little service to their cause. Marshal Daun, still at the head of a much superior army, intrenched in an inaccessible camp, was too cautious to give the king the least opportunity of so much as making an attempt. His majesty endeavoured to draw him to a battle, but all his efforts were in vain; so that after one of the longest, most laborious, and bloody campaigns, that ever was conducted, the king of Prussia distributed his troops into winter quarters.

In the mean time, the duke of Broglio, who having obtained the marshal's staff, now commanded the french army, determined to take advantage of the hereditary prince's absence to make an attack upon duke Ferdinand's posts. On the 24th, he attempted it by surprise; but found so warm a reception, and every post so well guarded, that he retired to his former quarters, without being able to effect any thing.

In this glorious and successful manner, did prince Ferdinand finish the campaign. The superiority of his genius appeared very evidently in its conclusion: there hardly ever being a bolder action than the detaching 12,000 men, so great a distance, from an army so much inferior to its enemy; nor did the abilities of the hereditary prince shine less conspicuously, in conducting that rapid march, during such severe weather. This action in the face of one superior army, and the taking Munster in the presence of another, particularly distinguishes the generalship of duke Ferdinand.

This was the most fatal campaign to the king of Prussia, of any he had made since the beginning of the war. All Europe was with great reason surprised, to see the immense efforts he made against such formidable enemies, even after having sustained four capital defeats in one campaign. Before this war, the power of the house of Brandenburg was supposed to be merely artificial; under any other sovereign, that supposition would perhaps have been true; but the resources which his prussian majesty found in his own genius, made up for those that are wanting in his dominions. Every one knows, that his territories, Silesia excepted, are some of the most barren tracts of country in Germany. And yet, this monarch was able for three years to carry on a most successful and glorious war, against four of the most powerful states in Europe; and, even in the fourth campaign, though not victorious, yet he displayed his vast abilities, in finding resources, more than in any of the former; for, although he lost four battles in that campaign, yet Dresden was the only fruit that his enemies gained by as many victories.

CHAP. XXV.

Preparations at Vannes and Breſt for an invaſion. Sir Edward Hawke blocks up the port of Breſt. He is driven from his ſtation. The french fleet comes out of Breſt. Battle of Belleiſle. French fleet defeated. War in the Eaſt-indies. Surat ſurrenders to captain Maitland. French attempt to dethrone the nabob of Bengal. Are defeated by colonel Clive. Major Ford takes Maſſulipatam. Battle at ſea, between Pocock and d'Aché. The french defeated. Affairs in Europe. Sad ſtate of France. Kings of Great Britain and Pruſſia offer to hold a congreſs for peace. Refuſed by the other belligerent powers. Reflections on the events of the year 1759.

I Before mentioned the preparations which the court of France had made for ſome time, in all their ports, to invade Great Britain. The battle of cape Lagos checked them; but they were far from being diſcontinued. The defeat which the french army in Germany met with at Minden, ruined their ſchemes of making a good peace, by means of the poſſeſſion of Hanover; they then found that their only hope depended on the ſucceſs of the invaſion, they had planned againſt England; and therefore redoubled their efforts to get their ſquadron at Breſt in all poſſible forwardneſs. The forces were to be tranſported from Vannes. The winter did not in the leaſt delay theſe preparations; it was that ſeaſon wherein the french court hoped to be able to put their deſign in execution; as they thought the engliſh fleet, which had been cruiſing ſome time before the harbour of Breſt, would then be obliged to take refuge in its own

own ports; and leave the sea open to the french fleet to come out, and land their forces in England.

The french were not wholly disappointed in their expectations; for sir Edward Hawke was forced from his station by a violent storm, and driven into Torbay. The french admiral, Conflans, took immediate advantage of his absence, and put to sea the 14th of november. This was an event which alarmed the whole british nation; the consequences of the whole war, were put at once to the stake; and this was the critical moment, that was to determine the fate of the two kingdoms: if the french were able to execute their plan; all the success which had attended the arms of Britain, since the beginning of the war, would be entirely overthrown. But though the nation was alarmed, yet it was far from being dejected; their fear only produced the most cool and regular methods of defence, no disturbance was heard of, and every one was emulous to distinguish himself in the service of his country. Orders were issued for guarding all such parts of the coast of England, as were most likely for the french to attempt to make a descent on; for which purpose, troops were every where put in motion; and all the ships of war in harbour were ordered out.

One remarkable instance of gallant behaviour at this period, is worthy to be recorded. Admiral Saunders came into port from his Quebec expedition, just after sir Edward Hawke had sailed. Neither the tedious length of his late voyage, the fatigues he had undergone in so severe a campaign, nor the want of the necessary orders, could deter him from putting to sea with ten ships, to partake the honour and the danger of the ensuing engagement; he was not however so fortunate as to join the english fleet time enough for it.

As sir Edward concluded, that the first rendezvous of the french fleet would be at Quiberon bay, the instant

stant he received intelligence of their having sailed, he left Torbay the 14th and (the same day as the french came out of Brest) directed his course thither, with a prest sail. At first the wind blew hard, and being contrary, drove him considerably to the westward. But on the 18th and 19th, though variable, it proved more favourable; so that on the 20th, at 8 o'clock in the morning, one of his frigates made the signal for an enemy's fleet in view. But, although the admiral was now so happy as to have the enemy in sight, yet there was an infinity of dangers to encounter, even before he could possibly engage them. The whole coast is sown very thick with sands and rocks, the english pilots were not well acquainted with it, and the wind blew little less than a violent storm; the sea running mountain high: the enemy's squadron was very strong, and on their own coast, with which they were perfectly acquainted. These dreadful difficulties only animated the english admiral; in circumstances less dangerous, some commanders would have avoided an engagement; but sir Edward Hawke knowing that this was the most critical moment of the whole war, determined to venture every thing in the service of his country: he was in one of the finest ships in the world, and commanded the flower of the british navy *, he was seconded by many of the

bravest

* English fleet.

Ships.	Guns.	Men.	Commanders.
Royal George	100	880	Sir Edward Hawke, Captain Campbell.
Union	90	770	Sir Charles Hardy, Captain Evans.
Duke	90	750	Captain Graves,
Namure	90	780	Captain Buckle,
Mars	74	600	James Young, esq. commodore.
Warspright	74	600	Sir John Bentley,
Hercules	74	600	Captain Fortescue,

Torbay

braveſt and moſt experienced officers in the ſervice, and every man carried in his breaſt the remembrance of thoſe glorious ſucceſſes, which had ſo particularly diſtinguiſhed the britiſh arms during the war. When the french fleet was firſt diſcovered, it was bearing to the northward, between the iſland of Belleiſle, and the main land of France.

The admiral obſerving, that on his firſt diſcovering them, they made off, threw out the ſignal for the ſeven ſhips neareſt them to chace, and draw into a line of battle a-head of him, and endeavour to ſtop them, till the reſt of the ſquadron ſhould come up,

who

Ships.	Guns.	Men.	Commanders.
Torbay	74	600	Hon. capt. Keppel,
Magnanime	74	700	Right hon. lord Howe,
Reſolution	74	600	Captain Speke,
Hero	74	600	Hon. capt. Edgecumbe,
Swiftſure	70	520	Sir Thomas Stanhope,
Dorſetſhire	70	528	Captain Denis,
Burford	70	520	Captain Gambier,
Chicheſter	70	520	Captain Willet,
Temple	70	520	Captain W. Shirley,
Revenge	64	480	Captain Storr,
Eſſex	64	480	Captain Obrien,
Kingſton	60	400	Captain Shirley,
Intrepid	60	420	Captain Mapleſden,
Montague	60	420	Captain Rowley,
Dunkirk	60	420	Captain Digby,
Defiance	60	420	Captain Baird,
Rocheſter	50	350	Captain Duff,
Portland	50	350	Captain Arbuthnot,
Faulkland	50	350	Captain Drake,
Chatham	50	350	Captain Lockart,
Minerva	32	220	Captain Hood,
Venus	36	240	Captain Harriſon,
Vengeance	28	200	Captain Nightingale,
Coventry	28	200	Captain Barſlem,
Maidſtone	28	200	Captain Diggs,
Sapphire	32	220	Captain Strachan.
	2030	15900	

French.

who were also to form as they chased, that no time might be lost in the pursuit. M. Conflans had it in his power, either to fly, or stand and fight it out; but, through cowardice or misconduct he did neither perfectly; for some time he appeared as if he meant to fight; but after giving the british ships time to come near him, when it was too late, he crowded all the sail he could carry; and at the same time, he shewed an attention to keep all his squadron together.

French fleet.

Ships.	Guns.	Men.	Commanders.
Le Soliel Royal	80	1200	M. Conflans, admiral.
Le Tonnant	80	1000	M. Beaufremont, vice-admiral.
Le Formidable	80	1000	M. de St. André de Verger, rear-admiral.
Le Orient	80	1000	M. Gubriant, chef d'Escardre.
Le Intrepide	74	815	
Le Glorieux	74	815	
Le Theseé	74	815	
Le Heros	74	815	
Le Robuste	74	815	
Le Magnifique	74	815	
Le Juste	70	800	
Le Superbe	70	800	
Le Dauphin	70	800	
Le Dragon	64	750	
Le Northumb.	64	750	
Le Sphinx	64	750	
Le Solitaire	64	750	
Le Brillant	64	750	
Le Eveillé	64	750	
Le Bizarre	64	750	
Le Inflexible	64		
Le Hebe	40		
Le Vestale	34		
Le Aignette	36		
Le Calypso	16		
	1612	16740	

The action began with great fury, about half an hour after two. The english admiral ordered his ship to reserve her fire, to pass by all the others, and to be laid along-side of the Soliel Royal, the best ship in the french navy. The master remonstrated on the great danger of the coast. Hawke answered, "You have done your duty in this remonstrance; " now obey my orders, and lay me along-side of the " french admiral." The captain of the Superbe, a french man of war of 70 guns, in a gallant and generous manner put himself between them. Hawke was obliged to bestow here, the fire he had reserved for a greater occasion, and at one broadside sunk her to the bottom. The crew of the Royal George gave a cheer, but it was a faint one; the honest sailors were touched at the miserable fate of 800 poor creatures, out of which number, only 20 were saved in some pieces of the wreck. Sir Edward having made this dreadful beginning, continued bearing down on M. Conflans; before he could engage him, he received the fire of six other ships; at last Conflans gave him his broadside; it was returned with great spirit, and after two or three exchanges the french admiral sheered off. Sir Edward then received the fire of their vice-admiral; but he soon followed the example of his superior. Another and another did the same, but all were equally unable to stand against the steady, but dreadful fire of the Royal George. The Formidable, in which was the french rear-admiral, was the only ship in the french fleet that fought fairly; captain Speke of the Resolution, did not force her to strike till towards the dusk of the evening. The Torbay was singly engaged with the Theseé; but at the second broadside sent that unfortunate ship to the bottom. About five the Heros struck, and came to an anchor; but it blowing hard, no boat could be sent on board.

Night

Night saved the remainder of the french fleet; the english admiral being on a part of the coast, among islands and shoals, of which they were totally ignorant, the greatest part of the squadron without a pilot, and the wind blowing hard upon the lee shore, made the signal to anchor. Every thing concurred to make the night which succeeded the action, completely dreadful. A violent storm blew all night long. It was a pitchy darkness; a dangerous coast surrounded them on all sides. A continual firing of distress guns was heard, without knowing whether they came from friend or enemy, and on account of the badness of the coast, and the darkness of the night, the english sailors were equally unable to venture to their assistance.

When the morning of the 21st came, they found that the french admiral and the Heros, which under cover of the night had anchored among the english ships, cut and run ashore to the westward of Crozie. On the latter's moving, sir Edward made the Essex's signal to slip and pursue her; but she unfortunately got upon some rocks, called the Four, and both she and the Resolution were irrecoverably lost, notwithstanding all the assistance the weather would permit, was sent them. The enemy it was found, had seven ships of the line at anchor, between Penris Point and the river Villaine; on discovering them, the english admiral made the signal to weigh, in order to work up and attack them; but it blowed so hard from the N. W. that instead of daring to cast the squadron loose, he was obliged to strike top-gallant masts. Most of these ships appeared to be on ground at low water; but on the flood, by lightening them, and the advantage of the wind under the land, they got into the river Villaine.

The weather being moderate on the 22d, the admiral sent the Portland, Chatham, and Vengeance to destroy the Soliel Royal and Heros. The french, on the approach of the english set the first on fire, and soon after the latter met the same fate from their enemies.

enemies. Sir Edward employed the 23d in reconnoitring the entrance of the river Villaine, which is very narrow, and only twelve feet water on the bar, he difcovered feven or eight line of battle fhips about half a mile within, quite light, and two large frigates moored a-crofs, to defend the mouth of the river, the latter only having guns. He fitted out 12 long boats to attempt burning them; but the weather being bad, and the wind contrary, it was found impracticable. The admiral then detached capt. Young to Quiberon bay, with five fhips to watch the enemy's ftraggling fhips, and made up a flying fquadron to fcour the coaft to the ifle of Aix. Sir Edward concludes his account of this action with thefe words:
" In attacking a flying enemy, it was impoffible in
" the fpace of a fhort winter's day, that all our fhips
" fhould be able to get into action, or all thofe of the
" enemy brought to it. The commanders and com-
" panies of fuch as did not come up with the rear
" of the french on the 20th, behaved with the great-
" eft intrepidity, and gave the ftrongeft proofs of a
" true britifh fpirit. In the fame manner I am fatis-
" fied, thofe captains would have acquitted them-
" felves, whofe bad going fhips, or the diftance they
" were at in the mooring, prevented from getting
" up. Our lofs by the enemy is not confiderable;
" for in the fhips that are now with me, I find only
" one lieutenant, and 39 feamen and marines killed,
" and about 202 wounded. When I confider the
" feafon of the year, the hard gales on the day of
" action, a flying enemy, the fhortnefs of the day,
" and the coafts we are on, I can boldly affirm, that
" all that could poffible be done, has been done. As
" to the lofs we have fuftained, let it be placed to the
" account of the neceffity I was under of running
" all rifks to break this ftrong force of the enemy.
" Had we had but two hours more day-light, the
" whole had been totally deftroyed or taken; for
" we

" we were almoſt up with their van, when night
" overtook us."

In this glorious and ſuccefsful manner was concluded this remarkable action, in which the french had four capital ſhips deſtroyed, one taken, and the whole of their formidable navy, in which confiſted the laſt hope of their marine, ſhattered, diſarmed, and diſperſed. The invaſion, which they had been ſo long at work to effect, and which was to repair their loſſes in every part of the world, was now entirely diſſipated; with their laſt hope, the ſpirit of the people ſunk, and the credit of their arms was broken along with their forces. On the contrary, the behaviour of the engliſh admiral, captains, and ſeamen was ſuch, as reflected the greateſt honour on their country; and added as much to the glory, and to the arms of Britain as to its ſafety. In ſhort, thoſe who were engaged, and thoſe who were not ſo fortunate, gave proofs that they were equally ardent in the ſervice of their country. This engagement, the ſurrender of the pruſſian troops at Maxen, and the taking of Munſter, happened on the ſame day, the 20th of november.

The ſuccefs of the engliſh was equally great in the Eaſt-indies. In that country, the two nations had been more upon an equality than any where elſe, ſince the commencement of the war; but yet the advantage was on the ſide of the engliſh. In the beginning of february, captain Richard Maitland of the royal regiment of artillery, was ordered by the governor and council of Bombay, to undertake an expedition againſt the city and caſtle of Surat. He embarked with 850 artillery and infantry, and 1500 ſeapoys, the 9th of february, and in eight days landed them ſafe at a place called Dentilowry, diſtant from Surat about nine miles, where he encamped for the refreſhment of his troops three or four days. Being poſſeſſed of a proper ſpace of ground, he immediately raiſed a battery of two 24 pounders and a mortar, which played very briſkly againſt the wall for three days.

days. Finding this method of attack tedious, he, with the advice of a council of war, ordered his little fleet to warp up the river in the night, and anchor in a line of battle, oppofite one of the ftrongeft fortified pofts they had got, called the Bundar, which being executed, a general attack begun from the veffels and battery at the appointed time, and the troops being fafely landed, foon became mafters of that poft, and the outer town. Having fucceeded thus far, the captain bombarded the caftle and town as foon as pofble, with fuch brifknefs, that it furrendered to him after little or no oppofition. This conqueft was of vaft importance to the englifh Eaft-india company, Surat being one of the richeft cities in India, carrying on a flourifhing and extenfive trade.

In the mean time, colonel Clive, who had before fo often diftinguifhed himfelf in this country, continued to command fuccefs againft the french. That nation had fet up a perfon in oppofition to the nabob, whom the colonel had placed upon the throne of Bengal, and having affifted him with men and money, he laid fiege to Patua. Clive being informed of the attempt, marched from Calcutta with great expedition, and obliged the pretender to retire with the greateft precipitation. He then detached major Brereton, with fome troops to harrafs the rear of general Lally's army, which had not long before raifed the fiege of Madrafs. This and fome other detachments foon after joined the englifh army, about thirty miles from Madrafs; many endeavours were ufe to bring Mr. Lally to an engagement, who, though fuperior in number declined it. Major Brereton marched foon after to Vandewafh, a country fort about 40 miles from Pondicherry, garrifoned by the french, hoping thereby to draw the enemy from their ftrong camp. M. Lally, having returned to Pondicherry, major general Soupire commanded the french army, he gave into the defign of major Brereton, and followed him into the neighbourhood of Vandewafh.

The

The englifh army directly marched againft him, drawing up in order of battle, in fight of the french. But Soupire intrenched himfelf fo ftrongly, it was impoffible to attack him. Major Brereton finding an action impracticable, made a forced march the 16th of april, to Conjeveram, where the enemy had 700 feapoys; after a fhort cannonade, the place was ftormed, and many of the garrifon made prifoners of war. The french army afterwards returned to Arcot, and having no pay, and but bad provifions, it occafioned great difcontent and difertion. On the 20th of june, general Lally joined his army at Arcot, and moved towards Conjeveram, where the two armies cannonaded each other for four days; but the french general finding his men continued to defert, retreated in the night to Pondicherry. The englifh army remained cantoned in Conjeveram, till the 1ft of auguft, when part of it, under major Monfon, advanced to the attack of Couvereepaut, which after two days he took, granting the french garrifon a capitulation. At the fame time, major Caniland marched with 200 europeans, and fome black troops, to diflodge the enemy from Tirupoty; which he did with the lofs of a few feapoys. To conclude this train of fucceffes, major Ford made himfelf mafter of Maffulipatam, taking it by ftorm, where he killed about 200, and took prifoners about 300 french. The operations in the remainder of the year by land, were not of very great importance; the only action of any confequece was, an attack made by major Brereton, on the village of Vandewafh. He marched the 24th of feptember, with about 400 europeans, 7000 feapoys, 14 pieces of artillery, 70 european and 300 black horfe. The french, to the number of about 1000, were intrenched under a fort, which mounted 20 pieces of cannon. Notwithftanding this ftrength, major Brereton attacked them on the 30th, in three different places, and carried the village. But in the night, the pioneers miftaking

taking his orders, neglected to throw up an intrenchment to cover the troops, which when the french perceived, they returned to the charge with great fury, and being seconded by the fire of the fort, drove the english out again, with the loss of 310 men killed, and wounded, so that they were obliged to retreat directly to Conjeveram. Notwithstanding this repulse, the english East-india company found themselves on the whole infinitely successful. They commanded in Bengal a whole kingdom, and were in possession of all its trade, which produced them immense riches. From Bengal, up the coast as far as Madrass, was likewise at their discretion, an extent of 800 miles, and the best part of the coast for trade and wealth. It was in this part of it that the french subsisted after they had lost their possession in Bengal; but in the loss of Massulipatam they were merely confined to Pondicherry, Carakat, and some few places to the southward.

By sea the two fleets were more upon an equality in point of force; though that of the french under M. d'Aché was superior to admiral Pocock: nevertheless, the latter sailed to the southward in quest of d'Aché, on the 1st of september; the very next day he discovered the enemy's fleet, but was not able to bring on an action. Mr. Pocock continued eight days using all his endeavours to bring the french admiral to an engagement. At last, on the 10th he effected it, when both admirals made the signal for battle. The english fleet consisted of nine sail of the line, but three of them were only 50 gun ships. The french consisted of eleven sail of the line of battle ships. The english line carried 536 guns, and 4035 men; the french 728 guns, and 6400 men. As soon as the signal was out, both squadrons began to cannonade each other with great fury, and continued hotly engaged for two hours, when the french rear began to give way; their center very soon after did the same, their van following;
the

the whole french squadron bore away with all the sail they could make.

Many of the english ships being greatly disabled in their yards and rigging, admiral Pocock was in no condition to pursue them; but having repaired the several damages of his ships, he once more sailed in quest of the enemy, and discovered them in Pondicherry road; d'Aché declined coming to a second engagement, stretching away to the southward. Mr. Pocock determined, with the advice of the rear admiral and captains, to return to Madrass, as the condition of the fleet would not permit him to follow the enemy to the southward. The loss in the engagement was considerable on both sides, but fell heaviest on the french, who had 1500 men killed and wounded, as reported by a deserter; the english had 569 killed and wounded, and both squadrons were very much shattered.

If we turn our eyes on the state of the french nation in Europe, we shall find their condition still more deplorable. The battle of Minden, which proved so fatal to their designs, having destroyed all their hopes in Germany for that campaign*, their court found it absolutely necessary to recruit, cloath, and pay their troops; articles as difficult to be effected, as the necessity was urgent; but by contracting the plan of their operations, they resolved to make every effort in their power, to render marshal Broglio's army as formidable as possible. To a nation without trade as France was, the supplies to support so great a charge were excessively difficult to be raised. The vast sums which had been sent out of the kingdom in subsidies to their allies, and in the pay of their troops, had extremely impoverished the nation; but still they would not have exhausted it, had France

---

* They were obliged to trust to their marine, as the last effort; but the defeat of their grand fleet under Conflans, ruined all their schemes.

been in the possession of a flourishing commerce: so far was this from being the case, that their foreign trade was entirely ruined; the principal of their colonies torn from them; and almost universal bankruptcy ensued throughout the whole kingdom. Such being the exhausted state of that kingdom, it was found impossible to raise such great sums as were necessary, by regular means only; recourse therefore was had to the most fatal and extraordinary ones. On this occasion, they did not scruple to break in upon the public faith, and to find supplies for one year, in an expedient that struck at the sources of all future credit. The ministry stopped payment upon public bills and funds*. But even this resource, was insufficient; the king threw his own plate into the public stock as an example, and a request that others should contribute in the same manner from their private fortune, to the necessities of state. Many of the nobility, gentry, churches and convents actually carried their plate to the mint; but still it was very far from being universal; there was a general reluctance to forward this method of supply, and to trust the public with so considerable a part of their substance, at the instant when they saw it so notoriously break its faith in other particulars. These miserable resources, however, enabled the ministry still to continue the war in Germany; and to refuse the offers of peace which the

---

* The following are the public debts, of which the french court have stopped payment:

1. The three kinds of rents created on the posts. 2. The constituted upon the chest of redemptions. 3. The coupons of bills on the same chest. 4. Those of the two royal lotteries. 5. The reimbursement of bills, drawn to bearer, on the same chest. 6. The bills of the two royal lotteries. 7. The rents created on the two sols per pound of the 10th penny. 8. Reimbursements of the capitals of rents. 9. The payments of bills dischargeable in nine years, known under the name of annuities. 10. Those of the new actions on the benefit of the farms. 11. All the bills drawn by the colonies upon the government, amounting to 1,333,000 l.

kings

kings of Great Britain and Pruſſia * made them at the end of the year: for as they did not expect, from their

* The following declaration was delivered by his ſerene highneſs duke Lewis of Brunſwick to the miniſters of the belligerent powers reſiding at the Hague, in the name of the two kings.

"Their britannic and pruſſian majeſties, moved with compaſſion at the miſchiefs which the war, that has been kindled for ſome years, has already occaſioned, and muſt neceſſarily produce; ſhould think themſelves wanting to the duties of humanity, and particularly to their tender concern for the preſervation and well-being of their reſpective kingdoms and ſubjects, if they neglected the proper means to put a ſtop to the progreſs of ſo ſevere a calamity, and to contribute to the re-eſtabliſhment of public tranquility. In this view, and in order to manifeſt the purity of their intentions, in this reſpect, their ſaid majeſties have determined to make the following declaration, viz.

"That they are ready to ſend plenipotentiaries to the place, which ſhall be thought moſt proper, in order there to treat conjointly, of a ſolid and general peace, with thoſe whom the belligerent parties ſhall think fit to authoriſe, on their part, for the attaining ſo ſalutary an end."

This declaration was made at the end of november, and no anſwer appeared to it, till about four months after, when the following declaration was made by the oppoſite party. Having mentioned the above offer, it goes on, "Her majeſty, the empreſs queen of Hungary and Bohemia; her majeſty, the empreſs of all the Ruſſia's; and his majeſty, the moſt chriſtian king, equally animated by the deſire of contributing to the re-eſtabliſhment of the public tranquility on a ſolid and equitable footing, declare in return;

That his majeſty, the catholic king, having been pleaſed to offer his mediation in the war, which has ſubſiſted for ſome years between France and England; and this war, having beſides, nothing in common with that which the two empreſſes with their allies, have likewiſe carried on for ſome years againſt the king of Pruſſia.

His moſt chriſtian majeſty is ready to treat of his particular peace with England, through the good offices of his catholic majeſty, whoſe mediation he has a pleaſure in accepting.

As to the war which regards directly his pruſſian majeſty, their majeſties the empreſs queen of Hungary and Bohemia, the empreſs of all the Ruſſia's, and the moſt chriſtian king, are diſpoſed to agree to the appointing the congreſs propoſed. But as by virtue of their treaties, they cannot enter into any engagement relating to peace, but in conjunction with their allies, it will be neceſſary, in order that they may be enabled to explain themſelves definitively upon that ſubject, that their britannic and pruſſian majeſties, ſhould previously be

their situation very advantageous or honourable terms, they resolved still to hold out, and determined to hazard the last extremities, hoping something favourable from the fortune of their allies, since their own had deserted them. This was the reason of their delaying (in conjunction with the two empresses) to answer the declaration of duke Lewis of Brunswick, near four months; had they been inclined to peace, they might very easily have found means to do it, in much less time; but as they could not, with a good grace reject those overtures, they had recourse to delays. The formal invitation which they require, should be made to the kings of Poland, and Sweden, plainly evinces this; for had a congress been appointed, there is no doubt, but those two princes, especially the former, would gladly have sent plenipotentiaries to it, where their pretensions might have been fairly discussed; but by this affected delay, three or four months must be lost; and if those difficulties had been removed, pretences would not have been wanting to put it off for some months more. It plainly appeared, that as the affairs of France were in such a bad situation, that court was resolved to try the event of another campaign, hoping to be able to get possession of Hanover, and thereby conclude a peace on more advantageous terms than she could at that time expect.

Before I take my leave of the transactions of this year, so gloriously marked in the annals of Great-Britain; I must observe, how extremely successful the british arms were, in every part of the world. The conquest of Quebec, the capital of the french dominions in America, was as advantageous to our

be pleased to cause their invitation to a congress to be made to all the powers, that are directly engaged in war against the king of Prussia, and namely, to his majesty the king of Poland, elector of Saxony, as likewise to his majesty, the king of Sweden, who ought specifically to be invited to the future congress."

interest, as it was glorious to the brave soldiers, by whose conduct and courage it was won. The success which attended our arms under general Amherst, contributed greatly to secure our colonies from the depredations of the french and their indians, and brought under the dominion of Britain, an immense tract of country, of the greatest importance. The acquisition of Guardaloupe, was as highly advantageous to the trade and commercial interest of this kingdom, as it was fatal to that of France. That memorable victory obtained in the plains of Minden, through the admirable conduct of duke Ferdinand of Brunswick, and the gallant behaviour of the english infantry, not only threw the whole kingdom of France into the utmost consternation, but obliged them to have recourse to their marine for an invasion of Britain, as the only hopes they had left, of being able to retrieve the many and desperate losses they had sustained. Lastly, the action at cape Lagos, under admiral Boscawen; but more particularly that remarkable victory at Belleisle, wherein, sir Edward Hawke acquitted himself so much to the satisfaction of his own honour, and the expectations of his country, blasted every sanguine hope of our distressed enemies; and involved them in the most despairing confusion. They were no longer able to carry on the war, either with the ordinary revenue of the kingdom, or those extraordinary sums, which are always raised in France, to support a war; but were obliged to have recourse to the most unprecedented and illegal means of raising money; equally fatal to the credit of their government, and insufficient to supply their pressing necessities.

CHAP. XXVI.

Affairs in Europe, in the beginning of the year 1760. *Thurot sails from Dunkirk. Lands in Scotland. Re-embarks. Lands in Ireland. Carrickfergus surrenders. Is plundered by the french. They re-imbark. Captain Elliot takes Thurot's squadron. Court martial on lord George Sackville. Sentence on his lordship. Affairs in north America. French prepare to besiege Quebec. Motions of brigadier general Murray. Action on the heights of St. Abraham. The trenches opened. The siege raised. Affairs in the East-indies.*

IN speaking of the french scheme for an invasion, I before mentioned, that there was to be a small squadron dispatched from Dunkirk, under M. Thurot, (a man who had rendered himself truly celebrated by his vast success, while commander of the Belleisle privateer), to make an attempt on Scotland or Ireland, in order to divide the attention of the british ministry. An english squadron, under commodore Boys, was stationed for some time before Dunkirk, to prevent Thurot's getting out. But the frenchman seizing a lucky opportunity, slipped out, and sailed directly northward. Boys followed him as soon as possible; but was not able to prevent his getting into Gottenburgh, in which harbour, and in that of Bergen, he took refuge some time, waiting an opportunity to get out. He effected it at last; and, on the 17th of february appeared off the island of Illa, in Argyleshire. In the evening they shewed english colours, which induced two gentlemen to go on board, whom they detained. Soon after,

after, some of their boats put off for the shore. In their way they boarded two small sloops, lying at anchor in a small bay of the island, which they plundered; the crews of the boats next landed on the island, and while Thurot remained on it, he behaved in every respect more like a friend than an enemy. He payed for every thing he took, even beyond their value; he allowed thirty shillings for every cow, half a crown for every goose, one shilling for a hen, and in proportion for flour, and other things. He kept the best discipline, and prevented pillaging as much as possible. He enquired very anxiously concerning the fate of Conflans's fleet, and was much surprised to hear, that that admiral had suffered himself to be beat without striking a blow. As Thurot's fleet consisted only of four small ships, the largest of which, did not mount above 50 guns, it was not in his power to make any attempt of consequence in Scotland.

On the 21st, he appeared with only three ships off the isle of Magee, standing in shore for the bay of Carrickfergus, in Ireland. At that time the small number of troops belonging to the garrison, were at exercise about half a mile on the road to Belfast; and about eleven o'clock the guard was turned off, to relieve that on the french prisoners in the castle; the rest of the men remaining in the field of exercise. The commanding officer no sooner received advice of three ships being seen so near the coast, and of their having detained some fishing boats, than he sent immediate orders to the castle, for both guards to continue under arms, and double the centries over the french prisoners that were confined there. A lieutenant with a reconnoitring party took post on a rising ground, to discover whether the ships were french; he soon perceived eight boats landing armed men; and that they drew out in detachments and took post on all the dykes, hedges, and rising grounds, from whence they could have the most extensive views; having ordered his corps to resist them as long as they were able, in case they were attacked, he hastened to lieutenant colonel Jennings, the commanding officer, to acquaint him with what he had discovered. The lieutenant colonel was with his troops on the parade of Carrickfergus, who immediately ordered detachments to the gates of the town, and took every precaution in his power to prevent the enemy from making themselves masters of it; ordering the french prisoners to be removed with all speed to Belfast.

By this time, the french, to the number of about 1000 men, were in full march for the town; they attempted to enter the gates, but were repulsed; and again made two different attacks, with the like ill success, being kept back as long as the troops of the garrison had ammunition. Lieutenant colonel Jennings then ordered his men into the castle; and the french immediately appeared in the market place; where they might have been attacked with great advantage, had it not been for the most scandalous want of ammunition. The french finding the fire of the garrison so weak, attacked the gates of the castle sword in hand, which from the battering of the shot on both sides, were knocked open, and the the enemy marched in; but lieutenant colonel Jennings, with some officers, and about 50 men repulsed them, and the men from a half moon near the gates, after their ammunition was gone, threw stones and bricks. Had this attack of the enemy been supported with the least degree of courage, they must certainly have succeeded in it; but they retired back under cover, leaving the gates open, and the garrison drawn up in their front. Jennings would have sallied, had they had ammunition; but without it the enterprise was too dangerous. And as the breach in the castle wall could not be defended, as it was 50 feet long, it

was

was agreed to beat a parley; and accordingly lieutenant colonel Jennings marched out with the honours of war, agreeing that an equal number of french prisoners should be sent to France in lieu of the garrison. By an article of the capitulation, the mayor and corporation were to furnish the french with provisions; but they not executing that article to the french general's satisfaction, the town was plundered. On the 22d, they sent a flag of truce to Belfast, and made a demand of several articles of provisions, and other necessaries to be delivered that day, promising to pay for them, and threatening, in case of refusal, to burn Carrickfergus, and afterwards to come up and burn Belfast also. With which demands, the inhabitants thought it best to comply. The french lost about 60 men in their attack on Carrickfergus; and having carried the mayor and some of the principal inhabitants aboard their ships, as a security for having the french prisoners sent to France, they re-embarked their troops, and set sail the 26th.

In the mean time, this handful of french troops, inconsiderable as they were, alarmed the whole kingdom of Ireland, and all the western coast of England. The rich towns of Liverpool and Whitehaven, were in fear for their ships and effects; twelve hundred men of the neighbouring militia marched to Liverpool, as soon as it was known that Thurot was landed in Ireland. There were at that time 200 sail of ships in the harbour of Whitehaven, and nothing to defend them; the neighbouring gentlemen, to protect the town and country, raised and armed 600 men. Ships were dispatched from several ports in quest of the french commodore; and the duke of Bedford, lord lieutenant of Ireland, issued the necessary orders for the forces in the northern part of that kingdom, to march towards Carrickfergus; and dispatched an express to Kinsale, to inform Capt. Elliot,
who

who commanded three men of war there, that Mr. Thurot was upon the coast.

Elliot directly set sail from Kinsale, with the Æolus of 32 guns, and the Pallas and Brilliant of 36 guns each: he made the entrance of Carrickfergus bay the 26th; but could not get in, the wind being contrary, and very bad weather. The 28th, at four in the morning, he got sight of them, and gave chace. About nine he got up along-side the french commodore, off the isle of Man, and in a few minutes after the action became general, and lasted about an hour and a half, when they all three struck their colours; although Thurot was killed by a cannon ball, yet his ship the Belleisle was fought so very bravely, that it was feared she would sink before she could be got into port; she mounted 44 guns, and carried 545 men, including troops; the la Blonde carried 32 guns and 400 men; and the Terpsichore of 26 guns and 300 men. The english officers and sailors, as well as those of the french, fought very bravely. The loss of the conquerors was trifling, that of the french amounted to about 300 men killed and wounded. Thurot was one of the bravest men that had appeared in France since the beginning of the war; he was remarkable for his mild and generous treatment of the prisoners he took while commander of the Belleisle privateer.

Before I dismiss this subject, I must observe, that Carrickfergus is the only magazine in the north of Ireland, from which all the troops in that part of the country were supplied with powder, &c. The fortifications were so much out of repair, that it was impossible to defend it better than was done by lieutenant colonel Jennings, so that what reason there could be for the expression in the London Gazzette; " Had " suffered himself with four companies of major " general Strode's regiment, to be made prisoners of " war:" I cannot find out. " Suffered himself,"

plainly

plainly implies his having made a bad defence. The parliament of Ireland had at different times, lately granted 450,000 l. for repairing the fortifications of the kingdom; therefore there muſt have been ſome very fatal neglect in this place's not having been put in a better poſture of defence. Some having imagined that Thurot was driven into Carrickfergus by ſtreſs of weather, and want of proviſions; but its much more probable, he landed there by deſign, he might very likely be acquainted with the weak ſtate of the place; and have had in his eye the wealthy city of Belfaſt juſt by it, as a proper object of his expedition: the preparations made by the lord lieutenant to prevent his penetrating further into the country, might have been the reaſon of his not attempting it.

In the mean time, the attention of all ranks of people was entirely engroſſed by the proceedings of a general court martial, appointed by his majeſty to ſit on the trial of lord George Sackville. His lordſhip as I before mentioned, had petitioned for one as ſoon as he arrived in England, after the battle of Minden; but it was not found convenient to aſſemble it till the beginning of march: as many officers were to be called home from Germany as witneſſes; beſides ſome other reaſons of a different nature. It was a point very much diſputed, whether a man, diſmiſſed from all his military employments, could be tried for an offence, committed while he was in the army; and as opinions differed extremely, the caſe was laid before the judges: it was ſuppoſed from their anſwer, that he might legally be tried. Accordingly, a court martial, conſiſting of the following members, met the 29th of february, for that purpoſe:

Lieutenant general Onſlow, preſident.
         Sir Charles Howard,
         Campbell,
                                Lieutenant

Lieutenant general lord Delaware,
　　　　　　　　　　Cholmondeley,
　　　　　　　　　　Stuart,
　　　　　　　　　　earl of Panmure,
　　　　　　　　　　Ancram,
　　　　　　　　　　Harrington,
　　　　　　　　　　Abercrombie,
　　　　　　　　　　Albemarle.
　　Major general Leighton,
　　　　　　　　　　Carr,
　　　　　　　　　　earl of Effingham,
　　　　　　　　　　Belford.

On lord George Sackville's being ordered into court, the judge advocate informed him, that all the members of the court were sworn, except general Belford, who was omitted on account of an objection which his lordship said he should make to his being a member of the court. Lord George Sackville having given his reasons * for making such an objection; general

* They were as follow: " When I was appointed lieutenant general to the ordnance, the duke of Marlborough ordered me to take the care of the artillery regiment upon me, as being one part of my duty. I represented to his grace, that when lord Ligonier was lieutenant general of the ordnance, the care of the regiment was left entirely to the colonel commandant; the duke of Marlborough said, that he could not in decency have desired my lord Ligonier, who was his superior in the army, and had been for many years at the head of the ordnance, to enter into such a regimental detail; but that he had no scruple in desiring me to do that part of my duty, and to report regularly to him. I expressed my readiness to obey; but said, that, previous to my undertaking it, his grace must give the proper orders for recalling that power, which was at present in general Belford, as colonel commandant. It was accordingly done; and when I began to execute my duty, general Belford expressed his disapprobation of it, thinking any diminution of his authority might be looked upon as some degree of disapprobation of his conduct. I explained to him what had passed upon the subject, between the master general and me, and he appeared better satisfied; and, as I afterwards had an opportunity of representing his services so favourably to his majesty,

as

neral Belford replied, that he was far from defiring to fit when objected, but only defired to know what the objection was: the court thereupon took the affair into confideration, and were unanimoufly of opinion, that lord George Sackville's objection was infufficient to exclude general Belford from fitting as a member; but as the general continued to exclude himfelf from fitting, the court agreed to it.

There was fitting at this time another court-martial on lord Charles Hay, for fome offences committed by him in north America, under lord Loudon, of which general Onflow was alfo a member; and his lordfhip behaving in a ftrange abfurd manner *, it provoked Onflow, a man of great dignity, and equal fpirit, to fpeak very warmly to lord Charles Hay: and his warmth coft him his life; for he had hardly concluded his fpeech, but he dropped down of an apoplectic fit, and being inftantly carried home, died

---

as to obtain a confiderable increafe of emolument to him. I did imagine any little difference that had happened had been entirely forgot; but perfons in my fituation are apt to watch little attentions, which at other times would be too trifling to regard; and as, upon my return to England, general Belford was the only field officer of the regiment, with whom I was acquainted, that did not fhew me even the common civility of a vifit; and, as the firft act he did, after my quitting the fervice, was recommending another aid de camp to my lord Granby, in preference to the artillery officer, who had attended me in that capacity, I confefs thefe circumftances induced me to think, that general Belford ftill retained fome degree of ill-will towards me; and though I am far from fufpecting that he would knowingly permit his judgment to be in the leaft influenced by fuch confiderations; yet, as there is fuch a biafs in the minds of men, when there is any prejudice in their breafts, that it often affects their actions, unknown to themfelves; I fhould hope the general would decline fitting upon this trial; I do not offer what I have faid as a legal objection, but rather fubmit my reafons to the court, and to him for their confiderations."

* He fwore by G—d they were not a legal court martial, but a fanguinary court of inquifition. General Cornwallis has faid, that he afked him fome crofs queftions, in hopes that he would throw the inkftand, &c. at his head, and by fome fuch action, put an end to fo ridiculous a court martial.

in a few days. He was a great loss to the court martial on lord George Sackville, as no man was ever more proper for a president of one.

There was a new warrant issued the 6th of march, appointing sir Charles Howard president, and adding to the former number of members, the major generals lord Robert Manners, lord Robert Bertie, and Julius Cæsar. I have already given the reader some particular points of this trial, in my account of the battle of Minden, from the evidence of several witnesses; the shortness of the plan of this work will not permit me now to be particular in regard to the trial*.

The

---

* There were some remarkable articles of evidence which deserve to be remembered.

It was observed, not only by the members of the court, but by all present, that lieutenant colonel Sl—p—r gave his evidence with great acrimony, and was to appearance, much prejudiced against the prisoner; this was what occasioned lord George Sackville's saying in his defence, "In what manner his evidence was given, I need not remind "the court." And again, "If his own behaviour has not entirely "destroyed the credit of his testimony." Lieut. col. Sloper, in his evidence, says, that as soon as capt. Ligonier had delivered the duke's order to lord George Sackville, he (Sloper) said to him, "For God's "sake, sir, repeat your orders to that man, (meaning lord George "Sackville), that he may not pretend not to understand them, for it "is near half an hour ago, that he has received orders to advance, and "yet we are still here," adding, "But you see the condition he is in." Being afterwards desired to explain what he meant by these last words; he answered, that his opinion was, that lord George Sackville was alarmed to a very great degree, that when his lordship ordered him to advance, he seemed in the greatest confusion.

Lord G. SACKVILLE. Sir Charles Howard, if I may be allowed to say a few words, touching this gentleman's (Sloper's) evidence before I go any further.

Gen. CHOLMONDELEY. I am never against any indulgence to the prisoner.

Lord G. SACKVILLE. It is a little hard for me to be sitting here, and have a witness come against me, with an opinion of this nature, and I forced to remain entirely silent. I shall only say a few words. This sort of attack, I never heard before, from any one gentleman whatever, excepting from the private insinuations of this gentleman,

The prisoner, during the course of it, behaved with great conduct, and discovered infinite abilities; he endeavoured

now before the court; I have heard of it since he has been in London. I am glad that he has mentioned it in court. I, ———

Lord ALBEMARLE. Your lordship will have an opportunity of observing upon that in your defence; but, I am afraid we are going into an irregularity.

Lord G. SACKVILLE. I will only say now, that I will prove my conduct that day, with regard to every branch of it, and I will shew that gentleman to the court in such colours, for truth and veracity.

Lord ALBEMARLE. My lord, this is being very irregular.

Lord G. SACKVILLE. Your lordship may imagine, that what I must feel on such an occasion; and it is difficult not to express it instantly.

Lord ALBEMARLE. I am very sensible of what your lordship must feel, and sorry to interrupt; but the course of proceeding.———

Lord G. SACKVILLE. I submit to the opinion of the court, and must beg leave to suppose, for the present, that no such evidence has been given. I shall now go on as if nothing of this sort had happened, and shall treat that gentleman, in that part of his evidence, with the contempt it deserves.

In another place his lordship makes an observation, on the evidence of colonel Sloper, in the following words: " Having mentioned col. " Sloper's evidence, I am obliged to take notice of the aspersion he " has thrown upon my character. Imputations of that nature were " very little to be expected from one, who had the honour of arriving " at the rank of a lieutenant general, after a course of some duty " and service. It is hard upon a man to be obliged to speak of his " own actions, or of his own merit or character in the service; but " what makes it on this occasion absolutely unnecessary, is, that most " of the generals, who compose this court, have either commanded " me, or I have had the honour of commanding them; and I am " persuaded, they will feel a generous indignation in my behalf, and " declare, whether my former conduct ought not to have exempted " me from so mean an attack."

During the course of the defence, lord George Sackville asked his witnesses such questions as he thought would contradict the aspersions thrown on him by lieutenant-colonel Sloper; endeavouring to prove his evidence false in several particulars. As soon as he had finished examining his witnesses, the judge advocate observed that his lordship had, in his defence, impeached the lieutenant-colonel's credibility; proposing by way of reply, to support the credibility of the witness, when his lordship had summed up his defence; but lord George wanted to have the fresh evidence examined before he concluded his defence, that he might answer any thing new, that appeared; or else that

endeavoured where ever he could introduce them, to throw reflections on duke Ferdinand, implying, that he

that the court would promise to permit him to make a rejoinder to the judge advocate's reply. Amongst other things which his lordship said,
—— " I find upon my trial a question proposed of very great con-
" sequence. I did not care at that time to give an answer to it.
" The natural inference is, that the court will go on, and afterwards
" consider of it. My reason for desiring the court to go on now is,
" that I am desirous of hearing all that is to be said. As to the evi-
" dence I have given, I do not know how far the court will admit of
" evidence in reply to it; and suppose if any thing is offered by way of
" reply that is new, it may be necessary for me to ask for a rejoinder.
" I am frightened every time I talk of law; I am told, if the court
" lets the prosecutor into new matter in supply, it will bring on a
" rejoinder, that is, to answer the new matter; if that is the case, I
" shall have the same indulgence that every prisoner has in any court
" of justice."

JUDGE ADVOCATE. In order that the reply may be properly made, I should be glad to hear what lord George has to offer in his observations.

As to a rejoinder, it is common in civil cases, if any new matter is introduced, the prisoner will have a right to answer that; I mentioned that particularly before.

I should be glad his lordship would not talk of law, I am not a military person, I do not really see why that should be thrown out, I have not the honour of wearing a military garb; but I hope I have endeavoured to conduct the prosecution with tenderness and candour.

As to the reply, it is agreeable to law, and practice founded in reason, that the prosecutor should be at liberty to establish the credit of his witnesses, and to reply to any new matter introduced in the course of the defence.

If the credibility of a witness is to be impeached, and his credit not to be established, I don't know to what purpose it would be to prosecute at all.

Lord G. SACKVILLE. As to the judge advocate, I wish, as he observes, he either wore a military garb, or were a person of such eminence and reputation in the profession of the law, as might entitle him to lay down the rules and practice of the courts of justice, in such a manner, as the prisoner might have no doubt of the truth of what was asserted to be law. I wish one of the judges of England was to sit here, the prisoner then would have been certain of being tried by the real laws of this land, and not by laws made occasionally for him; I desire therefore, no middle term. The judge advocate is very able in his post; but I do not apprehend he knows the rules and practice of courts in general. Here what do you do?

If

he had posted the cavalry of the right wing where it could be of no service; but such insinuations were
very

If there is a point of law, you refer to the judge-advocate; why, because you don't know law, not because he does. I know as little; I used the word rejoinder, I got it but the other day myself, and the court seemed to start when I mentioned it. When there is a difficulty, you refer to the judge-advocate, who is to determine; other courts never determine in any matter, without the advantage of being informed of what can be offered on both sides; this court, ignorant themselves of a matter of law, can only receive their information from the prosecutor. I have a great respect for Mr. Gould's character as judge-advocate, and think he sits there, and executes his office, as ably as any man I ever saw in his place. For the sake of the precedent it would make, I might say something; because every witness, whose character may be said to be impeached in a controverted proceeding, will by this means, have an opportunity of bringing in fresh evidence of fresh facts, and the prisoner must stand a second trial upon the same charge. As to my own part, if the court thinks fit to admit it, let them say that this does not affect me; let them say that the credit of the witness is impeached; by contradicting his facts; let them say, that such is the practice of courts-martial; I shall lament the fate of those who are to be tried by courts-martial; but with regard to myself, it is impossible for me to object to the determination. What I have proved, is the shewing the opinion of those about me, to whom I gave orders, with whom I was during the whole day, that is a direct contradicton of the fact; it includes the time of which col. Sloper speaks, the evidence now offered, is not to support this fact, it relates to another time.

Indeed the judge-advocate has said, it is not matter for the court, but for the publick, it is so. It is food for clamour, for which reason I wish to see the bottom of it. I should not have stood here, a prisoner at this bar, if I had been afraid of any thing that could be said, conscious innocence is my support.

Notwithstanding all that I have suffered, that innocence still supports me. I feel myself injured, and I know myself innocent. I feel myself before a court, that is to punish the guilty; but the most amiable part of their jurisdiction, is to protect the innocent.

I have confidence in every set of gentlemen, who are upon oath, to do justice; no gentleman can be under any influence.

In this court a prisoner has an additional security; he is sure, their honour will bind them, if their oath did not; standing under that security, I defy the prosecutor.

very little regarded, as the contrary was known to be the truth. As to his guilt, the court adjudged him by their sentence unfit to serve his majesty in any military capacity whatever. * As it is not the custom for land courts-martial to draw up a set of resolutions by way of reasons for their sentence; we cannot here so readily determine the nature of his lordship's guilt. That he was guilty, is indisputable; he most undoubtedly disobeyed the orders of duke Ferdinand. His serene highness ordered him to advance through the trees on his left, to form a third line, and support the infantry. Now it was very evident that the infantry were to be supported; and if that was the case, the time must consequently be extremely critical.
Could

Let col. Sloper stand forth, and from a witness become the agent of a prosecution. Let his character be supported by the testimony of opinion; opinion not founded upon facts, will only shew a readiness to form an opinion to a man's disadvantage. It is not proof, it is not a foundation for a court of justice to determine upon; it could not be brought hence, but with another intention.

If the court will establish the precedent, I submit; but out of regard to the profession I once was of, I oppose it.

Permit me to say, when I take my leave of the profession, that though I shall submit it to the decision of the court, I shall lament the jurisdiction.

The court determined that no new witnesses should be called in to prove that Lord George Sackville appeared alarmed. But that they would admit evidence to prove col. Sloper's having declared these facts the day after.

I shall conclude what I have to say on the subject of colonel S———r's evidence, with observing, that there had been formerly a quarrel between lord George Sackville and him, which was never made up.

* The court upon due consideration, of the whole matter before them, is of opinion, that lord George Sackville is guilty of having disobeyed the orders of prince Ferdinand of Brunswick, whom he was by his commission and instructions directed to obey, as commander in chief, according to the rules of war; and it is the farther opinion of this court, That the said lord George Sackville is, and he is hereby adjudged, unfit to serve his majesty, in any military capacity whatever.

CHARLES HOWARD.

Could this reasonably be thought a season for requiring an explanation of his orders, when they ought instantly to have been put in execution? Had he not better have disobeyed his orders in part, by advancing forwards, and doing his duty, instead of turning to the left? But the misfortune was, he never stirred at all. If he had advanced, it would at least have shewn an inclination to obey.—— But I am arguing on a point too well established, to admit a doubt.——
The only article which will bear an argument, is the motive of his guilt: a topic certainly more curious than useful: I fear in this case I am of a different opinion from the generality of men. Lord G. S-ck-vill- had, before the battle of Minden, expressed his disapprobation of many of duke Ferdinand's orders, in such a manner as shewed that he did not at all relish a superior in command. I cannot help attributing his bad conduct at that battle, to his disgust at the duke's command. A motive which certainly fixes a greater stain than cowardice could possibly do. I cannot help thinking but such vast abilities would in a great measure get the better of his fear, when so much was at stake as in his command: but this is a point which I leave to philosophers to determine. His lordship concludes the introduction to his defence, in these words. " This
" defence is intended, not for the world, but for
" the information of the court. All I at present
" desire is, that mankind would suspend their judg-
" ment of my conduct, till the evidence is closed;
" then I trust in the goodness of my cause, which has
" supported me under a load of calumny, and em-
" boldened me to ask for this trial; that under your
" favourable judgment, the candid will with pleasure
" acquit me, the prejudiced be obliged to retract their
" rash censures, and that I shall again be restored to
" the good opinion of my country, and of my so-
" vereign."

" vereign." And again at the end of his defence, he says: " My witnesses cannot say what they have " said, without being convinced that it is truth, and " said in support of innocence. They can have no " motive of interest: what motives of interest can " there be on the side of one who is a prisoner, who " has been in great employments? Perhaps unwor- " thily! Employments, which had I continued in " power, might have procured good will, at least the " appearance of it. At present they can have no " temptation but the force of truth; and by their " appearing in that cause; and on these motives, " they deserve as great a degree of credibility, as any " witness at any bar. In justice to them I have trou- " bled the court thus far. I shall trouble them no " longer; but express my acknowledgments, not " only for their patience in hearing me, but for the " many instances of their indulgence. I can expect " no better security for my cause, than their unin- " fluenced determination. I have mentioned already, " that I have the security of their oath; I have a " stronger still, their honour: upon that I rely.——— " If I am guilty, let me be declared so. If I am not " guilty, let the court shew by their sentence, that " they will with pleasure protect the innocent."

'Tis well known what a natural aversion the king has to soldiers who don't do their duty; he no sooner confirmed the sentence of the court-martial, than he ordered lord George Sackville's name to be struck out of the list of the privy-council. His m———y had, during the whole course of the trial, expressed himself very anxiously on some particulars relating to their proceedings. He had been heard to say, " This " trial is not on lord G——— S———, but on me." It was remarked that l——— A———————, during the trial, asked only leading questions in favour of lord George Sackville; and on the contrary, g———
C———

C——— afked none, but thofe which were directly againſt him; the reaſon for the former's behaviour, when we confider his connections with the d——e, is eafily conjectured; nor were the general's motives ever thought to be impenetrable.

But it is now time to take a view of the military operations in North America; they were indeed of but fmall extent, but great importance. Nothing lefs depended on them, than the poffeffion of our darling conqueft, Quebec. General Murray was left governor of that city, on its falling into our hands, and had a garrifon with him of about 6000 men; a number not in the leaft too numerous, as the men were extremely fatigued and harraffed with one of the moft difficult campaigns that ever was conducted; and as the city was fo meanly fortified, that it was not entirely fecure againſt a coup-de-main.

No fooner was general Murray fettled in this government, than he began repairing the ruins of the city; he built eight redoubts of wood out of the city, made foot banks along the ramparts, opened embrafures, placed his cannon, blocked up all the avenues of the fuburbs with a ftockade, carried eleven months provifions into the higheſt part of the city, and formed a magazine of 4000 fafcines. As foon as thefe and many other labours, were in fome forwardnefs, the general fent out two detachments, to take poffeffion of St. Foix and Lorette, two pofts of great importance, as they fecured eleven parifhes in the neighbourhood of the city, which greatly contributed to furnifh them with frefh provifions during the winter; and alfo with wood, an article much wanted by the garrifon. During three whole months in the winter, they were employed in dragging wood into the city. This conſtant labour greatly diminiſhed them, fo that before the end of april, 1000 men were dead,

dead, and above 2000 of what remained, were totally unfit for any service.

In the mean time the french general, the chevalier de Lewis, soon got intelligence of the low state of the garrison, and resolved to attempt carrying the city in the depth of winter. In pursurnce of this scheme, he made all the necessary preparations; designing to make the attempt in february: but the success of the garrison in some skirmishes, which happened on several occasions, obliged M. de Lewis to alter his plan, and not to think of attacking the city till the spring was more advanced.

As general Murray found that Quebec could be looked upon in no other light than that of a strong cantonment, and that any works he should add to it would be in that style, his plan of defence was, to take the earliest opportunity of intrenching himself on the heights of Abraham, which entirely commanded the ramparts of the place, at the distance of 800 yards, and might have been defended by his numbers, against a large army. But de Lewis did not give the general time to take the advantage of this situation. In the middle of april, the general attempted to execute the projected lines, but found it impracticable, as the earth was still covered with snow in many places, and every where impregnably bound up by frost.

Murray was informed in the night of the 26th, that the enemy had landed at Point au Tremble 10,000 men, and 500 barbarians; their scheme was, to cut off the posts of the garrison; but the general by a judicious march, prevented them from executing it; and several reasons concurred, to induce him to give them battle: he considered that his little army was in the habit of beating the enemy, and had a very fine train of field artillery; that shutting himself up within the walls, was putting all upon the single

single chance of holding out for a considerable time a wretched fortification; a chance which an action in the field could hardly alter, at the same time that it gave an additional one, perhaps a better. If the event was not prosperous, he determined to hold out to the last extremity; and then to retreat to the isle of Orleans, with what was left of the garrison, to wait for reinforcements.

In consequence of this resolution, the general marched out the 28th, with all the force he could muster, which did not exceed 3000 men; forming them on the heights of Abraham, in order of battle; and observing that the french army was upon the march in one column, as far he could see; he thought this the lucky moment; and moved with the utmost order to attack them before they had formed. He soon beat them from the heights they had possessed, though they were well disputed. Major Dalling, who commanded a corps of light infantry, having forced the enemies grenadiers from a house and wind-mill, in attempting to regain the flank of the english army, was charged, thrown into disorder, retired to the rear, and from the number of officers killed and wounded, could never again be brought up during the action. Otway's regiment was ordered to advance immediately, and sustain the right wing, which the enemy in vain made two attempts to penetrate. While this passed there, the left was not idle; they had dispossessed the enemy of two redoubts, and sustained with unparralleled firmness, the bold united efforts of the enemies regulars, indians and canadians, till at last, fairly fought down, and reduced to a handful, they were obliged to yield to superior numbers. This disorder was soon communicated to the right; but the whole retired in such a way, that the enemy did not venture upon a brisk pursuit. Most of the cannon was left, as the roughness of the ground, and the wreaths of snow, made it impossible to bring them off; but what could not be brought off, were nailed up. The killed and wounded amounted to one third of those in the field; that of the french, by their own confession, exceeded 2500 men, which may be readily conceived, as the action lasted an hour and three quarters.

On the night of the 28th, the french opened the trenches before the town; some frigates which they were in possession of, anchored below their camp; for several days they were busy in landing their cannon, mortars, and other ammunition; they worked incessantly at perfecting their trenches, and raising batteries; and on the 11th of may, they opened three batteries of cannon, and one of bombs. The garrison were not idle; they made the necessary dispositions to defend the place to the last extremity; they planted cannon on every bastion, and even in the curtains; and raised new works; insomuch that before the enemy opened their batteries, they had 132 pieces of cannon, placed on the ramparts, mostly dragged there by the soldiery. Notwithstanding this formidable artillery, they were so circumstanced, that had a french fleet appeared first in the river, the place must certainly have fell.

A small squadron of ships had been some time on their passage to Quebec, under lord Colvil and commodore Swanton: general Murray depended on their arrival, to be able to oblige the french to raise the siege; it was the 9th of may before he received any intelligence of them. The 16th, two english frigates were ordered by commodore Swanton to slip their cables, and attack the french fleet, which immediately weighed anchor; but they were so closely followed, and so briskly attacked, that their whole squadron consisting of six ships, ran aground in different places, and several of them were destroyed.

This

This misfortune was like a thunder-bolt to the french; they raised the siege the same evening, and retreated with the greatest precipitation. They left their camp standing, all their baggage, stores, magazines of provisions and ammunition, 34 pieces of battering cannon, ten field pieces, six mortars, four petards, a large quantity of scaling ladders, and intrenching tools beyond number. Spies and deserters reported, that they wanted provisions and ammunition excessively, and that the greatest part of their canadians had deserted them. General Murray, at the head of five regiments, and the grenadiers and light infantry, pushed out in pursuit of them; but they had crossed the river Caprouge before they could get up with them; and retired to a place called Jaques Cartier, not having above 5000 men remaining. In this succesful manner was the siege of this celebrated city raised, by the conduct of the brave governor, with his intrepid garrison, and the assistance of so inconsiderable a naval force. All the officers and men distinguished themselves remarkably; there never being, perhaps, a more fatiguing winter to any troops; and succeeding such a laborious campaign.

The same success, which so remarkably distinguished the english arms in America, also attended their operations in the East-Indies. This war was more important, and of greater extent in that country, than is generally the case. Colonel Clive who commanded in chief, had, from his first entering on his command, been surprisingly succesful: the beginning of this year, he gave another specimen of his abilities. It seems the dutch had a great inclination to engross the salt-petre trade entirely to themselves. The share which they had of this trade, was carried on at Chincery, a strong fort and factory in the river of Bengal; but the english salt-petre trade was much more considerable at Calcutta. The governor of Batavia being informed,

informed, that the english ships were absent on the coast, thought this a fair opportunity to attempt executing this scheme. Under colour of reinforcing their garrisons, he sent a body of troops to the mouth of the river. Colonel Clive had suspected their designs; and on the arrival of the two first transports, which were ships of 36 guns, and full of men, the colonel informed the dutch commodore, that he could not allow him to land any forces, or to march up to Chincery, as he had from good authority been acquainted with their scheme. The dutchman only desired the liberty of refreshing his men ashore; which was granted him. In the mean time, five other dutchmen arrived in the river. The commodore now began to retaliate; he not only ordered the land forces to march directly to Chincery, but, the ships to take every english vessel that should appear on the river, which was executed on several. Soon after, the Calcutta, captain Wilson, an english East-india man, went down the river, bound for England. When he came a-breast of the dutch commodore, he was haild, and told, that if he offered to pass they would sink him. Captain Wilson directly returned up to Calcutta, where two other East-Indiamen were lying; and on his arrival, informed colonel Clive of his being stopped. The colonel with a becoming spirit immediately ordered the three Indiamen to prepare themselves for action, and to endeavour to take, burn, sink, and destroy every dutch ship they should meet in the river. The dutchmen, on their approach, drew up into a line to receive them; three mounted 36 guns, three 26, and one 16. The engagement began with great fury, and in a short time, the dutch commodore struck his flag; his example being followed by three others; and of the remaining four, two of them escaped, and the other ran ashore. The prisoners were carried to colonel Clive; who

being

being informed, that the land forces which the dutch had set on shore, amounting to about 1100 men, were in full march for Chincery, detached 500 men, under major Ford to oppose them. The same bad success attended the dutch arms by land as by sea: the major entirely defeated them, killed 400, and took all the rest prisoners. Colonel Clive compromised the affair with this perfidious enemy, and returned their ships, on their giving security to pay a large sum of money for the damage the english suffered in the two engagements. Had not this affair ended in so successful a manner, we might have expected to have had the tragedy of Amboyna acted in Bengal.

The british arms were equally successful against the french. Colonel Clive having resigned the command in these parts, (in which he had been so signally successful) to colonel Coote, he embarked for Europe. He was one of the richest subjects in Christendom; which is not to be wondered at, since he had possessed so many opportunities of making an immense fortune. Colonel Coote took the field at the head of an army, towards the end of november; and being informed that general Lally had sent a detachment of his army to the southward, and that that party had taken Syningham, and threatned Trichenopoly with a siege, he thought it adviseable to endeavour to draw the french from that quarter. Accordingly, on the 27th of that month, he invested Wondiwash, and became master of it in two days, making its garrison of between 8 and 900 men prisoners of war. On the 3d of december, he laid siege to Carangoly, and in seven days it surrendered. Mr. Coote having intelligence, that several considerable detachments of french were rendezvoused at Arcot, under brigadier general Bussy; and that general Lally was on the march to join them, he moved with the english

lish army towards Arcot, and encamped opposite to that city, the river Palla running between them. At the end of december, general Lally took the command of the french army; and by the 9th of january 1760, it was all in motion; the general marched towards Wondiwash, and detached a body of near a thousand men to attack Conjeveram: the commanding officer there informed colonel Coote of his danger; who, by making a forced march, saved the place; and strenthening the garrison, marched within a few miles of Wondiwash; which place he found invested by general Lally, who had began to raise his batteries.

The commanding officer in the town informed Mr. Coote, that a breach was made; and the colonel thereupon determined, if possible, to raise the siege; for this end, he advanced with all his cavalry, on the 21st, to reconnoitre. The enemy's situation was very strong; but colonel Coote, on the 22d, by a judicious movement, having got possession of a hill, that covered his right flank, began the attack with a smart cannonade; and in the conclusion gained a complete victory; the french having left him master of the field, together with all their cannon, amounting to 22 pieces, besides a large quantity of shot, with tumbrils, and all other implements belonging to the train. Brigadier general Bussy, and le chevalier Godeville, quarter-master-general were taken prisoners, the former reckoned the richest subject in Christendom; they lost besides, 800 men killed and wounded, and 240 prisoners. The loss on the side of the conquerors was very inconsiderable; that of the greatest consequence was in major Brereton, who was killed. General Lally retired with the shattered remains of his troops to Pondicherry; and towards the end of january, colonel Coote detached captain Vasserot with 1300 men, to the neighbourhood of that

that city, to deſtroy the french country, and marched himſelf with the main army to beſiege Chittiput, which ſurrendered to him the 29th. This ſucceſs only paved the way to a conqueſt of more importance; on the 5th of february, he opened his batteries againſt Arcot, the capital of the province, and became maſter of it the 10th, finding four mortars, 22 pieces of cannon, and a great quantity of all ſorts of military ſtores in it. Theſe ſignal ſucceſſes extended the dominion of the engliſh Eaſt-india company, much beyond any thing that was ever known before, and reduced the french in thoſe parts to the greateſt diſtreſs.

C H A P.

CHAP. XXVII.

Affairs in Germany. Situation of the king of Prussia and the empress queen. Motions of the armies under the generals Fouquet and Laudohn. Fouquet evacuates Landshut. Glatz blockaded. Battle of Landshut. Measures of count Daun. Motions of his prussian majesty. Marches for Silesia. Followed by Daun. His critical situation. Lays siege to Dresden. Raises the siege. Motions of general Laudohn. Besieges Glatz. It surrenders. Bombards Breslau. Retires on the approach of prince Henry. Motions of his prussian majesty. His fine march into Silesia. Battle of Merschwitz. Its consequences. Campaign between the allies and the french. Skirmishes. Marpourg taken by the french. Action at Corbach. Action at Erxdorff. Battle of Warbourg.

HIS prussian majesty had received so many severe blows in the last campaign, that it was not expected he would be very early in his operations this year; indeed, the several armies in Germany, never took the field so late, since the beginning of the war: and, as a peace was expected by some of the parties to take place, before the opening of the campaign, all were remarkably cautious in their conduct, at a season, when a misfortune might be attended with the most decisive consequences; but as all these hopes were found entirely delusive, the king of Prussia took his usual wise precautions, to have his armies on the best footing possible: the empress queen had, during the whole spring, employed herself in raising numerous recruits for her army in Saxony, and took every measure that foresight could dictate, to render the ensuing campaign decisive. To oppose her the king augmented his own army, which acted against

marshal

marshal Daun's, and placed his brother Henry at the head of 40,000 men, to defend the eastern parts of his dominions, against the russians; who, it was evident from their conduct, would again attack him. Another body of troops he opposed to the swedes; and it was with surprise, that all Europe saw him still able to defend himself against such numerous and powerful enemies.

His majesty had employed himself during some months, in fortifying his camp near Meissen, which was very strong by nature; but rendered impregnable by art. He made vast intrenchments in every part where it was accessible, and furnished them with such a numerous artillery, that in the front alone, there were near 250 pieces of cannon. Marshal Daun, though greatly superior in numbers to the king, followed his example, and fortified himself in a strong camp near Dresden. The respective armies had been so harrassed the last campaign, that it was the month of june, before either the prussian or austrian troops withdrew from their quarters of cantonment.

The empress queen had placed general Laudohn at the head of an army of about 40,000 men, who were encamped some time in Bohemia, on the frontiers of Lusatia. This corps was destined to attack Silesia. In the beginning of june, Laudohn marched into the county of Glatz, and advanced to Reichenberg, two miles from Schweidnitz. General Fouquet commanded a prussian corps near Landshut, which when augmented with a detachment from prince Henry's army, amounted to near 20,000 men; this general supposed M. Laudohn's design was to cut off the communication between Schweidnitz and Breslau; and with that idea, withdrew all his posts from Landshut, and that neighbourhood, in so precipitate a manner, that he left there a considerable magazine: an austrian general took possession of the town, as soon as it was evacuated. In this manner

ner Laudohn was prevented from attacking Schweidnitz.

That general placed a strong garrison and detachment at Friedland, to support them; he left his cavalry at Franckenstein, and sent his infantry into the county of Glatz: as he found himself unable to penetrate further into Silesia, he resolved to undertake the siege of Glatz, a strong town, the key of Bohemia and Silesia, and by its conquest to open the campaign with some eclat. General Fouquet, in order to relieve that town, advanced against Landshut, and after some resistance drove from thence the austrian generals Geisrugg and Jahnus, taking possession of it the 17th of june. In the night between that day and the 18th, Laudohn made a very brisk attack upon Glatz, but was repulsed with considerable loss; and finding that the siege was like to be of longer continuation, than he at first expected, and that general Fouquet would have it in his power, from his situation at Landshut, to interrupt his operations; he determined, before he advanced further in it, to attack Fouquet.

Pursuant to this resolution, he called in all his detachments, and leaving a small body of troops before Glatz, marched towards Landshut. Fouquet being desirous to maintain that post, took all measures immediately for making a good defence. He was obliged however, to send off general Ziethen, with four battalions and two squadrons towards Frauenstein, in order to preserve a communication with Schweidnitz, as well as major general Grant on the other side, with some cavalry; so that there were but few generals left with him, and part of his corps, the whole of which was so much weaker than the austrians. On the 23d, at about two o'clock in the morning, he was attacked by general Laudohn, at the head of all his forces. The prussian troops were intrenched on several heights, defended by redoubts; it was not till after

after a very vigorous resistance, that Laudohn made himself master of three of them; general Fouquet threw himself into the two which remained in his possession; where he was twice summoned on the part of general Laudohn to surrender with his men, which he refused complying with. In consequence of which, he was again attacked with great fury, and the austrians being so much superior, at last penetrated into the redoubts, which had been defended in a most gallant manner, for near six hours successively. General Fouquet, after having made as brave a defence as was possible in his circumstances, and having received two wounds, fell into the hands of the austrians; and victory declared for general Laudohn. The loss on either side in this battle was never exactly known; but it fell very heavy on the prussians, whose whole army, according to the austrian account, was all either killed, wounded, or taken prisoners; but this is vastly exaggerated. General Fouquet was at the head of not above 15,000 men, when the action happened, and it was supposed, that out of this number, not above 7 or 8000 escaped. Laudohn's army amounted before the battle to above 30,000 men; his victory was quite complete, all the camp, artillery, and baggage of the prussians falling into his hands.

No sooner was his prussian majesty informed of this unfortunate affair, than he clearly saw the necessity of his affairs would oblige him to march into Silesia. The victorious general Laudohn, it was feared, would speedily advance against Schweidnitz or Breslau; and as his operations would, in all probability be seconded by a formidable army of russians, who were in full march for Silesia, prince Henry's force was insufficient to defend that province against such numerous enemies. These circumstances had such weight with his majesty, that he determined, if possible, to relieve that province, the favourite part of his dominions.

dominions. But many difficulties lay in his way, which rendered his march extremely hazardous. Marshal Daun, when he heard of Laudohn's victory, immediately foresaw that the king would endeavour to march into Silesia, and took such measures as he thought were most likely to prevent his being able to effect it. He detached general Lascy with a strong corps to take post at Lichtenber; and distributed strong bodies of troops at all the defiles in Lusatia, which lead into Silesia; the situation of his own army, in his strong camp at Reichenberg, he knew would enable him to follow the king very speedily, in case his majesty was to attempt the march which he expected he would make.

Count Daun was not mistaken in this supposition; for the king leaving a strong corps in his camp near Meissen, under general Hulsen, began his march into Lusatia the 2d of July, crossing the river Pulsnitz, at the bridge at Cracau, and encamping that day on the heights near the town: His majesty designing to attack general Lascy, marched on the 4th to Koninsbruck, in his way to Lichtenberg; but Lascy, on having notice of his approach, retired. The prussian army crossed the Sprehe, near Grofs Dobzan, the 6th; and from thence occupied the camp at Doberschutz, about half a german mile from Bautzen.

It was at this place, that his majesty received advice on the 8th, that marshal Daun was at Gorlitz, and that his army was on the march for Lauban. That general had laid his plan so well, that he had gained two marches upon the king, and posted himself between Silesia and the prussian army. His prussian majesty directly perceived how excessively difficult it would be for him to force his way through a country, in which every defile was guarded, and commanded by a superior army, under an able general. Any other man would have been embarrassed with

these

these circumstances; he found he could not relieve Silesia; and to remain inactive in Lusatia, would be fatal to his affairs every where; add to these, it was so critical a conjuncture, that not a moment's time must be lost. His majesty's genius extricated him from these pressing difficulties, and changed a misfortune at least to the probability of gaining an advantage. In the morning of the 8th, he was acquainted with Daun's march, and in the evening he determined to make a forced march back into Saxony, and endeavour to possess himself of Dresden, before the marshal could arrive to succour it. At 8 o'clock the tents of the army were struck, and it repassed the Sprehe near Bautzen, moving the next day by Bischoffswerda to Harta, and arrrived after a most expeditious march, the 13th, at Grunau near Dresden; encamping in two lines, one towards Pirna, and the other towards Dresden. General Macguire, an Irishman, who had raised himself from the station of a common soldier by his bravery, commanded in Dresden. His majesty sent him a summons by one of his aid de camps to surrender, which he gallantly refused. In the night between the 14th and 15th the trenches were opened, and the batteries being completed, began to play the 18th. The next day marshal Daun appeared with his army, which he had strengthened by great detachments, drawn from Bohemia and Silesia. The prince of Holstein, with part of the prussian army occupied the posts of Nauendorff and Weisse Hirsch, in order to block up Dresden on the other side of the Elbe; after the approach of Daun this corps was in danger of being surrounded by the superior numbers of the austrians; so the king ordered the prince to repass the Elbe. Marshal Daun, having by this means a free communication with Dresden, and being come up to encamp with his army at a place called the Granges, and having also caused two bridges of boats to be built over the Elbe; the king

king of Prussia found that there was no further prospect of any success in the siege, and accordingly determined to raise it the 21st. That night marshal Daun threw sixteen battalions into the town, which early in the morning of the 22d made a general sally on the besiegers, with design to get possession of their cannon, but they were driven back with considerable loss. His majesty after withdrawing all his artillery from the siege, removed his head quarters from Grunau to Leubnitz. In this manner he was disappointed in his expectations of being able to make himself master of Dresden, before Daun came came up; and general Macguire had a much stronger garrison than the king of Prussia imagined: nevertheless, we cannot but admire the activity of his majesty's genius, which always prompts him, when his affairs wear but a bad face, to try every expedient possible to extricate himself from such perplexing difficulties.

In the mean time general Laudohn, after gaining the victory of Landshut, returned with great expedition to resume the siege of Glatz. The artillery was all placed on the batteries in the night of the 25th, and began a very brisk fire the next morning; which was designed to cover an attack on one of the outworks, which was made that morning: and succeeded so well, by being vigorously supported, that in a short time the garrison surrendered at discretion. The austrians found a large magazine in the place; and it proved an acquisition of great importance.

Laudohn had no sooner possessed himself of Glatz, than he prepared to march against Breslau; which yielded him the prospect of an easy conquest; the king of Prussia was in Saxony, and prince Henry encamped at a great distance from that city, waiting the approach of the russians; so that he had great reason to expect Breslau would fall before any succour could be received. Moved by the fair appearance

ance of succefs; he pushed forward very expeditiously towards that city, and arrived before it on the 30th of july. Major general Javentzien, the prussian commandant, was several times summoned to surrender *, but as constantly refused it; and Laudohn's heavy artillery not being come up, he began on the first of august a very severe bombardment, which reduced the king of Prussia's palace and several other public buildings to ashes, as well as the finest streets in the city.

Marshal Soltikoff, at the head of a numerous army of russians, was at this time advancing briskly, as if with intent to join Laudohn. The motions of this general induced his royal highness prince Henry, who commanded an army of about 40,000 prussians, encamped at Gleissen, to march to Glogau. The 27th of july he broke up his camp, and took the rout to Strapel, Reitscutz, Pudligar, and Linden; on his arrival at Glogau, he learnt that Breslau was besieged; and instantly determined to make forced marches to relieve it. The rapidity of his motions on this occasion was such, as had distinguished the prussian arms. On the 3d of august he arrived at Parchwitz, from whence an austrian general with 2000 men retired on his approach. The next day, the prince's vanguard arrived at Neumark; and he was there informed, that Laudon had raised the siege of Breslau, and retired with great precipitation to Canth. The prussian army moved the 5th to Lissa, and the next day crossed the Elbe at Breslau, having marched no less than 25 german miles in five days: detachments were sent out to harrass general Laudohn in his retreat, and some hundreds of austrians were taken, with a major general. Nothing but the great expedition used by prince Henry in his march could have saved Breslau, for the russians on the 6th were but five miles from that city; the prudent use of an important

* Vide appendix.

portant height stopped their progress; and his royal highness by his admirable motions was able to oblige them to retreat to a greater distance from Breslau, and protected that city from the attack of general Laudohn, who retreated towards Schweidnitz.

While his affairs were in this critical situation in Silesia, the king of Prussia was attentive to every motion of marshal Daun, and as his presence was much wanted in that province, he determined to take the first opportunity of marching into it. On the 30th of july he decamped, and took the rout of Meissen, without giving Daun any reason to suspect his designs. The 2d of august he arrived at Dalwitz, and the next day took the road to Silesia; the 7th, his army reached Buntzlau, having marched no less than 200 miles in five days; which expedition is astonishing. Marshal Daun on the first notice of the king's march, moved towards Silesia, to stop him, but although he got to Bautzen the 1st, yet he was not able to prevent his prussian majesty's entering Silesia before him; he took possession of the camp of Lignitz the 10th. This march of the prussian army, if maturely considered, will appear very surprising. All Lusatia, through which it lay, was in the hands of his enemies; general Reid at the head of one army, and Lascy with another, lying on each side of him; general Beck commanded a third in his front; and marshal Daun's parties were continually at his rear. So surrounded with enemies, his army, encumbered with above 2000 waggons, passed the Elbe, the Spree, the Neiss, the Queiss, and the Bober, without any loss; which may possibly be reckoned one of the most remarkable pieces of generalship ever performed; more particularly if we consider that Daun, at the head of an army much superior in number, had no other employment besides preventing his majesty's penetrating into Silesia.

The

The king on his arrival at Lignitz, found that the enemies troops occupied all the country between Parchwitz and Coffendau; so that marshal Daun with his army formed the centre, and occupied the heights of Wahlstadt and Hochkirk. M. Laudohn with his army covered the ground between Jeschkendorff and Coschitz: general Naukendorf that of the heights of Parchwitz; and M. de Beck, who formed the left, extended his troops beyond Coffendan. His majesty intended to have passed the Katzbach, and the Schartzwasser, but this advantageous position of the enemy prevented him; he therefore marched in the night of the 11th to turn them, and to reach Javer: for this purpose, the columns of the army was got as far as Hohendorff, from whence a new camp at Pransnitz was discovered, and his majesty received advice, that it was M. de Lascy's corps, which was just arrived from Lauban; the prussian army prepared immediately to attack him; but M. de Lascy made his dispositions with so much skill, and knew so well how to avail himself of the advantages the ground gave him, that he retreated to marshal Daun, without the king's being able to attack him with any prospect of success. His majesty finding that the attempt of turning the enemy was impracticable; returned with his army on the 13th back to the camp at Lignitz.

The king no sooner arrived there, than he perceived how disadvantageous it would be to wait for the enemy in that camp. He foresaw that M. de Lascy would have advanced upon his right, that marshal Daun, would have probably attacked his front, and M. de Laudohn have fallen upon his left, possessing himself at the same time of the heights of Plaffendorff. These considerations induced his majesty on the 14th, to take possession of those heights, drawing up his army in order of battle upon them. This motion changed the scene of operation, and disconcerted

certed the dispositions of the austrian generals. Scarce had the prussians taken this new position, when they were informed, about two o'clock in the morning, that M. Laudohn was in full march towards them. Whereupon the prussian army separated into two bodies; the right remained upon the ground where it had been formed, to observe Daun. Sixteen battalions and thirty squadrons turned about, in order to fall upon the corps under Laudohn.

According to the plan on which that general acted, he was to advance by those heights, where the prussian army was drawn up; and he expected only to meet with some weak detachments there. About three o'clock in the morning, his advanced parties attacked those of the prussians, and made them give way, and Laudon to push this success, hastened the movement of his main body, thinking to get possession of the heights without opposition. Whilst he was endeavouring to do this, day-light came on; and to his great astonishment discovered the prussian army drawn up in excellent order. This was an unexpected stroke, but it was then too late to retreat; therefore he prepared in the best manner he could for action. The battle lasted but two hours; Laudohn was obliged to retire before the superior abilities of the prussian monarch; and yielded him a complete victory. The loss of the conquerors was very inconsiderable; but that of the austrians amounted in killed, wounded, and prisoners to upwards of 10,000 men. Two generals, and more than eighty officers were amongst the latter. Eighty two pieces of cannon, and twenty three pair of colours were taken [*].

This victory, for which his prussian majesty was so much indebted to his own genius, in a great measure changed the face of affairs in Silesia. For although he was not able to oblige the austrians and russians to evacuate that province, yet he defeated their particular

[*] Vide appendix.

ticular defigns againſt Breſlau and Schweidnitz, and prevented the generals Soltikoff and Laudohn from joining their forces. The king won the battle of Merſchwitz with much ſuch a ſtratagem as prince Ferdinand uſed ſo ſucceſsfully at Minden. Immediately after the action, his majeſty marched to Parchwitz, and from thence to Neumark, by which means he opened a communication with prince Henry, and effectually covered Breſlau. Daun ſeemed for ſome days to have a deſign of beſieging Schweidnitz, but the king by a maſterly movement towards that town prevented him from executing it.

It is now time to give an account of the operations of the army under the command of his ſerene highneſs duke Ferdinand of Brunſwick, which acted againſt the french, commanded by marſhal Broglio: the actions performed by either of theſe armies for ſome months were of but little importance; nor can this be wondered at, when we conſider, that the only object of duke Ferdinand's operations was to prevent the french from poſſeſſing themſelves of the electorate of Hanover; and as his ſerene highneſs was at the head of a very fine army, we are not to ſuppoſe that the french general would be able to force him to a battle, under diſadvantageous circumſtances. It was the middle of may before the allies were out of their cantonments, nor were the french earlier in the field; duke Ferdinand's troops were encamped the end of that month at Fritzlar, where the head quarters were eſtabliſhed. The generals Inhoff and Gilſoe commanding each a ſeparate corps, the firſt at Kirchaynon on the Ohme, and the latter upon the Fulda near Hirſchfield. The head quarters of the french army had been fixed during the winter at Franckfort; but about this time their detachments advanced towards Gieſſen and Marpourg. The count de St. Germain commanded a ſtrong corps of french on the Rhine, near Keyſerſwert, and general Sporken at the head of
a body

a body of hanoverians was opposed to him, encamping at Dulmen.

Duke Ferdinand opened the campaign with some successful attempts to streighten the quarters of the french. Towards the end of may he drove them from Butzbach, and seized their magazines in that town; and detached the hereditary prince with near 20,000 men into the county of Fulda, which corps cleared that country of the enemy's troops. In opposition to these motions marshal Broglio determined to advance; and accordingly having called in his detachments, he encamped the 28th of june at Neustadt; and laid siege to Marpourg and Dillenburg; the former surrendered the 30th of june, and the latter the 16th of july.

The french army was so much superior in numbers to that of duke Ferdinand, that his serene highness was unable to prevent their advancing; the 8th of july, marshal Broglio quitted his camp at Neustadt, and marched towards Franckenberg, and a strong corps at the same time, under M. de St. Germain, advanced towards Brillon and Corbach. Duke Ferdinand, who had been encamped near Treysa, also marched his army the 9th, to the neighbourhood of Wildungen, in order to prevent the enemy from penetrating further by their new motions. His advanced corps under the hereditary prince of Brunswick, was sent forwards as far as Saxenhausen, after having been reinforced with some battalions and some squadrons, under major general Griffin. The allied army resumed its march early the next morning, and the hereditary prince at the same time advanced from Saxenhausen towards Corbach, where he found the french army already formed; but judging them not to be very numerous, and their whole force against him not to exceed 10,000 foot, and 17 squadrons, he formed a design of driving that corps, which was commanded by the french general M. Wal-

M. Waldner, back; and thus an engagement was brought on, which became extremely hot about two o'clock in the afternoon. The french being continually reinforced with fresh troops, and having the superiority of numbers, and a large artillery, the prince found it impossible to dislodge them from their post; and as there was no necessity of maintaining that which he himself occupied (the main army being arrived at Saxenhausen) and it not being practicable for them to come up in time to sustain the hereditary prince in his post, orders were sent him by prince Ferdinand to rejoin the army, part of which was then formed. Accordingly he made his dispositions for a retreat, which was attended with some confusion among some of the best battalions and squadrons. The french observing this, pressed very briskly upon the allied troops, both with their artillery and a large body of cavalry. The consequences of this might have been very bad, had it not been for the great bravery of the hereditary prince, who putting himself at the head of one of Bland's squadrons, and Howard's regiment of dragoons, charged the french so furiously as to enable the infantry to make a safe retreat. Fifteen pieces of cannon however fell into the hands of the conquerors; twenty by the french account, who also assert, that the allies lost 3000 men, dead on the spot, besides 800 wounded or prisoners; whereas the whole of the loss is calculated by the London Gazette, at about 500 men, most probably both these accounts were false. General count Kilmansegge, major general Griffin, the two british battalions of Brudenel and Carr; particularly one squadron of Bland's, commanded by major Mill, and Howard's regiment of dragoons, all distinguished themselves remarkably; and the troops in general shewed great good will and alacrity. The hereditary prince was wounded in the shoulder, but not dangerously. The success of the french in this action was

of

of very little consequence to them, in any other respect than that of raising the spirit of their troops, who regarded this good beginning as an omen of future success.

Never was the bravery of any general more conspicuous than that of the hereditary prince in this affair: his well judged and desperate attack on the french troops, covered so effectually the retreat of his infantry, that the enemy themselves could not but admire the stroke which stopped their career. His highness soon after had an opportunity of revenging this defeat.

Marshal Broglio having formed the design of possessing himself of Ziegenhayn, detached a corps for that purpose under major general Glanbitz, consisting of six battalions, and the regiment of Berchini. Duke Ferdinand, on receiving advice of this motion, detached the hereditary prince from the army at Saxenhausen, the 14th at night, for Fritzlar, at the head of six battalions; in his way he was joined by general Luckner, with his regiment of dragoons, and Elliot's light horse, which was just arrived from England. M. de Glaubitz was encamped at Erxdorff; in perfect security, and had neglected to place the proper advanced posts to prevent a surprise. The prince having advanced pretty near the enemy, reconnoitred; and then made a detour of near two leagues, with part of his force, in order to gain the left flank of the french, who thinking themselves very secure, were surprised in their camp. Their artillery, baggage, and tents being soon taken, they retired by Langenstein. His serene highness putting himself at the head of Elliot's light dragoons, and some other cavalry, pursued the enemy, and overtaking them on their march in a plain, he charged and broke through them four or five different times, and separating 500 men from the body, obliged them to lay down their arms; and surrounding M. Glaubitz

Glaubitz at the head of the remainder of his corps, he summoned him to surrender, which was accordingly complied with. Berchini's regiment was likewise either entirely taken or cut to pieces, by Luckner's hussars. Major general Glaubitz and the prince of Anhalt, a brigadier, were amongst the prisoners. Nine pair of colours (almost all taken by Elliot's regiment) five pieces of artillery and a haut-bitzer, were taken; the prisoners amounted to 177 officers, and 2482 private men. The loss of the allies was inconsiderable, not amounting to above 200 men killed and wounded.

This advantage was not attended with any great consequences, except just the loss of men, to the french; and what was worse, the loss of reputation, particularly as M. Glaubitz was surprised in such a scandalous manner. It had one effect in common with many other enterprises of the hereditary prince, to display still clearer every day his great abilities in the art of war. Elliot's regiment of light horse, which was but just raised, distinguished themselves extremely; and the infantry shewed throughout great courage and good will to march on and engage, though harrassed and almost exhausted by the fatigues of their march. Major Erskine in particular, who commanded Elliot's greatly distinguished himself*.

This action was not of consequence enough to prevent the french from advancing: Duke Ferdinand was yet obliged to retreat; he bent his march towards Cassel, and leaving a garrison in that town, retreated towards Warbourg. Marshal Broglio formed a design of cutting off his communication with Westphalia: to compass this end, he detached the chevalier de Muy, at the head of the reserve of the french army, amounting to about 35,000 men, to cross the river Dymel, and extend himself down the side of it; while the marshal himself advanced with the main army

* Vide appendix.

army towards duke Ferdinand's camp at Kalle, in the mid way, between Caſſel and Warbourg; and on the 30th his ſerene highneſs paſſed the Dymel with his army, between Liebenaw and Dringelbourg. The hereditary prince had paſſed that river the day before, and took poſt between Liebenaw and Corbeke, at the head of 24 battalions and 22 ſquadrons; and he immediately reconnoitred the poſition of M. de Muy; after which it was agreed, that the hereditary prince, aſſiſted by general Sporke, ſhould turn the left of the french, while duke Ferdinand advanced with his army upon their front; which was done with all poſſible ſucceſs, the french being attacked almoſt in the ſame inſtant by M. Sporcke, and the hereditary prince, in flank and in rear. The army marched with the greateſt diligence to make the attack in front; but the infantry could not get up in time; general Waldegrave, at the head of the britiſh preſſed their march as much as poſſible: no troops ever ſhewed greater eagerneſs to engage; many of the men, from the heat of the weather, and overſtraining themſelves to get on, through moraſſy and very difficult ground, ſuddenly dropped down on their march. The duke obſerving that the infantry would be too late, gave orders for lord Granby to advance, with the cavalry of the right; general Moyſton commanded under him, and although the diſtance from the enemy was five miles, yet they made ſo much expedition in bringing it up, on a full trot, as to have an opportunity of ſharing in the glory of the day. The french cavalry, though very numerous, retreated as ſoon as that of the allies advanced to charge them, excepting only three ſquadrons, that kept their ground with ſome firmneſs, but were ſoon broke. A part of the engliſh cavalry then fell upon the enemy's infantry, which ſuffered extremely, particularly a regiment of ſwiſs. Theſe atttacks were ſeconded in a ſurpriſing manner by the engliſh artillery, commanded

manded by captain Philips, who brought it up on a gallop. His serene highness, seeing the french begin to give way, ordered an attack to be made on the town of Warbourg; on which they retired with the utmost precipitation, leaving about 1500 men dead upon the field of battle, together with ten pieces of cannon, some colours, and about 1500 prisoners. The loss on the side of the allies was very moderate, it fell chiefly on the brave battalion of Maxwell's english grenadiers, which did wonders. Lord Grandby greatly distinguished himself.

The consequences of this battle were not so great as might have been expected; duke Ferdinand was still obliged to retreat: nor could he prevent the french from entering the electorate, and making themselves masters of Gottingen and Munden. An universal consternation once more seized the unhappy inhabitants of that exhausted country; every thing depended on the abilities of duke Ferdinand: he was at the head of a fine army; but that of the french was much the most numerous. Marshal Broglio advanced his detachments for some days; but by the good conduct of his serene highness, he was not able to push on with the main of the french army; so the electorate was saved by his excellent management. Marches, countermarches, and the making choice of posts proper for covering a country against a greatly superior army, perhaps require greater abilities than many battles; but the generality of the world seldom understand the one so perfectly as the other, as they are of less eclat, though not less importance. I shall here leave the operations of these armies, for the present, and take a view of the military affairs in other quarters, of no less consequence than those of which I have been treating.

C H A P.

CHAP. XXVIII.

Campaign in North America. Expedition under general Amherst against Montreal. Army embarks at Oswego. Isle Royale surrenders. Troops land at Montreal. General Murray arrives there from Quebec, and colonel Haviland from Isle aux Noix. Montreal capitulates. Canada conquered. Affairs in Germany. French surprised at Zierenberg. Battle of Campen. Armies go into winter quarters. Remarks on the campaign. Conclusion of the campaign between the prussians and austrians, &c. Action at Strehla. Motions of the russians. Lay siege to Colberg. Raised by general Werner. The swedes driven back. Berlin surrenders to the russians. Plundered. Their inhuman ravages. King of Prussia marches into Saxony. Battle of Torgau. Saxony recovered. Silesia evacuated by the austrians. Russians retire into Poland. Remarks on the campaign. Affairs in England. Great preparations at Portsmouth. The expedition fleet countermanded. Death of his majesty king George the second. Accession of his present majesty king George the third. King's speech. Reflections.

NOTHING but the unbounded trade of Great Britain could have enabled the nation to maintain so expensive a war. The parliament had in the beginning of the year, voted upwards of fifteen millions* sterling for the public expence. Enormous as these grants were, none but the discontented repined

* For the army,   6886000 l.
  For the navy,   4072000
  Sundrys,   4545000
                        £ 15503000

at the credit of the government; for it was found, that the money granted by parliament was applied to those services for which it was designed by the people; and the abilities of the ministers were such, that the war was every where successful, and the strength of the nation bent against the most national objects, and employed in the most advantageous manner.

The british arms had been particularly victorious the last campaign in north America; but still the French were not entirely conquered. Montreal, Trois Rivieres, and several other fortresses remained yet in the hands of the enemy; but general Amherst, his majesty's commander in chief in that country, had made the necessary preparations in the winter, and spring of the year, for opening the campaign with vigour. His excellency repaired to Oswego the 9th of July; which place was the rendezvous of his army, as the plan of their operations was to fall down the river St. Lawrence, and attack Montreal. It was the beginning of august before all the troops were arrived, but on the 10th, all the army embarked; the rear and the provincials were under the command of brigadier general Gage. About 60 miles from the lake Ontario, down the river St. Lawrence, is situated the isle Royale, whereon was built a strong fort: It was necessary to be master of this island, before the troops could proceed on their voyage; accordingly general Amherst attacked the fortress in a resolute manner, with his vessels, and batteries on shore, so that he got possession of it by capitulation, the 23d of august, two days after the first firing of his batteries.

At this place Mr. Amherst waited no longer than was necessary to repair the fort; on the 31st he proceeded on his voyage; the difficulty of the navigation occasioned his losing, on the 4th of september, 29 batteaus of men, and 17 of artillery and stores, besides 17 whale boats, and one row galley staved, 84 men by this unhappy accident were lost. The army landed on the island of Montreal in good order the 6th, and without opposition; and the next day, general Murray arrived with part of the garrison of Quebec, and a naval force under captain Deane; and with such extraordinary foresight and judgement had general Amherst planned this expedition, that colonel Haviland, who commanded a third corps (that was in possession of the isle aux Moix, in lake Champlain,) reached Montreal the next day. History can hardly produce a more striking instance of excellent military conduct in three separate expeditions against one place, by different routs, without any communication with each other, and through such a dangerous and difficult country, meeting almost at the same time at the destined rendezvous.

Before general Amherst could raise a single battery, the marquis de Vaudreuil offered to capitulate; and accordingly, on the 10th, the articles of capitulation*, not only for Montreal, but the whole province of Canada, were drawn up and signed: that immense country was surrendered to the king of Great Britain, and the british troops took immediate possession of all the fortresses in it, the french garrisons of which, were bound not to serve during the remainder of the war; the civil and religious rights of the inhabitants were guarantied to them. The 30th article of the capitulation contains perhaps the most insolent demand, ever made on such an occasion: " If by treaty of peace Canada should remain in the " the power of his britannick majesty, his most chri- " stian majesty shall continue to name the bishop " of the colony, who shall always be of the roman " communion, and under whose authority the peo- " ple shall exercise the roman religion." This impudent demand was refused by Mr. Amherst with the indignation it deserved.

In

* Vide appendix.

In this glorious and decisive manner was the campaign in north America concluded; that country in which the enemy had been so extremely formidable in the beginning of the war, as to baffle all the attempts of a nation so much superior in that part of the world, was now completely conquered. The unparallel'd success, which had here so constantly attended the british arms, during the two last campaigns, entirely wiped out the memory of those repeated defeats, and disgraces that we suffered in the beginning of the contest. Nor could the consequences of our victories be so great and advantageous in any other part of the globe as this. I have already explained the infinite inconveniencies which our colonies sustained from this country's being in the hands of the french; but by its conquest they were secured; and the british dominion and trade extended over one of the most extensive, and perhaps the finest countries in the universe.

The campaign in Germany between the allied and french armies, was not concluded with any great eclat. But there happened some actions, which though of no great importance, yet deserve to be mentioned. The beginning of september, marshal Broglio detached 20,000 men to make a grand forage in the neighbourhood of Geismar; but prince Ferdinand having received previous intelligence of their design, marched in person, with a corps of troops to oppose them; and though his serene highness was much inferior in numbers to the french, yet he took his precautions so well, by occupying some advantageous heights, and placing artillery on them, that he rendered the enemy's attempt totally ineffectual, notwithstanding a large part of their army was in motion to cover their foragers. The very same day, the hereditary prince, who had behaved with so much gallantry in several actions, which I have already related, being informed that a body of 1200 horse, and as many foot

foot of the french troops, were cantoned at Zierenberg, and being very near their grand army, thought themselves in perfect security; he formed a design to surprise them. Accordingly, his serene highness gave orders for six battalions and eight squadrons, to take different roads, and post themselves at the avenues to the town, which being performed in great order, it was completely surrounded before the enemy had the least intimation of their danger. Part of the grenadiers marching in profound silence towards one of the gates, were discovered by their trampling over the gardens, and fired upon by the garrison; whereupon, they rushed on, pushed the piquets, and having killed the guard at the gate, poured into the town, and drove every thing before them, at about two o'clock in the morning. Never was a more complete surprise. The expedition concluded with the carrying off M. de Norman, brigadier, who commanded the volunteers of Dauphine, and M. de Comeiras, colonel of those of Clermont, with about 40 more officers, and 400 private men; the number of killed and wounded was also very considerable, from an ill judged resistance of those that were in the houses; the party was obliged to retire with these advantages when day came on, as they might have been cut off by the french at Warbourg.

Prince Ferdinand to finish the campaign as advantageously as possible, by extending his quarters in the winter, and opening a communication with such countries on the lower Rhine, as might serve to furnish his army with forage, &c. and possibly to compass another end, which will be explained hereafter, detached the hereditary prince towards the end of september, into the duchy of Cleves, to clear that and the neighbouring countries of the french troops, and to besiege Wesel. The 29th, part of his serene highness's corps passed the Rhine at Roeroort, and
scoured

scoured the country to Rhynberg and Wesel; and other detachments took poffeffion of Rees and Emmerick. The 30th, the hereditary prince himself came before Wesel, and by the 3d of october, it was completely invested; the same day Cleves surrendered to another of his detachments, the garrison of 500 men being made prisoners of war.

His serene highness pushed on the siege of Wesel with as much briskness as possible; marshal Broglio thought it an object of such importance, that he resolved to raise the siege; for this end, he detached M. de Castries, with a strong corps towards the lower Rhine, which, when it had joined the straggling detachments in the country, amounted to 30 battalions, and 38 squadrons: by forced marches he arrived at Rhynberg the 14th. The hereditary prince had a party at that place, who were obliged to retire, on being attacked by the french, although the prince himself was at their head; the enemy advanced and encamped behind the convent of Campen: his serene highness formed the design of surprising M. de Castries in the night: accordingly he began his march at ten o'clock, but before he could reach the french camp, he found it necessary to overpower that corps that occupied the convent, about half a league in the front of it; in this attack the firing alarmed M. de Castries, who immediately put his troops hastily under arms. He was however attacked and drove back twice. A most terrible and well supported fire of musketry ensued; which lasted from five in the morning 'till about nine at night, without ceasing. At length his serene highness seeing, that it would be to no purpose to persist in the attempt of driving the enemy out of the wood, of which they had possessed themselves, and his infantry having spent all their ammunition, ordered a retreat; which was executed without a brisk pursuit from the enemy. The loss of the allies in killed, wounded, and prisoners,

prisoners, amounted to near 1500 men. The hereditary prince had his horse killed under him, and received a slight hurt by the same shot in his leg. Lieut. colonel Pitt, and lord Downe were wounded and prisoners. Lieut. general Waldegrave, major general Griffin, lord George Lenox, and several other officers distinguished themselves greatly. Major general Elliot, and several other officers of distinction were wounded. M. de Segur, lieut. general, M. de Wangen, brigadier general, with many officers, and some hundreds of private men of the enemy were made prisoners; and their loss on the whole was reckoned more considerable than that of the allies. This action happened on the 15th.

His serene highness was obliged in consequence of this action to raise the siege of Wesel, and on the 23d he fixed his head quarters at Brugzen, at which place he remained encamped sometime, watching the motions of M. de Castries; but nothing material happened between them. Duke Ferdinand attempted to finish the campaign with the possession of Gottingen, the only place in the electorate of Hanover, that was in the hands of the french; but after some unsuccessful skirmishes, he was obliged to withdraw his troops from before it; and the heavy rains having made the roads extremely bad, he distributed his men into winter quarters. His own head quarters he established at Eimbec, lord Granby's were fixed at Paderborn, and the hereditary prince's at Munster, the troops occupying all the adjacent country. The french went into quarters of cantonment about the same time as the allies; marshal Broglio's head quarters were at Cassel, and his army was distributed towards the upper Rhine. M. de Castrie's corps was cantoned on the lower Rhine from Cleves to Cologne. Although this campaign between the french and allies did not end with the same eclat as that of 1759; yet duke Ferdinand with a force much inferior to that of his enemy, my, was enabled by his great generalship to keep the french out of the electorate, the most material aim he had in view. Otherwise indeed, the campaign was rather unfortunate, as marshal Broglio, from the time he took the field to his going into winter quarters, kept constantly advancing; and there were several unsuccessful skirmishes during the course of it: but when we consider, that the great end of the war was answered, the preventing the french from possessing themselves of Hanover, and consequently of attacking the king of Prussia, and also the great superiority of the enemy, we may justly pronounce it successful.

In my last chapter, I left the king of Prussia, after the battle of Merschwitz, covering Silesia against the austrian army, under marshal Daun. His majesty having left a strong corps in Saxony, under general Hulsen, the duke of Deux Ponts, who commanded the army of the empire in Saxony, formed a design of falling on him, in the absence of the prussian grand army. For this end, he collected some austrian detachments together, and joining them to his own army, endeavoured to cut off Hulsen's communication with Torgau, who was posted at Meissen. The prussian general penetrating into this design, marched on the 17th of august to Strehla; and on the 20th was attacked by the combined army, which contained more than double the number of his men: by the good conduct of Hulsen, and the bravery of his men, the duke of Deux Ponts was defeated, with the loss of above 3000 men killed, wounded, and prisoners; that of the conquerors did not exceed 500 men. The prussian general being informed, that the duke of Wurtemberg, at the head of 10,000 men, was on his march to join the duke of Deux Ponts, retreated to Torgau, where he remained encamped.

His prussian majesty continually found new enemies springing up, in every part of his dominions. The russians, after prince Henry had defeated their design upon Breslau, seemed to lay aside the thoughts of prosecuting the campaign in Silesia, but in Pomerania they acted with fresh vigor; a considerable body of them sat down before Colberg, the beginning of september, while a russian fleet blocked up the port by sea. A vast army of these barbarians had once before endeavoured in vain to master this little town; and they were again foiled in their attempt. General Goltze, who commanded a small prussian army near Glogau, that watched the motions of the russian army in Silesia, detached general Werner with 6000 men to raise the siege. Werner made one of the most astonishing marches, for expedition, ever known; he reached Colberg from Glogau, which is above 250 miles in 11 days; and arriving before the place, on the 18th, the russians though much superior in number, raised the siege with the greatest precipitation, abandoning their tents, cannon, ammunition, baggage, forage, and provisions in very great quantities, to the prussians. This was not the only service performed by Werner; the swedes had, towards the end of the campaign, advanced into Brandenburg, and made themselves masters of some considerable towns, general Stutterheim, who commanded against them, being too weak to stop their progress, Werner marched against them, and obliged them to retire into their usual winter quarters at Stralsund.

His prussian majesty by some masterly movements, after the battle of Merschwitz obliged marshal Daun to retire among the mountains on the frontiers of Silesia; and as this confined situation of his army stopped the operations both of the austrian and russian armies, the russians were prevailed on to march into

into Brandenburg, and attack Berlin; hoping by that means to change the theatre of the war.

For this end the ruffian generals Czernichef and Tottleben, were detached with upwards of 20,000 men, and general Lafcy was fent againſt Berlin with 14000 from the auſtrian army. The whole ruffian army followed at a ſmall diſtance, to ſuſtain this grand enterprize. But each party wanting to get before the other, general Tottleben, without waiting the arrival of the large corps of troops, appeared on the 3d of october before Berlin, with 2000 light troops and ſome foot. He immediately ſummoned it, and upon its refuſing to ſurrender, he threw into the city ſome hundreds of royal grenades, bombs, and red hot balls, and at the ſame time made three aſſaults on one of the gates, but was repelled every time, and the flames which broke out in ſeveral parts were happily extinguiſhed. The ruffian general finding all his efforts vain, retired. Mean while, prince Eugene of Wurtemberg, and general Hulſen, had come to the aſſiſtance of the capital, and would probably have ſaved it, had not count Czernichef and general Lafcy with their reſpective corps came up. At the ſame time the grand ruffian army arrived at Franckfort on the Oder. The two pruſſian generals, ſeeing the great ſuperiority of the enemy, would not expoſe the city to the precarious iſſue of a battle. Accordingly they withdrew on the 6th to Spandaw, a ſtrong fortreſs in the neighbourhood. By the capitulation, which the governor and magiſtrates made with general Tottleben, it was agreed, that the town ſhould be delivered up to the ruſſians; that the garriſon of three battalions ſhould be priſoners of war; and that, on paying a contribution of 1,500,000 crowns, and 200,000 as a gratuity to the troops, the city ſhould enjoy full liberty, protection, and ſafety, while the enemy ſtaid in it.

The russian and austrian armies were no sooner in possession of Berlin, than they began to exercise all manner of inhuman barbarities on the innocent inhabitants, in defiance of the capitulation. By the third article it was agreed, that no soldier should be quartered in the city or suburbs; that the light troops should not be permitted even to enter the place: nevertheless, Berlin in a few days was overrun with cossacks, pandours, and every other species of irregular troops, who vied with each other in committing the most enormous outrages. They even lived at discretion, and used the most cruel treatment to force money from their landlords. All the king's palaces, stables, and country seats were desolated, the fine pictures, antique statutes, and rich furniture, with the king's coaches that could not be carried off, were entirely spoilt and demolished. The very graves did not escape the ravages of their merciless invaders, they broke open the vaults, and stripped the dead. Numbers of people of all ages and conditions were beat and cut in a miserable manner, and the women were dishonoured in the very presence of their parents and relations. All the neighbouring towns, and the adjacent country quite to Saxony and Poland was ravaged in this inhuman manner. It would fill volumes to be particular in an account of these infamous actions: but the king of Prussia published a memorial, setting in a clear light, before all Europe, the unmanly conduct of his enemies *.

In the mean time that monarch perceived the necessity of his marching to the defence of his dominions, as there was no force either in Brandenburg or Saxony able to withstand 80,000 russians, who were encamped in the former of those countries. Accordingly his majesty, having called in his detachments, began his march towards Brandenburg; he

* Vide appendix.

bent

bent his courſe acroſs Luſatia, and arrived at Dam the 20th of october, being followed by marſhal Daun at the diſtance of a few days march. On the king's approach, the ruſſians evacuated Berlin, retiring towards Poland; ſo that his majeſty found himſelf enabled by their abſence to remove the theatre of the war into Saxony. His affairs in that country greatly wanted his preſence; the army of the empire, in conjunction with a large body of auſtrians had made themſelves maſters of Leipſick, Wittenberg and Torgau, and in ſhort, all Saxony was in the hands of his enemies.

If we conſider the ſtate of this monarch's affairs at this period, we ſhall not wonder much at all Europe's giving him over as loſt beyond recovery. An army of 80,000 ruſſians was encamped in his electorate, all Saxony was in the hands of the auſtrians, part of Sileſia was likewiſe in their poſſeſſion; and general Laudon, whom Daun had left in that province with a ſtrong corps, threatened the remainder of it; in fine, marſhal Daun, at the head of a ſuperior army was ready to maintain affairs in their then ſtate, that he might be ready in the ſpring to overwhelm the king at once.

His pruſſian majeſty paſſed the Elbe, the 25th at Coſwig, between Wittenberg and Deſſaw, and having joined the corps of prince Eugene of Wurtemberg, and general Hulſen, he found himſelf at the head of 80,000 men. Marſhal Daun having joined general Laſcy, alſo croſſed the Elbe at Torgau, and advanced to Eulenburg, probably with a deſign to join the army of the empire, which had taken poſt under Leipſick; but he returning to his old camp at Torgau, the pruſſian army marched to Eulenburg, and general Hulſen driving the army of the empire from before Leipſick, took poſſeſſion of that city, and leaving a garriſon in it, rejoined the grand army. His majeſty now determined, if poſſible, to force

marſhal

marshal Daun to a battle, for he found that nothing but a victory could retrieve the sinking state of his affairs.

To execute this resolution, he marched towards the austrian army, the 2d of november; his scheme was to make two different attacks on it, so that either his right or left must take the enemy in rear, and close them in. Accordingly his majesty, the next day, with 70 battalions and 50 squadrons of his left wing took one road, and general Ziethen, with 30 battalions and 50 squadrons of the right, marched by another. Marshal Daun, being apprised of the approach of the prussians, by the skirmishing of his advanced parties, formed a front to oppose the king, who began the attack at two in the afternoon: he was received with a brisk fire of 200 pieces of cannon, but was repulsed the first time, after a very smart fire of artillery and small arms, the prussian grenadiers suffering much from the austrian carabineers. His prussian majesty made a second vigorous attack, but his infantry was again repulsed, and forced to give way. The king then ordered two regiments of horse to advance, who threw several austrian regiments into disorder, taking prisoners three others. Upon this attack marshal Daun advanced between sixty and eighty battalions towards Torgau, placing his left at Zinne, and his right at the Elbe. The prince of Holstein went to meet them, with the prussian cavalry, and at first made them give way; but at the second attack, he was himself forced to retire a little. Nevertheless, he returned a third time to the charge; and the third line of the prussian infantry attacked the austrian foot, in the vineyards of Supritz, whilst general Ziethen, with their right wing made his attack in their rear. These three attacks being executed at the same time, succeeded; the whole austrian army was thrown into great disorder, which was encreased by marshal Daun's being wounded in the thigh.

The battle ended about a quarter before ten at night, when victory declared for the king of Prussia. The night being uncommonly dark, his majesty had it not in his power to pursue his enemy; so they employed the rest of the night in crossing the Elbe with all speed, on three bridges of boats, which they threw over it at Torgau. Next morning at day break the prussian army entered that town, and seized 20 boats belonging to their bridges.

In this desperate battle, which was one of the bloodiest that had happened since the beginning of the war; the conquerors, by their own account lost 1500 men made prisoners, among whom were two generals, 2500 killed, 4900 wounded. The austrians, according to the same account, lost four generals, 200 officers, and 7000 men; 29 colours, one standard, and 40 pieces of cannon were also taken; but the number of their killed and wounded was never published by the prussians. The Vienna account of this battle, makes their loss 10,000 men killed, wounded and missing; and computes the king of Prussia's in the whole at 20,000 men. But both these calculations were probably false. If they owned their loss to amount to 10,000 men, it is more than probable, it was nearer 20,000, especially if they lost 7000 prisoners. Considering the situation of the armies, and the duration of the engagement, nothing can be more improbable than the conquerors losing double the number of the vanquished. I believe it will not be thought extravagant to calculate the loss of the prussians at 10,000 men, and that of the austrians at 20,000.

I cannot help observing here, how impolitic it was in marshal Daun, to chuse a camp where he might be forced to an action, unless the court of Vienna (which is most likely) gave him positive orders to engage: had he continued on the defensive, the king of Prussia, considering how surrounded he was with
enemies

enemies in his very dominions, muſt have loſt many men in the remainder of the campaign, and have opened the enſuing one under the greateſt diſadvantages. The ruſſians would probably have taken their winter quarters in Brandenburg. And if the allies had began the campaign with vigor, it would have been a miracle, had the king eſcaped ruin. Indeed the ruſſians played a very wavering game by retiring in ſo critical a time. It looked as if the court of Peterſburg had determined not intirely to demoliſh the king.

The conſequences of this great victory ſoon appeared. Marſhal Daun ſurrendered the command of the auſtrian army, as ſoon as he was wounded, to general Buccow, whoſe arm being ſhot off in a few minutes, it devolved on general ODonnel. The new commander retreated with great expedition towards Dreſden, and having provided for the ſafety of that city, took poſſeſſion of the ſtrong camp at Plauen. All Saxony, except a ſmall tract about Dreſden and the auſtrian camp, fell once more into the hands of his pruſſian majeſty, who advanced with his army to Freyberg. It was too late in the ſeaſon, his troops had been too much fatigued, and Dreſden too ſtrong, for him to attempt making himſelf maſter of it. But he detached 10,000 men, under general Forcade, through Thuringia, to aſſiſt duke Ferdinand in his operations againſt the french; but the roads proved ſo extremely bad, that this party was obliged to halt by the way. He alſo ſent another ſtrong detachment againſt the ruſſians, who thereupon retired into Poland, and he had the ſatisfaction to ſee his dominions freed from that terrible enemy for the remainder of the campaign. Another party of his troops took up their winter quarters in Mecklenburg.

Saxony and Brandenburg were not the only provinces that were cleared of his enemies, by the glorious victory of Torgau. Marſhal Daun had left
general

general Laudohn, with a strong corps in Silesia, who making a feint, as if he intended to besiege Schweselnitz, turned suddenly off, and laid siege to Coid- The prussian general Goltz, who commanded against him, was unable to raise the siege; but the battle of Torgau operated even at that distance. General Laudohn was no sooner informed of it, (and having made an unsuccesful attack) than he raised the siege, and retired into the county of Glatz.

In this great and glorious manner did that magnanimous monarch extricate himself from those formidable and impending dangers, that so lately had surrounded him. All his dominions except those that had been in the hands of his enemies from the very beginning of the war, were now entirely cleared. Much the greatest part of Saxony and Lusatia, as well as Mecklenburg and swedish Pomerania were in his possession; in these he had it in his power to raise large contributions and recruits for his army; so that his situation at the close of the campaign, was much more advantageous, than it was at the end of the last. During the year 1759, he sustained four capital defeats, and the most fatal of them, the surrender at Maxen, concluded the campaign; whereas in this of 1760, he gained two great and signal victories, and the campaign was finished in the most glorious manner. Indeed it was opened unfortunately by Fouquet's defeat, but the king and prince Henry, by their admirable movements prevented the austrians from receiving any great advantage from their victory. One cannot reflect on the seeming desperate face which this monarch's affairs wore during the greatest part of the campaign, and not be lost in amazement, when we consider the abilities that extricated him from all those perplexing difficulties.

In the mean time, in England the attention of all ranks of people was taken up with the very considerable

derable preparations that had been carrying on at Portsmouth, four months succeſſively; a large ſquadron of men of war, with tranſports ſufficient to carry 10,000 men were collected at Spithead. Troops, both horſe and foot marched from all parts of England to Portſmouth. Mortars, cannon, bombs, ammunition, and a multitude of all ſorts of warlike implements both for the field or a ſiege, were tranſported thither. The greatneſs of theſe preparations alarmed the french, who expected another viſit on ſome part of their coaſt, they prepared at all their ports to receive the enemy. About the middle of november, the troops, to the amount of about 8000 men, embarked, general Kingſley was appointed to command in chief by land, and commodore Keppel by ſea. The fleet lay wind bound at Spithead ſome days, and before they could ſail, the commanders received counter orders, directing the troops to be diſembarked, as the expedition was laid aſide 'till the ſpring. The nation in general was greatly ſurpriſed at theſe ſudden orders; nor could any indifferent perſon pretend to mention the deſtination of the armament. Numberleſs conjectures were formed; but many circumſtances conſidered, I think there is great reaſon to ſuppoſe that this expedition was deſigned to co-operate with that of the hereditary prince of Brunſwick, when he laid ſiege to Weſel. 'Tis probable the fleet were to land troops on the beach of Blankenburg, on the coaſt of the auſtrian Netherlands, from which place they might have marched to the Maeſe, to join the hereditary prince, and have enabled him to proſecute the war in thoſe parts with the greater vigor. There are more reaſons than one that favour this opinion; but particularly the ſmall number of troops employed, which was too inconſiderable to make an attempt on the coaſt of France, and by a detachment of the guards being embarked, and the lateneſs of the ſeaſon, it was plain their deſtination

stination was in Europe. But when it was found that the hereditary prince was prevented from executing his expedition, it might possibly be thought better to lay aside the naval armament till the spring, and then to send it against Martinico.

I come now to mention an event, which filled the nation with grief. His most sacred majesty George II. died on the 25th of October, at his palace at Kensington, in a very sudden manner; his death being occasioned by the bursting of the right ventricle of his heart. He finished a long and happy reign, in the midst of a period which abounded with great events. It is needless to say, that he was a good, a brave, a just, and a virtuous king; his many amiable qualities adorned the throne on which he sat so long, and which he left at a time so glorious for himself and his subjects. These particulars are too deeply imprinted on the hearts of a grateful people to require an eulogy. He departed this life in the 77th year of his age, and the 34th of his reign. He was succeeded in the imperial crown of these kingdoms by his grandson, George, prince of Wales, our present most gracious sovereign, who was immediately proclaimed with the usual ceremony, under the title of George III. All the lords and others of the late king's privy-council were sworn of his majesty's privy-council, who was pleased, on the first day of his accession, to make the following declaration to them.

"The loss that I and the nation have sustained by the death of the king, my grandfather, would have been severely felt at any time, but coming at so critical a juncture, and so unexpected, it is, by many circumstances, augmented; and the weight now falling upon me much encreased; I feel my own insufficiency to support it as I wish; but animated by the tenderest affection for this my native country, and

depending

depending on the advice, experience, and abilities of your lordships, and on the support and assistance of every honest man, I enter with chearfulness into this arduous situation, and shall make it the business of my life to promote, in every thing, the glory and happiness of these kingdoms, to preserve and strengthen both the constitution in church and state; and as I mount the throne in the midst of an expensive, but just and necessary war, I shall endeavour to prosecute it in the manner most likely to bring on an honourable and lasting peace, in concert with my allies."

This declaration was remarkably pleasing to all ranks of people; and the words, " This my native country," could not but be excessively grateful to british ears. His majesty began his reign in the most promising and popular manner. A proclamation was published for the encouragement of piety and virtue, and for preventing and punishing vice, immorality, and profaneness. His royal highness, the duke of York, and the earl of Bute, who was appointed groom of the stole to his majesty, were sworn into the privy-council the 27th; and, in a few weeks after, the earl of Huntingdon, who was made master of the horse, the honourable George Townshend, and the lord viscount Royston, were also made privy counsellors. Some other changes and promotions took place, but not of importance. On the 8th of november a proclamation was issued for proroguing the parliament to the 18th of that month, on which day his majesty went with the usual state, attended by the earls of Huntingdon and Bute, to the house of peers, and the commons being at the bar of that house, his majesty made a most gracious speech to them, in which, after mentioning the greatness of the loss the nation had lately sustained, he

proceeded

proceeded in these words, " Born and educated in this country, I glory in the name of Briton; and the peculiar happiness of my life will ever consist in promoting the welfare of a people, whose loyalty, and warm affection to me, I consider as the greatest and most permanent security of my throne." What words could be more pleasing to a british parliament than this declaration? The lords, in their address, have this paragraph.— " We are penetrated with the condescending and endearing manner, in which your majesty has expressed your satisfaction, in having received your birth and education amongst us. What a lustre does it cast on the name of Briton, when you, sir, are pleased to esteem it amongst your glories?" His majesty's whole speech was extremely affectionate and popular; and the address of the lords and commons as dutiful and loyal.

The period at which his majesty came to the throne was so extremely brilliant for Great Britain, that his accession promised a reign equally glorious to himself and advantageous to his subjects. He ascended the throne, at at a time, when his kingdoms were engaged in a truly national and fortunate war. He had the happiness to see faction banished from home, and his arms victorious abroad. That unparalleled unanimity which took place among all ranks of people, when the odious names of Whig and Tory were no more, but when every one was desirous to be distinguished by no other title but that of Briton; then it was, that our victorious arms carried terror and conquest to the furthest regions of the earth, and reduced France, our constant, and once formidable, enemy, to the low state in which we see her at present. It was reserved for his majesty to become the sovereign of these imperial realms, at a period, when they were dreaded and respected by all their neighbours; when british fleets sailed unresisted to the remoteſt regions; when her armies marched only to enjoy victory; and when a concatination of glorious events all tended to exalt her power, and extend her influence and dominion, and to raiſe her ſovereign to that pitch of proſperity, as juſtly formed him the greateſt monarch in the univerſe.

CHAP. XXIX.

Overtures for a peace prove abortive. Pondicherry taken. Surrender of the fort of Mahe on the coast of Malabar. Great defeat of the mogul's and french troops. Lord Rollo, and sir James Douglas, rear admiral, take the neutral island of St. Dominique, in America. Colonel Grant's great success in that country against the Cherokees.

THE last chapter closed with the military transactions of 1760; those of the succeeding year ought immediately to follow; yet, as some overtures for a peace took place this year, but proved abortive, it may be more convenient to give a short account of that matter here, rather than to interrupt the future course of our history with an account of it at different periods.

All Europe could not but be sensible, that at this time, France was in such an exhausted condition, as not to be able to continue the payment of the stipulated subsidies; nor punctually to fulfil the engagements she had entered into with her allies. This that power seemed as little desirous to conceal, as unable so to do; and accordingly was the first mover towards a peace. With France, the other parties in the war thought prudent to concur. Each of these powers prepared a declaration, which were all five signed on the 25th of march, 1761, at Paris; the last day of the same month, they were delivered at London, accompanied by a letter from the duke de Choiseul to mr. Pitt. As the conduct of the court of France, in this affair, had the appearance of candor and sincerity, there was no delay made on our part. For the eighth of april following, a counter letter and memorial were returned on the part of the court of Great Britain. The king of Prussia also made his declaration. Augsburg was chose as the most convenient city for all the parties to hold a congress. The english plenipotentiaries appointed for this purpose were, the lords Egremont and Stormont, and general Yorke; and the count de Choiseul, for France. But as this congress, to be held by the consent of the parties concerned in war on the continent, was only for the determination of that, and to restore a general peace to Germany, a distinct and separate negotiation was to be entered into between Great Britain and France, to examine and settle those matters in which they were mutually and particularly interested.

Accordingly mr. Stanley, on the part of Great Britain, and mr. Bussy, on that of France, set out for the two different courts, with plenipotentiary powers; they both arrived the latter end of may, the one at Marli, and the other at London. A negociation was accordingly entered on. The articles of the greatest consequence between the two powers, to be settled, were these three.

I. France strenuously insisted, that a recompence should be made to the french merchants, for those ships that had been taken from them by the english, previous to the declaration of war; but this was positively refused on our part.

II. England demanded, that Wesel and Guelders, and their dependant territories should be restored to the king of Prussia; but this was peremptorily refused on the part of France, as the former demand had been by our court.

III. Turned upon withdrawing all subsistence, as well in subsidies as in money, mutually, and bona fide, from their allies in Germany. This was a subject,

ject, however, not easily to be adjusted to the satisfaction of both parties.

The principal things to be settled by the other articles were these:

I. That all Canada should remain to England; according to its utmost boundaries, including the course of the Ohio.

II. That the nations hereafter to be considered as neutrals, between Canada, Carolina, and Louisiana, should be traced out by lines.

III. That the french should exercise the right of fishing, and dressing fish on the coast of Newfoundland, according to the 13th article of the treaty of Utrecht. And that the isles of St. Pierre and Michelon should be ceded to France; but without any fortification, or military establishment, for the said purposes.

IV. That the works added to the port of Dunkirk, since the beginning of the war, should be entirely demolished.

V. The neutral islands of Tobago, St. Lucia, Dominica, and St. Vincent, should be equally divided.

VI. That Senegal and Goree should be guarantied to Great Britain, as should the settlements of Anamaboo and Akra, on the coast of Africa, to France.

VII. That a treaty between the english and french East-India company should be immediately entered upon, concerning their mutual differences, to be settled and finished at the same time with that between the two nations.

VIII. That Great Britain should have Minorca restored, with all the artillery found in fort St. Philip at the time it surrendered.

IX. That Guadaloupe and Marigalante should be restored to France, in the same manner.

X. That the landgraviate of Hesse, county of Hanau, and town of Gottingen, should be evacuated, and restored to their respective sovereigns.

XI. That the french king should declare, he never had any intention of retaining Nieuport and Ostend after a general peace.

This separation of the disputes merely relative to England and France from those of the continent, and leaving the latter to be settled by the principal powers at war, in the congress of Augsburg and that without the interposition of the neutral powers, seemed to be such wise and prudent measures, as to have promised a successful conclusion. But the very contrary was the consequence. Nor is this so much to be wondered at, if we examine the matter a little closer. For as the concerns of France were, by this settlement, separated from the general cause, her own private interests became the more conspicuous; and she could not but be sensible how much they were likely to suffer in a treaty with a victorious power, such as England at this time was. And though France had been more successful on the continent, yet she could not promise herself such advantages from the settlement of affairs there, as might be sufficient to indemnify her for the concessions England might require her to make, particularly in America, where the principal matters in dispute between the two powers subsisted. This reduced her to think of some other resource. This was only to be found in Spain, and accordingly the interests of that power were artfully introduced. Thus in the fifth article of the french memorial, of july 15, 1761, are these extraordinary words, " England shall enter into pos-
" session, as sovereign over the island of Tobago, in
" the same manner as France over that of St. Lucia,
" saving, at all times, the right of a third person,
" with

" with whom the two crowns will explain themselves;
" if such a right exists."

I cannot help here remarking, that the politics of France, at this time, seemed likely to have been as fatal to England, as they have ever been, if not more so. For had a peace at this time taken place, France would have recovered 20,000 seamen, who might have been employed in a new war, under the pretence of being an ally to Spain, in favour of whom the above article appears to have been calculated, that the king of Spain might have a plausible pretence to quarrel with Great Britain. That this certainly was the intention of France, appears most convincingly from the private memorial of the same date; in which a negociation with Spain was formally introduced, and the following demands made.

I. The restitution of some captures made upon the Spanish flag.
II. The privilege of fishing on the banks of Newfoundland.
III. The demolition of the english settlements in the bay of Honduras.

" M. Bussy represented to mr. Pitt, that it would be very dangerous to determine the fate of the neutral islands without attending to the claims of Spain, with which his catholic majesty had recently acquainted the court of Versailles, but which might easily be relinquished, if the other three articles were adjusted to the satisfaction of that monarch. This blending of the concerns of Spain with the separate treaty between Great Britain and France, was very surprising at that time to the court of London. But it soon after appeared, that the kings and France and Spain had, even then, been negociating a family compact, in full contradiction to the spirit of the treaty of Utrecht, and in express violation of the rights of commerce
which

which Great Britain ought to enjoy. This extraordinary compact was signed at Versailles, on the 15th of august, and ratified on the 8th of september, twelve days before mr. Stanley broke off the negotiation with the duke de Choiseul. By this compact, a perpetual league, offensive and defensive, was established by these two powers, against all the world. It is sufficiently evident from the whole tenor of this compact, that any treaty between Great Britain and France, made at that juncture, must have been delusive, if not momentary; unless the dignity and interests of the former had been tamely sacrificed to the demands of Spain."

Whilst this ineffectual negotiation was carrying on between England and France, both parties continued the war rather with greater vigour; in hopes that, during its progress, some advantage would arise, that might be productive of a good peace; this seems to have been the view on each side. On the part of France, the duke of Brunswick was to prosecute the operations he had begun, in the winter, with the utmost vigour; whilst England prepared for a sea-expedition, seemingly of great importance, against the coasts of France.

Our first success, this year, was in the East-Indies, against Pondicherry, the only place of importance, at that time, remaining to the french in India; and the capital of their settlements on the coast of Coromandel. The town of Pondicherry, beautifully built, and strongly fortified, is four leagues in circuit. It is forty miles from Madrass, situated on the coast of Malabar. The first thing attempted, previous to the reduction of Pondicherry, was that of the fortresses adjacent to the town; and this was effected, and the inland country brought perfectly to our interests, by the total expulsion of the French. As when this enterprize was first undertaken (in 1760) the periodical rains were daily expected, a regular siege was

judged

judged impracticable. The town itself was also strongly fortified, defended by a good garrison, commanded by general Lally, an able and resolute officer, and one whose pride and obstinacy they did not doubt would prompt him to maintain the place to the utmost extremity; as indeed he did. A blockade was therefore determined on. Colonel Eyre Coote commenced it by land, with the forces under his command, as did admiral Stevens with his fleet at sea. This was continued with the best dispositions, and the most extraordinary patience, on both sides, for seven months. In this time the garrison and inhabitants suffered greatly by famine. They had devoured every animal from an elephant to a mouse. Camels, dogs and cats, had been for some time their common food. Sixteen roupies, that is, so many half-crowns, had been paid for the flesh of a dog; even rats sold for thirteen pence a-piece. Before they surrendered, they boiled and ate their leathern jars, called Dame Joan's, used for keeping oil and butter.

On the 9th of november, colonel Coote ordered a ricochet, for four pieces of cannon, to be erected to the northward, at about 1400 yards from the town, more with a design to harrass the enemy, than for any damage it could do to the works at so great a distance. On the 10th, the land-stores were begun to be landed, and every thing prepared for a vigorous siege. As the rains were over by the 26th, in order to increase the distress of the enemy, and fatigue the garrison, some batteries were erected on different quarters of the town, and so placed, that the shot might enfilade, that is, scour the works of the enemy, and our men and guns not be exposed to any certain fire from the enemy. These, when ready, were all opened together at midnight, and continued firing till day-light. The next day the enemy kept a warm fire on our batteries, but without doing much damage to them. Some time after, another battery was

begun

begun for ten guns and three mortars, to the northward, at about 450 yards distance from the town, against the north-west counter-guard and curtain. Matters were thus situated at the end of the year 1760.

On the first of january, a violent storm of wind and rain coming on about eight in the morning, which lasted till between three and four the next morning, rear-admiral Stevens found it necessary, for the safety of his ships, to cut their cables, and put to sea, where he parted company with the other ships of the squadron, and on the fourth returning into Pondicherry road, found that the ship, duke Acquitain, had foundered, as also the Sunderland, and most of the crew perished. The ships, Newcastle and Queenborough, with the Protector fireship, were drove ashore, and lost, but the crews saved, and most of the stores and provision. Several ships besides suffered in the storm, but were soon refitted. During this period, the admiral intercepted the following letter from general Lally to mr. Raymond, french resident at Pullicat, dated at Pondicherry, january 20, 1761.

" Mr. Raymond,
" The english squadron is no more, sir. Out of
" the twelve ships they had in our road, seven are
" lost, crews and all; the four others dismasted,
" and it appears there is no more than one frigate
" that hath escaped; therefore don't lose an instant
" to send us chelingoes upon chelingoes, loaded with
" rice. The Dutch have nothing to fear now;
" besides, according to the rights of nations, they
" are only to send us no provisions *themselves*, and
" we are no more blocked up by sea.
" The saving of Pondicherry hath been in your
" power once already. If you miss the present opportunity,
" it will be entirely your fault. Don't
" forget also some small chelingoes. Offer great
" rewards

" rewards. I expect 17000 Morattoes within three
" or four days. In short, risque all, force all, and
" send us some rice, should it be but half a garse at
" a time.
"(Signed)   LALLY."

The admiral, being possessed of this letter, immediately dispatched circular letters to the dutch and danish settlements, to acquaint them, that, notwithstanding the representations of general Lally, he had eleven ships of the line, and two frigates, under his command, in condition for service, holding the blockade of Pondicherry. And as that place was closely invested and shut up by land and sea; and as in that case, it was contrary to the law of nations, for any neutral power to give them any succour, or relief, he had determined to seize any vessel, or boat, that should attempt to throw any provisions into that place.

To return to the operations by land; some of the batteries having suffered by the storm, colonel Coote ordered them to be repaired, and put every thing in the best order the then situation of affairs would admit, and in a few days the blockade of Pondicherry, both by sea and land, was as complete as ever. Thus things went successfully on, till the 15th of january, 1762, when the town surrendered at discretion to colonel Coote. The next day, at eight o'clock in the morning, the grenadiers of Coote's regiment took possession of the Villenour-gate, and in the evening those of Draper's of the citadel. In this affair, happily, the sea and land commanders were perfectly united. An amazing quantity of artillery and ammunition was found in the fort and on the works; among which there were no less than 81 serviceable pieces of brass, and 436 of iron, ordnance. The sum total of the prisoners, including the king's troops, company's troops, and inhabitants, amounted to 2072.

At the time the town surrendered, the besieged had not more than one day's provision of any kind remaining.

By this glorious success, the power of the french, in India, became extinct, and the rich coast of Coromandel lay at our command. There was nothing now to obstruct our trading throughout the great peninsula of India, from the Ganges to the Indies, except the petty french settlement of Mahe, on the coast of Malabar. Nor were we much longer kept out of the possession of that. For, on the 10th of February following, M. Louet surrendered the fort of Mahe, to mr. Hodges, commander at Tellichery, and to mr. Munro, commander of the king's troops employed in that expedition.

It is observable, that on the very same day that Pondicherry surrendered, our forces also proved victorious over a numerous army of the Mogul's, supported by some french troops. To understand this affair, we must look back to the year 1757, when, after admiral Watson had taken Chandenagore, mr. Law, nephew to the Mississippi Law, put himself at the head of a few french fugitives, whom he at last increased to two hundred. With these he got into the heart of the country, and from time to time united with some or other of the princes of the country, as best suited his interest. He supported the credit of his little army by a series of success. The following incident, proved for a time, very lucky to him. The Morattoes, having made an irruption, deposed the great mogul; upon his death, which soon after followed, Sha Zadda, one of his sons, endeavoured to ascend the throne of his father. As in that extensive disunited empire there are many provinces, some declared for the young prince, whilst others opposed him. He had indeed no inconsiderable army of loyal subjects, but sensible of their deficiency in military skill, and apprehensive of the superiority

of

of his opponents in number, he thought, if he could gain the assistance of some Europeans, that their knowledge in the art of war might render him superior to his enemies. Mr. Law embraced this opportunity, joined him, and they together reduced several considerable provinces. Mr. Law, now, in his turn, thought of making him conducive to his interests. He insinuated to the young prince, that the reduction of the rich and flourishing country of Bengal, would most certainly secure to him the throne he sought. Sha Zadda was easily induced to listen to a man who had rendered him some real services. He accordingly entered the kingdom of Bengal, with 80,000 indians, and the french, under mr. Law, who were still but two hundred. It might perhaps have been better for the new mogul, had there been no french with him; for this was enough to determine the english in favour of the Nabob of Bengal. An army was immediately assembled, commanded by major John Carnac, consisting of about 500 english soldiers, 2500 seapoys, and 20,000 blacks; not much more than half the number that they were to oppose. The two armies came to an engagement near Patna, on the 15th of january, 1761; the young Mogul's army was entirely defeated, himself and mr. Law, and most of the french, taken prisoners.

In America, a successful attempt was made upon one of the neutral islands, called Dominica, or Dominique, but which the french had fortified and settled. This island was extremely convenient to the french, as it is well wooded and watered, and affords coffee, cocoa, and cotton. As the land is very high, if it was properly cultivated, it would certainly produce very good sugar-cane.

On the fourth of june, 1761, lord Rollo sailed with the troops under his command, from Guadaloupe, with the Dublin, Balliqueux, Sutherland and Montague, all ships of the line, and some frigates, for
the

the island of Dominica, under the command of sir James Douglas, and about noon, on the sixth, arrived within a league of Rosseau; when a summons was sent to the inhabitants. Soon after, two of the principal of them came off in a boat, who seemed not unwilling to resign the possession of the island: but in the afternoon, the inhabitants seemed to be disposed to stand upon their defence; being probably spirited up by the governor, monsieur Longprie. Upon this, the admiral ordered the ships to anchor as close as possible; and the necessary dispositions were accordingly made for landing the troops, which was effected about five in the evening, under cover of the shipping; and notwithstanding the enemy had four intrenchments upon the face of a steep hill, with two nine pounders on the upper one, there was not one single cannon, or musquet, discharged, till the enemy began to fire, just before the troops landed. The troops formed quickly on the beach, and while part soon after possessed the town, the corps of grenadiers, commanded by colonel Melvill, seized a flank-battery, and part of an adjoining intrenchment, which had been abandoned. The enemy annoyed our troops with some popping musketry from behind the trees and bushes, and fired from time to time from their battery overlooking their entrenchments, the town and shore. It was now pretty late, and the troops likely to be extremely harrassed during the night, and to suffer great loss, and probable that the enemy might be greatly reinforced before morning, having an excessive strong country in their favour, with four intrenchments behind and above each other, which might enable them to make a great defence. These circumstances considered, determined lord Rollo to order an attack immediately to be made by the grenadiers, supported by the battalion troops. This was done with so much order, rapidity and resolution, that the enemy, with very little loss, were driven successively

cessively in great confusion, from all their intrench‑ment-batteries, and from the head quarter above it, where colonel Melvill immediately took post with the grenadiers. M. de Longprie, the french commandant, their second officer, M. de la Couche, and some others, were taken prisoners; there was also a quantity of powder taken. As the place was carried by assault, lord Rollo only granted the inhabitants a protection till his majesty's pleasure could be further known.

Lieutenant-colonel Grant, of the 40th regiment of foot, on the 7th of june, 1761, marched from fort prince George, with near 2600 men, and in the course of the month, penetrated into the country of the Cherokees, and destroyed all their towns, eleven on the Etchoey * branch of the Tenassee, four on the Stickoe branch, called the back-settlements; fifteen in all; besides these, many little villages and scattered houses were burnt; upwards of 1400 acres of corn, beans and pease, were also destroyed, and near 5000 Cherokees, including men, women and children, were driven to the woods and mountains to starve; their only subsistence for some time past having been horse-flesh. The colonel's loss on this expedition, amounted to one subaltern, one serjeant, and nine private men killed; four subalterns, one drummer, and forty-seven private men wounded. In consequence of this defeat, the Cherokees gave up, at a small expence, one of the finest countries in the world; and at the latter end of the year, december 10, the nine principal headmen of the Cherokee nation arrived in Charlestown, and in a few days afterwards, the treaty between that nation and the province of South-Carolina, was finally ratified, in all its forms, by the lieutenant-governor, and those nine Indians, respectively.

* Etchoey had been destroyed the year before.

CHAP.

CHAP. XXX.

A noble exploit of general Luckner. General Mansberg obliged to quit Duderstadt to the French; who are afterwards expelled by general Luckner. Success of a French detachment from Gottingen. The french surprize Stadbergur, and other successful actions. The allied army marches to attack the french posts; enter Hesse and Thuringia; make an unsuccessful attack on Fritzlar. Fritzlar taken. The marquis of Granby takes Guderberg. Further success of the allies. Siege of Cassel. General Sporken's success. The progress of the allies at a stop; they retreat. The french make an unsuccessful attack upon Bremen. Situation of the two armies. An unsuccessful enterprize of prince Ferdinand. Brave action of the marquis of Granby. Another motion of the allies. Skirmishes. The French again in motion; take Warburg, Dringleburg and Paderborn. Situation of the allied army; attacked by marshal Broglio. The french defeated in the battle of Kirch-Denckern. Skirmishes. The allies surprise Dorsten; but soon after recovered by prince Soubise. The french seize on Embden; raise contributions at Osnabrug. Scharsfels surrendered to the french. Meppen and Wolfenbuttel capitulate. The siege of Brunswick raised, and Wolfenbuttel abandoned by the French.

WITH respect to the military transactions on the continent of Europe, I shall first take notice of those of the allied army.

On the 23d of december, 1760, general Luckner, who was posted at Heilgenstadt, with a body of between

between 3 and 4000 men, was attacked by count Broglio, at the head of 10,000 french. General Luckner, as the town was invested on all sides, had no other method of retreat, but by the road that leads to Witzenhausen, where, having gained an advantageous eminence, he cannonaded the french with such success, that he secured his retreat to Scharffenstein, without the loss of a single man or horse killed or wounded. But an officer, and 30 militia-men, who were left in the town, were taken prisoners. The french are supposed to have lost on this occasion about 300 men. General Luckner was detached the next day, the 24th, to Heilengenstadt, and finding the french had quitted it, retook possession of it.

On the second of January, 1761, count Broglio, with a large body of troops, and assisted likewise in his operations by lieutenant-general M. de Stainville, attacked the town of Duderstadt. General Mansberg was posted there, but found it necessary to quit the town, which the enemy entered. General Mansberg took possession of the heights of Herbishagen, where he maintained himself till the arrival of the generals Kilmansegge and Luckner, to his succour; who the the next day attacked the french in Duderstadt, drove them from thence, and pursued them as far as Witzenhausen. The loss of the french, in this action, was, according to their own accounts, 600 men; 200 of them were made prisoners; among whom were three complete companies of french grenadiers. The loss of the allies, about 190 men.

On the eigth of January, a detachment of 150 men, and two companies of grenadiers, under the command of the viscount de Belsunce, marched out of Gottingen, attacked a post of the allies near Gibelhausen, and made about 100 men prisoners; among whom were four officers. And, on the 27th of the same month, the french, under M. de St. Victor,

Victor, furprifed the poft of Stadbergen. Major Delaune, who commanded the garrifon, compofed of part of Lane's battalion, was killed in his chamber. On the 26th of march, the chevalier de Origny made a battalion of the britannic legion prifoners, at Wolfshagen, where he took one piece of cannon, and a magazine. The fame day the french royal legion made 300 prifoners at Alsfelt, who had been left there for their recovery. A battalion of Hanoverians, that blocked up the caftle of Arolfen, was, for the moft part, taken or deftroyed. The next day colonel Colignon abandoned Nordheim to the garrifon at Gottingen, and in his retreat loft 220 men, with two pieces of cannon.

The fituation of the french, at the beginning of the campaign this year, was extremely advantageous for them; and confequently very bad for the allied army. The former enjoyed the entire poffeffion of the territory of Heffe; they had alfo added to the ftrength of feveral places in it, by fome new works, and had amaffed very great magazines in fuch parts as were moft convenient for them. They had, on their left, driven the allies from the Rhine, whofe quarters they ftreightened, and prevented all efforts on that fide, by the great number of troops that they kept there. Gottingen, on their right, was alfo in their poffeffion, in which they had taken care to have a very ftrong garrifon. Thus were the allies alfo fhut up in this quarter; and his majefty's German territories entirely expofed to the defigns of the enemy.

The greater thefe difficulties were with refpect to the allies, the more neceffary it was to attempt a removal of them; prince Ferdinand, therefore, determined to march and attack the french pofts. But this feemed to be a very hazardous attempt; for, befides the advantages of the enemy, already mentioned, they were mafters of all the proper communications

munications neceſſary for their ſubſiſtence, with ſtrong places in their rear, and in both their flanks. But prince Ferdinand being determined to act with vigour, ſettled the places of rendezvous, one on the Dymel, another on the Rhine, and a third in Sauerland. He himſelf, the ſame day, february 9th, went to Gieſmar, where lieutenant-general Gilſac had marched, with the corps, according to his orders. The next day the troops halted, and the diſpoſitions for the march of the whole were communicated to the generals. On the 11th, the army marched off in four columns; his ſerene highneſs led the center; it penetrated directly into Heſſe, and marching by Zierenberg, and Durenberg, made its way towards Caſſel. Though the right and left of the army were each at a conſiderable diſtance from this body, yet they were ſo diſpoſed, as fully to co-operate in the general plan of this very extenſive operation. The hereditary prince, who commanded on the right, marched by Stadbergen, for Mengeringhauſen; and, leaving the country of Heſſe to the eaſtward, as the alarm was to be as ſudden, and as widely diffuſed as poſſible, he puſhed forward with the utmoſt expedition into the heart of the french quarters. At a greater diſtance to the left, general Sporken, with his corps, penetrated into Thuringia, by Daderſtadt, and Heiligenſtadt. This movement was deſigned to break the communication of the french with the army of the empire, to procure a communication with the Pruſſians, and to cut off all intercourſe between the enemy's grand army and their garriſon at Gottingen. The french, by this ſudden, extenſive, and vigorous attack, were thrown into the utmoſt conſternation, and fled on every ſide.

The vanguards, or piquets, of the four columns, being rejoined and augmented with ſome cavalry, the brave marquis of Granby was appointed to command that corps, and fixed it at Ehlen, from whence he ſent detachments to the cascade, and to Weissenstein. The hereditary prince cantoned his corps about Zuschen. Receiving advice that the garrison of Fritzlar was not prepared for an attack, he went thither with a few battalions, in hopes of being able to carry that place at once. He attacked it with great spirit; but the enemy defended it resolutely, taking all the advantages their situation afforded them. And now the prince found that he had been misinformed; he therefore thought it advisable to desist from the attempt, and to wait for the arrival of some cannon to reduce it. The army cantoned on the 13th, in the neighbourhood of Niedenstein. The marquis of Granby led his corps to Kirchberg and Metze. Lieutenant-general Gilsac remained in his former position. The hereditary prince cantoned his troops about Hademar, not far from Fritzlar. Lieutenant-general Breidenbach took possession of a magazine of 40,000 rations at Rosenthal, and advanced towards Marpurg. He made an attempt upon that town; but, as the enemy were upon their guard, did not succeed; and the general himself was killed in the attack. General Okeim succeeded to his command. However these two severe checks at the beginning of their enterprize, did not intimidate them; they were only the more cautious, and more expeditious.

The army halted on the 14th; when the hereditary prince detached major general Zastrow to Feltzberg, and ordered the cavalry to pass the Eder. Cannon and mortar being now brought before Fritzlar, and some bombs thrown into the town, colonel de Narbonne offered to capitulate, if the most honourable terms were allowed him. He was answered, that, in consideration of his brave defence, such should be granted him; but the garrison should not serve during the present campain; and that the battalions of Waldeck and Wildungen should be included in the capitulation. But the commandant refusing

refusing to submit to this condition, a brisk cannonade was begun again, and continued for half an hour, after which, the terms were accepted, and the place surrendered; but the commandant having declared he had no command over the two garrisons abovementioned, that demand was dropped. A magazine was found at Fritzlar.

At this time, the allies had driven the french every where before them, for the space of about 40 miles, leaving Gottingen, Cassel, Waldeck, and some places of less note behind them; being persuaded, that when the main army was driven back, those garrisons would fall of course. With this view, the allies resumed their march, february the 17th, covering from their right to left a vast tract of country, of more than seventy miles in extent, and driving all before them; where-ever the allies approached, the enemy fled, setting fire to their magazines, and abandoning their provisions, insomuch that the allies found plenty for their subsistence in every town thorough which they had occasion to pass. At Melsungan, a post about fifteen miles from Cassel, prince Ferdinand found a considerable magazine of meal and forage.

At Over-Weimer, near Marbourg, the enemy made a shew of standing their ground; but M. d'Oheim, on the eighteenth, put himself in motion, and having defeated their advanced guard, M. de Mopeau, who commanded their main body, gave way, and the allies having halted a day or two, to refresh their troops, continued their pursuit. In the night between the 19th and 20th, M. Broglio abandoned Hirschfeldt, after setting fire to the grand magazine that had been established there for the assistance of the troops. This magazine, which had consisted of 80000 sacks of meal, 50000 sacks of oats, and a million of rations of hay, was most of it saved by the allies, who entered the town almost as soon as quitted by the french.

In the mean time, the marquis of Granby was succefsfully employed in reducing the caftles and fortreffes in the nighbourhood, particularly Guderfberg, in which was a garrifon of 200 men. Here he found fome provifions and forage.

The allied army refolutely advanced, and the french continually retired; abandoning poft after poft, and fell back almoft to the Mayne. In their retreat, they fet fire to their own magazines; but the allies purfued them with fo much rapidity, that they faved five capital ftores; one of which contained no lefs than 8000 facks of meal, 50000 facks of oats, and a million of rations of hay; a very fmall part of which had been deftroyed. This proved a very great help to the allied army in its progrefs; but Caffel ftill remained to be reduced. In this town the french had a garrifon of feventeen battalions, befides fome other corps, commanded by count Broglio; the enemy not only confided in thefe, but alfo in the feverity of the feafon. The fiege of this place was of too much importance to be delayed; as foon therefore as marfhal Broglio had been driven out of Heffe, and had retreated towards Frankfort, prince Ferdinand made a ftop. As Marpurg and Zeigenhayn ftill held out, the prince ordered them to be blockaded. He then formed that part of his army which was with him into a chain of cantonments. His front was towards the enemy, ftretching from the river Lahn, to the river Ohm, and from the latter to the Fulda. By this means, he was enabled, not only to watch the motions of marfhal Broglio's army, but alfo to cover the fiege of Caffel; and the two blockades of Marpurg and Ziegenhayn.

The trenches were opened before Caffel the firft of march, under the direction of the count of Lippé Schaumberg, a fovereign prince of the empire, and a very great engineer; from whofe fuccefsful management

nagement of the artillery at Thornhausen, much was now expected. On the seventh, the french made a sally, took possession of the trenches, carried off four mortars, nailed up one piece of cannon, and destroyed the works of the grand battery.

But at length the enemy was forced back into the town. They afterwards made two other unsuccessful sallies; suffering considerably in both. The garrison of Gottingen also made a motion, and attacked Duderstadt, where the allies had a post, forced it, and made the garrison prisoners. The garrison of Waldeck also made a succesful attack on a party of the allies that were patrolling in the neighbourhood of that city; for captain Willenius, who commanded the party, having the misfortune to be dangerously wounded in the first onset, the advantage was on the side of the enemy, who took thirty horses and two waggons belonging to the convoy.

Major-general Schluter, in order to straiten the fortress of Ziegenhayn, formed the design, on the third instant, of getting possession of the suburbs. Though he succeeded with very little loss, yet M. de Zuemantel, who commanded in the town, regardless of the houses, fired against them with great fury, and obliged the general to retire, with his troops, into his old quarters.

Whilst these matters were carrying on, M. Sporken, who commanded the detachment of the allied army to the left, advanced, with an intrepidity equal to the rest, on the side of Saxony. He was soon joined by a body of prussians, and the united army lost no time to clear the Werra and the Unstrut, of the bodies of french and saxons, which occupied the most important post upon these rivers. As the enemy was advantageously posted, and could be supported on one side by the garrison of Gottingen, and on the other, as they promised themselves, by the army of the empire, they maintained their ground, and a

sharp

sharp action soon ensued. The allies attacked a large body, february 14, advantageously posted, at Langensaltze, upon the Unstrut, with great success. The prussians took three whole battalions of saxons, and seven pieces of cannon. General Sporken took two battalions, and six pieces of cannon. The whole loss of the enemy was computed at 5000; but that of Sporken's at little more than one hundred.

The following days they continued pursuing the enemy, driving them everywhere before them, killing many, and making many prisoners. The army of the empire, which was in the neighbourhood of Gotha, when general Sporken attacked the enemy at Langensaltze, made a precipitate retreat; at Eysenach a very large magazine was found; general Luckner, on the 24th, took three hundred prisoners at Fulda, and the neighbouring villages, in most of which the enemy left their forage behind them. Sporken had divided his corps into two columns, one commanded by count Kielmansegge, and the other by lieutenant general Wagenheim; major Luckner commanded the advanced guard. Kilmansegge's corps pressed forward with such rapidity, that he soon came in sight of a body of troops, commanded by marshal Broglio in person; but being too weak, did not attack it. General Luckner had still made greater haste, possessed himself of Asschaffenbourg, and, on the next night, march the 7th, threw a bridge over the Mayne, at Selligenstadt. Hitherto almost every thing had succeeded, according to the wishes of the allies; but things now began to change.

At the same time that this division was pursuing the enemy to the left, the prince, and the marquis of Granby, were moving with greater caution in the center. The forts and castles that were not tenable, were deserted one after another. Marshal Broglio, with the main body, continued his march, with the

the utmost precepitation, till he arrived at Bergen, within a few miles of Franckfort. Here the marshal began to fortify himself, and here he made a stand till the reinforcements arrived from the Lower Rhine, to enable him to make head against the allies, and either to give them battle, or recover the ground he had lost.

On the 20th of march, the several divisions of the allied army joined. The main body had its position on the heights of Homberg; the head-quarters were at Schwansberg; the marquis of Granby at Kirchayn; general Hardenberg behind Redechen; and the hereditary prince formed the van, in the neighbourhood of Grunberg, almost in sight of the enemy. Marshal Broglio, at the same time, occupied the country along the Rhine, from Gladenbach to Allendorf.

The reinforcement that the marshal received from the Lower Rhine, consisted of 12,000 French troops. This at once put a stop to the career of the allies, and ennabled marshal Broglio, not only to make a stand, but to advance and drive, in his turn, his pursuers before him. Prince Fedinand had now three strong posts of the enemy in his rear, and their grand army perfectly united on his front; he was therefore obliged to call in Sporken's body. The prince contracted his operations, and caused a field of battle to be marked out, near Homberg, to which the troops were ordered to repair on the first notice. But the want of subsistence, in a place already exhausted both by friends and foes, would admit of no delay, and it became absolutely necessary either to march forwards to meet the enemy, or to fall back, and relinquish all the advantages which had been acquired, by a desperate, and ill-concerted, enterprize. A retreat was determined on; in which the hereditary prince, who covered the rear, was attacked by a superior number of the enemy, near the

village

village of Strongerode, in the neighbourhood of Grunberg, and the corps under his command broken and difperfed. The attack was made by the enemy's dragoons, the firft fhock of which broke the whole foot, confifting of nine regiments of hanoverians, heffians, and brunfwickers. The french in this action made 3000 prifoners, and poffeffed themfelves of feveral trophies of victory. However, few were killed or wounded on either fide. Prince Ferdinand himfelf owed his own efcape to the intrepid behaviour of two of his officers. The fieges of Caffel, Gottingen, and Zeigenhayn, that had been fuccefsfully begun, were now no longer fupportable. Town after town was relinquifhed, many were killed, many made prifoners, and not a few perifhed through want and fatigue.

In the city of Marbourg, when the allies quitted it, a pound of bread was not to be purchafed for 1000 ducats. In this difgraceful manner were the allies expelled Heffe, and forced to take refuge in Weftphalia, where the want of magazines, and the natural poverty of the country, would not permit the french to purfue them. Thus the two armies being feparated, both found it neceffary to go into winter quarters of cantonment, as well to refrefh the troops, as to procure fubfiftence. The places adjacent to the two armies, were filled with the fick and wounded; of whom many more died than recovered, for want of proper accommodations. Upwards of 2000 horfes died in the allied army in a fortnight; the enemy's army alfo fhared in the fame misfortune.

However, the french having loft fo many magazines, were unable, for a long time, to reap any advantage from their fucceffes in the preceding campaign, or from their late victory. The greateft part of the month of june elapfed, before they found themfelves in a condition to act.

In

In the mean time, however, a few skirmishes happened. Towards the latter end of april, a detachment of 3000 men, from the garrison of Gottingen, attacked a battalion of the british legion, in the village of Feldhaven, near Uslar, and made one hundred prisoners; but were afterwards dislodged from that post by the hanoverians. The first week in may, general Luckner, with an hundred hussars, came up with 300 horse of the garrison of Gottingen, entirely routed them, made one officer and thirty troopers prisoners, and took sixty horses. The same day, may the 5th, captain Brinsky attacked them on their return, with one hundred hussars, and fifty brunswick cavalry, drove them before him into Gottingen, and made three officers and fifty-three dragoons prisoners. The vicomte de Belsunce, their commander, narrowly escaped being taken in the pursuit. The village of Spielen, beyond the Fulda, was taken by captain Riedesel, with an hundred men of brunswick hussars, and the garrison, consisting of fifty men, were killed, or made prisoners. In this action the allies sustained very little loss. In the same month, one hundred horse of the allied army took, near Nordheim, a french lieutenant colonel, thirty-four dragoons, and forty horse; M. de Belsunce himself narrowly escaped being taken prisoner. In the middle of june, general Luckner took eighty-four oxen under the walls of Gottingen, forced the garrison back, killed and wounded an hundred men, and took prisoners fourteen private men, and one captain. The next day, M. Sheiter crossed the Rhine, with only thirty-six horse; and, in the space of ninety-three hours, set fire to the french magazines at Xanten, and other places, and plundered a great quantity of baggage. The magazines which he destroyed, amounted to 1,635,000 rations of hay and straw, near 6000 sacks, and several thousand rations, of oats.

About

About the same time, the french took 245 prisoners at Luhnen and Kamen, and two pieces of cannon.

But now some more considerable actions began to take place; as soon as the french had taken proper measures for their subsistence, the prince of Soubise caused his troops to pass the Rhine, and to advance on the side of Munster; not far from which city, the hereditary prince of Brunswick was posted to oppose him. Marshal Broglio assembled the forces under his command, at Cassel, and moved towards the Dymel, in order to effect a junction with the body under the prince of Soubise. General Sporken, who, was, with a strong detachment, advantageously posted on the Dymel, in front of the allied army, on the approach of marshal Broglio, quitted his situation, and attempted to retire; being inferior to the enemy in number. But the french were too quick for him, overtook, and attacked, his rear, june the 29th. The general was soon routed; the enemy made eight hundred prisoners, took nineteen pieces of cannon, four hundred horses, and above an hundred and seventy waggons. The french passed the Dymel the same day. Prince Ferdinand being discouraged by this misfortune, fell back to the Lippe; and thus gave the enemy an opportunity to possess themselves of Warburg, Dringleburg, and Paderborn.

About a fortnight after, a body of french troops, under the command of M. Chabot, intending to surprise M. de Luckner, near Samle, was attacked and defeated by that general; when 150 men were made prisoners, and 200 horses taken. The day after, captains Kampen and Engel, captain-lieutenant Sanders, and lieutenant Muller, with two hundred and twenty horse, in different detachments, burnt upwards of thirty carriages of bacon and provisions; destroyed, or gave away, a prodigious quantity of bread and meal, took seven hundred horses, ruined two thousand more, and, in their return to the allied army, made two hundred and fifty recovered men of the enemy's troops, prisoners.

Prince Ferdinand continued some time posted to the south of the Lippe, between Ham and Lipstad, that he might get between the prince of Soubise, and the Rhine, as marshal Broglio had, by occupying the places on the Dymel, got between him and Hanover. His view in this was, or at least seems to have been, that, in case the marshal made any attempt upon the electorate, he might fall upon the places the enemy occupied upon the Dymel, and so draw them back to their protection. At length, marshal Broglio, with a view to fall upon the allied army, made a junction with Soubise, at Soest, a place between Lipstadt and Ham. Prince Ferdinand, therefore, in order to strengthen his situation, established his left wing on the isthmus between the rivers of the Lippe and the Aest; the left extremity of this wing, under general Wutgenau, by which it was perfectly secured, as the right was supported by the village of Kirch-Denkern, situated immediately on the Aest. In this wing the marquis of Granby commanded, assisted by lieutenant-general Howard, and the prince of Anhalt, who were posted towards the village. Behind the little river was placed the center, on a considerable eminence, commanded by general Conway. On the same eminence, the right wing, under the hereditary prince, extended towards the village of Werle, well defended on the flank by rugged, bushy, and almost impracticable ground. The greatest part of the artillery was placed in the left wing, by the direction of the count of Lippe, as was also the strength and flower of the army, as being most exposed to the attack of the enemy; an event which prince Ferdinand wisely foresaw; and which happened as follows:

Marshal

"Marshal Broglio decamped on the 15th of July, at break of day, from Erwite, and attacked lord Granby's camp in the evening, with great briskness. His lordship sustained the efforts of the enemy with resolution and success, till the arrival of lieutenant-general Wurgenau, who had received orders to march to his support. The french being now taken in flank, they could no longer withstand the firmness of these generals, with whom prince Ferdinand was in person, but were driven back into the woods, after a fire of artillery and small arms, which lasted till late in the night. The action was renewed at three the next morning, and continued till nine. M. Wurtgenau's corps, against which the french made redoubled attacks, maintained its ground with intrepidity. At last M. Broglio appeared to have a design of planting some batteries upon an eminence opposite to lord Granby's camp, which was not enclosed within the lines. To prevent the bad consequence of such a design, prince Ferdinand ordered the nearest troops to advance upon the enemy, which they did with such courage, that the french soon gave way, and retreated precipitately, abandoning their dead and wounded. Maxwell's battalion of grenadiers took the regiment of Rouge, consisting of four battalions, prisoners, with their cannon and colours. Upon the news of this defeat on the right, the left of the french army, under the prince de Soubise, which was opposed to the hereditary prince, desisted from the attack. Two hundred men, commanded by major Limburg, defended the village of Scheidengen, on that side, against all the attacks of the enemy."

The loss of the french in killed, wounded, and prisoners, was computed at about five thousand men; five pieces of cannon, and six pair of colours were taken. The brigades of the king, Auvergne, Belfunce and Nassau, suffered the most. The duke of
Havre,

Havre, and his son-in-law, the marquis of Cirrac; the marquis of Rouge, lieutenant-general, and his son, the colonel, were killed. Their loss, in officers, was very considerable. The place of battle was the field of Kirch-Denckern, near Hiltrup, and at no great distance from Ham. The allies had three hundred and eleven men killed, one thousand and eleven wounded, one hundred and ninety-two made prisoners, and three pieces of cannon taken. The allies, after this battle, kept their ground for some time, whilst the French retreated, and both parties remained quiet for some time, except some skirmishes, which proved in favour of the allies.

A great convoy of provisions was destroyed by colonel Freytag, between Cassel and Warbourg. The Brunswick hussars ruined two french magazines upon the Werra, and major-general Luckner, in his retreat from Neuhaus near Paderborn, the day after the battle of Kirch-Denckern, had a smart engagement with the enemy, and made one hundred and fifty prisoners. Colonel Freytag, in a second expedition, july 19 to 20, destroyed a great quantity of ammunition and corn belonging to the French, on the Fulda and the Werra, without the loss of a man. And on the last day of july, but one, general Luckner attacked marshal Broglio's rear-guard, at Lipsprinck, and destroyed the corps of volontaires de Broglio. In one of these skirmishes, july 20th, young prince Henry of Brunswick was mortally wounded. In the beginning of august, prince Ferdinand attacked liutenant-general Stainville, who had between sixteen and eighteen battalions, and as many squadrons under his command, and obliged him, after a warm dispute of three or four hours, to abandon the post of Stadtbergen. The day after, a detachment of hunters belonging to colonel Freytag's corps, attacked, and took, a convoy of two

P p   hundred

hundred and fifty waggons, going towards the Weser.

About the middle of auguſt, general Luckner, having reached the heights near Daſſel, with his corps, ordered his own regiment towards the right wing of the french, and colonel Freytag, with all the light horſe, towards their left. The enemy, under the command of M. Belſunce, drew back their forces towards the foreſt of Solling, having firſt detached a large body of horſe and foot to the high road that leads to Eimbeck. Luckner's huſſars immediately attacked, and totally routed this body. General Luckner himſelf, in front, attacked the french, whilſt they were drawn up in order of battle; upon which they quickly retired, and advanced nearer to the foreſt of Solling. Colonel Freytag obliged their light horſe to diſperſe themſelves in the foreſt; whither they were preſently followed by general Luckner. In the Solling they met with a warm reception from lieutenant-colonel de Stockhauſen, who had previouſly poſted himſelf there, with his hunters, and who defeated them. In their retreat thither, they were ſucceſsfully harraſſed by the Brunſwick huſſars, who had purſued them. In theſe different attacks, the french loſt three pair of colours, had eight hundred of their horſes taken; beſides forty-four officers, and ſeven hundred and fifty-nine private men, taken priſoners by the allies.

However, all the advantage was not on the ſide of the allies; for on the 18th of auguſt, the caſtle of Waldeck ſurrendered to the french. And on the ſame day, the marquis de Conflans attacked the rear-guard of a detachment of the allied army, in its march from Munſter to the lower Embs, made ſome priſoners, took the tents belonging to Scheiter's cavalry, and thirty baggage-waggons.

Prince Soubiſe ſtill perſiſted in the deſign he had formed to beſiege Munſter, notwithſtanding the obſtacles

stacles he had met with. He therefore began to make the previous preparations at Dorsten. Upon this, the hereditary prince laid hold of the first opportunity to attack this place. This was accordingly done on the 30th of august, when the garrison, consisting of a battalion of french troops, and some piquets, commanded by M. Vierset, made a brave defence, but was forced to yield to the resolute attack of the allies, and surrender prisoners of war. The prince totally destroyed the ovens which were established there. By this means, the enemy were not only prevented from their design on Munster, but even to retire from the Lippe for a time. The day after, the french attacked the corps under the generals Luckner and Freytag, and colonel Stockhausen, and obliged them to abandon several posts in the defiles of the Hartz mountain.

The allies did not long retain their possessions of Dorsten, for, on the third of september, four days after they had taken it, the vanguard of the prince of Soubise retook that place, made one hundred and eighty of the allies prisoners, and took one piece of cannon. And on the 14th of the same month, a body of the french, consisting of eight, or nine, thousand, under the command of the marquis de Conflans, appeared unexpectedly before Embden, and, the burghers refusing to join in defending the place, the garrison, consisting of two hundred english, made an honourable capitulation for themselves, and embarked immediately for Bremen. The french, being now masters of the town, extorted contributions by every act of violence, insomuch that the country rose upon them, and drove them off; but in a few days they returned, and, with greater fury than ever, plundered the inhabitants of every thing they could carry off; and what they could not remove, they broke and destroyed: such are the miseries of war!

On the 24th of the same month, a body of french appeared suddenly before Wolfembottle, and having summoned the city, and received a refusal, began bombarding the place, which so terrified the inhabitants, that many of them retired to Zell. In a few days after, Brunswick was formally invested by a body of the enemy. Osnabrug being unable to satisfy their exorbitant demands, was given up to be pillaged. The next month, the strong castle of Scharsfels, in the Hartze mountains, surrendered, after a siege of eight days, to the french, who demolished its fortifications. Mippen capitulated to the prince of Conde, in which five hundred of the allies were made prisoners of war. Wolfenbuttel also surrendered to prince Xavier, of Saxony, after a siege of five days, who, after levying exorbitant coutributions, quitted it, and returned to Seesen.

The french having thrown up intrenchments at the pass of Oelpher, for covering the siege of Brunswick, prince Ferdinand, with all the expedition in his power, dispatched the hereditary prince to its relief. General Luckner, having joined this prince, by forced marches, arrived in time, and attacked the french in the intrenchment, october 13, and in the end obliged prince Xavier, not only to raise the siege of Brunswick, but also to abandon Wolfenbuttel. Many of the enemy were killed; and one major-general, several officers, upwards of two hundred private men, and one piece of cannon, were taken.

The allies were under no little concern for Bremen, as it had but a weak garrison, and was a place of great consequence to the enemy; for there was in it immense magazines, and it was advantageously situated on the Weser; so that if the french had got possession of this trading town, they would have had the command of the Weser, and have shut up the allies in a barren country, in the very center of Germany, deprived of every resource, and environed by
their

their enemies. The enemy, encouraged by the succefs they had met with at Embden, through the timidity of the inhabitants, made an attempt upon it, but met with a very different reception from what they had found at Embden; for the inhabitants, alarmed at the cruel behaviour of the french at the abovementioned place, timely joned the garrison, and the enemy were forced to make a hasty retreat. But to prevent a second attack, a strong reinforcement was immediately thrown into the place.

Prince Ferdinand, the beginning of november, still kept the same position, at Ohr, upon the left of the Weser, the same that he had taken possession of after the battle of Kirch-Denckern, which he prudently and resolutely kept, in spight of the motions and stratagems, and endeavours of the enemy, to force him to remove. His head quarters were at Buhne, and his army reached from thence towards Hammelen. By this situation, he kept possession of the course of the Weser, and thereby prevented the enemy from taking either Hammelen, or Minden.

M. Broglio's position upon the right of the Weser, was as follows; "The Hartz was occupied by two thousand men; lieutenant-general Stainville was encamped at Seesen, with sixteen battalions; prince Xavier at Ganderfheim, with nineteen battalions; M. Broglio with eight battalions, at Eimbeck, which made the center; and general Chabot, with fifteen battalions, at Escherfhausen. The rest of the infantry, with the cavalry, cantoned in the village behind the above camps. General Rochembeau was left at Caffel, with eight battalions, and the Irish brigade upon the Eder, in order to secure the communication with Hesse and Franconia.

As the french army was thus dispersed, prince Ferdinand formed a very judicous, but unsuccessful, plan, to prevent their collecting in a body; he, purposing to surprise the count Chabot and his fifteen bat-

battalions, ordered generral Luckner to march, so as to be opposite to M. Stainville's corps at Seesen, on the 5th of november, that he might intimidate him from marching, or, in case he did, pursue him. The hereditary prince's directions were to march on the 3d, in order to get possession of the heights of Eimbeck, by the 5th. The brave marquis of Granby, who had also a share in this expedition, was directed to force the post of Cappelnhagen, and get to Wickensen by the 5th, that he might block up the defile, which leads from Eschershausen to Eimbeck. The marquis bravely entered upon his appointment, and, after a smart engagement, forced the post the enemy held at Cappelnhagen, and arrived, even at the hour appointed, on the 5th, at Wickensen. These several bodies, had been, for some time, upon the right of the Weser; those upon the left crossed the river; prince Ferdinand, with the main body, passed it on the 4th; as did lieutenant general Conway, and general Scheele, on the same day. On the morning of the 5th they all joined at Halle. The method the prince proposed to carry his design into execution, was to cut off the body of troops, under the command of the count de Chabot, encamped at Eschershausen; with this view, he, on the 5th, continued his march. The count, apprehensive of the prince's design, quitted his camp, and moved towards Wickensen, that he might reach Eimbeck, and join marshal Broglio. But, as he was endeavouring to effect this junction, he met, to his surprise, the marquis of Granby, with his corps. He had now no other way to escape, but by turning to the right toward Stad-Odendorp; with this view he fell back upon the road to Escherhausen. However, had the whole plan of prince Ferdinand been happily executed, he would have been interrupted in his march, and must have been entirely routed; for lieutenant general Hardenberg was to have passed the

the Weser, on the 4th at night, at Bodenwerder, in order to have reached Amelunxborn in the morning of the 5th; but unhappily, as he was on the way to Eskerhausen, the pontoons, on which he was to have passed the river, overturned, and delayed him. In the interim, the count de Chabot escaped to Eimbeck, by the way of Daffel, and getting there at noon, took his post upon the Huve. By this accident, the hereditary prince was also disappointed in his design upon Eimbeck; for he arrived opposite the Huve at two o'clock; and, at four in the afternoon was joined by the marquis of Granby, and lieutenant general Conway; a brisk cannonading was begun, which continued till night. But as circumstances were now changed, and the french marshal had time to collect a great number of troops, the hereditary prince thought it was not adviseable to attempt the passage of the Huve.

The same day at night, prince Ferdinand encamped at Eskerhausen, where he was joined by general Hardenberg. The next day there happened some skirmishes on both sides, with different success. The next day, the 7th, prince Ferdinand ordered the marquis of Granby to march from Weutzen to Foorwohle, and the hereditary prince to Ammensen. Marshal Broglio, considering this as a retreat, pursued the hereditary prince; but without attempting to attack him. The marquis was likewise pursued by count Broglio, who attacked him, just as he was on the point of encamping, after a fatiguing march through snow and difficult roads, at Foorwohle, and drove in his out-posts. The noble marquis, not only made a brave resistance, but repulsed the enemy, and even drove them back to the Huve.

Prince Ferdinand judging it impracticable to attack the enemy in their present position, resolved to attempt getting round their left flank, that he might oblige them either to attack him, or abandon Eimback, beck, and the country about it. Having therefore reconnoitred on all sides, on the 7th, and 8th, he, at three in the morning of the 9th, marched to the heights between Mackensen and Lithorst. The hereditary prince marched to replace lord Granby at Foorwohle; and general Luckner to occupy the hereditary prince's camp at Ammensen. But in the morning, before he could march to follow the army, lord Grandby was again attacked upon his left; but received the enemy with so much spirit and conduct, that he again repulsed them, and made them retreat with a considerable loss. In this action, major Fraser greatly distinguished himself.

The french marshal finding, by his detachments, which were driven off the heights of Lithorst, that prince Ferdinand had gained his flank, and was partly in his rear, having it at his option either to risk an action, or retire, chose the latter. He accordingly quitted Eimbeck the 9th, in the night, and all the adjacent country. Before the marshal quitted these parts, he ordered the gates of Eimbeck, and the additional works to be blown up, by which general Werner was killed, and the marshal himself was very near being destroyed. Nothing further of any consequence happening between the two opposite armies for some time, the severity of the season, and other circumstances necessarily obliging both parties to remain inactive, naturally puts a period to this Chapter.

CHAP.

CHAP. XXXI.

Position of the king of Prussia, prince Henry, marshal Daun, and the russians. Tottleben takes Steten and Burwalde. A large body of imperialists defeated by prussians. Skirmishes. The Swedes in motion; take Demminn. Motions of the armies in Silesia. Breslau attacked. Laudohn marches towards the Lower Silesia. Colberg besieged. The russians take Coslin and Schweidnitz. Colberg taken. The several armies go into winter-quarters.

FROM the advantageous conclusion of the last campaign of the king of Prussia, as I related in the twenty-eigth chapter, after the great victory that his majesty obtained at Torgau, one might reasonably have expected a succession of important and interesting events; and cannot therefore but be surprised to see the campaign of 1761, move on so languid and heavy, that one would almost have thought that the cautious soul of marshal Daun had passed into that of his prussian majesty.

The king lay strongly intrenched in Upper Silesia, near Schweidnitz; the fortresses in the lower part of the country were well secured with garrisons. Prince Henry, who commanded in Saxony, was strongly entrenched under Leipsic. Marshal Daun was encamped near Dresden. The russian army was divided into two strong bodies; that led by count Tottleben marched towards Pomerania; Butterlin, who commanded the other, entered into the Upper Silesia, advancing towards Breslau. On the opposite part to them, baron Laudohn entered the same province. These armies intended to unite, either to attack the king, or to take Breslau, or Schweidnitz.

The whole country was overspread by the russians, who every-where raised heavy contributions; this was their position in the summer.

I shall now be a little more particular as to their movements, and go back to the beginning of the year. So early as january, count Tottleben entered Pomerania, with ten thousand russians, and made himself master of Stetin and Burwalde. On the second of march, the imperialists, to the amount of six battalions, and eight hundred horse, having, on the approach of the left wing of the allied army, changed their position, were followed by a body of the prussians, under general Sybourg, and another corps, commanded by general Schenkendorf, who attacked them near Saalfeld. The prussians planted their batteries to so much advantage, that the enemy, being attacked on all sides, were soon routed and dispersed. The prussians, in the pursuit, killed many of them, and took eight hundred prisoners, among whom were one colonel, one major, and twenty-nine other officers; besides four pair of colours, and a great quantity of baggage. Zeithen's hussars, under major Hundt, particularly distinguished themselves. As soon as the king of Prussia received the news of this success, he ordered the two generals abovementioned to march immediately with their troops, each having ten thousand men, to the assistance of the allies, who, at this time, had been obliged to post themselves behind the Dymel.

Marshal Daun had not as yet taken the field; but was now preparing with all diligence. In the mean time, the prussians were successively filing off regiments towards Lusatia; having not less than 100,000 between Meissen and Leipsick; and 25000 between Fribourgh and Thuringen; yet were so cautious as to intrench themselves near Meissen and Friberg; and not only repaired the old, but also erected new, works. In the following month, april, a body of imperialists, under general Guasco, near Plaven in the

the Voightland, were attacked by a detachment of pruffians, who defeated them, and took prifoners, one colonel, eight officers, and one hundred and fifty men, befides four pieces of cannon, and all their baggage. But in this fuccefsful action, the pruffians had the mortification to lofe the brave major Hundt, of Zeithen's huffars, one lieutenant, and thirty private men. In the courfe of the fame month, the pruffians had their line that they had formed near Milbitz, forced, an hundred of the men killed, and forty made prifoners, by Reid, an auftrian general. But the next month, the auftrians fuffered in their turn, for colonel Kleift advancing towards Freyberg, the auftrians abandoned it, and the colonel took eighty-four men, and one hundred horfes. The fame colonel, a few days after, attacked a poft of general Guafco's troops at Schellenberg, and made three officers, and one hundred and eighteen men prifoners. This month, the king of Pruffia took an auftrian magazine of meal, at Bautzen. Towards the end of the fame month, a body of pruffians, on the Queifs, near Greiffenberg, were attacked by general Beck, and fix hundred men were killed and wounded, and as many made prifoners, befides the lofs of four pieces of cannon. About a month after, the pruffian flying camp near Schweidnitz, was furprifed by two thoufand auftrians, who took prifoners two hundred men ; befides three hundred horfe, and fome other booty. About this time, an army of ruffians, under general Tottleben, marched into Pomerania, and made a furious, but unfuccefsful, attack upon Belgrade. In the mean time, fome ruffian detachments appeared upon the frontiers of the New-Marche, and occupied Landfberg, upon the Wartha; but thefe detachments being too weak, were obliged to abandon their new acquifitions, and the country being totally ruined before, and affording but little

plunder,

plunder, they changed their rout, and marched to join their main body.

The swedes, about this time, who had done little more this war than plunder the country they had occupied, began to renew their incursions. This obliged the few prussian troops, who were appointed to oppose them, and restrain the Mecklenburgers, to fortify themselves in the best manner they could, to prevent a surprise; and to defend the poor inhabitants from further violences.

About the beginning of july, general Zeithen reconnoitred the russian army, skirmished with an advanced post, killed two hundred men, and afterwards made good his retreat to his camp, at Storknest, in Poland. A little after, marshal Butterlin, having detached some regiments of hussars from his headquarters, at Pristame, with a design to cut off the retreat of colonel Lossow, who had been reconnoitring the russians; the latter fell upon them by surprise, killed twenty men, took two officers, fourteen subalterns, two surgeons, and one hundred and six private men prisoners; besides an hundred horses; and dispersed the remainder of the troops. Two days after, colonel Belling, and lieutenant colonel Goltz, gained some advantage over the swedes. The next day, the swedes took Demmin, and made an hundred of Hordt's battalion prisoners of war. The prussian lieutenant-colonel Goltz lost one hundred men at Malchin; and at Damgarten, a lieutenant and twenty prussian hussars were taken prisoners. The next day, his majesty of Prussia made a forced march, attacked general Brentano's cavalry, near Munsterberg, took possession of the camp that general had the very same day marked out for the austrians, under general Laudohn, and took one hundred and fifty four prisoners.

On the 21st of july, general Laudohn, having received a reinforcement, began his march, in order to to join the russians, who had advanced so near Breslau, as to be within one day's march of it; but his prussian majesty took such measures, as prevented their junction at this time; however, they effected this on the twenty-fifth of august following. On the first of august, a detachment of russians, with a large train of artillery, began to cannonade Breslau from seven batteries. But the governor Tauenzien, marched out with seven battalions, under his command, fell furiously upon the besiegers, and forced them to retire; who, in their retreat set fire to two villages. In order to be well prepared, in case of another such visit, the fortifications of Breslau were put into a thorough repair, the place well garrisoned, and further covered by Knoblauche's troops.

Laudohn finding it impossible to execute his plan in the Upper Silesia, where his prussian majesty, at this time, commanded, suddenly decamped, and, to oblige his majesty to divide his forces, marched to the Lower Silesia. The king of Prussia, on the 3d of august, passed the Neisse, drove part of the austrian army as far as Hoff, in Moravia, and made one hundred prisoners.

General Laudohn, at this time, made use of every stratagem to divert his prussian majesty from his post, and to bring him to a disadvantageous action. At one time he seemed determined to join the austrians; at another, to make an attempt upon Schweidnitz; but neither of these succeeding, he made as if he proposed to fall upon the Lower Silesia, and therefore made a movement, as mentioned above, in hopes that, at least, he might induce the king to divide his forces; but his majesty still kept his resolution to continue in the same situation. In the interim, the other grand division of the russians marched unopposed, into Pomerania. As Tottleben (who was suspected, and even said to have been convicted, of having carried on a secret correspondence, with his
prussian

prussian majesty) was now removed, and general Romanzow appointed to command in his stead; it was expected their operations would be vigorous.

The czarina considering the siege of Colberg, as an object of the greatest importance, had sent a fleet of ships to convey artillery, ammunition and stores, and transports to carry forces; but some of them perished in the passage by bad weather; the rest were landed at Rugenwalde, and employed against the fortifications of Colberg*. And now Colberg was blockaded by a fleet of forty sail, of all kinds; whilst the army of general Romanzow formed the siege by land. On the 19th of august, this general took possession of the town of Coslin, near Colberg, in Pomerania. A few days before, as thirty squadrons of austrian cavalry, and ten battalions of grenadiers, were on their march to join the russians at Finkenstein and Czelteritz, some prussian regiments attacked them, took a great number of them prisoners, and so dispersed them, that only ten squadrons escaped to the place of their destination. General Knoblock took two regiments of russian infantry prisoners, much about the same time.

As to Colberg, the king of Prussia was under such great apprehensions about it, that, though Laudohn and Butterlin found sufficient employment for all his forces, he resolved to send general Platen, with a considerable body of troops, to the assistance of Colberg. General Platen had a further commission; this was to pass through Poland, and, if possible, destroy some magazines that the russians had erected there; and by which their army in Silesia was wholly supported. The general so far succeeded, as to take three principal magazines; he also attacked and destroyed a large convoy of the enemy's

---

* This strong town is the key to his prussian majesty's dominions on the side of New Marche.

waggons, destroyed five hundred, and burnt or dispersed the provisions they carried; though the convoy wrs guarded by five thousand men, the greater part of whom were either taken prisoners, or killed. The general afterwards quickened his march to Pomerania.

It was at this time that the russians and austrians had effected their junction, which had been for some time retarded by the king of Prussia, as already related. But this misfortune obliged them to separate again, and desist from their intentions upon Breslau, to repass the Oder, near Sleinau, on the 9th of September, and make what haste they could into Poland, to save their remaining magazines; that they might not be totally deprived of their subsistence. Butterlin, who commanded that body, proposed to follow the next day; nor indeed had the junction of the austrians and russians during its continuance, proved of any service to them, for the king still maintained his camp at Buntzelwiltz, between Striegau and Wurben, and made head against all the force of the enemy in such a manner, that they did not dare to attack him, or form any new enterprize.

Skirmishes still fell out between the two parties. In the middle of september, general Platen destroyed several large magazines at Colbin and Gostin, attacked five thousand waggons at a convent near the latter place, defeated the convoy, consisting of four thousand men, killed a great number of them, and took two thousand prisoners, including brigadier general Czerapow, three majors, and twenty inferior officers; besides taking five haubitzers, and two pieces of cannon. A few days after, general Romanzow attacked a redoubt, which covered one of the flanks of the prince of Wertemberg's camp, and carried it. Encouraged by this success, he made a second attack on the prince's intrenchments; but
was

was repulsed with the loss of near three thousand men, and of the redoubt that he had taken the day before. The same month, a body of russians defeated general Werner, and took him prisoner, whilst he was endeavouring to rally the regiment of Wertemberg, that had been thrown into disorder during the engagement. General Romanzow made another attempt upon the prussian intrenchments before Colberg, but unsuccessfully.

The king of Prussia, on the retreat of Butterlin, thought he had greater freedom to act, and being in want of provisions in his camp, near Schwiednitz, ventured to draw near to the Oder, that he might be the more easily supplied. He pitched his head quarters at Strehlin, fortified his camp in the plain of Canth, to preserve his communication with Breslau. He even ventured to draft four thousand men from the garrison of Schweidnitz. He thought, that if the enemy should attempt to lay siege to that place, that the time the preparations for it would take up, would be sufficient for him to provide against it; especially as he was still at so little distance from the place. But general Laudohn, the austrian general, who had all along carefully watched for a favourable opportunity to strike some important blow, immediately determined to take the opportunity of the king's absence, and attempt the reduction of the strong town of Schweidnitz, by a coup de main.

Accordingly on the first of october, Laudohn bebegan the assault at three in the morning. The austrian troops observed so much precaution in their approach, that the garrison was not aware of them, till they scaled the four out-works, all at one time. This was executed with so much quickness, that the besieged had hardly time to fire a few cannon. The assailants did not fire a gun; but in one of the outworks, the fire of the small-arms accidentally set fire to a powder magazine, which blew up, and destroyed
three

three hundred auſtrians, and as many pruſſians. The out-works being carried, the auſtrians prepared to aſſault the body of the place. They burſt open the gates, and, after firing a few ſhot, got poſſeſſion of the town. Lieutenant-general Zaſtrow, governor of the fortreſs, and three thouſand ſeven hundred and ſeventy-one men, were made priſoners of war. One hundred and eighty-one pieces of cannon were found in the place, and a large magazine of meal. The auſtrians loſt, on this occaſion, two hundred and ſeventy-nine men killed; beſides one thouſand and ſeven wounded, and one hundred and forty miſſing. The ruſſians who were concerned in this affair, had fifty-one men killed and forty-five wounded. The ruſſian grenadiers behaved remarkably well.

This was a heavy blow on the king of Pruſſia, and of which he ſeemed to be extremely ſenſible. He foreſaw the ſeveral hurtful conſequences of it; that the auſtrians would now winter in Sileſia; and that, without leaving Breſlau, and the whole of Upper Sileſia, in the moſt imminent danger, he could make no motion in favour of any other part of his dominions. He was, at firſt, confounded at the news of this capital loſs; but, recovering himſelf, ſaid, with an air of pleaſantry, " It is a fatal blow; we muſt " endeavour to remedy it." He alſo ſeemed to entertain ſome doubts as to the governor, general Zaſtrow; but, at the ſame time, could not help reflecting that he had hitherto thoroughly approved himſelf as a faithful ſervant. However, he wrote to him in theſe terms. " We may now ſay, what " Francis I. of France wrote to his mother, after " the battle of Pavia: *We have loſt all, except our* " *honour.* As I cannot comprehend what hath hap- " pened to you, I ſhall ſuſpend my judgment; the " thing is very extraordinary."

After this affair, nothing very material happened for ſome time. The king continued his head quarters

ters at Strehlen, and general Laudohn encamped at Freyberg. Both parties even thought they might safely send out detatchments; the king sent twenty thousand men to prince Henry in Saxony, and general Laudohn sent as many to marshal Daun. The swedish and russian fleets were, by the badness of the weather, driven from before Colberg, and the russian general Romanzow left to continue the siege wholly by land. During the absence of these fleets, Colberg happily received, by sea, a fresh supply of provisions and stores, which enabled the garrison to make that vigorous and obstinate defence which they afterwards did. But they were not so successful by land; for as a convoy of upwards of one thousand waggons, laden with stores, and guarded by a large body of troops, was making its way from Stetin to Colberg, it was attacked by the russians, near Golnow, and forced to retire back to Dam, and two companies of general Platen's corps were surprised and taken; and the general himself was obliged to retreat to Stargard. The next day, the russian light troops having blown up eighty-five waggons loaded with bombs and gunpowder, and destroyed an hundred more filled with provisions and other stores, afterwards got possession of the town of Golnow, and burnt the suburbs: in this town they found forty thousand bombs and balls.

On the twenty-first of october, and the two preceeding days, the russians made several furious attacks upon Colberg, and likewise upon the prince of Wirtemburg's intrenchments; but to very little purpose. The main army of the russians making a movement towards Treptow, the prussian general Knoblock threw himself into that place. But the russians detached, from before Colberg, lieutenant general Romanzow, who attacked and took the town, and general Knoblock, with three battalions and a body of cavalry, four thousand in all, were made

prisoners

prisoners of war, with the loss of six prussian colours and ten pieces of cannon. A few days after, the russians dislodged the prussians from Stepnitz. Colonel Combiere, who commanded the van-guard of general Platen's troops, consisting of six thousand men, had penetrated as far as Golnow; but, at the village of Sanglow, was surprised by the russian general Berg, who took him prisoner, with thirty six officers, and one thousand men; besides taking six pieces of cannon. Four days after, Berg made an attack upon general Platen himself, between Stargand and Pyritz; but now was defeated in his turn, with the loss of five hundred men killed and wounded.

The king of prussia, at the beginning of the campaign, had detached prince Eugene, of Wurtemburg, with twelve thousand men, to cover Colberg. This prince caused very strong intrenchments to be made by general Thadden, an able engineer, which surrounded the town from the Baltic sea to the river Persante, and from thence to the other side of that sea. In these intrenchments, the prince of Wurtemberg maintained his ground against the united force of the russian and swedish fleets, and a body of twenty five thousand russians, commanded by general Romanzow, which, during all the time, blocked up the town. The different assaults, made from time to time by that general, were always repelled with loss. At the latter end of september, general Platen, with ten thousand men from the king of Prussia, arrived to the relief of Colberg. This general, soon after his arrival there, and the prince of Wurtemburg beginning to want provisions, the latter marched towards Stetin, in quest of the convoys which were held ready at that place; but, in his return back thither, was attacked by a large body of russians, as already related, and obliged to retire to Stargard.

Thus the prince of Wurtemberg was left alone to cover Colberg, and, though reduced to great straits, rejected with disdain the capitulation which was offered him on the second of november, by general Romanzow.

The advantages the ruffians had gained over the generals Platen and Knoblock, greatly animated the ruffians. Field-marfhal count Butterlin quitted his quarters at the village of Sturgorth, near Colberg, on the second of november, and marched with the main body of his army towards Schiefelbein, and general Fermor towards Noremberg and Templebourg, having firſt ſent a reinforcement to general Romanzow, who continued before Colberg. As to the prince of Würtemburg, he, after revictualling Colberg, and reinforcing the garriſon, being fearful left his army, which had been unable to relieve the town, by continuing longer under its walls, ſhould only ſhare its approaching unhappy fate, reſolved, while his men were in their vigour, to make his way through a part of the ruſſian army, and leave Colberg to make the beſt terms it could. He accordingly forced his way, and got to Grieffenberg, where he was joined by general Platen's troops, and marched immediately to the neighbourhood of Regenwalde, in order to annoy general Romanzow's rear, cut off his ſubſiſtence, and to force him to raiſe the ſiege of Colberg; but this was not the conſequence.

The ſiege of Colberg had now continued near ſix months, during which time it had been bravely defended by Heyde, the governor; but now its impending fate approached, and, on the ſeventeenth of december, it ſurrendered to the auſtrians, without a blow. But this event was rather the conſequence of famine, than of the valour of the aſſailants. The month before, general Romanzow took the fort of Munde, at the entrance of the river Perſante, and thereby cut off all
com-

communication by water between Stetin and Colberg. In the beginning of december,* the ruffians also took Minden, under Colberg, towards the sea. The consequence of this loss was, that the entry of any prussian vessel with provisions into Colberg, was now extremely dangerous and uncertain. Prince Wurtemberg indeed made an attempt to relieve the garrison, and to throw in stores and provisions; but failed in the enterprize.

* On the first of this month a plan was laid for seizing the king of Prussia in the suburbs of Strehlin. "A silesian gentleman, named Wargotsch, who had an estate near Strehlin, came often to the prussian camp, where he was well received by the king of Prussia, and by his officers. He informed himself, with great exactness, of every thing that passed in the army; and particularly of the dispositions made of the troops in their quarters of cantonment; and, as the country thereabouts was well known to him, he formed a project of surprising his prussian majesty, in the night of the 18th of december, which was to have been executed in this manner. A small body of resolute cavalry were to penetrate, in the night, into the suburbs of Strehlin, where his prussian majesty lodged, to which they were immediately to set fire; and, during the confusion that this must necessarily occasion, to endeavour to seize and carry off the king of Prussia; which Wargotsch thought was very practicable, as the quarters were, at that time, but slightly guarded.

The whole affair is reported to have been accidentally discovered by one of Wargotsch's own servants, who had often been employed to carry letters to a popish priest, in a neighbouring village. These letters were directed to an austrian lieutenant-colonel, and the priest had the care of transmitting them. The servant observing, when his master gave him the last letter, he was uncommonly anxious about the safe delivery of it, and appeared to be in great agitation of mind, began to suspect that he was employed in a dangerous service; however, he took the letter, and promised to deliver it as usual; but, instead of that, carried it directly to Strehlin, where he put it into the hands of M. de Crucemark, the adjutant-general, who immediately sent out two small parties of dragoons, to seize Wargotsch and the priest, who were both made prisoners, but escaped afterwards."

I have transcribed this *verbatim* from the account published by authority.

On the 13th of december, general Romanzow attempted to take the place by storm, but failed. But the town being now reduced to the last extremity, the garrison exhausted, provisions low, the fortifications in many places battered to pieces, the army, that defended it, driven back, on which they depended as their last resource, no hope of supply left by sea, or land, and no possibility of dislodging the enemy, who still continued firm; colonel Heyde, the governor, sent out articles of capitulation to the russians, on the 17th of december, 1761, which were immediately accepted. The brave garrison, consisting of 79 officers, and 3000 private men, were made prisoners of war. In the arsenal were found 146 pieces of cannon; forty pair of colours, and four standards were taken. Colonel Heyde acquired great honour by his spirited defence of this fortress, during a siege which lasted upwards of five months. According to the russian account, general Romanzow made 3000 prisoners in the course of the campaign, exclusive of 5000 deserters; though not without the loss of many of his own men during the time of the siege.

The russians, in consequence of the reduction of this important place, got possession of the New Marche, part of Pomerania, and of all Prussia. In short, the russians, by possessing Colberg, possessed every thing. They were masters of the Baltic, and had now a post by which their armies could be well provided. The road lay almost open to Brandenburg; Stetin alone stood in their way. The russians immediately began to repair the fortifications of Colberg; 18000 of their troops occupied Stargard, and the right of the Oder, to the neighbourhood of Stetin. The russians, now for the first time, wintered in Pomerania.

After

After the reduction of Colberg, the prussian general, Platen, took the route of Berlin, in his way to join prince Henry in Saxony; and the prince of Wurtemberg filed off to the dutchy of Mecklenburg Schwerin. Prince Henry established his head quarters at Hoff; as did the prince of Wurtemberg at Rostock; and those of colonel Belling at Gastrow; and all parties now took up their winter quarters; where for the present we shall leave them.

Brave actions of the Unicorn, Seahorse, and of capt. Hood, in the Minerva, and of his majesty's ship the Vengeance, commanded by capt. Nightingale. The English make an attempt upon Belleisle, Fortifications of Aix destroyed. Parliamentary grants for the war of 1761.

I AM now to record the naval atchievements of this year 1761; and cannot help observing on this occasion, that we are apt to be so attentive to naval operations of greater importance, such as that of one fleet with another, as to overlook the brave and noble actions of single ships, whose heroic feats ought surely to have a place in a work of this nature, and whose names ought to be transmitted to posterity with honour. I shall therefore not omit giving an account of those as they come in my way.

The beginning of this year opened with two actions of this kind. Capt. Hunt, of his majesty's ship the Unicorn, of twenty-eight guns, and two hundred men, being cruizing off the Penmarks, discovered at eight o'clock in the morning, january 8, a sail to the northward, to which he gave chace; and found it to be the Vestal, a French frigate, commanded by M. Boisbertelot, mounting twenty-six twelve and nine pounders upon her lower deck, and four six pounders upon her quarter-deck and forecastle, with two hundred and twenty men. At half an hour past ten the Unicorn came up with, and began to engage, her, and continued in close action two hours, when the enemy struck. Capt. Hunt, and the french captain, were both mortally wounded; the

the former died an hour after the action was over. Capt. Hunt received a gun shot wound in his right thigh, when lieutenant Symons took the command; and fought the enemy with great courage and conduct during the remainder of the engagement; for which he was rewarded with the command of the Mortar sloop. The Unicorn, notwithstanding the length and sharpness of the engagement, had only five men killed, six dangerously, and four slightly, wounded; but the Vestal had many more killed and wounded. Two days after, capt. James Smith, of the Seahorse, and only twenty guns, and one hundred and sixty men, engaged at the distance of thirty-four leagues S. W. from the Start, the Opale, a french frigate, of thirty-six guns, and three hundred and fifty men, commanded by the marquis d'Ars; when after a warm engagement of an hour and a quarter, in which the ships were board and board three different times, the enemy seeing the Unicorn coming up, left the Seahorse, and made all the haste she could from her. The Opale had her captain killled, and one hundred and fifty of her men killed or wounded. Eleven only of the Seahorse were killed, and thirty-eight wounded, but many of them very dangerously. Capt. Smith was afterwards detained at home, that his bravery might be rewarded with the command of a larger ship. In the course of the same month, the 23d at day-light. Capt. Alexander Hood, of the Minerva, of thirty-two guns, and two hundred and twenty men, being in the lat. of 45 deg. 22 min. N. Cape Pinas bearing S. by E. distant 30 leagues, saw, and gave chace to, a large ship, which afterwards proved to be the Warwick, which formerly belonged to us. She had thirty-four guns, but pierced for sixty, having on board two hundred and ninety-five men, seventy-four of whom were king's troops, with two other officers, and four passengers, that was bound to the isle of France and Bourbon,

with

with provisions, ammunition, and stores. At twenty minutes after ten in the morning, with a fresh gale easterly, and a great sea, capt. Hood began a close engagement with her. At eleven her main and foretop-mast went away; and soon after she came on board the starboard-bow of the Minerva, and then fell along side; but the sea soon made a separation, when the enemy fell a-stern. About a quarter after eleven the Minerva's bowsprit went away. These unfortunate accidents made capt. Hood almost despair of being able to attack the enemy again. However, determined to do his utmost, he ordered the wreck to be cut away as soon as possible; and about one o'clock cleared the ship of it by the loss of one man, and the sheet anchor. He then wore the ship, and stood for the enemy, who was then about three leagues to the leeward of him. At four o'clock he came up close to the enemy, and renewed the attack. About a quarter before five she struck, and the captain immediately got possession of her. The enemy had fourteen killed, and thirty-two wounded. On board the Minerva, the boatswain and thirteen other men were killed; and the gunner and thirty-three wounded; the latter and two seamen died on the 27th following.

Capt. Nightingale, of the Vengeance, of twenty-eight guns, nine and four pounders, on the 23d of march, took two prizes. One named the Entreprenant, pierced for forty-four, but carrying only twenty-six guns, twelve and six pounders, with two hundred and three men, being equipt for war and merchandize, and loaded with various goods for St. Domingo. The other a small privateer, four carriage and four swivel guns, with forty-five men. Capt. Nightingale fell in with them off the Lizard on the 23d; and at five in the afternoon began the attack, which lasted for three quarters of an hour; during which time the Vengeance was five times on fire;

fire; twice, as was supposed, from the enemies wads setting fire to the main rigging. The Vengeance's rigging and sails, by these accidents, being so much shattered, the enemy run his bowsprit over her, and offered for boarding, but was prevented; and the Vengeance sheered off to repair her rigging and sails. As soon as the ship was in condition, capt. Nightingale got up again close to the enemy, and the engagement was renewed for an hour, when the enemy sheered off, and bore away. The Vengeance, being a second time disabled in her masts and rigging, was some time in wearing. But at length she wore, and got again within pistol-shot of the enemy, and renewed the engagement, which continued for an hour and a half, when the enemy called for quarter. There were fifteen men killed, and twenty-four wounded, on board the Entreprenant. The Vengeance had six killed, and twenty-seven wounded, most of them dangerously; two of whom afterwards died. The captain brought his two prizes to Plymouth the twenty-seventh of the same month.

At the latter end of the last year, 1760, an expedition, the object of which was then kept a secret, was prepared with great diligence in England; but it was supposed to be against the coast of France and Belleisle * on the coast of Bretagne in particular; and

---

* One of the largest of all the European islands subject to the king of France; being between twelve and thirteen leagues in circumference. The middle of it lies in 47 deg. 20 m. north, 3 deg. 10 m. west of London,

This island originally belonged to the earl of Cornouaille, but has since been yielded to the king of France. It contains only one little city, called le Palais; three country towns, an hundred and three villages, and about five thousand inhabitants.

The town of Palais, so named from a castle belonging to the marquis de Belle-Isle, in its neighbourhood, but now converted into a citadel, which is a regular and strong fortification, fronting the sea, composed principally of horn-work, and provided with two dry ditches, the one next the counterscarp, and the other so contrived

and indeed it proved so to be. But this fleet did not sail till the spring of 1761, march 29. The land forces were commanded by major-general Hodgson, and the fleet by the honourable commodore Keppel. This fleet came to an anchor in the great road off Belleisle, on the 7th of april, about twelve o'clock. Soon after their arrival, the commodore and general took a view of the coast, and at their return agreed, that

as to secure the interior fortifications. In this citadel was a strong garrison of french soldiers. The citadel is divided from the largest part of the town, by an inlet of the sea, over which there is a bridge of communication from the other part of the town, and which is the most inhabited; it is only divided by its own fortifications and a glacis. There are here two magazines; one, which is called the higher magazine, has two floors, and serves as a granary for the corn belonging to the proprietor of the island. The lower buildings are employed for pressing and salting pilchards, and consist of a long row of low buildings, standing upon the sands near the shore.

At the mouth of the harbour there is a jettée, or pier, of cut stone, about thirty feet in breadth, and two hundred in length. There are in this island three nominal harbours; those of Palais and Sauzon, which lie on the N. and N. W. parts of the island, from the point des Poulains to that of Locmaria; and a third, called Goulfard, on the south side.

Each of these labour under some capital defect, either in being exposed, shallow, or dangerous to be entered. The road of Palais is the best anchoring ground, but hazardous in bad weather, because there is always then a high sea; which, together with the violence of the winds, often renders it impossible for the boats and sloops to come out to the assistance of the ships. Besides, if the wind happens to blow fresh from the N. or N. E. they are obliged to get out to sea, or run the hazard of being driven upon the coast. Sloops of twelve or fifteen tons cannot enter this harbour of Palais, except at full sea; and they are dry at low water.

The harbour of Sauzon is surrounded with very high hills which secures it from all winds, and could admit vessels of forty, or fifty, tons burthen; yet these are also dry at low water.

The harbour of Goulfard, though capable of admitting fifty gun ships every tide, is seldom entered by any ships, but in desperate situations, when there is no other visible means of avoiding shipwreck; the entrance into it being so very dangerous on account of rocks; nor is it covered from south winds, which, on this coast, are the most dangerous and violent.

that the port of St. Andro, near point Locmaria, was the moſt likely place at which to attempt a deſcent. It was accordingly ſettled between them, that ſir Thomas Stanhope, with ſome of the ſhips of war, and the tranſports, with Stuart's and Grey's battalions, and marines on board, ſhould make a feint at Sauzon, at the ſame time that a real attack ſhould be made on St. Andro. But as it was late in the day, nothing more was done than giving orders to prepare for the embarkation of the troops early the next morning, in the flat-bottomed boats, as ſoon as the ſhips ſhould have ſilenced a four gun battery, which commanded the entrance of the bay. The next morning, being the 8th, the wind N. by E. the boats were ready for the reception of the troops. The ſignal was made early in the morning for them to aſſemble at the rendezvous; and three ſhips, with two bomb veſſels, were ordered to proceed round the point of Locmaria, at the S. E. part of the iſland, and attack the fort and other works in the ſandy bay, round the beforementioned point.

Captain Barrington, in the Achilles, got firſt, and ſoon ſilenced the fire from the fort, and from the ſhore; and then, as directed, made the ſignal for his having done ſo. Now no time was loſt, and the troops in the flat-bottomed boats were puſhed to the landing with great briſkneſs and ſpirited behaviour, at three different places, near each other, by captain Barton, whom the admiral appointed to command the boats. But upon entering the bay, they found the enemy ſo ſtrongly intrenched on each ſide of the hill, which was ſo exceſſively ſteep, and the foot of it ſcarped away, that it was impoſſible to get up to the breaſt-work. And the enemy being ſtrongly intrenched on the heights, and in the little fort, the troops ſoon met with ſuch a repulſe, that it became neceſſary, as well as prudent, to deſiſt from the attempt

tempt for that time*. They accordingly retired with the flat-bottomed boats, in which they were well covered by the ships and bombs.

One of these boats landed sixty of Erskine's grenadiers, who got up a very difficult place to the top of the hills, where they formed with great skill, but were immediately routed by a much more numerous body of the enemy, so that all attempts to succour them were ineffectual, any further than the boats bringing from the rocks about twenty of them.

In the mean time, sir Thomas Stanhope, with four ships of war, the battalions of Grey's and Stuart's, with five hundred marines in transports, were opposite Sauzon, at the northern part of the island. Here troops were embarked in the boats, if possible, to divert the enemy from the principal object. A gale of wind coming on very quick, after the retiring from the shore, we received much damage among the transports, by loss of anchors and flat boats; twenty-two of the latter were lost. The loss of our troops on this occasion was, in killed, wounded, and prisoners, four hundred and thirty-four.

However, this repulse neither disheartened the commanders nor the soldiers. They resolved not to give up their design; and therefore determined diligently to search the whole coast to find a place more favourable for a second attack. It was a considerable time before the weather afforded an opportunity to make another attempt. At last a convenient part was found on the coast, not indeed less strong than the rest; on the contrary, the commanders founded their hopes on the excessive steepness and difficulty of the rocks. For the admiral and general were of opi-

* General Hodgson, in his account of this affair, says the whole island is a fortification; and that the little nature had left undone to make it such, has been amply supplied by art; the enemy having been at work upon it ever since sir Edward Hawke appeared before it in the winter of 1760.

nion,

nion, that attempting mounting the rocks where it was just possible, and where the enemy were not otherways prepared, from the impracticable appearance it had to them, than by a body of troops to annoy the boats in the attempt, would be the most likely means to succeed; and by making a disposition for the attack of their intrenched bays, and at Sauzon at the same time with the light horse, they might possibly gain a footing.

A rocky shore near the point of Locmaria was pitched upon: besides the principal attack, two feints were made at the same time to distract the enemy; whilst the men of war directed their fire with great judgment, and no less effect, on the hills. This gave brigadier general Lambert an opportunity of climbing up a rock with a handful of men. The difficulty of mounting had made the enemy least attentive to that part. Beauclerk's grenadiers, with their captain, Patterson, climbed a rock, and made good their landing april 23. at five o'clock, before the enemy saw what was intended. Having gained the top of the rock, they formed in good order, and bravely opposed three hundred of the enemy who came upon them, till the rest of brigadier Lambert's grenadiers got up to them; with whose assistance they repulsed the enemy, took three brass field pieces, and some wounded prisoners, with the loss of not above thirty men. Captain Patterson lost his arm.

In a short time all the rest of the English forces made good their landing with very little loss. The enemy indeed, in one or two places, made some opposition, but the english light horse soon forced them back to the town, and cleared their way up to the very intrenchments. The cannon with great difficulty were brought forward, being obliged to be dragged up the rocks, and then two leagues further over a rugged and broken road. And now the siege of Palais was commenced; at this time there were

2600

2600 french troops in the citadel, commanded by a brave and experienced officer, the chevalier de St. Croix. From the character of this gentleman it was reasonable to suppose that this place would not be soon surrendered; nor indeed was it. In one of the sallies, which the enemy made, they were so lucky as to take prisoners major-general Crawford, his two aid de camps, and fifty more, as they were reconnoitering in the night; the enemy had with them in this sally 300 men, and came upon Crawford's party by surprise. Notwithstanding the tediousness of the siege, the English forces were not dispirited; nor indeed did the besieged appear to be disheartened. They still hoped that a fleet would arrive to their assistance; but our ships kept so close a watch, as to prevent all relief from the continent.

A vigorous assault was made upon the lines that covered the town, when a body of new raised marines behaved with uncommon, and unexpected, bravery; and the lines were carried with very little loss. And now the condition of the besieged was become very desperate, yet the brave commander consulted his honour more than his unhappy situation, and held out till the 7th of June, when seeing no prospect of relief, and the place untenable, he asked, and obtained, an honourable capitulation, after a defence of two months. He was granted for himself and garrison all the honours of war, and were transported to the continent at the expence of his britannick majesty. The british prisoners were declared to be free, from the moment of the capitulation; but the french prisoners were to be exchanged according to the cartel of Sluys. In this expedition we are supposed to have had eighteen hundred men killed and wounded; though some accounts make the killed to have amounted to 2000; among these was sir W. Peere Williams, whose loss was much lamented. He was shot in the night by having
care-

carelesly approached too near a centinel of the enemy. The captains Bell, Wightwick, and Collins, of the marines, were promoted to the rank of majors in the army, for their gallant behaviour. It is said that the marines, though newly raised, behaved in the attack upon the French lines with so much bravery, that no action of greater spirit and gallantry had been performed during the whole war. In the course of the siege out of 2600 troops that at first composed the french garrison, 922 were killed, wounded, or taken prisoners.

With respect to this expedition, very various were the reasonings at home upon it. Whilst it was yet in embrio, the expectations of the public were greatly raised, who hoped something very capital was going to be undertaken against the enemy. But as soon as the destination of it was known, many thought contemptibly of it; and their disgust was increased at the delay that attended the taking of Belleisle, and the expence of men and stores. They did not think that the acquisition of it would be of any considerable service to England in time of peace, if kept, or of any great injury to the enemy during the continuance of the war. They judged, that it could not be taken without a considerable loss, or kept without a very great expence; and, on the whole, they apprehended that when exchanges came to be made, it would be considered by France as of but little value. Whilst others reasoned thus; that though the harbours in that island were bad, yet small privateers might lie there, and occasionally molest the french coasting trade; and that an english fleet might ride between it and the continent in a well secured road. They further supposed, that though the loss of the island might not be of great detriment to the interest of France, yet that her pride would be sensibly mortified by it; and that those reasons, which had formerly induced her to be at great expence in strengthening the fortifications of it, and when alarmed with an invasion, to put a strong garrison into it, might make her set some value on it when it should come under consideration in the treaty for a peace.

Others again disliked this expedition, because as a treaty for a peace was then in agitation between the two courts, they thought this insult upon the court of France would rather exasperate them, and irritate their pride to renew these efforts which their great losses had obliged them to suspend. But however, this event does not seem to have had any prejudicial effect upon the treaty; and the breaking it off does not seem, in the least, to be charged to that transaction. But notwithstanding all these different reasonings upon this event, the news of the taking of the place no sooner arrived in England, than a general joy diffused itself throughout the whole kingdom, and the city of London addressed his majesty upon the acquisition. The general, and the land and sea officers concerned in the expedition, were universally praised, for having so bravely struggled with, and at last overcome, the great difficulties that they had to encounter, and for not being dispirited at their first repulse, but still nobly renewing the attack under circumstances nearly as discouraging as those they had at first experienced.

The loss of Belleisle was not the only injury the french suffered from us this year; in the month of july part of commodore Keppel's squadron, under Sir Thomas Stanhope, demolished the works and fortifications on the isle of Aix. A captain of the furnace bomb, on this occasion, bravely distinguished himself.

Before I conclude this chapter, which also concludes the history of the war for the year 1761, I shall add the grants of parliament for the expences of the war during that period.

For

	l.	s.	d.
For 70,000 seamen, including 18,355 marines for 13 months, at 4 l. per man, per month	3,640,000	00	00
For the ordinary of the navy and half-pay	258,624	7	10
Towards building and rebuilding of ships, for 1761	200,000	00	00
For the charge of the ordnance office	302,267	9	00
For the extra expence of that office	426,449	4	9
For 64,971 men, including 4008 invalids, for guards, &c.	1,576,985	10	7
For the forces in the plantations, Africa, and the East-Indies, and provisions for garrisons	843,756	12	9
For three irish regiments in North-America	22,179	00	0
For general and general staff-officers, and officers of the hospitals for land-forces	72,896	14	2
For the embodied militia from dec. 25, 1760, to april 25, 1761; 122 days	140,350	19	4
For clothing for ditto 1761	56,568	15	2
For 39,773 hanoverians, for 1761	463,874	19	1
For 2120 horse, and 9900 foot, hessians, with artillery, officers, &c.	268,360	8	8
For an additional corps of 1576 horse and 8808 foot,	147,071	5	2
For 1205, horse, 2208 foot troops of Brunswick, together with subsidy	57,798	16	00

	l.	s.	d.
For five battalions serving with the king's army in Germany, and artillery for 1761	25,504	6	8
For reduced officers of land forces and marines	34,854	9	2
For allowance to reduced horse-guards and regiment of horse	2,973	19	2
For pensions to reduced officers and widows	1,922	00	00
For out-pensioners of Chelsea-hospital	18,360	2	11
For the embodied militia from april 1761, to december 24	298,668	9	10
Upon account of the militia when unembodied, and for cloathing of the militia now unembodied, for the year beginning at Lady-day, 1761	70,000	00	00
To the king of Prussia, pursuant to convention	670,000	00	00
To certain provinces in North-America	200,000	00	00
To the East-India company for defraying the expence of a military force in their settlements	20,000	00	00
For Nova Scotia for 1761	10,595	12	9
For Georgia for 1761	4,357	10	00
To the African forts and settlements	13,000	00	00
To the landgrave of Hesse-Cassel	120,000	00	00
Total £.	9,084,520	3	00

In the foregoing account I have only inserted such articles as provided for the expences of the ensuing year, omitting those which provided for the arrears, and past expences due upon account of the war, and other deficiencies, a supply of credit of one million, and other expences incident to government; the whole grants for the year 1761, being as follows:

Total for navy, ordnance, land service, eighteen millions eight hundred and sixteen thousand one hundred and nineteen pounds nineteen shillings and nine pence three farthings.

CHAP. XXXIII.

Debates relative to Spain. Mr. Pitt resigns. Abstract of the family-treaty between France and Spain. Great Britain and Spain declare war against each other.

IN the twenty-ninth chapter of this work, I mentioned a treaty between England and France for a peace, and the occasion of its being broken off, and at the same time took notice of the family compact entered into between France and Spain. In consequence of this treaty failing between England and France, the proposed congress at Augsbourg never took place. Mr. Pitt, who at this time had the principal direction in the ministry, and who was, perhaps, the greatest minister, and undoubtedly the honestest, that England ever had, plainly saw into the artifice of France in this negociation, and the designs of Spain, being fully satisfied that Spain would be entirely led by France; and that a war with Spain was, for that reason, absolutely unavoidable. This affair naturally brought on a very serious, and, in the end, a very warm debate among those whose duty it was to consider the matter. Mr. P's opinion upon this occasion seems to have been this : " That if Spain for the present rather delayed declaring war, than laid aside their hostile intentions, it was in order to strike the blow at their own time, and with the greater effect; that therefore their reasons for delaying to act, were the very motives which ought to induce us to act with the utmost speed and vigour. That we ought to consider the evasions of that court as a refusal of satisfaction, and that refusal as a declaration of war. That we ought, from prudence as well

well as from spirit, to secure ourselves the first blow, and to be practically convinced, that the early and effective measures which had so large a share in reducing France to this dependance upon Spain, would also be the fittest for determining, or disabling, Spain from affording any protection to France. That their flota had not yet arrived, and that the taking of it would at once disable theirs, and strengthen our hands. That this proceeding, so suitable to the dignity of the nation, and the insults it had received, would be a lesson to Spain, and to every other power, how they should presume to dictate in our affairs, and to intermeddle with a menacing mediation, and an officiousness as insidious as it was audacious. That he would allow our enemies, whether secret or declared, no time to think and recollect themselves." *

Most disinterested and unprejudiced persons highly approved of these sentiments so worthy of the resolute and enterprising patriot who delivered them. But, to others, they appeared in a very different light. Who argued, in reply, with some shew of reason, " That they admitted that we ought not to be terrified from the assertion of our just demands by the menaces of any power. They acknowledged, that France had taken a very extraordinary and

* About two months before this debate, Mr. Pitt, in his letter of the twenty-eighth of July, had directed lord Bristol, then embassador at Spain, to demand of Mr. Wall a full and explicit explanation of the tendency of the Spanish armaments, and of the views of that court in relation to Great-Britain. Mr. Wall acquainted lord Bristol, that France had made a voluntary offer of assisting Spain, with all her force, in case of a future rupture between the courts of London and Madrid; and that the king his master had received so friendly an offer with cordiality; but that Spain was not looking out for an occasion of quarrelling with Great-Britain, in the time of her greatest glory and power; on the contrary, she was desirous of connecting a mutual friendship: but we shall soon see that this answer was all cant and deceit.

very unjustifiable step; but that we ought to admit, and even to wish for an explanation. That this court, upon a sober, yet spirited remonstrance, might recall that rash proposition into which they had been, perhaps unwarily, seduced by the artifices of France; that to shun war, upon a just occasion, was cowardice; but to provoke or court it, was madness. And if to court a war was not, in general, a very wise measure, to desire it with Spain, if possible it could be avoided, was to overturn the most fundamental principles of the policy of both nations. That this desire of adding war to war, and enemy to enemy, whilst we had our hands already as full as they could hold, and whilst all our faculties were strained to the utmost pitch, was ill to calculate the national strength of our country; which, however great, had its limits, and was not able to contend with all the world. That, whilst we were calling for new enemies, no mention was made of new allies, nor indeed of any new resource whatever." It was further urged, " that to plunge into such measures, in the manner proposed, and upon no better grounds, could not fail to scandalize and to alarm all Europe; and that we could possibly derive no advantage from this precipitate conduct, which would not be more than counter-ballanced by the jealousy and terror it would necessarily create in every nation near us. As to the flota, it was not to be reckoned upon, as, at the very time of that deliberation, it might be expected to be safe in its harbour; and, perhaps, if we could succeed in seizing it, we might perform a service not very agreeable to neutral nations, and as little advantageous to our own commerce. If Spain, blind to her true interests, and misled by french councils, should give, in a more decisive manner, into the designs of that court, and obstinately refuse a reasonable satisfaction, it would then be the true time to declare war, when all the neighbouring and impartial powers
were

were convinced that we acted with as much temper as resolution; and when every thinking man at home should be satisfied, that he was not hurried into the hazards and expences of war, from an idea of chimerical heroism, but from an inevitable necessity; and that, in such a case, he might depend upon the utmost support which the nation could give to an administration that depended upon its strength, and yet dreaded to waste it wantonly, or to employ it unjustly."

The minister, irritated at this opposition, is said to have warmly replied in these terms: "That this was the time for humbling the whole house of Bourbon; that, if this opportunity was let slip, it might never be recovered; and, if he could not prevail in this instance, he was resolved that this was the last time that he should sit in that council. He thanked the ministers of the late king, for their support; said, he was himself called to the ministry by the voice of the people, to whom he considered himself as accountable for his conduct; and that he would no longer remain in a situation which made him responsible for measures he was no longer allowed to guide."

The minister was immediately answered, with no less vigour and spirit, by a noble lord since deceased; but who then presided in this council, and whose advanced age seemed to have had no effect on his great understanding, in these terms, as it is said:

" I find the gentleman is determined to leave us, nor can I say I am sorry for it, since he would otherwise have certainly compelled us to leave him; but, if he be resolved to assume the right of advising his majesty, and directing the operations of the war, to what purpose are we called to this council?"

" When he talks of being responsible to the people, he talks the language of the house of commons, and forgets,

forgets, that, at this board, he is only responsible to the king. However, though he may possibly have convinced himself of his infallibility, still it remains that we should be equally convinced, before we can resign our understandings to his direction, or join with him in the measure he proposes."

On the division, the minister and a noble peer, closely connected with him, were the only voices in favour of the immediate declaration for war; the rest being unanimously against it. Mr. Pitt and lord Temple, adhering to their first opinion, delivered their reasons in writing, and resigned their employments, on the eighteenth of September 1761. Perhaps so general, and such a national concern, never before appeared in this or any other kingdom, on the resignation of a minister of state, as now prevailed. If any future historian should be disposed to represent the present age, as corrupt and degenerate in morals and understanding, sure this instance of the sense of the public on the loss of a good and able minister must prevent, or, should he venture the acusation, give the lye to it.

Nor does it appear, that a very great person thought less of his intrepidity, or had a less sense of his abilities; for, on his resignation of the seals, he was treated in the most amiable manner; and though his majesty, upon the noblest principles, approved of the opinion of the majority, yet Mr. Pitt had the next day a pension of three thousand pounds a year settled upon him, for three lives; at the same time, a title was conferred upon his lady, and her issue; from hence we may judge, what the best of kings thought of the best of ministers. Should any one be disposed to write a panegyric on this minister, he has no more to do than to relate this fact, that, whilst he was concerned in the affairs of government, this country carried on the most important war England was ever engaged in without an ally, more to her honour,

honour, and with greater success, than she ever did before in the most successful war, and with the most powerful assistance. Yet this great man has his calumniators; but when their memories, as well as their carcasses shall stink, his memory will be odoriferous with the wise and good.

But to continue the affair with Spain; on the twenty-eighth of september, lord Bristol wrote that he was pressed by Mr. Wall, to give the strongest assurances at home of their readiness to adjust their differences with us, if we would only abandon our recent settlements on the coast of Honduras, to save the spanish puntondor.* In two letters, of the twenty-eighth of october, lord Egremont gave directions, by the king's orders, to lord Bristol, to demand a communication of the treaty of Versailles; or, at least, of those articles of it which had an immediate, or distant, relation to the interests of Great-Britain; and to couch that demand in the most polite and friendly terms, rather insinuating than urging his arguments. But lord Bristol, before he received these letters, informed lord Egremont, in one of his own to him, that the style and sentiments of Mr. Wall were greatly altered, and that he had told lord Bristol, that we were intoxicated with our successes, and had, in consequence thereof, refused the reasonable concessions made us by France in the late negociation; that we had formed a design to ruin France, and then to tread upon the power of Spain; that, therefore, he would be the first to counsel his master not to suffer his subjects to remain in a defenceless condition; that it was now high time for Spain to open her eyes, and not to suffer a neighbour, an ally, a parent, and a friend, to submit to the rigid laws imposed by an insulting conqueror. That the court of Versailles had communicated to that of Madrid, punctually and mi-

---

* Or point of honour.

nutely,

hutely, every step that had been taken at Paris and London, during the negociation for peace; and that his catholic majesty had judged it expedient, to renew his family compacts with the most christian king. This animated discourse was occasioned by the advice which Spain had received of Mr. Pitt's resignation, and of the motives on which it was founded; construing the cautious, and perhaps too scrupulous, attachment of our councils to the strictest rules of justice, to a fear of the power of Spain. The whole court of Spain was immediately in a ferment, having always considered themselves as the aggrieved party, and never imagining that the English would be the first to propose or begin the war.

Lord Bristol, in answer to this letter, was directed to insist, in his majesty's name, on an immediate, clear, precise, and categorical answer from the court of Spain to this question, "What were their intentions, relative to Great-Britain?" short and spirited enough. His lordship, at the same time, was directed to avoid all harshness in the manner, yet to maintain a proper firmness in the matter of the demand, and to act, *fortiter in re, suaviter in modo*. And, in case he did not receive proper satisfaction, immediately to quit Madrid, without staying to take leave. Lord Bristol, agreeable to his instructions, attended on Mr. Wall, and had a cool and candid conference with him; in which Mr. Wall acknowledged the caution we had observed, in declining the attack of those french settlements which had any connection with the territory of Spain, and agreed with his lordship concerning the public nature of what had passed in the british councils on the change of the ministry; but at the same time declared, that the copy, which he had already given, of his own dispatch to the count de Fuentes, in London, was the only answer he was at liberty to return to his lordship's enquiries.

In

In this copy, which Mr. Wall referred to, he used these words:

"You know how easy it would be for the king to give a positive answer, but his own dignity hinders him from it; considering this demand as a necessary condition for entering upon a negociation with Spain, on differences which, they own, have subsisted a long time."

Upon the whole, Mr. Wall strongly expressed his wishes, that some temperament might be found out for adjusting their mutual disputes; and he promised to lay before the king, faithfully and minutely, the disposition and sentiments of his britannic majesty. Two days after, Mr. Wall acquainted lord Bristol, in a second conference, that his majesty of Spain was sensible of all the assurances of friendship, and marks of attention, which had been conveyed through his means; but that his catholic majesty did not think it expedient to give any other answer, with regard to the treaty, than that which had been communicated in the dispatch of the count de Fuentes. Lord Bristol then found himself obliged to apply, in form, for that full categorical answer which the court of London had ordered him to demand; and he pressed Mr. Wall, with address and energy, to go in person to his catholic majesty, and to enlarge upon all those arguments, in favour of his demand, which he had made use of with him in their several conferences.

Mr. Wall, on the tenth of December, informed lord Bristol, by letter, that since he had demanded, in writing, a positive and categorical answer to this question: "If Spain thought of joining herself with France, against England?" and had declared, at the same time, that he should look upon the refusal as a declaration of war, and, in consequence, leave the court of Madrid; he was therefore to acquaint him, that the spirit of haughtiness and discord which had
dictated

dictated that inconsiderate step, and which, for the misfortune of mankind, still reigned so much in the british government, was what made, in the same instant, the declaration of war, and attacked the king's dignity; that he might retire when, and how, it was convenient to him; which was the only answer his majesty had ordered him to give. A copy of this letter was received in London, on the twenty-fourth of december; and, the next day, the count de Fuentes delivered the following note to lord Egremont.

Translation of a note delivered to the earl of Egremont, by the count de Fuentes, december 25, 1761, as published in the London-Gazette.

"The count de Fuentes, the catholic king's ambassador to his britannic majesty, has just received a courier from his court, by whom he is informed, that my lord Bristol, his britannick majesty's ambassador at the court of Madrid, has said to his excellency Mr. Wall, minister of state, that he had orders to demand a positive and catagorical answer to this question, viz. If Spain thinks of allying herself with France against England? And to declare, at the same time, that he should take a refusal to his demand, for an aggression and declaration of war: and that he should, in consequence, be obliged to retire from the court of Spain. The above minister of state answered him, that such a step could only be suggested by the spirit of haughtiness and of discord, which, for the misfortune of mankind, still reigns but too much in the british government: that it was in that very moment that the war was declared, and the king's dignity violently attacked, that he might retire how, and when he should think proper.

The count de Fuentes is, in consequence, ordered to leave the court and the dominions of England, and to declare to the british king, to the english nation, and to the whole universe, that the horrors into which the Spanish and English nations are going to plunge themselves, must be attributed only to the pride, and to the unmeasurable ambition, of him who held the reins of government, and who appears still to hold them, although by another hand: that, if his catholic majesty excused himself from answering on the treaty in question, between his catholick majesty and his most christian majesty, which is believed to have been signed the 15th of august, and wherein it is pretended, there are conditions relative to England, he had very good reasons: first, the king's dignity required him to manifest his just resentment of the little management, or, to speak more properly, of the insulting manner with which all the affairs of Spain have been treated during Mr. Pitt's administration; who, finding himself convinced of the justice which supported the king in his pretensions, his ordinary and last answer was, That he would not relax in any thing, till the Tower of London was taken sword in hand.

Besides, his majesty was much shocked, to hear the haughty and imperious tone with which the contents of the treaty were demanded of him: if the respect due to royal majesty had been regarded, explanations might have been had without any difficulty: the ministers of Spain might have said frankly to those of England, what the count de Fuentes, by the king's express order, declares publicly, viz. That the said treaty is only a convention between the family of Bourbon, wherein there is nothing which has the least relation to the present war: that there is in it an article for the mutual guaranty of the dominions of the two sovereigns; but it is specified therein, that that guaranty is not to be understood but of the dominions which shall remain to France after the present war

shall

shall be ended: that, although his catholick majesty might have had reason to think himself offended, by the irregular manner in which the memorial was returned to M. de Bussy, minister of France, which he had presented, for terminating the differences of Spain and England, at the same time with the war between this last and France, he has, however, dissembled; and, from an effect of his love of peace, caused a memorial to be delivered to my lord Bristol, wherein it is evidently demonstrated, that the step of France which put the minister, Pitt, into so bad a humour, did not at all offend either the laws of neutrality, or the sincerity of the two sovereigns: that, further, from a fresh proof of his pacific spirit, the king of Spain wrote to the king of France, his cousin, that, if the union of interest in any manner retarded the peace with England, he consented to separate himself from it, not to put any obstacle to so great a happiness; but it was soon seen, that this was only a pretence on the part of the English minister, for that of France continuing his negociation, without making any mention of Spain, and proposing conditions very advantageous and honourable for England, the minister, Pitt, to the great astonishment of the universe, rejected them with disdain, and shewed, at the same time, his ill-will against Spain, to the scandal of the same british council; and, unfortunately, he has succeeded but too far in his pernicious design.

This declaration made, the count de Fuentes desires his excellency, my lord Egremont, to present his most humble respects to his britannick majesty, and to obtain for him the passports, and all other facilities, for him, his family, and all his retinue, to go out of the dominions of Great-Britain, without any trouble, and to go by the short passage of the sea, which separates them from the continent.

Translation

Tranflation of the anfwer delivered to the count de Fuentes by the earl of Egremont, Dec. 31, 1761, as publifhed in the London Gazette.

" The earl of Egremont, his britannick majefty's fecretary of ftate, having received from his excellency the count de Fuentes, ambaffador of the catholic king at the court of London, a paper, in which, befides the notification of his recal, and the demand of the neceffary paffports to go out of the king's dominions, he has thought proper to enter into what has juft paft between the two courts, with a view to make that of London appear as the fource of all the misfortunes which may enfue from the rupture which has happened: in order that nobody may be mifled by the declaration, which his excellency has been pleafed to make to the king, to the englifh nation, and to the whole univerfe; notwithftanding the infinuation, as void of foundation as of decency, of the fpirit of haughtinefs and of difcord, which, his excellency pretends reigns in the britifh government, to the misfortune of mankind; and notwithftanding the irregularity and indecency of appealing to the englifh nation, as if it could be feparated from its king, for whom the moft determined fentiments of love, of duty, and of confidence, are engraved in the hearts of all his fubjects; the faid earl of Egremont, by his majefty's order, laying afide, in this anfwer, all fpirit of declamation and of harfhnefs, avoiding every offenfive word, which might hurt the dignity of fovereigns, without ftooping to invectives againft private perfons, will confine himfelf to facts with the moft fcrupulous exactnefs: and it is from this reprefentation of facts, that he appeals to all Europe, and to the whole univerfe, for the purity of the king's intentions, and for the sincerity of the wishes his majesty has not ceased to make, as well for the moderation he has always shewed; though in vain, for the maintenance of friendship and good understanding between the british and spanish nations.

The king having received undoubted information, that the court of Madrid had secretly contracted engagements with that of Versailles, which the ministers of France laboured to represent, in all the courts of Europe, as offensive to Great-Britain; and combining these appearances with the step, which the court of Spain had, a little time before, taken towards his majesty, in avowing its consent, (though that avowal had been followed by apologies) to the memorial presented the 23d of july, by the Sieur de Bussy, minister plenipotentiary of the most christian king, to the king's secretary of state; and his majesty having afterwards received intelligence, scarce admitting a doubt, of troops marching, and of military preparations making in all the ports of Spain, judged that his dignity, as well as his prudence, required him to order his ambassador at the court of Madrid by a dispatch dated the 28th of october, to demand, in terms the most measured, however, and the most amicable, a communication of the treaty recently concluded between the courts of Madrid and Versailles, or at least of the articles which might relate to the interests of Great-Britain; and, in order to avoid every thing, which could be thought to imply the least slight of the dignity, or even the delicacy, of his catholic majesty, the earl of Bristol was authorised to content himself with assurances, in case the catholic king offered to give any, that the said engagements did not contain any thing that was contrary to the friendship, which subsisted between the two crowns, or that was prejudicial to the interests of Great-Britain, supposing that any difficulty was made of shewing the treaty. The king
could

could not give a less equivocal proof of his dependance on the good faith of the catholic king, than in shewing him an unbounded confidence, in so important an affair, and which so essentially interested his own dignity, the good of his kingdoms, and the happiness of his people.

How great, then, was the king's surprise, when, instead of receiving the just satisfaction, which he had a right to expect, he learnt from his ambassador, that having addressed himself to the minister of Spain for that purpose, he could only draw from him a refusal to give a satisfactory answer to his majesty's just requisitions, which he had accompanied with terms that breathed nothing but haughtiness, animosity, and menace; and which seemed so strongly to verify the suspicions of the unamicable disposition of the court of Spain, that nothing less than his majesty's moderation, and his resolution taken to make all the efforts possible to avoid the misfortunes inseparable from a rupture, could determine him to make a last trial; by giving orders to his ambassador to address himself to the minister of Spain, to desire him to inform him of the intentions of the court of Madrid towards that of Great-Britain in this conjuncture, if they had engagements, or formed the design to join the king's enemies in the present war, or to depart, in any manner, from the neutrality they had hitherto observed; and to make that minister sensible, that, if they persisted in refusing all satisfaction on demands so just, so necessary, and so interesting, the king could not but consider such a refusal as the most authentic avowal, that Spain had taken her part, and that there only remained for his majesty to take the measures which his royal prudence should dictate for the honour and dignity of his crown, and for the prosperity and protection of his people: and to recal his ambassador.

Unhappily for the publick tranquility, for the interest of the two nations, and for the good of mankind, this last step was as fruitless as the preceding ones; the spanish minister, keeping no further measures, answered dryly, "That it was in that very moment that the war was declared, and the king's dignity attacked, and that the earl of Bristol might retire how, and when, he should think proper."

And in order to set in its true light the declaration, " That, if the respect due to his catholic majesty had been regarded, explanations might have been had without any difficulty, and that the ministers of Spain might have said frankly, as Monf. de Fuentes, by the king's express order, declares publicly, that the said treaty is only a convention between the family of Bourbon; wherein there is nothing, which has the least relation to the present war; and that the guaranty, which is therein specified, is not to be understood but of the dominions, which shall remain to France after the war:" It is declared, that, very far from thinking of being wanting to the respect, acknowledged to be due to crowned heads, the instructions given to the earl of Bristol have always been to make the requisitions, on the subject of the engagements between the courts of Madrid and Versailles, with all the decency, and all the attention possible; and the demand of a categorical answer was not made till after repeated, and the most stinging, refusals to give the least satisfaction, and at the last extremity; therefore, if the court of Spain ever had the design to give this so necessary satisfaction, they had not the least reason, that ought to have engaged them to defer it to the moment, when it could no longer be of use. But, fortunately, the terms, in which the declaration is conceived, spare us the regret of not having received it sooner; for it appears at first sight, that the answer is not at all conformable to the demand: We wanted to be informed, *if the court of Spain intended to join the french, our enemies, to make war in Great-Britain, or to depart from their neutrality:* whereas the answer concerns one treaty only, which is said to be of the 15th of august, carefully avoiding to say the least word, that could explain, in any manner, the intentions of Spain towards Great-Britain, or the further engagements they may have contracted in the present crisis.

After a deduction, as exact as faithful, of what has passed between the two courts, it is left to the impartial public to decide, which of the two has always been inclined to peace, and which was determined on war.

As to the rest, the earl of Egremont has the honour to acquaint his excellency the count de Fuentes, by the king's order, that the necessary passports for him shall be expedited, and that they will not fail to procure him all possible facilities for his passage to the port which he shall think most convenient."

As the treaty between France and Spain has been the subject of much political debate, and partly the occasion of a war with Spain, I imagine an abstract of it may not be unacceptable.*

---

* Abstract of the treaty of friendship and union concluded between the kings of France and Spain, august 15, 1761, under the denomination of a family convention, the ratifications of which were exchanged on the 8th of september following.

" The preamble sets forth the motives for concluding this treaty, and the objects of it. The motives are, the ties of blood between the two kings, and the sentiments they entertain of each other. The object of it is, to give stability and permanency to those duties which

On the 2d of January, 1762, the king in council signed a declaration of war against Spain. On the 5th which naturally flow from affinity and friendship; and to establish a solemn and lasting monument of that reciprocal interest which ought to be the basis of the desires of the two monarchs, and of the prosperity of their royal families.

The treaty itself contains twenty-eight articles.

1. Both kings will, for the future, look upon every power as their enemy, that becomes the enemy of either.

2. Their majesties reciprocally guaranty all their dominions, in whatever part of the world they be situated; but they expressly stipulate, that this guaranty shall extend only to those dominions respectively, of which the two crowns shall be in possession the moment they are at peace with all the world.

3. The two kings extend their guaranty to the king of the Two Sicilies and the infant duke of Parma, on condition that these two princes guaranty the dominions of their most christian and catholic majesties.

4. Though this mutual inviolable guaranty is to be supported with all the forces of the two kings, their majesties have thought proper to fix the succours which are to be first furnished.

5, 6, 7. These articles determine the quality and quantity of these first succours, which the power required engages to furnish to the power requiring. These succours consist of ships and frigates of war, and of land forces, both horse and foot. Their number is determined, and the posts and stations to which they are to repair.

8. The wars in which France shall be involved in consequence of her engagements by the treaties of Westphalia, or other alliances with the princes and states of Germany and the North, are excepted from the cases in which Spain is bound to furnish succours to France, unless some maritime power take part in those wars, or France be attacked by land in her own country.

9. The potentate requiring may send one or more commissaries, to see whether the potentate required hath assembled the stipulated succours within the limited time.

10, 11. The potentate required, shall be at liberty to make only one representation on the use to be made of the succours furnished to the potentate requiring: this, however, is to be understood only of cases where an enterprize is to be carried into immediate execution; and not of ordinary cases, where the power that is to furnish the succours, is obliged only to hold them in readiness in that part of his dominions which the power requiring shall appoint.

12, 13.

5th following, the count de Fuentes, the Spanish ambassador, sailed from Dover to Calais; the earl of Bristol

12, 13. The demand of succours shall be held a sufficient proof, on one hand, of the necessity of receiving them; and, on the other, of the obligation to give them. The furnishing of them shall not, therefore, be evaded under any pretext; and without entering into any discussion, the stipulated number of ships and land forces shall, three months after requisition, be considered as belonging to the potentate requiring.

14, 15. The charges of the said ships and troops shall be defrayed by the power to which they are sent: and the power which sends them, shall hold ready other ships to replace those which may be lost by accidents of the seas, or of war; and also the necessary recruits and reparation for the land forces.

16. The succours above stipulated shall be considered as the least that either of the two monarchs shall be at liberty to furnish to the other: but as it is their intention that a war declared against either, shall be regarded as personal by the other; they agree, that when they happen to be both engaged in war against the same enemy, or enemies, they will wage it jointly with their whole forces; and that in such cases they will enter into a particular convention suitable to circumstances, and settle as well the respective and reciprocal efforts to be made, as their political and military plans of operations, which shall be executed by common consent, and with perfect agreement.

17, 18. The two powers reciprocally and formally engage, not to listen to, nor to make, any proposals of peace to their common enemies, but by mutual consent; and, in time of peace, as well as in time of war, to consider the interests of the allied crown as their own; to compensate their respective losses and advantages, and to act as if the two monarchs formed only one and the same power.

19, 20. The king of Spain contracts for the king of the Two Sicilies, the engagements of this treaty; and promises to cause it to be ratified by that prince; provided that the proportion of the succours to be furnished by his sicilian majesty, shall be settled in proportion to his power. The three monarchs engage to support, on all occasions, the dignity and rights of their house, and those of all the princes descended from it.

21, 22. No other power but those of the august house of Bourcon shall be invited or admitted to accede to the present treaty. Their respective subjects and dominions shall participate in the connection and advantages settled between the sovereigns, and
shall

Bristol had quitted Madrid on the 17th of december. The spanish declaration of war against Great-Britain was published on the 18th of january 1762, at Madrid; in consequence of this new war, one also took place between Spain and the king of Portugal.*

On shall not do, or undertake, any thing contrary to the good understanding subsisting between them.

23. The Droit d'Aubane shall be abolished in favour of the subjects of their catholic and sicilian majesties, who shall enjoy in France the same privileges as the natives. The french shall likewise be treated in Spain and the Two Sicilies, as the natural born subjects of these two monarchs.

24. The subjects of the three sovereigns shall enjoy, in their respective dominions in Europe, the same privileges and exemptions as the natives.

25. Notice shall be given to the powers, with whom the three contracting monarchs have already concluded, or shall hereafter conclude, treaties of commerce, that the treatment of the french in Spain and the Two Sicilies, of the spaniards in France and the Two Sicilies, of the sicilians in France and Spain, shall not be cited nor serve as a precedent; it being the intention of their most christian, catholic, and sicilian majesties, that no other nation shall participate in the advantages of their respective subjects.

26. The contracting parties shall reciprocally disclose to each other their alliances and negociations, especially when they have reference to their common interests; and their ministers at all the courts of Europe shall live in the greatest harmony and mutual confidence,

27. This article contains only a stipulation concerning the ceremonial to be observed between the ministers of France and Spain, with regard to precedency at foreign courts.

28. This contains a promise to ratify the treaty.

* At this time another great event took place; on the fifth of january, her imperial majesty of all the russias died at Petersbourg, which occasioned a remarkable alteration in the affairs of Europe, and was attended with very serious consequences. By her death the king of Prussia, who, at this time, was reduced almost to the last distress, was delivered from a formidable and determined enemy. For Peter the third, her successor, adopted not only a different but an opposite system. As soon as the new czar was proclaimed at Petersburg, he sent orders to the russian generals in Germany,

On the declaration of war against Spain, all Europe was in agitation; the dutch began to be alarmed, expecting succours would be demanded of them from more quarters than one. France found it necessary to exert all her force; whilst Spain marched troops to her frontiers, and collected seamen and shipping every where, at whatever pains and whatever price.

Germany, to engage in no new enterprize against the king of Prussia, untill further orders. He also sent an extraordinary courier, with a very satisfactory letter, to that monarch, to inform him of the death of the empress, and of his own accession to the throne; in consequence of which, his prussian majesty immediately dispatched two ambassadors extraordinary to congratulate him on that event.

CHAP.

CHAP. XXXIV.

Martinico taken by rear-admiral Rodney and major-general Monckton. The island of St. Lucia surrenders to capt. Harvey, at discretion. Surrender of the island of Grenada, together with the Grenadillas and their dependencies, to brigadier-general Walsh, and commodore Swanton. Island of St. Vincent taken by Walsh. An english frigate attacks four french ships, under a fort in Tiberone-bay; burnt one, sunk another, and took the other two. The french take Newfoundland; retaken by the English. A descent upon the banks of the river Orne, in Lower Normandy. Brave action of captain Read.

REAR-admiral Rodney arrived at Barbadoes on the 22d of November 1761, having parted company with the squadron under his command, in a hard gale of wind, a few days after he had left the british channel; the other ships of his squadron followed him soon after. But the Temeraire and the Actæon, with the troops from Belleisle, did not arrive till the 14th of december. Ten days after, major-general Monckton also arrived there, with the forces from North-America. A few days having been spent in watering the ships and refreshing the men, and in making other necessary dispositions, the fleet with the troops on board set sail, and arrived off Martinico, the place of their destination, on the 7th of january 1762, and the next day anchored in St. Ann's bay, the ships under Sir James Douglas having silenced the forts of that coast. But, in doing this, the Raisonable, a 64 gun ship, formerly taken from the french, was lost as she was leading in for one of the enemy's enemy's batteries, through the pilot's ignorance of a little reef of rocks which took her up; but the crew and stores were saved.

The fleet and army having, by this motion, got possession of an excellent harbour, and secured a landing on the weathermost part of the island, that might be made tenable at any time, and thereby greatly alarmed the enemy; the admiral, at general Monckton's request, dispatched commodore Swanton, with a squadron of ships and two brigades, to the bay of Petite Ance, in order to take post there. Captain Hervey, of the Dragon, having silenced the battery of the grand Ance, landed his marines and seamen, who attacked it also from the shore, and took possession of the fort. The two brigades, under the command of brigadiers Haviland and Grant, marched to the ground opposite to the island; but finding the wood impassable for cannon, which were necessary for the reduction of that island, the general judged it best to proceed, having first reconnoitered the shore, and landed near the Cafe de Navires, which was effected on the 16th, without any molestation, the ships of war having silenced the batteries. With the above command were the light infantry, under lieutenant Scot, who were advanced the night the command remained there, and were attacked in the night by three companies of grenadiers, some free-booters, negroes, and mulattoes, which the enemy had passed over from Port Royal; but they were so warmly received, that they retreated precipitately, leaving some dead; and a serjeant and three of their grenadiers taken prisoners, without any loss on our side.

On the 14th the admiral followed with the whole fleet and army, after destroying the enemy's batteries at St. Ann's bay; when, the admiral having reconnoitered the port along with the general, they came to a resolution to make an attempt between point
Negroe

Negroe and the Cas de Pilotte, which the admiral ordered to be attacked on the 16th, and, very successfully and with very little loss, silenced the batteries. General Monckton then landed with the greatest part of his forces by sun-set, and the whole army got on shore a little before day-light the next morning, with such necessaries as they were most immediately in want of. The admiral also landed two battalions of marines, consisting of four hundred and fifty men each. The boats used in landing the forces, were commanded in the center by commodore Swanton, captain Shuldham on the right wing, and captain Hervey on the left.

General Monckton intending to attack the enemy in the strong posts they occupied on the opposite heights, and the Morne Tartenson leading to fort Royal, got the necessary batteries ready to assist them in passing a very deep and wide ravine, or gully, which separated the enemy from them. The disposition for the attack being made, on the 24th of january, at break of day, the troops advanced, under a brisk fire of their own batteries. The grenadiers, under brigadier Grant, first falling in with the enemy's advanced posts, began the attack. Brigadier Rufane on the right, with his brigade and the marines, was to advance and attack the redoubts along the coast; a thousand seamen, in the flat-bottomed boats, rowing up as he advanced. Lord Rollo's brigade supported the grenadiers; as did brigadier Walsh, with his brigade, the light infantry, under lieutenant-colonel Scott, to attack the left of the plantation, and to endeavour to get round the enemy.

The light infantry succeeded in their attempt, and, while the grenadiers were driving the enemy from post to post, they got upon the left of the enemy; which helped to complete the event of the day. The enemy's works were now successfully attacked with
the

the most irresistable impetuosity, so that by nine o'clock an entire possession of all their works was obtained, and the strong ground of Morne Tartenson, consisting of many redoubts mounted with cannon, and advantageously situated, to assist the natural great strength of the country. The enemy retired, in the greatest confusion, to the town of Fort Royal and to Morne Garnier. This is a higher hill than the Morne Tartenson, and separated from it by a deep ravine, covered with a very thick brush, and a rivulet at the bottom. From this hill they thought they were never to be dislodged, on account of its natural strength, and the works and batteries it had on it. But the spirit of the grenadiers in this attack was such, that some of them even pursued the enemy to the bridge of the town, and brought off prisoners from thence. Whilst this was doing on this side, brigadier Haviland, with his brigade, two battalions of highlanders, and a corps of light infantry, formed from the several regiments commanded by major Leland, were ordered by the general to cross the ravine a good deal to the left, as the passage was reported to be practicable, and then to attack a body of the enemy, posted on several heights opposite to them, and to endeavour to get on their left, and by that means divide their force.

Though they began their march at two o'clock in the morning, the access was so difficult that it was late before they effected it. As soon as the general perceived that the enemy were giving way on all sides, he ordered lieutenan-colonel Scott's light infantry, Walsh's brigade, and a division of the grenadiers, to a plantation more to the left, where brigadier Haviland was to have come down. They drove off some of the enemy posted there, and the light infantry possessed themselves of a very advantageous post, opposite to Morne Garnier. To support them, general Monckton ordered Haviland's corps, which had now passed, to their right; Grant's division of grenadiers, and Walsh's brigade, kept possession of this upper plantation, and communicated with Haviland's corps. The marines which the general had taken from brigadier Rufane, he posted to cover the road between the two plantations. On the 25th, in the morning, they began to erect batteries on Morne Tartenson, against the citadel of Fort Royal; but were much annoyed, on that and the following day, by the enemy from Morne Garnier. Finding that it was absolutely necessary to attack this place to the left, where the corps of light infantry and brigadier Haviland's brigade were posted, the general determined immediately to erect batteries against those of the enemy which annoyed us, and which might also cover our passage of the ravine.

The enemy, on the 27th, about four o'clock in the evening, under cover of their batteries, with the greatest part of their force, had the temerity to attack the two corps of light infantry, and Haviland's brigade, in the posts they occupied. But were received with such steadiness, that they were immediately repulsed; and such was the ardour of the troops, that they passed the ravine with the enemy, seized their batteries, and took post there; being reinforced by Walsh's brigade, and the division of grenadiers under brigadier Grant, who immediately on the attack had marched to support them. Night was now come on; but major Leland moving on the left, with his light infantry, and finding no opposition, continued his rout towards the enemy's redoubt, which he soon came up to and took possession of, the enemy having abandoned it; except a few grenadiers, who were made prisoners. Their troops retired into the town and citadel, and the militia dispersed in the country. The brigadiers Walsh, Grant, and Haviland, immediately moved up to support the light infantry; so that at nine o'clock at night the british troops were in

possession

possession of this very strong post; which entirely commanded the citadel. The enemy made so precipitate a flight, that they left a mortar loaded, and eight or nine guns unspiked, with a quantity of ammunition and provisions. The cannon and mortar we made use of against the citadel the next morning. This advantageous post, from which the enemy had so greatly annoyed us, being thus gained, and two batteries on Morne Tartenson, of 14 guns and three mortars, completed, they were opened on the thirtieth.

But finding that the distance was too great, and having now possession of Morne Capuchin, not four hundred yards distant from the fort, as well as possession of the town, the general immediately resolved to erect batteries at both these places, the sooner to reduce the citadel; and, for the easier conveyance of our cannon by water, ordered major Leland, with his light infantry, to take post on the river Monsieur. The enemy perceiving our designs, and for reasons best known to themselves, on the evening of the 3d of february, beat the chamade; in consequence of which, the gate of the city was delivered up to his majesty's troops the evening of the 4th, and at nine next morning the garrison marched out, the terms of capitulation being settled. It consisted of about 300 men, grenadiers, marines, militia, and free-booters. About one hundred and fifty of the garrison were killed and wounded during the siege. The regulars were put on board the fleet, to be sent to France; the other forces were made prisoners of war, till the reduction of the island.

These several attacks cost the French 1000 men, in killed, wounded, and prisoners. The loss of the british troops amounted to no more than 96 killed, including seven officers; 389 wounded, including 32 officers and eleven private men missing. Four, rank and file, died afterwards of their wounds. The gallant last seamen made no difficulty in carrying mortars, and the heaviest ship's cannon up steep mountains, and even a-cross the french line of fire. On the 7th of february, Pidgeon Island, one of the defences of the harbour, surrendered, and nine quarters of the island capitulated, on terms advantageous to the inhabitants, and honourable to the conquerors. Fourteen stout privateers were taken in Fort-Royal bay, and many more in the different ports of the island, were to be delivered up by virtue of the capitulation. The artillery and stores, taken in this conquest, were considerable. The grenadiers in three divisions, headed by the lieutenant-colonels Fletcher, Massey, and Vaughan, together with the light infantry and rangers, under the command of lieutenant-colonel Scott, major Leland, and captain Kennedy, had the greatest share in the course of this successful and important affair. Indeed all the troops, of which this brave army was composed, exerted the same noble spirit, which the several corps of it had so providentially displayed in the reduction of Louisbourg, Crown-Point, Quebec, Montreal, Guadaloupe, and Belleisle.

Though the reduction of Fort-Royal was immediately followed by the submission of much the greatest part of the island, yet St. Pierre * or St. Peter, as we call it, and the territory adjoining, still held out. M. Le Vassor de la Touche, the governor-general, with the greatest part of his forces, retired thither, and gave out that he was determined either to die sword in hand, like the brave Montcalm before Quebec, or preserve the place. But the inhabitants soon after forced the governor to surrender the place. Accordingly, he sent his brother and others to Fort-Royal to offer terms of capitulation for the whole island, on the 12th of february, just as general

* Situated, in what the natives call the Basse-Terre, about 20 miles by land from Fort-Royal.

Monckton,

Monckton was going to embark in order to reduce that place. The general and admiral Rodney returned their answer to the proposals, which were carried back to St. Pierre, and on the 14th the two deputies returned with the capitulation, formed and signed on the 13th and 14th. In consequence of which, general Monckton left Fort-Royal the 15th, with the grenadiers of the army, and the second brigade; and on the following day took possession of this large and opulent town, with all the ports in the neighbourhood.

Thus the defection of the inhabitants, by compelling the surrender of the fort, happily saved the town from destruction. Three hundred and twenty grenadiers marched out with the honours of war, to be embarked immediately for France. M. La Touche, governor-general, Monsieur Rouillé, lieutenant-governor; and the officers of the staff, were to follow them soon after. In the forts Royal and St. Pierre, the redoubts and the batteries, there were found 435 pieces of serviceable cannon of different sizes and 1463 barrels of gunpowder, including filled cartridges for cannon, together with a proportionable quantity of all other stores, ammunition, and implements of war.

Commodore Swanton being at this time off the island of Granada, with a squadron of men of war, general Monckton immediately sent brigadier-general Walsh, with the 5th brigade, and the corps of light-infantry, under lieutenant-colonel Scott, to assist in the reduction of that and the other islands.

Soon after the reduction of Martinico, the island of St. Lucia surrendered at discretion to captain Hervey.

General Walsh arrived off the island of Granada on the 3d of march with the troops under his command, when, according to his orders, and in conjunction with commodore Swanton, he sent lieutenant-colonel Scott the same day on shore, to summon the governor, with the troops and inhabitants, to surrender, and accept the favourable terms offered to them

from

from general Monckton. The commodore had, before Walsh's arrival, summoned them, but they then refused to submit; but the inhabitants now thought proper to take the benefit of the capitulation, and accordingly signed it on the 4th. They abandoned a very strong and advantageous post, commanding the fort, which the governor, with the regulars and free-booters, had determined to defend. The next day the general landed at day-break with the grenadiers, light infantry, and 27th regiment, and got possession of a favourable post. The governor finding himself abandoned by the inhabitants, and the communication with the country, and every supply cut off, submitted, without firing a gun, to the terms granted to Martinico. Thus we became masters of the island of Granada, together with the Grenadillas and their dependencies; and this conquest was made without the loss of a man; though the fort, and the intrenched hills above it, might have been more obstinately defended. Brigadier Walsh afterwards took possession of the island of St. Vincent.

The Hussar frigate, on the 3d and 4th of april, attacked four ships in Tiberon Bay; one of them of 16 guns was burnt, another of 14 sunk, the third of 16, and the fourth of 12 guns, laden with flour and indigo, were cut out, and carried into Jamaica; but the french crews got on shore in their boats during the engagement. The enemy had seventeen killed, and thirty-five wounded; the Hussar had only one man killed and thirty-five wounded. But unhappily the Hussar, captain Casket, in may following, being on a cruize off Hispaniola, struck upon the shore, and was lost. Three men were drowned; but the captain and the rest of the crew were taken prisoners.

The french, greatly concerned at the loss of Newfoundland, and determined to recover it, sent the chevalier de Ternay, from Brest, with the Robuste of 74, L'Eveille of 64, La Garonne of 44, the Licorne of 30, and a bomb-ketch, to retake that place. His squadron left Brest on the 8th of may, and three days after met with the East-India, West-India, and North-American fleets, under convoy of the Superbe of 74 guns, the Gosport of 44, and the Danae of 38. But the french, notwithstanding the superiority of their force, declined an engagement, in order to preserve their full strength for the expedition against Newfoundland. They came in sight of that island on the 20th of june, and on the 24th, landed a body of troops, under the count de Hauffonville, in the bay of Bulls, seven leagues distant from St. John's. After possessing themselves of a small settlement in that bay, the count, at the head of these troops, marched straight to the town, and presented himself before the fort. The governor was three times summoned to surrender; but would hearken to no proposals, and fired on the french troops. The count de Hauffonville putting himself at the head of the grenadiers, and disposing his troops for an assault, the garrison and inhabitants capitulated, on the 27th, to be prisoners during the war, unless sooner exchanged, and to be secure in their persons and properties. The rest of the island, particularly Placentia, the capital of it, was afterwards reduced. After the surrender of the fort of St. John, the enemy's ships entered the harbour, having broken the chain that defended the entrance. They found in it the Countess of Grammont frigate, formerly a privateer of Bayonne, which the crew had run on shore, but which was got off. They took besides a great number of other vessels which the french admiral made use of to burn, in the north and south harbours, all the vessels, scaffolds, and other works, employed in the fishery, and then fortified himself at St. John's.

The loss of this place occasioned great uneasiness here, and the public were highly displeased that so insufficient a force had been left to secure it after our having taken it. However, they did not long remain in the possession of it; for lieutenant-colonel Amherst, under the orders of Jeffery Amherst, sailed on the 18th of september, with the transports from New-York, and got into the harbour of Hallifax, on the 26th of august, after the fleet under lord Colville had left it. Not having a sufficient number of transports with him, he took up shipping to the amount of 400 tons, reached Louisburg the 5th of september, and sailed out of that harbour, with his whole embarkation, on the 7th. He joined lord Colville on the 11th, a few leagues to the southward of St. John's. He landed his troops, on the 13th, at Torbay, about three leagues to the northward of St. John's; a party of the enemy fired some shots at the boats as they rowed. The light infantry of the regulars landed first, gave the enemy one fire, and drove them towards St. John; the battalions landed, and our forces marched. The path for four miles was very narrow, through a thick wood, and over very bad ground. Captain O'Donnell's light infantry came up with some of the party that had been drove from the landing place. They had concealed themselves in a wood, from whence they fired, and killed three of our men; but O'Donnell's corps rushed in upon them, took three prisoners, and drove the rest off.

The country opened afterwards, and the army marched to the left of Kitty Vitty. As soon as the right of the army was close to this place, the enemy fired from a hill on the opposite side. Colonel Amherst sent a party up a rock, which commanded the passage over, and, under cover of their fire, which drove the enemy up to the hill, and pursued them on that side towards St. John's; when the colonel perceiving a body of the enemy coming to their support, ordered over the remainder of the first battalion,

talion, upon which the enemy retreated, and the english forces had just time to take post before dark. Ten prisoners were taken. The troops lay this night on their arms. The next morning, the 14th, the channel was opened, where the enemy had sunk the shallops. On the 15th the enemy were dislodged, with great resolution, by captain O'Donnell, from a steep and difficult hill in the front of colonel Amherst's advanced posts. Lieutenant Schuyler was killed, and the captain himself wounded in this gallant action. In the night the french fleet under M. de Ternay, though equal in number to the british squadron, and superior in guns and men, made their escape by a shameful flight, after having been blocked up by lord Colville in the harbour of St. John for three weeks. They afterwards got safe to Corunna. Colonel Amherst, on the 16th, acquainted the count d'Haussonville by letter, that in case he executed his intended design of blowing up the fort when he quitted it, every man of the garrison should then be put to the sword. On the night of the 17th a mortar battery was opened against the fort; and the next day it capitulated, before any other batteries had begun to play.* M. de Ternay, flying in the utmost

---

* The letters which passed on this occasion, between colonel Amherst, and the count d'Haussonville, and the articles of capitulation, were as follows:

Camp before St. John's, sept. 16, 1762.

Sir,

"Humanity directs me to acquaint you of my firm intentions.

"I know the miserable state your garrison is left in, and am fully informed of your design of blowing up the fort on quitting it; but have a care; for I have taken measures effectually to cut off your retreat: and so sure as a match is put to the train, every man of the garrison shall be put to the sword.

"I must have immediate possession of the fort, in the state it now is, or expect the consequences.

I give

most confusion, left his anchors and the grenadiers of the army behind him. The garrison amounted to 689 men, staff and other officers included.

The

"I give you half an hour to think of it. I have the honour to be, sir, your most obedient humble servant,

To the officer commanding at St. John's.   WM. AMHERST."

Letter from the count d'Hauſſonville to lieutenant-colonel Amherſt; dated at St. John's, ſept. 16, 1762.

' " With regard to the conduct that I ſhall hold, you may, ſir, be miſinformed. I wait for your troops and your cannon; and nothing ſhall determine me to ſurrender the fort, unleſs you ſhall have totally deſtroyed it, and that I ſhall have no more powder to fire. I have the honour to be, ſir, your moſt humble, and moſt obedient ſervant,

The count D'HAUSSONVILLE."

Count d'Hauſſonville to lieutenant-colonel Amherſt.

SIR,

" Under the uncertainty of the ſuccours which I may receive either from France or its allies, and the fort being entire, and in a condition for a long defence, I am reſolved to defend myſelf to the laſt extremity. The capitulation which you may think proper to grant me will determine me to ſurrender the place to you, in order to prevent the effuſion of blood of the men who defend it.

" Whatever reſolution you come to, there is one left to me, which would hurt the intereſts of the ſovereign you ſerve. I have the honour to be, your moſt obedient humble ſervant,

Fort St. John, ſept. 18, 1762.   Count D'HAUSSONVILLE."

Camp before St. John's, ſept. 18, 1762.

SIR,

" I have juſt had the honour of your letter. His britannic majeſty's fleet and army co-operating here, will not give any other terms to the garriſon of St. John's than their ſurrendering priſoners of war.

" I don't

The total number of french prisoners made on this occasion were near 800; a very fine body of men,

"I don't thirst after the blood of the garrison; but you must determine quickly, or expect the consequences; for this is my final determination. I am, Sir, your most obedient humble servant,

To count d'Hauſſonville. Wm. Amherst."

Letter from count d'Hauſſonville, to colonel Amherst; dated at St. John's, september 18, 1762.

"I have received, Sir, your letter, which you did me the honour to write to me.

"I am as averse as you to the effusion of blood. I consent to surrender the fort in a good condition, as I have already acquainted you, if the demands, which I enclose herewith, are granted to my troops. I have the honour to be, Sir, your most humble and most obedient servant,

Le compte d'Haussonville."

ARTICLES of CAPITULATION.

Demands of the garrison of St. John, and, in general, of the troops that are in it.

The french troops shall surrender prisoners of war.————— Agreed to.

The officers and subalterns shall keep their arms, to preserve good order among their troops.————Agreed to.

Good ships shall be granted to carry the officers, grenadiers, and private men, either wounded or not, to France, in the space of one month, on the coast of Brittany.————Agreed to. Lord Colville will, of course, embark them as soon as he possibly can.

The goods and effects of both the officers and soldiers shall be preserved————His britannick majesty's troops never pillage.

The gate will be taken possession of this afternoon, and the garrison will lay down their arms.

This is to be signed by lord Colville, but will remain at present, as afterwards, in full force.

Camp before St. John's,   Signed,
  sept. 18, 1762.   Wm. Amherst.
                               Le compte d'Haussonville.

men, and almoſt as numerous as the regulars of the britiſh army. On the part of the engliſh, one lieutenant and eleven rank and file were killed; three captains, two ſerjeants, one drummer, and thirty-two rank and file were wounded; in all fifty.

In the ſummer of this year, july 12th and 13th, five hundred marines of commodore Young's ſquadron made a deſcent upon the banks of the river Orne in Lower Normandy, with a deſign to deſtroy thirteen veſſels guarded by two battalions at the mouth of that river. They ſucceeded in nailing up the cannon of the batteries, but were obliged to re-imbark without carrying their deſign upon the veſſels into execution.

In the month of auguſt captain Read, in the King George privateer of 26 nine pounders, and only 130 men, took the Tyger frigate, captain Fabre, from St. Domingo for Bourdeaux, of 26 nine pounders and near 240 men, valued at between two and three millions of livres. The engagement laſted two hours and a half; the King George had only three men killed, and thirty-two wounded; but the Tyger had about 80 men killed and wounded. The beginning of the next month, ſept. 2, captain Lebras in the Lion, took the Zephyr frigate of 26 guns, which had on board 200 troops, braſs mortars and cannon, ammunition and ſtores, and was bound from Breſt for St. John's in Newfoundland. Having thus related the principal naval tranſactions of this year between us and the french; I ſhall in the next chapter proceed to the hiſtory of the war with Spain.

The grants for the ſervice of this year, 1762, were as follows:

	l.	s.	d.
For navy ſervices in general, including 70,000 ſeamen and marines	4,112,226	00	00

For

	l.	s.	d.
For hire of transports, and victualling forces in transports	835,025	00	00
Ordnance land service, including last year's extra	642,916	00	00
Towards discharging the debt of the navy	1,000,000	00	00
For 67676 land forces, including 4,008 invalids	1,629,320	00	00
For forces in plantations	873,780	00	00
Four regiments on irish establishment, now in North-America	23,284	00	00
For augmentation of 9,370 men	163,711	00	00
General and staff-officers in Germany	72,896	00	00
Embodied militia and scotch highlanders	443,952	00	00
Cloathing of embodied militia	60,706	00	00
Cloathing and paying of unembodied militia	20,000	00	00
Half-pay of land officers	34,383	00	00
Superannuated and reduced horse-guards	2,952	00	00
For 39,773 men from Hanover, Wolfembuttle, Saxe-Gotha, Buckelbug, and employed in Germany	465,638	00	00
Five battalions serving in Germany	25,504	00	00
For hire of 1,464 horse, 2,330 foot from Brunswick	68,008	00	00
For hire of 2,120 horse, and 9,900 foot, from the landgrave of Hesse Cassel, with artillery, &c.	268,360	00	00

For

	l.	s.	d.
For hire of 1,576 horse, and 8,800 foot, additional troops from Hesse-Cassel	147,071	00	00
Towards assisting his majesty to grant reasonable succours in money to the landgrave of Hesse-Cassel	50,000	00	00
Extraordinaries of the land forces to nov. 1761, over and above one million granted by parliament	1,353,662	00	00
Forage, bread, and extraordinaries of the combined army in Germany under prince Ferdinand	1,000,000	00	00
Extraordinaries there from nov. 24, 1761, to dec. 24, following	958,384	00	00
For extraordinaries of the war in 1762, and to assist the king of Portugal	1,000,000	00	00
For compensation to certain provinces in North-America, for levy, cloathing, and pay of troops raised there	133,333	00	00
To the East-India company in lieu of a regiment	20,000	00	00
For Anamaboo and other forts in Africa	13,000	00	00

The above grants, with others, for officers widows, pensioners, the chapel at Gosport, hospital at Plymouth, and for other exigencies of government, amounted, in the whole, to sixteen million seven hundred ninety-four thousand one hundred fifty-three pounds eighteen shillings and eleven pence halfpenny.

CHAP.

CHAP. XXXV.

Spanish ships taken. Spain declares war against Great-Britain. Memorials between the courts of Spain, France, and Portugal. The declaration of war by Portugal against Spain and France; of Spain and France against the former. Foundation of the Spanish claim to Portugal. Progress of the war between Spain and Portugal. The former take Miranda, Braganza, Torre de Moncorvo, and Chaves. Valença taken by brigadier-general Burgoine. Success of the Spaniards; their encampment near Villa Velha, forced and taken by general Burgoine. The Spaniards retire, and afterwards entirely withdraw their troops, on the signing the preliminaries for a peace.

WITH the commencement of the new year we found ourselves engaged in a new war;[*] but which happily proved both successful and short. But could our two united enemies have acted as powerfully as they boasted, our fate had been very bad indeed, and both England and Ireland would soon have become the seats of war, and made to feel the horrors of it; for great armaments and powerful invasions were mightily talked of. But the same good providence still prospered the bravery of our men, and fresh enemies but gave us new opportunities to shew that we still could conquer.

The declaration of war by Spain against Great-Britain, was published at Madrid on the 18th of January, sixteen days after that of our court. This

---

[*] On the 2d of january, 1762, his majesty king George in council signed a declaration of war against Spain.

rupture between Great-Britain and Spain was a very interesting and important event to Portugal, who soon saw she must take part with one of these powers. She accordingly soon found herself strongly solicited, both by Spain and France, to declare war against England.

The spanish ambassador and the minister plenipotentiary of France presented a joint memorial to his most faithful majesty, dated at Lisbon the 16th of march, 1762. In which they represented, "that the two sovereigns of France and Spain being obliged to support a war against the English, found it proper and necessary to take indispensable measures to curb the pride of the english nation; that the first measure they had agreed on, was to have the most faithful king in their offensive and defensive treaty, and to desire him to join their majesties forthwith: that they expected, the most faithful king would acquiesce therein, since his subjects feel, much more than other nations, the yoke which Great-Britain lays, and which she means to extend, over all those, who have possessions beyond sea: that they desired the most faithful king to declare himself united with them in the present war against the english, to break off all correspondence and commerce with them as the common enemy of all three, and even of all maritime nations; to send away all their men of war and merchant ships; and to join to the forces of France and Spain, those which the most High has put in his hands." His catholic majesty makes this reflection to the most faithful king; that he is the brother of the queen his wife, a true friend, a moderate and quiet neighbour, who has made this proposal to him; considering the interests of the most faithful king as his own. "How much more glorious and useful will it be, (continues the memorial) for the most faithful king to have for his ally a catholic king, his near relation, his neighbour in Europe and America, to assist each other

mutu-

mutually and with ease, than the english nation, incapable, by their haughtiness, of considering other sovereigns with equality, and always desirous to make them feel the influence of their power? and what occasion can the most faithful king have for the assistance of England, when, by an offensive and defensive league, he shall be united with Spain and France? These considerations are so strong, that the catholic king thinks, there can be no doubt, but that the most faithful king will yield to them, without stopping a moment; so much the more, as his catholic majesty has caused troops to march to the frontiers of Portugal, so that, in a few days, they may garrison the principal ports of the kingdom, to prevent the danger which the maritime places of Portugal might run, when the part taken by his most faithful majesty should come to the knowledge of the english."

This memorial was signed on the part of Spain by Don Joseph Torrero, and on that of France by Jacques Bernard O Dun.

The two ministers added to the memorial, that they were ordered by their courts to demand a categorical answer in four days, and that every day beyond that term would be considered as a negative.

This memorial was answered on the part of his most faithful majesty, by don Lewis de Cunbra, secretary of state to his majesty of Portugal, in a memorial signed at the palace on the 20th of march following.

In which, having briefly recapitulated the substance of the foregoing memorial, it is said, " That his most faithful majesty, having taken the contents of the aforesaid memorial into consideration, in the precise time of four days, has ordered his secretary of state to represent, that his most faithful majesty is sensibly affected at seeing the flames of war kindled between the powers with whom he is closely connected by ties of blood,

blood, of friendship, and of solemn treaty, such as Spain, France, and Great-Britain."

His majesty then wishes to mediate between them a renewal of the conferences broke off at London. And then adds, " that the court of Portugal having ancient and uninterrupted alliances with the British court, for many years past, by solemn and public treaties, purely defensive, and, as such, innocent; and not having received offence on the part of Great-Britain, his faithful majesty could not enter into an offensive league against that court, without being wanting to the public faith, religion, fidelity, and decorum; besides, that loving his subjects as a father, and being obliged to attend to their preservation as a king, he would be wanting both to one and the other, if he should oblige them to endure the calamities of an offensive war, which they are not in a condition to support, after the misfortunes which have happened in Portugal, by the long sickness of the late king, by the earthquake in 1755, and by the horrible conspiracy of 1758."

" That his majesty, upon these principles, has given orders to repair his ports and maritime places, and to equip a sufficient number of ships of war to protect them; caused his troops to be held ready to prevent, in the said ports and maritime places, those accidents which might happen there; and all for the common advantage of the powers of war, without distinction of any. That his most faithful majesty, since the accession of his catholic majesty to the throne of Spain, has always given him the most distinguished marks of a brother who loves him, of a brother-in-law who esteems him, of a sincere friend, and of a neighbour, who has forgot nothing to cultivate an intimate correspondence with him, even so far as to stipulate, by the last treaty of the 12th of February of the preceeding year, even when the acquisitions of the king were in question, " That he preferred, to

every

every other interest, that of removing the smallest occasion that might become an obstacle to, or alter, not only the good correspondence due to his friendship, and to the strict ties of blood, but that might prevent an intimate union between their respective subjects."

"The king hopes, that the moment his catholic majesty shall have reflected upon all these marks of love, he will see on the one hand, that these reasons alone, which exceed the limits of the king's power, hinder him from entering into the league proposed to him; and that it is impossible for any thing to be done in the ports of this kingdom, contrary to the interests of his catholic majesty, and to the firm neutrality which this court considers as a necessary principle of her system."

Another memorial, dated the 1st of April, from Spain and France, by the same ambassador of Spain and minister of France, was delivered to the portuguese secretary; in which it was represented, "That if there should be a new negociation, their catholic and christian majesties would accept the mediation of his most most faithful majesty, out of regard to his sacred majesty; but the partiality which his ministry has shewn for the english, would make his most christian majesty fear, with reason, that the mediation of his most faithful majesty would not be favourable to him. That their catholic and most christian majesties believe, and their enemies also know, and take advantage of, his most faithful majesty's aversion to war. That the defensive alliances with the court of London are not an obstacle, because no alliance is obligatory, when the question is to shake off a yoke; the project, already far advanced, of England on Portugal. That Portugal had received an offence from England, by that power's having attacked a french squadron in one of the ports of Portugal; an insult sufficient to give right to a declaration

claration of war against his britannic majesty. That these alliances are not so innocent, though called purely defensive, because they become in reality offensive, since the convenience of the portuguese ports enable the english squadrons to cruize on the principal coasts for cutting off the french and spanish navigation, which they otherwise could not do at all seasons. That these islanders would insult all the maritime powers of Europe; they would let others enjoy their possessions and their commerce, if all the riches of Portugal did not pass into their hands. Consequently, Portugal furnishes them with the means to make war; and their alliance with the said court is offensive. The said alliances were made in the beginning of this century, when there were animosities and oppositions, occasioned by the preceding possession of Spain, and for as long as they might last. These animosities, however, are now ended, and two brothers possessors of Spain and Portugal; necessity might then have authorized the king of Portugal to adopt an alliance contrary to his true system, and to his decorum. Now he ought to be glad of the necessity, which others lay upon him, to make use of his reason, in order to take the road of his glory and common interest. That their majesties might, however, complain of the preference given to England, to send succours to Portugal, for the object of these same precautions; to keep at Lisbon an english general, several aids de camp, and other officers; since it is not possible but that they will concert military projects, according to the solicitations of the Portuguese minister at London, which are public, and which the english themselves do not conceal. But as his most faithful majesty is still in time to embrace the most just party, the two monarchs of France and Spain flatter themselves, that the preparations of the king of Portugal may acquire an ally; being well assured that they will give him but little umbrage, and, on the contrary, that they

will

will produce much advantage to him. Finally, the ambaffador of Spain, and the minifter plenipotentiary of France, repeat what they have already fet forth in the memorial of the 16th of march. They infift on the demand therein contained, and they declare to the moft faithful king, that, without further reprefentations, or his confent, the Spanifh troops, already on the frontiers, will enter Portugal, for the fingle object of advancing, till they fhall obtain that the ports of Portugal be not at the difpofal of the enemy, having, at the fame time, the moft precife orders not to commit, without reafon, the leaft hoftility againft the fubjects of the moft faithful king. It remains for his moft fathful majefty to choofe, either to receive thefe troops as allies, or to refufe them entrance, or fubfiftence, and to oppofe them as enemies. For then the two allies will take all poffible precautions, on thefe fufpicions, already too much founded, that the court of Lifbon, by intelligence for fome time paft with that of London, will march out to meet them, with Englifh forces, in order to hinder their juft defigns, and to make them bloody, contrary to the fentiments of their hearts.

Lifbon, the 1ft of april, 1762.

Signed,
Don Joseph Torrero,
Don Jaques O'Dun."

This memorial, which breathed rather the fpirit of a declaration of war than the remonftrances of friends, was very fmartly anfwered on the part of Portugal, by Don Lewis, fecretary of ftate to his moft faithful majefty, in a memorial dated the 5th of april, 1762; which fets forth,

"That his faithful majefty, notwithftanding a declaration fo furprifing and unexpected, perfifts in the fentiments which he has always at heart, of complying with the wifhes of their catholic and moft
chri-

christian majesties; nevertheless, he cannot persuade himself that it is in his power to break the defensive treaties which he has with Great-Britain, without that court's having given him motives so strong as to oblige him to undertake a war. That he can no more persuade himself that the said treaties are offensive, as is insinuated in this last memorial, on account of the commerce which Portugal allows to the English subjects; it being generally known to all the world, that these sort of treaties consist of engagements between the powers, to enable them the better to defend and maintain themselves, by the succours which one receives from the other, either in troops or money, or in something else which may be of advantage to them; and this is the case of the treaties of league and commerce between Portugal and Great-Britain, and is what the law of God, of nature, and of nations, and the universal practice of all nations, have always deemed innocent.

"That the unbounded confidence which his most faithful majesty has always had in the ties of blood, the friendship, and the good neighbourhood which he has always cultivated with his catholic majesty, cannot be better proved than by the silence and tranquillity with which the king has seen, for a long time past, his frontiers almost blocked up and infested, the commerce of corn prohibited, the spanish magazines upon the said frontiers filled with all sorts of military stores, and the places swarming with troops, without his most faithful majesty's having given the least order to his ambassador at Madrid, to know the object of these preparations.

"That, after having acted with such sincerity, tranquillity, and good faith, at the time only when his most faithful majesty saw that it was necessary for him to listen to the clamours of his subjects, and to preserve his royal decorum from the universal censure of all Europe, which had spread even into every public news-paper. And, at the same time, that it was known to all the world, that the kingdom of Portugal was in want of experienced officers, his most faithful majesty invited over lord Tyrawley; he also took some English officers, and of other nations, to exercise his troops, as has been constantly practised in this kingdom, and as their catholic and most christian majesties, and all sovereigns in general, practise also, without there arising any suspicious distrust from such a proceeding.

That his most faithful majesty hopes, that the solidity of these reasons will make, upon the minds of their catholic and most christian majesties, an impression worthy of their religion, and of their humanity; and that they will perceive the crying injustice of pursuing, against Portugal, the war kindled against Great-Britain. And that his most faithful majesty, under these circumstances, could not recede from the neutrality which he adopts for his system, without losing, even with their catholic and most christian majesties, that good opinion which he prefers to every other opinion.

That, for these reasons, and, in the unexpected case of the spanish troops entering Portugal, under any pretence whatever, not only without his most faithful majesty's permission, but contrary to his express declaration made in the memorial of the 20th of march, and repeated by the present, making a declared and offensive war against him, by this violent and unexpected invasion. In such a case, his most faithful majesty, no longer able to avoid doing his utmost for his own defence, has commanded his forces to hold themselves in readiness, and to join with those of his allies, in support of the neutrality, which is the only and single object for which they shall be employed.

His most faithful majesty declares, finally, that it will affect him less, though reduced to the last extremity,

mity, of which the supreme judge is the sole arbiter, to let the last tile of his palace fall, and to see his faithful subjects spill the last drop of their blood, than to sacrifice, together with the honour of his crown, all that Portugal holds most dear; and to submit, by such extraordinary means, to become an unheard-of example to all pacific powers, who will no longer be able to enjoy the benefit of neutrality, whenever a war shall be kindled between other powers, with which the former are connected by defensive treaties."

On the 23d of april, the spanish ambassador, Torrero, with the french minister, O'Dun, presented a third memorial to the court of Portugal, to the following effect:

" The said ambassador and minister having lost all hope that their masters should prevail with the king of Portugal to unite his forces with theirs, and shake off his prejudicial dependance upon England, Portugal being so accustomed to this evil as not to perceive it, or the English having gained a despotic power over her understanding, since she will not admit the reasonings of France and Spain; and knowing that, though easy, it would be useless to refute the last memorial of Portugal, of the 5th of april, they make to that memorial only the following general reply.

" The king of Portugal has confessed, that England has given him cause to break the defensive treaties, by saying, that it does not outweigh the calamities of a war; but Portugal will not incur equal calamity by waging a war against England, as by waging a war against France and Spain; and yet though England has given him offence, and France and Spain have given him none, except by persuading him to regard his interest, he has chosen a war

with

with France and Spain, rather than a war with England.

"The king of Portugal cannot see, because he will not see, that his defensive treaties with England are offensive with regard to Spain and France, the preceding memorials in which they are proved to be so, being unanswerable.

"Notwithstanding the king of Portugal insists, that there is no difference between her neutrality and that of other powers, and that he cannot be justly forced out of it; yet such neutrality cannot be regarded with indifference, on account of the inconveniencies experienced by Spain in other wars with England.

"Since the king of Portugal founds his honour upon not delivering himself from the yoke of England, the kings of France and Spain found theirs on attempting it; and will maintain it with as much inflexibility as the king of Portugal resolves to do, when he declares, he will, rather than give it up, see the last stone of his palace overturned, and the last drop of blood in his dominions shed.

"Lastly, the king of Portugal having determined, rather to resist the spanish forces as enemies, than admit them as friends, it is not fit a spanish ambassador, or a french plenipotentiary, should continue longer at Lisbon, and the necessary passports are therefore required for their departure."

To this memorial, Portugal replied, in substance as follows, on the 2d day after its delivery, april 25.

"His majesty the king of Portugal finds nothing new in the preceding memorial that should cause him to alter his resolutions; nor is he surprised at the effective rupture now owned by Spain and France, in the progress of an unexampled negociation, which was opened by notifying to his majesty, that it was agreed between Spain and France, without any previous notice, to make the neutral kingdom of Portugal the theatre of war.

"The king of Portugal places his honour solely in being faithful to his word, and in fulfilling the duties of his crown, of religion and humanity, which forbid his entering into an offensive war against any power which has not given him just cause, though not allied by reciprocal treaties, which have been kept inviolable for ages past, as those with England have been.

"That no part of the memorial of the 5th of april, can, without the grossest perversion of the sense and intention of it, be tortured into a confession, that England had given cause to break the treaties; because, on the contrary, his portuguese majesty owes to England all that good harmony which is the natural effect of those ancient alliances.

"His majesty sees no other difference between his neutrality and that of other powers, than the manner in which his frontiers are beset, under no other pretence, than that it is convenient for France and Spain that Portugal should violate her treaties.

"His majesty's sole view is to defend and preserve himself in peace, which by all the laws of God, of nature, and nations, he has a right to do; and he has the same right to defend his kingdom from invasion, as every private person has to defend his house against any body that should attempt to enter it against his consent, and that he will do it with his utmost efforts, assisted by those of his allies.

"He orders the necessary passports for the spanish and french representatives to be ready when they shall send for them; and declares, that in such case, he will send expresses to recall his ambassador and plenipotentiary from Spain and France."

On the 23d of may, his portuguese majesty issued the following declaration of war against Spain:

"Whereas the ambassador of Castile, Don Joseph Torrero, in conjunction with Don Jacob O'Dun, minister plenipotentiary of France, by their representations, and the answers I have given thereto, it appears, that one of the projects agreed on between the aforesaid powers in the family pact was, to dispose of these kingdoms as if they were their own; to invade them, to occupy them, and usurp them, under the incompatible pretext of assisting me against enemies, which they supposed for such, that never existed; and whereas different general officers of his catholic majesty have successively, since the 30th of april last, spread various papers through my dominions, prescribing laws and sanctions to my subjects, invading at the same time my provinces with an army divided into various bodies, attacking my fortified places, and perpetrating all the aforesaid hostilities, under the pretence of directing them to the advantage and glory of my crown and of my subjects; and in such light even the catholic king himself has represented the case to me; and whereas, notwithstanding all these contradictory and unheard-of motives, an offensive war has been made against me, contrary to truth and justice, by the aforesaid two monarchs, through mutual consent: I have ordered it to be made known to all my subjects, that they hold all disturbers, or violaters, of the independent sovereignty of my crown, and all invaders of my kingdom, as public aggressors and declared enemies; and from henceforward, in natural defence, and necessary retortion, they be treated as aggressors and declared enemies in all and every sense; and that to oppress them in their persons and effects, all military persons, and others, authorised by me, make use of the most executive means, which, in these cases, are supported by all laws; and that, in like manner, all said military, and every other person or persons, of whatever rank, quality, or condition they be, quit all communication and correspondence with the said enemies, under the penalties decreed against rebels and traitors. I likewise order that all the subjects of France and Spain that reside in this city, or in the kingdoms of Portugal and Algarva, retire within the precise term of fifteen days, to reckon from the day of the publication of this decree, otherwise they shall be treated as enemies, and their effects confiscated; and that in all the wet as well as dry ports of this kingdom, all commerce and communication cease with the aforesaid monarchies of France and Spain, and all fruits, manufactures, or goods, of any kind, of the produce of the said monarchies, be deemed contraband, and the entry, sale, and use of them be prohibited.

"Ordered, that this decree be affixed and transmitted to every country, that it may come to the knowledge of all my subjects. I have given orders to the intendant-general of the police, to grant passports to all the aforesaid, who have entered these kingdoms, bona fide, on their business, that they be permitted to retire unmolested.—Palace of Nossa Senhora da Ajuda, 18th may, 1762.

With the rubrick of his majesty,
ANTONIO LUIZ DE CORDES."

On the 15th day of june, the king of Spain issued the following declaration of war against Portugal.

"Neither my representations, founded in justice and utility, nor the fraternal persuasives with which I accompanied them, have been able to alter the king of Portugal's blind affection for the english. His ministers, engaged by long habit, continue obstinate in their partiality, to the great prejudice of his subjects;

jects; and I have met with nothing but refusals, and been insulted by his injurious preference of the friendship of England to that of Spain and France. I have even received a personal affront, by the arresting of my ambassador, Don Joseph Torrero, at Estremos, who was detained there in violation of his character, after he had been suffered to depart from Lisbon, and had arrived on the frontier, in virtue of passports from that court; but notwithstanding such insults were powerful motives for me to keep no longer any measures with the king of Portugal, nevertheless adhering to my first resolution of not making an offensive war against the portuguese, unless forced to it, I deferred giving orders to my general to treat them with the rigours of war; but having read the edict of the king of Portugal, of the 18th of last month, in which, misrepresenting the upright intentions of the most christian king and myself, he imputes to us a pre-concerted design of invading his kingdoms, and orders all his vassals to treat us as enemies, and to break off all correspondence with us, both by sea and land; and forbids the use of all protections coming from our territories, confiscating the goods of the french and spaniards, and likewise ordering them to leave Portugal in a fortnight, which term, however strait, has been further abridged, and many of my subjects have been expelled, plundered, and illtreated, before the expiration of it; and the marquis de Sarria having found, that the portuguese, ungrateful to his goodness and moderation, and the exactness with which they have been paid for every thing they have furnished for my troops, have proceeded so far as to excite the people and soldiery against my army; so that it would be dishonourable to carry my forbearance any farther: for these causes I have resolved, that from this day my troops shall treat Portugal as an enemy's country, that the property of the portuguese shall be confiscated throughout

my

my dominions, that all the portuguese shall leave Spain in a fortnight, and that all commerce with them shall be prohibited for the future."

On the 20th day of june the french king issued his declaration of war against Portugal, as follows:

" The king and the catholic king being obliged to support a war against England, having entered into reciprocal engagements to curb the excessive ambition of that crown, and the despotism which it pretends to usurp, in every sea, and particularly in the East and West-Indies, over the trade and navigation of other powers.

" Their majesties judged that one proper step for attaining this end would be, to invite the king of Portugal to enter into their alliance. It was natural to think that the proposals, which were made to that prince on this subject, in the name of his majesty and of his catholic majesty, would be readily accepted. This opinion was founded on the consideration of what the most faithful king owed to himself and to his people, who, from the beginning of the present century, groaned under the imperious yoke of the english. Besides, the event hath but too clearly shewn the necessity of the just measures taken by France and Spain with regard to a suspicious and dangerous neutrality, that had all the inconveniencies of a concealed war.

" The memorials presented to the court of Lisbon on this subject have been made public: all Europe hath seen the solid reasons of justice and conveniency which were the foundation of their demand on the king of Portugal: to these were added, on the part of Spain, motives of the most tender friendship and assiduity, which ought to have made the strongest and most salutary impression on the mind of the most faithful king.

But

" But thefe powerful and juft confiderations were fo far from determining that prince to unite with his majefty and his catholic majefty, that he abfolutely rejected their offers, and chofe to facrifice their alliance, his own glory, and the good of his people, to his unlimited and blind devotion to the will of England.

"Such conduct leaving no doubt concerning the king of Portugal's true intentions, the king and the catholic king could confider him, from that time, only as a direct and perfonal enemy, who, under the artful pretext of a neutrality which would not be obferved, would deliver up his ports to the difpofal of the englifh, to ferve for fheltering places for their fhips, and to enable them to hurt France and Spain with more fecurity, and with more effect.

" Neverthelefs, his majefty and his catholic majefty thought it their duty to keep meafures with the moft faithful king; and if the fpanifh troops have entered Portugal, this invafion, which was become indifpenfably neceffary, was not accompanied with any declaration of war; and the troops have behaved with all the circumfpection that could be required even in a friendly and neutral ftate.

" All this moderation hath been thrown away: the king of Portugal hath juft now declared war in form againft France and Spain. This unexpected ftep forced the catholic king to make the like declaration againft Portugal; and the king [of France] can no longer defer taking the fame refolution.

" Independent of the motives which are common to the two monarchs, each hath feparate grievances to alledge againft Portugal, which of themfelves would be fufficient to juftify the extremity to which their majefties fee themfelves with regret obliged to proceed.

" Every one knows the unjuft and violent attack made by the Englifh in 1759, on fome of the french king's fhips, under the cannon of the portuguefe forts

at

at Lagos. His majesty demanded of the most faithful king to procure him restitution of those ships: but that prince's ministers, in contempt of what was due to the rules of justice, the laws of the sea, the sovereignty and territory of their master, (all which were indecently violated by the most scandalous infraction of the rights of sovereigns and of nations) in answer to the repeated requisitions of the king's ambassador on this head, made only vague speeches, with an air of indifference that bordered on derision.

"At the same time the court of Lisbon, pretending to be ignorant that sovereigns, who hold their rank of their birth only, and the dignity of their crown, can never permit, under any pretext, any potentate to infringe prerogatives and rights belonging to the antiquity and majesty of their throne, hath pretended to establish, without distinction, an alternative of precedence between all the ambassadors and foreign ministers about the king of Portugal. The king being informed by his ambassador of the notification that had been made to him of this extraordinary and unexampled regulation, signified in writing to the most faithful king his just dissatisfaction; and his majesty declared that he would never suffer any attempt to be made to diminish the right essentially inherent in the representative character with which he is pleased to honour his ambassadors and ministers.

"However justly the king was authorised to express, at that time, his displeasure on account of these grievances, and several other subjects of complaint which he had received from the court of Portugal, his majesty contented himself with recalling his ambassador, and continued to keep up a correspondence with the most faithful king, which he very sincerely desired to render more intimate and more lasting.

"That prince, therefore, can only blame himself for the calamities of a war, which he ought, on every
account

account to have avoided, and which he hath been the firſt to declare.

"His offers to obſerve a ſtrict neutrality might have been liſtened to by the king and the catholic king, if paſt experience had not taught them to guard againſt the illuſion and danger of ſuch propoſals.

"In the beginning of the preſent century, the court of Liſbon was very forward to acknowledge king Philip V. of glorious memory, and contracted formal engagements with France and Spain. Peter II. who at that time filled the throne of Portugal, ſeemed to enter cordially into the alliance of the two crowns: but after diſſembling his ſecret intentions for three years, he broke all his promiſes, and the neutrality which he had afterwards ſolicited, and which, in a letter to the republic of the United Provinces, he had even adviſed her to embrace, and joined the enemies of France and Spain. The ſame confidence, and the ſame ſecurity, on the part of the two crowns, in the preſent ſtate of things, would undoubtedly have been followed by the like defection in the court of Liſbon.

"United to the catholic king by indiſſoluble ſentiments of tender friendſhip and common intereſts, the king hopes that our united efforts will be favoured by the God of Hoſts, and will in the end compel the king of Portugal to conduct himſelf on principles more conformable to ſound policy, the good of his people, and the ties of blood, which unite him to his majeſty and his catholic majeſty.

"The king commands and enjoins all his ſubjects, vaſſals, and ſervants, to fall upon the ſubjects of the king of Portugal; and expreſsly prohibits them from having any communication, commerce, or intelligence with them, on pain of death; and accordingly his majeſty hath from this date revoked, and hereby revokes, all licences, paſſports, ſafeguards, and ſafe-conducts, contrary to theſe preſents, that may have been granted by him or his lieutenant-generals, and other officers; declaring them null and void, and to no effect; and forbidding all persons to pay any regard thereto. And whereas, in contempt of the 15th article of the treaty of peace between France and Portugal, signed at Utrecht, april 11, 1713, (and by which it is expressly stipulated, That in case of a rupture between the two crowns, the space of six months shall be granted their subjects respectively to sell, or remove, their effects, and withdraw their persons, if they think fit) the king of Portugal hath just now ordered, that all the french who are in his kingdom should leave it in the space of fifteen days, and that their effects shall be confiscated and sequestered; his majesty, by way of just reprisals, commands, that all the portuguese in his dominions shall, in like manner, leave them within the space of fifteen days from the date hereof, and that all their effects shall be confiscated."

On june 25, the king of Spain sent to the viceroy of of Navarre, and to the governors of the provinces of Spain, an order in the following terms:

" Since the portuguese, through an inveterate hatred for the spanish name (a hatred founded only on hereditary prejudice) have carried their barbarity to such extremities, as to cut off the ears and noses, or in other cruel manner to mutilate several spaniards who were leaving Portugal, in consequence of the declaration of war, who are arrived on our frontiers thus mutilated and disfigured; and as the portuguese government has endeavoured to shake, by motives of interest, that fidelity and love which good subjects owe their country, by publishing, on the 17th, at Yelves, and without doubt through all their frontiers, that any spaniard banished from Spain, who would retire with his wealth to Portugal, should enjoy all sorts of franchises, and be treated as a native there:

although

although his majesty believes that he has no subject so unworthy the name of a spaniard as to be tempted by such offers; if, however, there should be any one so base, be it known to him from this hour, that if he should at any time return to Spain, he shall suffer the infamy and punishment due to traitors and deserters of their country. His majesty orders you to publish the present edict throughout your jurisdiction.

D. RICARDO WALL."

"The reasons which the court of Madrid published to the world, are hardly to be paralleled but by those which Peter the Great alledged against Charles the twelfth; that he, the Czar, had not received sufficient honours when he passed *incognito* through Riga, and that provisions had been sold too dear to his ambassadors.

"Family connections, and the various distresses of Portugal, ought to have prevented the desolation of that kingdom. A fatal earthquake; a daring and wicked attempt upon the life of the sovereign; the very dreadful punishments afterwards inflicted upon the noble families which were concerned in that attempt; the expulsion, and total ruin, of the jesuits; all these working together, had weakened, to a great degree, that reciprocal affection and confidence which constitute the true happiness of prince and people. In this ferment of men's minds, the consequence of an irruption, on the part of Spain, was dubious. Such an irruption, unprovoked and cruel as it was, might have given spirit and power to disaffection, or it might have called back the court and nation to their mutual interest, and have at least united a wretched country before it was subdued. Upon the whole, it seems to have done neither; the king maintained his prerogative, and the subject abandoned himself to his cowardice.

Perhaps

"Perhaps there never was a more flagrant and outrageous inftance of ftate-cafuiftry and political injuftice, than in the behaviour of the king of Spain to his portuguefe majefty. All the arguments advanced in the fpanifh memorials, to palliate the invafion of Portugal, are a daring infult upon common fenfe, and betray a weaknefs of judgment almoft equal to the incapacity of the meafure which they were intended to fupport. It may not be improper to prefent the reader with a fhort account of the foundation upon which his catholic majefty might be fuppofed to have laid his claim to Portugal. Don Henry, cardinal bifhop of Evora, came to the crown upon the death of the unfortunate Don Sebaftian, and reigned a year and an half. He was the laft of the royal blood of Portugal, in the male line. The title to the fucceffion lay between the iffue of Mary and Catherine, daughters of prince Edward, the fon of king Emanuel; and between Philip the fecond of Spain, fon of the princefs Ifabella, the daughter of that king. Mary was married to the duke of Parma, from whom the prefent king of Spain is naturally defcended. But the general affembly of the ftates of Portugal, paffed a famous law, A. D. 1139, by which it was enacted, that the eldeft daughter of the king, in cafe of failure of iffue male, fhould have the right of fucceffion in her, if fhe married a portuguefe nobleman; but, if fhe married a prince or nobleman of any foreign nation, fhe fhould then forfeit all that right. The reafon of this limitation is thus expreffed: " Becaufe our people fhall not be obliged to obey a king who is not a portuguefe by birth; fince they were our own countrymen and fubjects who gave us a king, without any foreign affiftance, by their own valour, and at the expence of their blood.

"This is the fundamental law of Portugal, and Philip the fecond admitted the validity of it, when he himfelf infifted that a fpaniard was no foreigner. Catherine,

therine, the younger sister of Mary, became the wife of the duke of Bragança, from whom the present king of Portugal is lineally descended. Such was the state of the several claims. Whoever had the firmest pretensions, Philip had indisputably the greatest power. His wealth, his established character for political abilities; and, above all, his situation, enabled him to take possession of Portugal in the close of 1580; and that kingdom remained in his family till 1640, when the tyranny of the spaniards, and the spirit of the portuguese, raised the duke of Bragança to the throne. The battle of Montijo in 1644, that of St. Miquel in 1658, the vigorous attack made upon the spanish lines before Elvas, by the marquis of Marialva, in 1659; all these were proofs of the resolution and fortune, with which the portuguese troops acted, in the assertion of their recovered freedom.

"The spaniards, exhausted by the success of France, having ended their war with that nation by the peace of the Pyrennees, were left at liberty to bring their whole force against Portugal. The actions of Canal and of Amexial in 1663, were still favourable to the portuguese; but the great general Schomberg was the person who put a period to the flattering expectations of Spain. He came with 4000 french troops into Portugal. With this choice body of experienced soldiers, he joined, in 1665, the portuguese forces, under the marquis of Marialva, gained a complete victory at Montes Claros, over the spanish army commanded by the marquis of Carracena, and fixed the throne in the house of Bragança. The firmness, constancy, and zeal of the portuguese, were conspicuous in the whole course of this war, which lasted twenty-eight years.

"It is easy to imagine how difficult a work it must prove, notwithstanding any advantages, to force the neck of such a people into a yoke which they have once shook off; and to bring those again into subjection, who are equally animated by a detestation of their enemy, and a remembrance of their former glory. However, we shall not find in the course of this new war between the Portuguese and Spaniards, that the former, some of the peasants and regulars excepted, behaved with that spirit of bravery, which so nobly animated their ancestors."

Great Britain, ever faithful to her treaties, took care to send a timely succour of troops and officers to Portugal, in the month of may. With respect to the war between Spain and Portugal, I shall content myself with giving a short account of the principal events of it.

The Spaniards on their entering into Portugal are said to have committed unheard-of barbarities among the small villages, robbing and murdering the inhabitants, setting fire to their crops, and not even sparing the sacred furniture belonging to their chapels. In the course of this invasion, they made themselves masters of Miranda*, Braganza, Torre di Moncorvo, and Chaves. They demolished the fortifications of the two former cities, and left a strong garrison in the latter. On their retreat from Braganza, they plundered the college and church, as well as the houses of several of the principal people; whom, together with several priests, they carried with them to Spain. They also killed several peasants of that neighbourhood in cold blood. But his catholic majesty being informed of the sacrilege committed by his army, ordered all the sacred furniture to be restored

* Whilst the marquis de Sarria, commander of the spanish forces, was preparing to besiege Miranda de Douro, in the province of Tras-os-Montes, a powder magazine blowing up, the portuguese governor determined to capitulate; upwards of 800 men were either destroyed by the explosion, or obliged to surrender prisoners of war.

to

to the bishop of the diocese, and that the churches should not be profaned.

The spaniards divided their forces, which were in the province of Tras-os-Montes, into three parts. The principal corps was encamped near Miranda; the second, consisting of 5000 men, at Torre di Moncorvo; the third, of the same number, near Chaves. Another body of 8000 men entered the portuguese frontier near Almeyda: this corps suffered by desertion, and its detached parties were often repulsed by the militia of the country. The summer months in that warm climate are unfavourable to military expeditions, and the spaniards could do little more than chastise the peasants of several villages, whose natural aversion overcame the oath of obedience which they had taken, and who did every thing in their power to cut off the convoy of provisions designed for their camp. These, and the portuguese companies, called auxiliaries, were easily defeated and dispersed. At length the spaniards opened the trenches before Almeyda, a frontier town, in the province of Tras-os-Montes, sixteen miles from the spanish city of Cividad Rodrigo. On the 25th of august the fortress was surrendered, after a siege of nine days, and before a practicable breach had been made, by the governor Alexandro de Pallares Coello di Brito, for which he was afterwards put under confinement at Coimbra. Fifteen hundred regulars, and two thousand peasants, were permitted to retire with the honours of war, on condition of not serving against the king of Spain for six months. They found there eighty pieces of cannon, eleven of iron, nine brass mortars, and one of iron for grenades; seven hundred quintals of powder, and other implements of war, together with a quantity of ammunition and provisions.

As a counterbalance to this advantage, the count de Lippe, (who now commanded the british and portuguese troops, lord Tyrawley being returned to England) caused Valençia d'Alcantara to be attacked by the british troops. Brigadier-general Burgoine, who was appointed to this brave exploit, ordered part of his regiment of light dragoons to push into the town sword in hand. The attack was so brisk and sudden, that the guards in the square were all killed, or taken prisoners, before they could use their arms. After the body of the english regiment was come up, and formed in the square, some desperate persons attempted an attack, but all of them were destroyed, or taken. The general gave no quarter to those who fired single shots from the windows of the houses: at last he forced some priests through the town, to declare to the people, that he was determined to set fire to it at the four corners, unless all the doors and windows were instantly thrown open. This menace had the desired effect. Major-general don Michael d'Irumberrri and Balança, with his aid de camp; one colonel and his adjutant; two captains, seventeen subalterns, and fifty-nine private men, were made prisoners; the rest of the regiment of Seville were destroyed. Three colours were taken. The dragoons were sent into the country to bring in all who had escaped. A detached serjeant, and six men only, fell in with a spanish subaltern and twenty-five dragoons, who were unbroken, and prepared to receive them; of these they killed six, made the rest prisoners, and took all their horses.

The loss of the english in the attack of Valença was inconsiderable, only lieutenant Burk, of colonel Frederick's, one serjeant, and three private men, were killed; but two serjeants, one drummer, and eighteen private men, were wounded; ten horses were killed, and two wounded. Brigadier Burgoine and colonel Somerville conducted the troops in person. The british grenadiers, under the command of lord Pulteney, since dead, dislodged the enemy's infantry from

from the houses, and captain Singleton distinguished himself in this affair. The spanish officers themselves publicly commended the generosity of general Burgoine in handsome terms; and indeed the generosity and courage of the british troops, on this occasion, were highly worthy of admiration. This success would probably have been attended with more, if circumstances, that could not well be expected, had not retarded the march of sixteen portuguese battalions, and three regiments of cavalry.

The field-marshal, count de Lippe, on this occasion, in the orders of the day, august 29, declares, that " he thinks it his duty to acquaint the army with the glorious conduct of general Burgoine, who, after having marched fifteen leagues without halting, had taken Valença sword in hand, made the general, who was to have invaded Alentejo, prisoner, destroyed the spanish regiment of Seville, taken three standards, a colonel, many officers of distinction, and a great number of soldiers, prisoners. The marshal makes no doubt but the whole army will rejoice at this event, and that every one will, in proportion to his rank, strive to imitate so glorious an example."

The marquis de Sarria had hitherto commanded the spanish army, but having solicited and obtained his dismission, with the order of the golden fleece in recompence of his past services, he was succeeded in his post of general by the count d'Aranda. The portuguese on the 28th of september abandoned Celorico. The spaniards afterwards took possession of Penamacor, Salvaterra, and Segura. In Salvaterra there was a garrison of upwards of 400 men, which capitulated on the condition of not serving against the king of Spain, or his allies, for the term of six months.

The spaniards, early in october, also made themselves masters of the defile of St. Simon, and of Villa Velha, a moorish castle near the Tagus. Brigadier Burgoine

Burgoine for some time supported the latter across the river. The garrison, consisting of upwards of three hundred men, surrendered prisoners of war. The portuguese infantry, under the count de St. Jago, being obliged to file off by the road of Sobreira Formosa, lord Loudon, with four british regiments, six companies of portuguese grenadiers, some light dragoons and portuguese cavalry, brought up the rear guard, and kept the spaniards in awe. The portuguese grenadiers merited upon this occasion the approbation of lord Loudon, who spoke advantageously of them. Colonel Lee, between the 5th and 6th of october, with one hundred grenadiers, two hundred royal volunteers, fifty british dragoons, and fifty of St. Payo's horse, all under the orders of brigadier-general Burgoine, marched up to, attacked, and forced a small spanish encampment near Villa Velha, burnt some magazines, spiked up six pieces of cannon, brought off about sixty artillery mules, a few prisoners, and a quantity of valuable baggage. Lieutenant Maitland, of Burgoine's dragoons, bravely distinguished himself in this affair, and repulsed the enemy's cavalry. The british troops lost only one corporal killed, eight private men wounded and missing. The spaniards, according to their own account, had two lieutenants killed, one colonel and one ensign wounded, one captain and one subaltern taken prisoners; the loss of their private men uncertain. Great commendations are due to the abilities of general Burgoine, and the resolution of the british troops commanded by colonel Lee, in this operation.

The surprise of the spanish encampment near Villa Velha, as above related, effectually defeated the scheme they had formed of passing over the Tagus into the province of Alentejo; and the heavy rains which fell afterwards, obliged them to retire from Castella Branco, and to repass the mountains which separate the provinces of Estremadura and Beira.

Some time this month, october, his portuguese majesty, by a letter under his own hand, having requested a further succour from our court, orders were given for three thousand light troops to march to Portsmouth, and embark immediately for Lisbon, under convoy of the Neptune man of war.

These troops were actually embarked, but the preliminary articles for a peace between Great-Britain, France, and Spain, being signed in the interim, orders were sent for their disembarkation. The preliminaries of peace were received with great joy at the court of Portugal, and by the whole portuguese nation, though not so by ours, and the spaniards immediately began to withdraw their troops out of that kingdom.

(680)

CHAP. XXXVI.

Two Spanish ships taken. Brave action of captain Mead in the Fowey. Capture of the Hermione, a rich Spanish register-ship. Gallant action of two privateers. Transports for the Havannah taken by the French. Sir George Pocock and lord Albemarle take the Havannah. Further actions against the Spaniards. Treaty of peace between Great-Britain, France, and Spain, revived. The duke of Bedford goes to the court of France, and the duke of Nivernois arrives in England. Preliminary articles of peace between Great-Britain, France, and Spain. Cessation of arms. The definitive treaty of peace.

THE first act of hostility on the part of Great-Britain, after the declaration of war against Spain, committed upon the spaniards by us, was the taking a large spanish store-ship, of 800 tons burthen, laden with cannon, powder, small arms, and ordnance stores for la Guayra. Captain Ourry, in the Actæon, under the orders of admiral Rodney, fell in with, and took her off Tobago. Captain Elphinston, in the Richmond, march 3, brought into the Madeira a spanish ship, called the Il Castil de la Marr, in her passage to the West-Indies. The captain offered sixty thousand pounds sterling for her ransom. She had on board one hundred tons of Campeachy logwood, two thousand raw hides, and about seventy thousand dollars, besides indigo, coffee, and bale goods.

This was followed by a brave action of captain Joseph Mead, in the Fowey. On the 13th of march he met with the la Ventura, a spanish frigate of 26 guns,

guns, twelve pounders, on one deck, and 300 men, commanded by captain Don Joseph de las Casas, on her return from the Havannah, from whence she had been sent with money for the payment of the spanish king's troops at Porto Rico and St. Domingo. The Fowey had only 24 guns, nine pounders, and but 134 men, two of whom were sick, and incapable of service. However, captain Mead began the attack, at about six or seven leagues from Cape Tiberone. The engagement lasted about an hour and an half, when both ships sheered off to repair the damages they had received. At ten at night captain Mead bore down a second time upon the Ventura, and exchanged a few broadsides with her; but the darkness preventing him from forming a satisfactory judgment of her motions and distance, he made sail to windward, and kept his men at quarters, to observe her as closely as possible during the night.

On the dawn of the next morning, the 14th, the engagement was renewed for the third time, when the Fowey went as near to the enemy as she could do, without falling on board of her. The dispute was long, and well maintained; but at last, about half an hour after eight, the La Ventura struck her colours. She was at this time reduced almost to a wreck, and had received several shots between wind and water, one of which was afterwards discovered to have penetrated into her magazine: and indeed the Fowey was herself so much damaged in her masts and rigging, that she was obliged to undergo a thorough repair at Jamaica. When the Ventura struck, neither ship had a boat that could swim, or tackle left to hoist one out with. However, captain Mead contrived, by nailing a tarpaulin over the shot holes of a small boat, to get a midshipman and six men on board the prize, and to receive the captain of the ship, the captain of the soldiers, and six or seven more prisoners on board his own ship. The midshipman

was

was obliged to employ good usage, and some art, to induce the spaniards to assist him in bringing the Ventura into Port-Royal harbour.

In the above action, the La Ventura lost about forty or fifty men. The Fowey had but ten killed, and twenty-four wounded; two of the latter died soon after of their wounds. The lieutenant, two mates, and twenty private sailors were in the harbour. The master got drunk, and disappointed the captain of his assistance, and the gunner was wounded in the first part of the engagement. Under all these disadvantages, the capture of so strong a frigate may be justly reckoned among the gallant actions of the war*.

In may following, the 21st, captain Sawyer, in the Active frigate, and captain Pownall, in the Favourite sloop, took off Cape St. Vincent, and carried into Gibraltar, the Hermione, a spanish register ship, of 26 or 28 guns, bound from Lima to Cadiz, having on board 2,600,000 hard dollars, registered for the court of Madrid.

Captain Crichton, in the Brilliant privateer, in company with the York privateer of Bristol, a sloop of ten three pounders, silenced a fort upon Cape Finisterre, mounting two eighteen pounders and eight nine pounders, struck the spanish, and hoisted english colours, sunk two vessels in the harbour, and brought away four others, loaden with wine for the spanish fleet at Ferrol: this gallant action was effected with the loss of but two men killed, and twelve wounded.

Five transports, being part of the second division from New-York for the Havannah, having on board

---

* Captain Mead, when he was an inferior officer, served under Mr. Moystyn, and was the inventor of a machine for cleansing a ship's bottom at sea, known to the sailors by the name of Mead's Hog. While he commanded the Crown store-ship, he gave repeated proofs of his diligence and conduct. He is the author of a little work, "An essay on currents at sea," for which he received the thanks of the lords of the admiralty.

three

three hundred and fifty regulars of Anstruther's regiment, were taken, july 21, by two french ships of the line, three frigates, and six sail of brigantines and sloops, near the passage between Maya Guannas and the north Caicos. Two days after, the Pallas, captain Clements, attacked two spanish chebecs at the entrance of the bay of Cadiz, one of which was of 34 guns, and the other of 24, and obliged them both to take shelter, with a considerable loss, under the cannon of their own forts.

The same month the Chesterfield, of 44 guns, and four transports, ran on Cayo Confite, the entrance of the Bahama streights, on the Cuba side, an hour before day-light, and were stranded; but all the seamen and troops got on shore, and were afterwards transported safe to the Havannah.

But I am now to relate a more glorious and capital event, which took place in the month of august, the surrender of the Havannah, and all its dependencies, and the ships of war and merchandize in the harbour, to sir George Pocock, and the earl of Albemarle. Sir George passed through the old streights of Bahama with his whole squadron, consisting of nineteen ships of the line, several frigates, and a large number of transports, between the 27th of may and the evening of the 5th of june. On the 2d of june the Alarm, captain Almes, engaged and took the Thetis, of 22 guns and 180 men, and the Phœnix store-ship, of 18 guns and 75 men, together with a brigantine and a schooner, all bound to Segoa in the Streights, to load with timber for the use of the fleet at the Havannah. The Thetis had ten men killed and fourteen wounded; the Alarm seven men killed and ten wounded. The army under lord Albemarle landed on the 7th of june without opposition, between two forts on the rivers Bocanao and Coximar, about six miles to the eastward of Moro castle. Captain Hervey, in the Dragon, silenced Coximar

mar caftle, and enabled the army to pafs that river unmolefted. On the 8th, a fmall corps, under colonel Carleton, repulfed and difperfed the fpanifh regiments of Edinburgh dragoons, two companies of grenadiers and many officers, together with a body of militia on horfeback, the whole amounting to near 6000 men, advantageoufly pofted upon a rifing ground between the britifh army and the village of Guanamacoa. On the 11th the fort of Chorera (on the weft fide) was abandoned by the fpaniards, after having been battered by the Belleifle, captain Knight; and colonel Carleton attacked a redoubt upon the Cavannos (an hill above Moro caftle) which he carried with little refiftance and lofs: a poft was eftablifhed here under the name of the Spanifh Redoubt. By the 12th the fpaniards had funk three fhips of the line in the entrance of the harbour's mouth, by which it was effectually blocked up and fecured. On the 15th a detachment of 1200 men under colonel Howe, and 800 marines under the majors Campbel and Collins were landed and encamped at Chorera, about feven miles weftward of the Havannah, where they engaged the attention of the enemy, and proved of confiderable fervice. After the previous and neceffary preparations were completed, which employed the time of the army from the 12th of june to the 1ft of july, the artillery began to play upon the Moro Caftle. The enemy landed on the 29th of june two detachments from the Havannah of 500 men each, confifting of grenadiers and chofen troops, together with armed negroes and mulattoes, to interrupt the befiegers in their operations. One of thefe detachments marched upon the right under the Moro; the other upon the left near the Lime-kiln, where the befiegers had raifed one or two batteries to remove the fhipping to a greater diftance which had annoyed them confiderably: the picquets and advanced pofts repulfed thefe detachments, wounded many, and killed

or

or took prisoners 200 men, with the loss only of 10 men killed and wounded on their side. On the first of july the Cambridge of 80 guns, Dragon of 74, and Marlborough of 66, all under the command of captain Hervey, attacked the north-east part of the Moro castle for the space of near six hours, when they were called off. The two former ships received great damage from the height of the fort, whilst the fort itself suffered very little from their fire. This attack divided the attention of the garrison, and enabled the army to obtain a superiority of guns on the land side. Captain Goostry, of the Cambridge, was killed in the beginning of the engagement; and his place was supplied by captain Lindsay of the Trent, who acquitted himself with honour during the remainder of the action. The conduct of captain Campbell, of the Stirling Castle, was censured by captain Hervey, and ordered to be examined into by a court-martial. 42 seamen were killed, and 140 wounded in this desperate service. Captain Mackenzie, of the Defiance, brought the Venganza frigate of 26 guns, and the Marte of 18, out of the harbour of Port Mariel, after some firing. All but 20 men had left them. The harbour of Port Mariel is about seven leagues to the leeward of Chorera, and was afterwards taken possession of by sir George Pocock as a place of security for the shipping against the dangers of the season, in which he was at that time advanced. A schooner loaded with coffee, and bound from Hispaniola to New Orleans, fell into the hands of the cruizers belonging to the fleet. On the 2d of july the grand battery caught fire, and the labour of 5 or 600 men for 17 days was destroyed. Had not this accident intervened, the castle would probably have been reduced in a short time. On the 11th the merlons of the grand battery again caught fire, and the whole was irreparably consumed. Amidst these difficulties, and the uninterrupted communication which the castle

main-

maintained with the town of the Havannah and the ships, together with the nature of the soil, which was all rocky, and the consequent necessity of carrying on all the approaches above ground, the siege proved a work of time. From the 17th to the 22d the besiegers proceeded against the Moro by sap and mines. About four in the morning of the 22d, fifteen hundred men made a sally from the Havannah, divided into three parties; two of these parties were repulsed and driven back into the town; the third retreated without venturing upon an engagement. Lieutenant-colonel Stuart, of the 90th regiment, at the head of 30 men only, sustained the attack of one of these parties for an hour, when he was supported by about 100 sappers and the 3d battalion of royal Americans. The loss of the spaniards was computed at near 400 men in killed, drowned and taken: that of the british troops amounted to about 50 killed and wounded; brigadier Carleton was among the latter. On the 26th a two-decked spanish merchant ship was sunk by an howitzer; and on the 28th a large merchant ship was destroyed by lightning in the harbour. The works were continued from the 23d to the 30th, and the usual advances were made, step by step; on the 30th two mines were sprung; one in the counterscarp, the other in the right bastion; the latter had the most considerable effect, and made a practicable breach. Orders were immediately given for the assault. Twenty-two officers, 15 serjeants, and 281 rank and file commanded by the gallant lieutenant-colonel Stuart of the 90th regiment, together with 150 sappers under a captain's command; all sustained by 17 officers, 14 serjeants, and 150 rank and file, making in the whole 499 men, mounted with the greatest resolution, formed expeditiously on the top of the breach, drove the enemy from every part of the ramparts, and planted his majesty's standard upon the bastion. Thus fell Moro castle after a siege of

29 days. Of the fpaniards, Don Louis de Velafco, captain of the Reyna, colonel and commander in chief of the caftle, was mortally wounded in defending the colours fword in hand; a brave officer, defervedly regretted both by friends and enemies; the marquis Gonzales, captain of the Aquilon, colonel and fecond in command in the caftle, was killed; their lofs in the affault amounted to 343 killed or drowned, 37 wounded, and 326 made prifoners; in all, 706. The lofs of the britifh troops was trifling, confifting in 14 killed, and 28 wounded. On the 10th of Auguft in the morning, the batteries being prepared to play from the Cavannos on the eaft fide, and ground being ready to be opened on the weft fide, lord Albemarle fummoned the governor of the Havannah to capitulate, who returned a civil but refolute anfwer; the next day, the artillery men and failors filenced, in about fix hours, all the guns in the Punta fort and the north baftion of the town. The governor hung out a white flag and beat a parley. The capitulation was figned on the 13th, by which the town of Havannah, with all its dependencies furrendered to his majefty's arms; all fhips in the harbour, all money and effects whatever belonging to the king of Spain; all the artillery, arms, ammunition, and naval ftores without referve, and all the catholic king's flaves, were to be delivered up to fir George Pocock and lord Albemarle; the regular troops, failors and marines, all making part of the garrifon, were to be tranfported to the neareft port of Old Spain at the expence of his britannic majefty, and the militia were to deliver up their arms to the commiffary appointed to receive them. The Tigre, Reyna, Soverano, Infante, and Aquilon of 70 guns, the America, Conqueftado, San Genaro and Santo Antonio of 60 guns, fell into the hands of the conquerors; the Neptuno of 70, the Afia of 64, and the Europa of 60, were funk in the entrance of the

harbour;

harbour; there were two more ships of war on the stocks, and several merchant ships. The regulars who capitulated, were composed of the second regiment of Spain, the second regiment of Arragon, the Havannah regiment, artillery companies, Edinburgh and Havannah dragoons, amounting to 936, exclusive of the prisoners on board the men of war, and the sick and wounded on shore. In the course of the siege, the loss of the british troops consisted in 11 officers, 15 sergeants, 4 drummers, and 260 rank and file killed; 19 officers, 49 serjeants, 6 drummers, and 176 rank and file wounded; 39 officers, 14 serjeants, 11 drummers, and 632 rank and file dead of diseases and the climate; and one serjeant, 4 drummers, with 125 rank and file missing; 4 officers, 1 drummer, and 51 rank and file died of their wounds. The whole amounted to 1822. The officers of note were, the lieutenant-colonels Thomas, Gordon, and Leith; the majors M'Neil, Mirrie, and Ferron; the captains Suttie. Tyrwhitt, Schaak, M'Donald, Menzies, Crofton, Windus, and Goreham, dead; captain Strachey, killed; brigadier Carleton and the captains Balfour, Morris, Spendlove and Gordon, wounded. 351 pieces of brass and iron ordnance were found in the Moro castle, Punta, and the town of Havannah. Major-general Keppel commanded the attack of Moro castle. Sir George Pocock, commodore Keppel, lieutenant-general Elliot in particular; and, in general, every officer, soldier and sailor, carried on the service with the greatest spirit and zeal. The seamen chearfully assisted in landing cannon and ordnance stores, manning batteries, making fascines, and supplying the army with water. The unanimity which subsisted between the army and fleet cannot be better described than in Sir George Pocock's own words. " Indeed, (says he) " it is doing injustice to both, to mention them as " two corps; since each has endeavoured, with the
" most

"most constant and chearful emulation, to render
"it but one; uniting in the same principles of ho-
"nour and glory for their king and country's ser-
"vice." This capture of 12 great ships of the line,
(including the three which were sunk) besides two
men of war on the stocks, three frigates, and an
armed storeship, was a more severe blow to Spain
than that which she felt from England in 1718, when
sir George Byng and captain Walton took or burnt
off Cape Passaro, and on the coast of Sicily, one ship
of 74 guns, one of 70, four of 60, two of 54, one
of 44, three of 40, one of 36, one of 30, and one
of 24; in all, fifteen: and if the situation of the
Havannah, and the treasure found in it, are considered, perhaps it may be safely affirmed, that the
spaniards have not suffered such a sensible and humi-
liating loss since the defeat of their celebrated Ar-
mada. The narrow pass between the town and castle
having been closely watched, a letter was intercepted
from the governor of the former to the governor of
the latter, desiring him to maintain himself in the possession of the castle, and expressing his own inability
to make any defence. After the castle was gallantly
taken by assault, lord Albemarle acquainted the governor of the town, that he had been well informed
of the weak state of the place, and that it would save
much bloodshed to surrender. This was, however, refused; upon which lord Albemarle sent his own letter to him, which immediately brought on the capitulation.

During the course of this summer, the following
action happened between us and the dutch. The
Hunter sloop, cruizing off the Texel, fell in with four
dutch ships under the convoy of a man of war, in
the month of august, and desired leave to search
them, but was refused. The Hunter, on proper sig-
nals being made, was joined between the 23d and
the 26th by the Trial sloop, the Diana, and the
Chester,

Chester, and two cutters; when captain Adams, of the Diana, acting as commodore, politely demanded the usual permission to search the merchantmen; but the commander of the dutch man of war persisting in his refusal, captain Adams prepared himself for force, and ordered the boats of the ships, with an english jack hoisted in each, to search the convoy, threatening the dutch captain with a broadside, if he insulted the english flag. However, the dutchman immediately fired two shot at the Hunter's boat, which captain Adams answered by a single shot, which the dutchman violently returned by a whole broadside. This brought on a regular engagement, which continued about a quarter of an hour, when the man of war and convoy struck, and were brought into the Downs. Not one man was killed, or wounded, on board the Diana; but on board the dutchman two were killed, and the captain and two others were wounded. The dutch frigate was called the Dankbuarheld of 26 guns, commanded by Solomon Dedel the younger; she did not strike till she received the fire of the Chester, according to the dutch account.

Captain Hotham, in the Æolus, attacked in Aviles bay, on the 2d of september, the St. Joseph, a spanish ship of above 1200 tons, capable of carrying 60 guns, though mounting but 32, bound from the Caraccas to Port Passage, with a cargo of hides and cocoa. After a faint resistance, the enemy took to their boats, and abandoned their ship; which being now in the possession of the english, the spaniards quitted a battery of three guns, erected upon an eminence, and lieutenant Campbell, with a party of marines, went on shore in the evening and spiked the guns. Captain Hotham was obliged to burn this valuable prize; she having bulged in the night.

But now the appearance of a peace once more revived. His most christian majesty having nominated
the

the duke de Nivernois to come here to treat of a peace, his britannic majesty was pleased to name the duke of Bedford to go to Paris for the same purpose: the latter accordingly set out for Dover the first week in september, and a few days after the duke of Nivernois arrived in London. On the 3d of november the preliminaries of peace were signed at Fontainbleau by the count de Choiseul,* secretary of state for foreign affairs, on the part of France; by the duke of Bedford, minister plenipotentiary, on the part of Great-Britain; and by the marquis de Grimaldi, ambassador and plenipotentiary from the court of Madrid, on the part of Spain. For the sake of comparing them with the definitive treaty itself, in order to see how they differ, I shall here insert

The Preliminary Articles of peace, between the kings of Great-Britain, France, and Spain.

[Published by Authority.]

"In the Name of the most Holy Trinity.

"THE king of Great-Britain, and the most christian king, animated with the reciprocal desire to re-establish union and good understanding between them, as well for the good of mankind in general, as for that of their respective kingdoms, states, and subjects, having reflected, soon after the rupture between Great-Britain and Spain, on the state of the negociation of last year, (which unhappily had not the desired effect) as well as on the points in dispute between the crowns of Great-Britain and Spain; their britannic and most christian majesties began a

---

* The most christian king rewarded the services of the count de Choiseul in this negociation, by creating him a duke and peer of France, with the title of duke de Praslin.

correspondence to endeavour to find means to adjust the differences subsisting between their said majesties. At the same time, the most christian king having communicated to the king of Spain these happy dispositions, his catholic majesty was animated with the same zeal for the good of mankind, and that of his subjects, and resolved to extend and multiply the fruits of peace by his concurrence in such laudable intentions. Their britannic, most christian, and catholic majesties, having, in consequence, maturely considered all the above points, as well as the different events which have happened during the course of the present negociation, have, by mutual consent, agreed on the following articles, which shall serve as a basis to the future treaty of peace. For which purpose, his britannic majesty has named and authorized John duke and earl of Bedford his britannic majesty's minister plenipotentiary to his most christian majesty; his most christian majesty Cæsar Gabriel de Choiseul, duke of Praslin; and his catholic majesty has likewise named and authorized Don Jerome Grimaldi, marquis de Grimaldi, his ambassador extraordinary to his most christian majesty: who, after having duly communicated to each other their full powers in good form, have agreed on the following articles:"

" Article I. As soon as the preliminaries shall be signed and ratified, sincere friendship shall be re-established between his britannic majesty and his most christian majesty, and between his said britannic majesty and his catholic majesty, their kingdoms, states, and subjects, by sea, and by land, in all parts of the world. Orders shall be sent to the armies and squadrons, as well as to the subjects, of the three powers, to stop all hostilities, and to live in the most perfect union, forgetting what has passed, of which their sovereigns give them the order and example: and, for the execution of this article, sea passes shall be given, on each side, for the ships, which shall be dispatched

patched to carry the news of it to the respective possessions of the three powers."

"II. His most christian majesty renounces all pretensions, which he has heretofore formed, or might have formed, to Nova-Scotia, or Acadia, in all its parts, and guaranties the whole of it, with all its dependencies, to the king of Great-Britain: moreover, his most christian majesty cedes and guaranties to his said britannic majesty, in full right, Canada, with all its dependencies, as well as the island of Cape Briton, and all the islands in the gulf and river St. Laurence, without restriction, and without any liberty to depart from this cession and guaranty, under any pretence, or to trouble Great-Britain in the possessions abovementioned. His britannic majesty, on his side, agrees to grant to the inhabitants of Canada the liberty of the catholic religion: he will, in consequence, give the most exact and the most effectual orders, that his new Roman catholic subjects may profess the worship of their religion, according to the rites of the Roman church, as far as the laws of Great-Britain permit. His britannic majesty further agrees, that the french inhabitants, or others, who would have been subjects of the most christian king in Canada, may retire, in all safety and freedom, wherever they please; and may sell their estates, provided it be to his britannic majesty's subjects, and transport their effects, as well as their persons, without being restrained in their emigration, under any pretence whatsoever, except debts, or criminal prosecutions: the term limited for this emigration being fixed to the space of eighteen months, to be computed from the day of the ratification of the definitive treaty."

"III. The subjects of France shall have the liberty of fishing and drying on a part of the coasts of the island of Newfoundland, such as it is specified

in

in the XIIIth article of the treaty of Utrecht;* which article shall be confirmed and renewed by the approaching definitive treaty, (except what regards the island of Cape-Breton, as well as the other islands in the gulf of St. Laurence:) and his britannic majesty consents to leave to the most christian king's subjects the liberty to fish in the gulf of St. Laurence, on condition that the subjects of France do not exercise the said fishery, but at the distance of three leagues from all the coasts belonging to Great-Britain, as well those of the continent, as those of the islands situated in the said gulf of St. Laurence. And as to what relates to the fishery out of the said gulf, his most christian majesty's subjects shall not exercise the

---

* The 15th article in the treaty of Utrecht, here alluded to, is as follows:

"Article XIII. The island called Newfoundland, with the adjacent islands, shall from this time forward belong of right wholly to Britain; and to that end the town and fortress of Placentia, and whatever other places in the said island are in the possession of the french, shall be yielded and given up, within seven months from the exchange of the ratification of this treaty, or sooner if possible, by the most christian king, to those who have a commission from the queen of Great-Britain for that purpose. Nor shall the most christian king, his heirs and successors, or any of his subjects, at any time hereafter, lay claim to any right to the said island or islands, or to any part of it, or them. Moreover, it shall not be lawful for the subjects of France to fortify any place in the said island of Newfoundland, or to erect any buildings there, besides stages made of boards, and huts made necessary and useful for drying of fish. But it shall be allowed to the subjects of France to catch fish, and dry them on land, in that part only, and in no other besides that, of the said island of Newfoundland, which stretches from the place called Bonavista to the northern point of the said island; and from thence, running down by the western side, reaches as far as the place called Point Riche. But the island called Cape Breton, as also all others, both in the mouth of the river St. Laurence, and in the gulph of the same name, shall hereafter belong of right to the french; and the most christian king shall have all manner of liberty to fortify any place or places there."

fishery,

fishery, but at the distance of fifteen leagues from the coasts of the island of Cape-Breton."

" IV. The king of Great-Britain cedes the islands of St. Peter and of Miquelon, in full right, to his most christian majesty, to serve as a shelter for the french fishermen; and his said majesty obliges himself, on his royal word, not to fortify the said islands; to erect no buildings there but merely for the conveniency of the fishery; and to keep there only a guard of fifty men for the police."

" V. The town and port of Dunkirk * shall be put into the state fixed by the late treaty of Aix la Chapelle, and by former treaties: the Cunette shall remain as it now is, provided that the english engineers, named by his britannic majesty, and received at Dunkirk by order of his most christian majesty, verify, that this Cunette is only of use for the wholesomeness of the air, and the health of the inhabitants."

" VI. In order to re-establish peace on the most solid and lasting foundation, and to remove for ever every subject of dispute with regard to the limits of the british and french territories on the continent of America; it is agreed, that, for the future, the con-

---

* It is stipulated in the ninth article of the treaty of Utrecht, " that all the fortifications be rased, that the harbour be filled up, and that the sluices and moles which serve to cleanse the harbour be levelled, and that at the said king's own expence, within the space of five months after the conditions of peace are concluded and signed: that is to say, the fortifications towards the sea within the space of two months, and those towards the land, together with the said banks, within three months, on this express condition also, that the said fortifications, harbours, moles, or sluices be never repaired again."

The 17th article of the treaty of Aix la Chapelle, allows that Dunkirk shall remain fortified on the broad side in its present state, and for the sea side on the footing of ancient treaties.

fines between the dominions of his britannic majesty, and those of his most christian majesty, in that part of the world, shall be irrevocably fixed by a line drawn along the middle of the river Mississippi, from its source, as far as the river Iberville, and from thence, by a line drawn along the middle of this river, and of the lakes Maurepas and Pontchartrain, to the sea; and to this purpose, the most christian king cedes in full right, and guaranties to his britannic majesty, the river and port of Mobile, and every thing that he possesses, or ought to have possessed, on the left side of the Mississippi, except the town of New Orleans, and the island in which it is situated, which shall remain to France; provided that the navigation of the river Mississippi shall be equally free, as well to the subjects of Great-Britain, as to those of France, in its whole breadth and length, from its source to the sea, and that part expressly, which is between the said island of New Orleans, and the right bank of that river, as well as the passage both in and out of its mouth. It is further stipulated, that the vessels belonging to the subjects of either nation shall not be stopped, visited, or subjected to the payment of any duty whatsoever. The stipulations, in favour of the inhabitants of Canada, inserted in the second article, shall also take place, with regard to the inhabitants of the countries ceded by this article."

"VII. The king of Great-Britain shall restore to France the islands of Guadalupe, of Mariegalante, of Desirade, of Martinico, and of Belleisle, and the fortresses of these islands shall be restored in the same condition they were in when they were conquered by the british arms; provided that the term of eighteen months, to be computed from the day of the ratification of the definitive treaty, shall be granted to his britannic majesty's subjects, who may have settled in the said islands, and other places restored to
France

France by the definitive treaty, to fell their eftates, recover their debts and to tranfport their effects, as well as their perfons, without being reftrained on account of their religion, or under any other pretence whatfoever, except that of debt, or of criminal profecutions."

" VIII. The moft chriftian king cedes and guaranties to his britannic majefty, in full right, the iflands of Grenada, and the Grenadines, with the fame ftipulations in favour of the inhabitants of this colony, as are inferted in the fecond article for thofe of Canada: and the partition of the iflands called Neutral, is agreed and fixed, fo that thofe of St. Vincent, Dominico, and Tobago, fhall remain in full right to England, and that of St. Lucia fhall be delivered to France, to enjoy the fame in like manner in full right: the two crowns reciprocally guarantying to each other the partition fo ftipulated."

" IX. His britannic majefty fhall reftore to France the ifland of Goree, in the condition it was in when conquered: and his moft chriftian majefty cedes in full right, and guaranties to the king of Great-Britain, Senegal."

" X. In the Eaft-Indies, Great-Britain fhall reftore to France the feveral comptoirs which that crown had on the coaft of Coromandel, as well as on that of Malabar, and alfo in Bengal, at the commencement of hoftilities between the two companies in the year 1749, in the condition in which they now are, on condition that his moft chriftian majefty renounces the acquifitions which he has made on the coaft of Coromandel, fince the faid commencement of hoftilities between the two companies in the year 1749.

His moft chriftian majefty, on his fide, fhall reftore all that he fhall have conquered from Great-Britain, in the Eaft-Indies, during the prefent war;
and

and he also engages not to erect any fortifications, or to keep any troops in Bengal."

"XI. The island of Minorca shall be restored to his britannic majesty, as well as fort St. Philip, in the same condition they were in when they were conquered by the arms of the most christian king; and with the artillery that was there at the taking of the said island, and of the said fort."

"XII. France shall restore all the countries belonging to the electorate of Hanover, to the landgrave of Hesse, to the duke of Brunswic, and to the count of La Lippe Buckebourg, which are or shall be occupied by the arms of his most christian majesty: the fortresses of these different countries shall be restored in the same condition they were in when they were conquered by the Faench arms; and the pieces of artillery, which shall have been carried elsewhere, shall be replaced by the same number, of the same bore, weight, and metal. As to what regards hostages exacted or given during the war, to this day, they shall be sent back without ransom."

"XIII. After the ratification of the preliminaries, France shall evacuate, as soon as it can be done, the fortresses of Cleves, Wezel and Gueldres, and in general all the countries belonging to the king of Prussia; and, at the same time, the british and french armies shall evacuate all the countries which they occupy, or may then occupy, in Westphalia, Lower Saxony, on the Lower Rhine, the Upper Rhine, and in all the empire; and each shall retire into the dominions of their respective sovereigns: and their britannic and most christian majesties further engage and promise, not to furnish any succour, of any kind, to their respective allies, who shall continue engaged in the present war in Germany."

"XIV. The towns of Ostend and Nieuport shall be evacuated by his most christian majesty's troops,
imme-

immediately after the signature of the present preliminaries."

"XV. The decision of the prizes made on the spaniards by the subjects of Great-Britain, in time of peace, shall be referred to the courts of justice of the admiralty of Great-Britain, conformably to the rules established among all nations, so that the validity of the said prizes, between the british and the spanish nations shall be decided and judged, according to the law of nations, and according to treaties, in the courts of justice of the nation who shall have made the capture."

"XVI. His britannic majesty shall cause all the fortifications to be demolished, which his subjects shall have erected in the bay of Honduras, and other places of the territory of Spain in that part of the world, four months after the ratification of the definitive treaty: and his catholic majesty shall not, for the future, suffer the subjects of his britannic majesty, or their workmen, to be disturbed, or molested, under any pretence whatsoever, in their occupation of cutting, loading, and carrying away logwood; and for this purpose, they may build without hindrance, and occupy without interruption, the houses and magazines necessary for them, for their families, and for their effects; and his said catholic majesty assures to them by this article, the entire enjoyment of what is above stipulated."

"XVII. His catholic majesty desists from all pretensions which he may have formed to the right of fishing about the island of Newfoundland."

"XVIII. The king of Great-Britain shall restore to Spain all that he has conquered in the island of Cuba, with the fortress of the Havanna: and that fortress, as well as all the other fortresses of the said island, shall be restored in the same condition they were in when they were conquered by his britannic majesty's arms."

" XIX.

"XIX. In consequence of the restitution stipulated in the preceding article, his catholic majesty cedes and guaranties, in full right, to his britannic majesty, all that Spain possesses on the continent of North-America, to the east, or to the south-east, of the river Mississippi. And his britannic majesty agrees to grant to the inhabitants of this country, above ceded, the liberty of the catholic religion: he will, in consequence, give the most exact and the most effectual orders that his new Roman catholic subjects may profess the worship of their religion, acccording to the rites of the Roman church, as far as the laws of Great-Britain permit. His britannic majesty farther agrees, that the spanish inhabitants, or others, who would have been subjects of the catholic king in the said countries, may retire, in all safety and freedom, wherever they please; and may sell their estates, provided it be to his britannic majesty's subjects, and transport their effects, as well as their persons, without being restrained in their emigration, under any pretence whatsoever, except debts, or criminal prosecutions: the term, limited for this emigration, being fixed for the space of 18 months, to be computed from the day of the ratification of the definitive treaty. It is further stipulated, that his catholic majesty shall have power to cause all the effects, that belong to him, either artillery, or others, to be carried away."

"XX. The king of Portugal, his britannic majesty's ally, is expressly included in the present preliminary articles. And their most christian and catholic majesties engage to re-establish the ancient peace and friendship between them and his most faithful majesty: and they promise,

1st, That there shall be a total cessation of hostilities between the crowns of Spain and Portugal, and between the spanish and french troops, on the one side, and the portuguese troops, and those of their allies, on the other, immediately after the ratification of thefe preliminaries: and that there fhall be a like ceffation of hoftilities between the refpective forces of the moft chriftian and catholic kings, on the one part, and thofe of the moft faithful king, on the other, in all other parts of the world, as well by fea as by land: which ceffation fhall be fixed on the fame epochs, and under the fame conditions, as that between Great-Britain, France, and Spain, and fhall continue till the conclufion of the definitive treaty between Great-Britain, France, Spain, and Portugal.

2d, That all his moft faithful majefty's fortreffes and countries in Europe, which fhall have been conquered by the fpanifh and french armies, fhall be reftored in the fame condition they were in when they were conquered: and that, with regard to the portuguefe colonies in America, or elfewhere, if any change fhall have happened in them, all things fhall be put again on the fame footing as they were before the prefent war. And the moft faithful king fhall be invited to accede to the prefent preliminary articles as foon as fhall be poffible."

" XXI. All the countries and territories, which may have been conquered, in any part of the world whatfoever, by the arms of their britannic and moft faithful majefties, as well as by thofe of their moft chriftian and catholic majefties, which are not included in the prefent articles, either under the title of ceffions, or under the title of reftitutions, fhall be reftored without difficulty, and without requiring compenfations."

" XXII. As it is neceffary to affign a fixed epoch for the reftitutions, and the evacuations, to be made by each of the high contracting parties, it is agreed, that the britifh and french troops fhall proceed, immediately after the ratification of the preliminaries, to the evacuation of the countries which they occupy in the empire or elsewhere, conformably to the 12th and 13th articles.

The island of Belleisle shall be evacuated six weeks after the ratification of the definitive treaty, or sooner if it can be done.

Guadaloupe, Desirade, Mariegalante, Martinico, and St. Lucia, three months after the ratification of the definitive treaty, or sooner if it can be done.

Great-Britain shall likewise, at the end of three months, after the ratification of the definitive treaty, or sooner if it can be done, enter into the possession of the river and of the port of Mobile, and of all that is to form the limits of territory of Great-Britain, on the side of the river Mississippi, as they are specified in the VIth article.

" The island of Goree shall be evacuated by Great-Britain three months after the ratification of the definitive treaty; and the island of Minorca by France, at the same epoch, or sooner if it can be done. And according to the conditions of the IVth article, France shall also enter into possession of the islands of St. Peter and of Miquelon, at the end of three months.

" The comptoirs in the East-Indies shall be restored six months after the ratification of the definitive treaty, or sooner if it can be done.

" The island of Cuba, with the fortress of the Havanna, shall be restored three months after the ratification of the definitive treaty, or sooner if it can be done: and, at the same time, Great-Britain shall enter into possession of the country ceded by Spain according to the XIXth article.

" All the fortresses, and countries, of his most faithful majesty, in Europe, shall be restored immediately after the ratification of the definitive treaty: and the portuguese colonies, which may have been conquered, shall be restored in the space of three months in the West-Indies, and of six months in the

East-

East-Indies, after the ratification of the definitive treaty, or sooner if it can be done.

"In consequence whereof, the necessary orders shall be sent by each of the high contracting parties, with reciprocal passports for the ships which shall carry them, immediately after the ratification of the definitive treaty.

"XXIII. All the treaties, of what nature soever, which existed before the present war, as well between their britannic and most christian majesties, as between their britannic and catholic majesties, as also between any of the above-named powers and his most faithful majesty, shall be, as they are in effect, renewed, and confirmed, in all their points which are not derogated from by the present preliminary articles, notwithstanding whatever may have been stipulated to the contrary by any of the high contracting parties: and all the said parties declare, that they will not suffer any privilege, favour, or indulgence, to subsist, contrary to the treaties above confirmed.

"XXIV. The prisoners made respectively by the arms of their britannic, most christian, catholic, and most faithful majesties, by land and by sea, shall be restored reciprocally, and *bona fide*, after the ratification of the definitive treaty, without ransom, paying the debts they shall have contracted during their captivity. And each crown shall respectively pay the advances which shall have been made for the subsistence and maintenance of their prisoners, by the sovereign of the country where they shall have been detained, according to the receipts and attested accounts, and other authentic titles which shall be furnished on each side.

"XXV. In order to prevent all causes of complaints and disputes, which may arise on account of ships, merchandizes, and other effects which may be taken by sea, it is reciprocally agreed, that the ships, merchandizes, and effects which may be taken in the channel, and in the north seas, after the space of 12 days, to be computed from the ratification of the present preliminary articles, shall be reciprocally restored on each side.

" that the term shall be six weeks for the prizes taken, from the channel, the british seas, and the north seas, as far as the Canary islands inclusively, either in the ocean or in the Mediterranean.

" Three months, from the said Canary islands as far as the Æquinoctial line, or Æquator.

" Lastly, six months, beyond the said Æquinoctial line, or Æquator, and in all other parts of the world, without any exception, or other more particular description of time and place.

" XXVI. The ratifications of the preliminary articles shall be expedited in good and due form, and exchanged in the space of one month, or sooner if it can be done, to be computed from the day of the signature of the present articles.

" In witness whereof, we the underwritten ministers plenipotentiary of his britannic majesty, of his most christian majesty, and of his catholic majesty, in virtue of our respective full powers, have signed the present preliminary articles, and have caused the seal of our arms to be put thereto.

" Done at Fontainebleau, the third day of november, 1762."

BEDFORD, C. P. S.
(L. S.)

CHOISEUL, DUC DE PRASLIN.
(L. S.)

EL MARQ. DE GRIMALDI.
(L. S.)

Declara-

Declaration, signed at Fontainebleau, the third of november, 1762, by the french plenipotentiary, relating to the XIIIth article of the preliminaries.

" His most christian majesty declares, that in agreeing to the XIIIth article of the preliminaries, signed this day, he does not mean to renounce the right of acquitting his debts to his allies; and that the remittances made on his part, in order to acquit the arrears that may be due on the subsidies of preceding years, are not to be considered as an infraction of the said article.

" In witness whereof, I, the underwritten minister plenipotentiary of his most christian majesty, have signed the present declaration, and have caused the seal of my arms to be put thereto.

" Done at Fontainebleau, the third day of november, 1762."

CHOISEUL, DUC DE PRASLIN.
(L. S.)

On wednesday the 25th of november, the duke de Nivernois, ambassador extraordinary and plenipotentiary from the most christian king, had an audience of his majesty to deliver his credentials; on this occasion he made, in french, the following speech to his majesty.

" SIR,

" A cordial reconciliation between two powerful monarchs, formed to love each other; a permament union of system between two great courts, attracted to one another by their interest rightly understood; and a sincere and lasting conjunction of two respectable nations, whom unhappy prejudices have too long

long divided, from the glorious æra of the commencement of your majesty's reign: and this æra will, at the same time, be that of happiness restored to the four quarters of the world. Your majesty's name, your glory, and your virtues, will be inseparably joined in history, with universal felicity: and posterity will there read, with sentiments of respect, that treaty which will be distinguished, above all others, by good faith, without equivocation, and by permanent stability.

"Permit me, Sir, to felicitate myself at your feet, on being chosen, by the king my master, to serve, between your majesty and him, as the organ of the noble sentiments of two hearts so worthy of each other; and to be employed in this blessed work, which insure your majesty's glory, by giving happiness to the whole world."

On the 26th of november, his britannic majesty issued a proclamation, declaring the cessation of arms, as well by sea as land, between his majesty and the most christian king and the catholic king.

The day before, his majesty went to the house of peers, and opened the session of parliament with a speech; in which he was pleased to acquaint the house with the steps relative to a peace, in these words:

"My enemies have been brought to accept of peace, on such terms as, I trust, will give my parliament entire satisfaction. Preliminary articles have been signed by my minister, with those of France and Spain; which I will order, in due time, to be laid before you.

"The condition of these are such, that there is not only an immense territory added to the empire of Great-Britain, but a solid foundation laid for the increase of trade and commerce; and the utmost care

care has been taken to remove all occasions of future disputes between my subjects and those of France and Spain, and thereby to add security and permanency to the blessings of peace.

"I have made peace for the king of Portugal, securing to him all his dominions; and all the territories of the king of Prussia, as well as of my other allies in Germany, or elsewhere, occupied by the armies of France, are to be immediately evacuated."

On the 26th of the same month, a messenger arrived here from the duke of Bedford, with the ratifications of their most christian and catholic majesties, of the preliminary articles, signed the second instant, which were exchanged with his grace, the 22d, at Versailles.

The cessation of arms was proclaimed, on the 1st of december, at the Royal Exchange, and the usual places in London and Westminster. On the 10th of december, the house of peers waited on his majesty, with their address in relation to the peace; as also did the house of commons, on the 13th following.

However desireable in itself a peace might be, yet the prospect of the present one was far from giving a general satisfaction; great and public complaints were made against it. It was strongly urged, that we had returned to France almost every thing that had been taken from them, at the expence of so much blood and treasure. The dispute was warmly supported by several political papers; which were but weakly answered by others. However, this must be acknowledged, that there never was a war by which the interest of so many individuals was supported, as by the late war: it is therefore no matter of wonder, that there were so many to oppose a peace. Nor, indeed, is the acquisition of territories so much to be wished for by a treaty of peace, as the permanency of it. If, therefore, "care has been taken to remove all occasions of future disputes between the subjects of Great-Britain, France, and Spain, and thereby to add security and permanency to the blessings of peace,*" we shall have reason both to be content and thankful for it; and that such care has been taken, we have the highest assurance.

On the 19th of february, Richard Neville, Esq; secretary to the embassy at the court of France, arrived at Whitehall with the definitive treaty of peace, signed at Paris on thursday the 10th of the same month, by his grace the duke of Bedford, the duke de Praslin, and the marquis de Grimaldi, ambassadors extraordinary and plenipotentiaries on the part of his britannic majesty, the most christian king, and the catholic king; to which M. de Mello, ambassador and minister plenipotentiary of his most faithful majesty, acceded the same day. And on the 15th of March one of the king's messengers, dispatched by his grace the duke of Bedford, arrived with the ratifications of their most christian and catholic majesties of the definitive treaty of peace, signed on the 10th of February; and also those of the accession of his most faithful majesty to the treaty; which ratifications were exchanged with his grace, on the 10th of March, by the ambassadors and ministers plenipotentiary of the princes abovementioned, against those of his majesty; upon which occasion the Tower and Park guns were fired. But for this treaty I shall refer my readers to the end of the appendix to this work, where he will find it.

It must be confessed, that we entered into the late war with a spirit of languor and indolence, and that our affairs had a very melancholly appearance, till a

---

* See his majesty's speech, nov. 25, 1762.

certain

certain right honourable gentleman, whose remembrance must always be dear to a free and grateful people, came into the administration; we were then awakened from our lethargy; grand and noble designs were formed, and the most vigorous methods were pursued; success, honour, and riches, were the consequences to ourselves; and confusion, distress, and shame, the portion of our enemies. Less cannot be said upon the occasion, and more would be unnecessary, seeing my business in this work is that of an historian, and not of a politician.

These glorious events, with which the divine providence has been pleased to bless and crown our arms and cause, have not been purchased but at a very great expence. Though I have, in the course of this work, already mentioned in every year the supplies granted by parliament, yet it may not be improper to lay them before the reader, in one point of view, faithfully taken from the appropriating acts, as follows:

		£.	s.	d.
1st year of the war	1755,	4,520,327	12	8
2d	1756,	7,915,430	4	6¾
3d	1757,	8,330,906	6	5½
4th	1758,	10,475,007	0	1
5th	1759,	12,705,339	3	8½
6th	1760,	14,636,930	15	9¼
7th	1761,	17,301,119	19	9¾
8th	1762,	16,794,153	18	11½
Total		92,679,215	2	0½

However, this immense sum is not to be charged singly to the article of war; the annual supplies for the common exigencies of government are to be deducted from it; let us then multiply the sum total of the supplies granted for the last year of peace, viz. 1754,

1754, which was 2,265,016 l. 10 s. 2 d. $\frac{1}{4}$ by eight, the number of years the war continued, we shall find the total to be 18,120,132 l. 1 s. 4 d. which, deducted from the total of supplies for the last eight years supply, leaves the remainder 74,559,085 l. 0 s. 8 d. $\frac{1}{4}$, being the whole extra expence arising from the prosecution of the war.

I shall now proceed to relate, in the ensuing and last chapter, the progress of the war on the continent, from the last year of the war to the cessation of arms between the allied army and the french, to the end of the war between the king of Prussia and the empress queen, and to the peace concluded between those two powers, which will consequently put a period to this work.

CHAP. XXXVII.

General Luckner makes an excursion towards Meningen, and carries off a great number of male inhabitants. Skirmishes. The castle of Arensberg surrenders to the hereditary prince of Brunswic. Movement of the hereditary prince. Prince Ferdinand defeats the French. Skirmishes. Castle of Waldeck surrenders to general Conway. A body of french defeated. Motions of the french and allies, and skirmishes. An engagement between the hereditary prince of Brunswick, and the prince of Conde. Both armies change their position. The engagement at Amoenebourg, and surrender of that place to the french. Ziegenhayn besieged. Cassel surrenders. Cessation of arms. Campaign of 1762, by the king of Prussia. Cessation of hostilities between the russians and prussians in Pomerania; and between the russians and swedes for a short time. Treaty of peace between the emperor of Russia and the king of Prussia. Treaty of peace between Sweden and Prussia. Peter the third deposed, and the empress Catherine the second declared sovereign of Russia. A smart action between Pcille and Reichenbach. Action near Neisse. The prussians take Zittau. Prince Henry forced to repass the Mulda. Schweidnitz surrenders to the prussians. Battle of Rathswald. Battle near Freyberg. Peace concluded by the empress queen, the elector of Saxony, with the king of Prussia.

THE two armies in Westphalia remained pretty quiet till the 4th and 5th of january, when general Luckner, at the head of three or four thousand men, advanced on the side of Meningen, and put the french in a panic, by carrying off all the men in that part of the country, from the age of fifteen to forty. In this expedition two of his hussars were made prisoners, and his party took two of the enemy's. The French, pretending that the country-people favoured their falling into Luckner's hands, exacted of them 500 livres for each of these men. The French were very busy, the beginning of this year, in fortifying some places, raising magazines, exacting contributions, and making a show of having a numerous army in the field; and by fortifying their own frontiers, laying up provisions in their towns, and supplying them with fresh trains of artillery, seemed as if they were fearful that the seat of war would be removed into their own country, and that a retaliation would be made upon them of the ravages their own troops had committed on the neighbouring parts. Skirmishes now, april, began to take place between the french and the allies, and the former troops put themselves in motion, the martials d'Etrees and Soubise, commanding in Hesse, and the prince of Conde on the Lower Rhine. In the beginning of april, general Luckner, at the head of 1600 horse, came up with the marquis de Lortunge, as he was retreating to Gottingen with 1800 horse and 2000 foot, and immediately fell upon his rear, killed thirty, took eighty prisoners, and brought off 100 horses. Major Wintzingcrode, about the same time, took, in the country of Eichfield, fifty hussars and a french officer. About the middle of the same month the castle of Arensberg, defended by M. Muret, surrendered at discretion to the hereditary prince of Brunswick. On this occasion, 26 pieces of cannon were taken, 231 men, and nine officers.

The campaign was opened on the side of Westphalia, on the 9th of may, by the hereditary prince of Brunswick, who, being determined to raise contributions on the duchy of Berg, marched with a body of 7000 men, an hundred miles in two days, and appeared unexpectedly before Elberfeld. He dispersed the corps of Conflans, and the other french troops that were there; who retreated with precipitation, and not without loss. From thence the prince

prince advanced to Sclinguen, and, having first taken hostages for the payment of the contributions that he had demanded of the duchy of Berg, retired from thence.

The prince of Conde, on this movement, assembled such troops as were nearest at hand, and directed his march to Medman; but, on advice of the retreat of the hereditary prince, he sent back the troops to their respective garrisons. Soon after this exploit, the french generals received orders to begin their operations with the utmost vigour. The army in Hesse endeavoured to get possession of the duchies of Brunswick and Wolfenbuttel, whilst the army on the Lower Rhine made the utmost efforts to dislodge the allies from Westphalia. On the other hand, the troops of the allies were every-where in motion; so that some important action was now expected, and which soon after took place.

Prince Ferdinand, on the 24th of june, surprised and defeated the french army, commanded by the marshals d'Etrees and Soubise, in their camp of Grabenstein. General Luckner, with six battalions of grenadiers, four squadrons of dragoons, and his own regiment of hussars, marched from Hollenstadt, near the Seine, to Mareindorf, formed between the last place and Udenhausen, and attacked the marquis de Castries in the rear, who was posted at Carlsdorf to cover the right wing of the french. General Sporken, at the same time, with twelve hanoverian battalions and a body of cavalry, charged this corps of the enemy in flank; having marched from Sielem over the Dymel, and formed between Hombrexen and Udenhausen.

The marquis de Castries retired with little loss, and the two hanoverian generals continued their march, in order to take the camp at Grabenstein both in flank and rear. The marquis of Granby, with the reserve under his command, crossed the Dymel at Warbourg, and, passing by Zieremberg and Ziebersthausen,

hausen, possessed himself of an eminence opposite to Furnstenwalde, and was prepared to fall upon the enemy's left wing. Prince Ferdinand passed the Dymel, marched through Langenberg, and came upon the centre of the French, which occupied an advantageous eminence. In this critical situation, the enemy struck their tents, and retreated. M. de Stainville preserved their whole army, by throwing himself into the woods of Wilhelmstahl, but was forced to sacrifice the flower of his infantry to secure the retreat.

The grenadiers of France, the royal grenadiers, and the regiment of Aquitaine, suffered severely in this action. M. Reidesel entirely routed the regiment of Fitz-James's horse. The british troops consisted of the grenadier guards, the first, second, and third, battalions of guards, Welch's and Maxwell's grenadiers, Hodgson's and Barrington's regiments, Keith's and Campbell's highlanders, Frazer's chasseurs, the Blues, and Elliot's horse. The first battalion of grenadiers, belonging to colonel Beckwith's brigade, distinguished itself extremely. As to lord Granby, he behaved with his usual intrepidity, and had no little share in the victory.

The allies had, on this occasion, 108 killed, 271 wounded, and 318 missing, in all 697, of whom 437 were british. The enemy took two pieces of cannon, and three ammunition waggons: however, some standards and colours fell into the hands of the allies. The only officer of distinction who fell in this engagement was lieutenant-colonel Townshend, of the first regiment of foot-guards. The french retreated under the cannon of Cassel, and a great part of their army afterwards passed hastily over the Fulda. The enemy owned they lost near 900 men, killed and wounded; and, by the account published in the London Gazette, it appeared, that the number of their prisoners amounted to 2732; among whom were five colonels of the grenadiers of France, the viscount de Broglio

Broglio, and 156 other officers. The chevalier de Narbonne, lieutenant-colonel in the royal grenadiers, was killed; the duc de Picquigny, and the marquisses of Peyne and la Roche Lambert were wounded. The chevalier de Muy, and many other general officers, lost their baggage. The corps de reserve, under prince Xavier, of Saxony, which was encamped near Dransfeld, in the territory of Hanover, retired over the Werra, and joined the french main army, with the loss of its hospital, baggage, medicines, and the escorte that conducted them.

After the action, prince Ferdinand occupied Fritzlar, Feltzberg, Lohr, and Gudensberg. The day after the above action, the hereditary prince of Brunswick, at the head of 400 horse, attacked the french troop of Conflans at Recklinghausen, but was repulsed, and had 200 of his men taken prisoners, and twenty killed.

On the first of July, the brigades of infantry and cavalry under M. de Rochambeau, near Hombourg, were attacked and defeated by the brigade of the british grenadiers, Elliot's horse, the blues, and four hanoverian squadrons, all commanded by the marquis of Granby. Elliot's regiment made the first charge, and was in danger, till colonel Harvey, at the head of the blues, passed the village of Hombourgh on full gallop, overthrew every thing in his way, and came seasonably to its rescue. These two gallant regiments maintained an unequal combat, till the arrival of the infantry, when the enemy retreated in the utmost hurry. The loss of the allies, in killed, wounded, and taken, was under an hundred; but that of the french was considerable, the number of the prisoners alone amounting to upwards of two hundred and fifty. Lord Frederick Cavendish's corps came up during the retreat; and the hussars of Baver and Reidesel pushed on to Rothenbourg, where they destroyed a considerable magazine. Colonels Harvey and

and Erskine, and majors Forbes and Ainsley, distinguished themselves greatly in this engagement. The next day, lieutenant-colonel Reidesel burnt 150,000 rations of Hay, 40,000 rations of oats, and carried off seventy fat oxen, belonging to the french.

Two days after, the army under the prince of Conde made major Scheiter, two officers, and upwards of 120 men, prisoners of war; and afterwards took the little village of Rhene, in which there were some small magazines.

M. de Viomenil, under the orders of the prince of Conde, on the 6th and 7th of July, ruined many magazines belonging to the allied army, upon the lower Embs and the Haze, to the amount of seventy-six loaded waggons, 62,800 sacks of grain, 46,880 sacks of oats, and 4,000,000 rations of hay; to the value of four millions of livres. Soon after one of the largest magazines on the Embs, consisting of near two millions of rations of forage, was destroyed by a very small party of the french.

The same month, the count de Vaux attacked and defeated a large party of M. de Luckner's corps near Uslar, made one lieutenant-colonel, one captain, and eighty-one private men, prisoners; and took many horses.

On the other hand, general Luckner took the french partisan Monet, with his whole corps, at Schaffhoff, at the distance of 200 paces from Cassel. The marquis de Chamberant, on the 10th of july, destroyed part of the british bakery, and provision waggons, near Warbourg, took 210 horses, besides rendering 20 others unfit for service; the english commissary, and eighty-three other persons, were also made prisoners of war.

On the 11th of july, the castle of Waldeck, eleven leagues from Cassel, surrendered to general Conway, and the garrison, consisting of 160 men, capitulated upon condition of not serving for one year against
Great-

Great-Britain, or her allies. A few days after, M. de Valliere took 400 horses from the allied army, and entirely defeated, near Ulfen, one of their detachments.

On the 23d of July, in consequence of his serene highness's orders, general Zastrow and Gilsæ, with their respective corps, hanoverians and hessians, passed the Fulda at day-break, and attacked the right of the french army, composed chiefly of saxons, commanded by prince Xavier. General Waldhausen took post at Bonnefort, by which position, he not only kept in check the garrison of Munden, but was ready to fall upon the enemy's rear when occasion offered. Our troops passed the Fulda, under a heavy fire from the enemy, which they sustained with the greatest intrepidity, and soon got possession of a wood, which covered the enemy's right. Prince Xavier, finding his flank gained, after an obstinate resistance, began to give way, which general Waldhausen observing, he immediately attacked with his cavalry, and completed the victory. We took thirteen pieces of cannon in the pursuit, two standards, and about a thousand prisoners, among whom was the prince of Isenburg.

Lieutenant-general Stainville, who occupied the intrenched camp upon the Kratzenberg with 10,000 men, quitted his intrenchments to cover prince Xavier's retreat. Prince Frederick of Brunswick immediately entered the abandoned intrenchments, and totally demolished the strong lines on the heights of Kratzberg, and all the redoubts and other works. On this defeat, prince Soubise dispatched three couriers, one after another, to press the prince of Conde to quit his camp on the lower Rhine, and march to Marbourg, in order, if possible, to enable the french to keep their footing in Westphalia. In consequence of these orders, the dislocation of his army was made at Haltesen on the 25th, and the troops began their

march

march in three divisions, but so interlaced with each other, as to follow very close.

The hereditary prince of Brunswick, who commanded the army destined to oppose the prince of Conde, marched about the same time with his highness, and reached the neighbourhood of Marbourg on the first of august, within two hours march of the prince of Conde. In the interim, prince Ferdinand formed the design of attacking the french main army, before the arrival of that of Conde. He accordingly, on the 21st, at night, crossed the Eder, with three brigades of infantry, and eight squadrons of horse, and joined the marquis of Granby upon the heights of Falckenberg. The design was, if practicable, to attack the left flank of the main french army, posted between Hilgenberg and Melsungen, whilst general Sporcken should engage their front, and prince Frederick of Brunswick their right; but upon reconnoitring, so close to the enemy as to be exposed to the fire of three batteries, he found their disposition too strong, and too well provided with troops, to hazard the attack. Whilst prince Ferdinand was doing this, he left his army formed in columns, presenting the heads of the columns only to the enemy's view; but observing them to be embarrassed, he formed at eight in the evening, within cannon-shot, and general Sporcken began to cannonade them. At ten his highness withdrew the troops to the heights of Falckenberg, leaving the picquets advanced, to keep the fires burning to deceive the enemy. At two in in the morning he repassed the Schwalm at Harte, and the Eder at Nieder Melrick. Suspecting, however, that the French would take the opportunity of the night to decamp, he left lord Granby upon the Falckenberg, with orders to stay till day-light, and, in case the enemy retired, immediately to take possession of the high grounds of Melsungen. His lordship found the french had decamped, and executed

the

the orders he had received. Thus prince Ferdinand succeeded, in obliging the enemy to abandon a post they gave out was not to be forced, without risking a double action, and which could not fail to cost a great many lives.

The same day that prince Ferdinand marched to attack the french at Melsungen, july 25, general Stainville, with four regiments of dragoons, fell into an ambuscade at Morschen, where general Freytag commanded. These regiments were routed and dispersed with great loss by Freytag, whose troops made a considerable booty on the occasion; for the enemy, after a great slaughter, fled with precipitation, and left their baggage to the victors. However, general Stainville afterwards joined the prince of Conde, whose army moved both on the the right and left, to endeavour to restore the communication that had been left entirely at the mercy of prince Ferdinand. It was thought, that that prince would have pushed the french to a decisive action, but at the time when every thing was prepared for the attack, a sudden rain fell, which swelled the Fulda so as to render it unfordable.

His majesty's army, nevertheless, gained some advantages. A body of troops crossed the river, and took post opposite to the center of their army, whilst the prince marched with the greatest rapidity behind their army, and gained possession of Muhlchausen, Eschwege, and Wanfreid. The french army, under the marshals Soubise and d'Etrees, abandoned the banks of the Fulda, on the 17th at night, and marched away by their right, in the space which lies between Spangenberg and Liechtenau.

On the 18th, the army under prince Ferdinand followed them, and took up his head-quarters the next day in the morning at Homberg, and the hereditary prince was so posted as to be able to join him. The prince of Conde marched by his right towards the

town

town of Fulda, with a view to cover the retreat of the french army.

I should have taken notice, that on the 28th of july the count de Stainville defeated 400 light troops of the allies near Vacha, and that about the same time, Messrs. de Rochechouart and de Lostanges dispersed a detachment of the allies near Uslar, and made 200 prisoners. They afterwards divided their forces, and took, or destroyed, at Carlshaven and Beverungen, a magazine, and twenty-nine large boats, laden with provisions.

About the same time, M. de Verteuil ruined a magazine at Brackel, and took 120 horses, together with 60 soldiers. The baron du Blaisel marched from Giessen to Amoeneburg, and surprised and took prisoners 400 of the allies.

The french, on the second of august, made an unsuccessful attack upon the troops commanded by general Freytag, at Neumersten. On the 16th of the same month, the french garrison in Gottingen, having first destroyed the fortifications of the place, and set fire to the powder magazine, by the explosion of which 50 saxons were killed, retired to Witzenhausen; they left three brass guns, and a great quantity of all kinds of ammunition, in Gottingen. The night after, the french also abandoned Munden.

About the same time, colonel Reidesel dislodged M. Conflans from Pattenberg, where the latter lost 70 private men, and many horses. The hereditary prince of Brunswick, on the 22d of august, charged the vanguard of the prince of Conde, under the orders of M. de Levis, in which action the french lost 150 men. Three days after, the marquis d'Auvet bombarded Ham, in the dutchy of Cleves; but on the approach of 4000 men from the allied army, they thought fit to retreat, and the town was saved. The same day the prince of Conde gained a small advantage over the hereditary prince of Brunswick, and, after

after a smart cannonade, obliged him to retreat, with the loss of three field-pieces.

But a more important action took place between these two princes on the 30th of august. The hereditary prince, and general Luckner, with 19 battalions and 40 squadrons, engaged the different corps under the prince of Conde, count Stainville, and the chevalier de Levis, near Neuheim and Friedberg. At the beginning of the action, the french were driven from the steep mountains of Johannesberg into the plain below, by the vigorous charge of the allies; but a considerable reinforcement arriving from the grand army, under d'Etrees and Soubise, the attack was renewed with spirit and success, and the allies being repulsed in their turn, were obliged to repass the Wert. The hereditary prince, while he was endeavouring to rally his disordered troops, received a wound in his hip; the bullet entered on the right side, above the hip-bone, and came out on the back, four inches below it *. Prince Ferdinand, who seems to have had a better information of the situation of the french army than the hereditary prince, marched with a considerable part of his forces from his camp at Nidda, to support the allies, and arrived time enough to prevent the enemy from reaping the benefit of the advantage that they had gained. The only british troops concerned in this action, were Elliot's dragoons, and the chasseurs under lord Frederick Cavendish. Colonel Clinton, notwithstanding he was wounded, continued with the hereditary prince two hours afterward, and never mentioned the hurt he had received, till the prince desired him to carry an account of the battle to prince Ferdinand, when he acquainted him

---

* This wound proved more dangerous than was at first expected. About the beginning of October he was attacked by a fever, occasioned by the working of a splinter out of the wound. On the 13th, his fever began to go off, and he was declared out of danger; he continued mending, and, at last, happily recovered.

that he was unable to obey his orders. On the part of the enemy, M. de la Guiche, lieutenant-general, and commander of the brigade of Boisgelin, was taken prisoner. The french troops, in general, behaved in this action with intrepidity and spirit. The regiment of Boisgelin had a particular share in the suffering and glory of the day. The french, according to their own account, had not above 500 men killed and wounded, whilst they made the loss of the allies to amount to 600 killed, and 1500 prisoners, including 400 wounded, besides two standards, and 15 pieces of cannon, taken. But, according to the account of the allies, their loss in killed, wounded, and prisoners, amounted only to 1398 men, and ten small pieces of cannon taken.

The enemy, nevertheless, had been obliged to abandon Gottingen, and the neighbourhood of Cassel, in which they left a garrison of 10,000 chosen men, with orders to defend the place to the last extremity. However, prince Ferdinand prepared to lay siege to the latter; but the french threatened to set fire to the suburbs, if attacked upon the north-west quarter. In order to cover this siege, prince Ferdinand changed his position, in consequence of which the french armies repassed the Lohne, in the neighbourhood of Giessen, and advanced, on the 13th of september, near Marpourg. On the 15th, prince Ferdinand ordered an attack to be made on their left and rear, and every where driving them from their posts, obliged them to make a precipitate retreat over the Lohne. The siege of Cassel, that had been suspended on this occasion, was again resumed; the troops that had been detached from thence were ordered thither again, as also the heavy artillery that had been sent away.

A detachment of the french army, on the 9th and 10th, harrassed the allies in their retreat, drove two battalions out of Laubach, and took some pontoons and baggage. About the same time a body
of

of the french, under M. de St. Victor, attempting to intercept the bread waggon train belonging to the allies, between Alsfelt and Neustadt, were defeated by general Freytag. Prince Ferdinand marched to Wetter, through the same routs which the prince of Conde had opened for the french army, and on the 16th drove the enemy's garrison out of that place, and obliged the prince of Conde to repass the Lahne. The french abandoned Schweinberg on the same day.

From the 7th to the 21st of september, the armies were in perpetual motion, the french to open their communication with Cassel, the allies to cut it off. In this view, one of the most bloody contests happened that is any where recorded. Amoenebourg is a small fortress, but of great importance, as it opens the pass that leads to the adjacent country, which the motions of the french all tended to enter. Amoenebourg was occupied by a battalion of the british legion, and a detachment of 200 men from the reserve; Kirchayn, a more considerable place, had a garrison of 400 men; and the bridge over the Lahne, that separated these two places, was guarded by a detachment of 200 men; on one side of this bridge was a mill, called Bucker-Muhl, and on the other a small redoubt, in which 100 men only were placed, to defend the head of the bridge. About six in the morning of the 21st of september, the weather being extremely foggy, the enemy attacked the post at the Bucker-Muhl, without being able to carry it. They planted at the same time some cannon, at the foot of the hill of Amoenebourg, about 200 paces from the bridge, in order to bear on the redoubt. It appeared, that their intention at first, in taking possession of the mill, was only to cut off our communication with Amoenebourg; but the fog, with the fire of the cannon, giving it the appearance of a design of more consequence, we brought up several pieces

pieces of artillery. Lord Granby's whole corps moved that way: General Weiſſenbach marched to Kirchayn, and eight battalions and four ſquadrons entered the wood of Stautzenberg. In proportion as the number of our cannon increaſed, that of the enemy did ſo likewiſe, till they had brought up 20 pieces of heavy artillery. On our ſide, all the heſſian, and buckeburg, and half of the hanoverian artillery, were placed upon the height of Bucker-Muhl; and from break of day till dark night, a moſt terrible firing continued without intermiſſion. We maintained the redoubt, and the enemy the mill. Hiſtory can ſcarcely furniſh an inſtance of ſo obſtinate a diſpute; in which the loſs on either ſide may eaſily be conceived to be conſiderable. The troops in the redoubt were conſtantly relieved, after having fired 60 charges; and towards the cloſe of the day 17 complete battalions had been employed on the ſervice. The redoubt was expoſed to the fire of the enemy's artillery, at the diſtance of about 300 paces, and to that of all their ſmall arms, within 30 paces diſtance; beſides that, the troops, coming and going, were obliged to march near 400 paces, expoſed to the enemy's cannon, loaded with grape ſhot. The enemy's ſituation was nearly the ſame, excepting that the mill afforded them rather more ſhelter. The oldeſt ſoldiers ſay, they never ſaw ſo ſevere a cannonade; ſince, though there were near 50 pieces of cannon employed, their execution was confined to the ſpace of about 400 paces; and not only the fire of the artillery, but the muſquetry too of the two oppoſite poſts was not intermitted a ſingle minute for near fifteen hours. Towards the concluſion of the affair, the number of the killed and wounded, at the entrance of, and in the redoubt, on our ſide, ſeemed to exceed 500; ſo that the troops which came there late in the day, made uſe of the dead bodies to raiſe the parapet a little, which was almoſt levelled; and within a very

ſmall

small compass, 1700 of the enemy's balls were afterwards taken up.

While the enemy were attacking the redoubt, they played likewise some batteries on Amoenebourg, and assaulted it three times, but without success. On the 22d, every thing was quiet, and the works on both sides were repaired without molestation.

After a fire from the enemy, which lasted all night, and by which they had made a practicable breach, the garrison of Amoenebourg surrendered prisoners.

In consequence of which, on the 23d, the enemy pushed forward the right of their camp, and posted a body between Amoenebourg and Kleinseellieim.

The french account says, that their men fired till the barrels of their pieces were so hot, that they could not charge them.

On the 18th, the enemy pushed a considerable detachment to Ziegenhayn, and thought themselves strong enough to force major-general Freytag; but he attacked them, and pursued them to Alsfeldt, killing, wounding, and taking 400 men. It is supposed their intention was to load their waggons with meal for the relief of the garrison of Cassel, which was said to be in great distress. But notwithstanding their subsistance was only bread made of oats, and no great quantity remained of that; yet M. Diesbach, the commandant, rejected all terms of capitulation, so that the trenches were opened before it in the night of the 16th of october, with the loss only of 20 killed, and several wounded, since which the garrison made several unsuccessful sallies to interrupt the approaches.

With respect to the affair of Amoenebourg, there were employed, on the part of the allies, 17 complete battalions, at different times. Lieutenant-colonel Manlove, major M'Lean, the captains Twisleton and Reynell, and ensign Clive, brother to lord Clive, were killed; lieutenant-colonel Hale, the captains Peter,

Campbell, and Wyvil, together with seven inferior officers, were wounded. The total loss, including that of the hanoverian corps, amounted to 161 killed, 460 wounded, and 17 missing; in all 638, according to the returns in the London Gazette; tho' a subsequent general account makes it amount to near 800: 19 horses were killed, and four pieces of cannon were rendered unserviceable. The loss of the french, as they acknowledged, was 300 killed, and near 800 wounded; among the latter were the marquis de Castries, and the chevalier de Sarsfeld; but other accounts make the loss of the french to have amounted to near 2000 men.

The city of Osnabrug, having no garrison to defend it, was, on the 30th and 31st of october, taken and plundered by the french partisan Cambefort.

The motions that the allies had made a little before, to facilitate the siege of Cassel, proved successful, for on the 1st of november that city surrendered to prince Frederick of Brunswick, after the trenches had been opened before it from the 16th of the foregoing month. The garrison obtained all the honours of war, and were escorted by the nearest road to the french army under the command of the marshals d'Etrees and Soubise. They were allowed to carry with them all their baggage, two twelve pounders, and one four pounder, for the governor, and all the effects belonging to the officers, without searching. A separate capitulation was granted for the officers, in which every convenience was provided for the sick, and those who attended them.

Six days after the surrender of Cassel, prince Ferdinand acquainted his general officers, that the preliminaries between Great-Britain, France, Spain, and Portugal, were signed, and that the french marshals had received orders to cease all hostilities; upon which his highness sent orders to the commanding officers before Ziegenhayn to stop their operations
against

againſt that place. But this ceſſation was formally ſettled a few days after in the following manner.

Convention agreed upon between the army of his britannic majeſty, and the french army.

I. There ſhall be a ſuſpenſion of arms between the troops on both ſides, on the day of the ſignature and ratification of the preſent convention, and as ſoon as poſſible between the moſt diſtant detached parties.

II. There ſhall be a line formed between the two armies, the center of which ſhall be the Lahne, from its ſource to its junction with the Ohme, and from thence along that river to Merlau. This line ſhall extend as far as Nehem upon the Roer, by Unna, Dortmund, Halteren, and Coesfeld, and terminate at the frontier of the United Provinces.

III. The french garriſon at Ziegenhayn ſhall remain quiet, and pay ready money for every thing they may ſtand in need of, till ſuch time as they evacuate the town. A place ſhall be aſſigned them to cut wood, with which they ſhall be furniſhed at the current price of the country.

Done at Bruck-Muhl upon the Ohre, november 15, 1762.

  (L. S.) G. Howard, lieutenant-general.
  (L. S.) Le comte de Guerchy.

Having read theſe conditions contained in three articles, we declare them agreeable, and promiſe to execute them, bona fide, in all points.

At the bridge of Bruck-Muhl, november 15, 1762, at two in the afternoon.

     (Signed)
  (L. S.) Ferdinand, duke of Brunſwick
     and Lunebourg.
  (L. S.) L. M. d'Etrees.
  (L. S.) L. M. de Soubise.

Having thus related the history of the war between us and France and Spain, as well by land as sea, till terminated by a peace; it now only remains, to put a conclusion to this work, to take a view of the campaign of 1762, between our ally the king of Prussia and the austrians, to that period when a peace was also settled between them; and thus a general peace established throughout Europe.

The history of this part of the war, closed the last year with an account of the surrender of Colberg to the russians. As soon as they were in possession of this important place, they immediately began to repair the fortifications of it. Eighteen thousand of their troops occupied Stargard, and the right of the Oder to the neighbourhood of Stetin. General Platen, on the reduction of this fortress, took the route of Berlin, in his way to join prince Henry in Saxony, and the prince of Wurtemburg filed off to the duchy of Mecklenburg Schoverin. On the 8th, prince Henry met general Platen at Leipsic, and, after settling the quarters assigned to the corps which that general led into Saxony, the prince returned on the 11th to Hoff; where he established his head-quarters. Upon the prince of Wurtemberg's arrival at Mecklenburg Schwerin, the reigning duke returned to Lübeck, and ordered his mint to be transported to Entin, in ducal Holstein. The prince's head-quarters were established at Costock, and those of colonel Belling at Gastrow.

The prussian generals Platen and Wunsh, after having taken several places, on the 12th, penetrated within a league of Narembourg, which the army of the empire quitted, and retired towards Weimar, with the loss of men and baggage, which obliged the army of the empire to quit their quarters at Narembourg, Zeitz, Altemberg, and Gera. This expedition proved the enlargement of prince Henry's winter-quarters. M. Reid, on the 21st of january, attacked the advanced

vanced posts of the prussians in Saxony, in which the latter lost near 1000 men, in killed, wounded, and deserters, together with four pieces of cannon. And, four days after, the chevalier de Vosseil, with a detachment of sixty-five men, obliged 300 prussians to lay down their arms; for which brave action he was made a lieutenant-colonel.

The affairs of the king of Prussia had, for some time past, been in a very bad condition; but a fortunate event for him fell out the beginning of this year; the death of Elizabeth, empress of Russia, on the 5th of january. By her death he was delivered from a very powerful enemy. Peter the third, who succeeded her, immediately shewed himself to be his friend; and the russian general Zernichef soon received orders to quit Silesia, with the 12000 men that he commanded, and to return into Poland by the way of Moravia. His prussian majesty issued an order for releasing prisoners without ransom, and soon after a cessation of hostilities was settled between the russians and prussians, which was signed at Stargard on the 16th of april. A cessation of hostilities, till the fine weather should come on, was also concluded between the prussians and swedes; and likewise for three months between the commandant of Great Glaugou, and the austrian troops stationed along the Bober under general Beck. The amity between the emperor of Russia and the king of Prussia further appeared by all the prisoners throughout the dominions of the two sovereigns being released; with other acts of mutual friendship.

But, to return back to the progress of the war: on the 3d of february an austrian detachment attacked L'Abadie's independent battalion at Grofs Purdon, near Greinm, killed the greatest part of it, and took many prisoners. Six days after, prince Lobkowitz dislodged the prussians from Pegau, who lost, on that occasion, about 400 men; and the austrians had only twenty

twenty men killed, twenty-six wounded, and fifteen missing. On the 20th following, the austrians and imperialists dislodged the prussians from the post of Lomatsch, and burnt a magazine.

A treaty of peace was signed on the 5th of may at Petersbourg, by the baron de Goltze, in the name of the king of Prussia, and by the count de Woronzof, great chancellor, in the name of the emperor of Russia. In consequence of this treaty, 16,000 men, under the command of count Zernishew, received orders to join the king of Prussia in Silesia.

The prince Henry of Prussia opened the campaign in Saxony on the 12th, 13th, and 14th of may, by crossing the Mulda, surprising the left wing of the austrians near Dobeln. General Zetwitz, 43 officers, and 1536 men were taken, and three pieces of cannon. Prince Henry afterwards got possession of Freyberg; here he found a considerable magazine. The austrian general, Maguire, retired from Freyberg to Dippoldswalda. General Luzinski, on the 21st, defeated the prussian major-general de Bendemar, and took prisoners one lieutenant-colonel, 14 officers, about 5 or 600 private men, and afterwards got possession of Chemnitz. A treaty of peace was signed, may 22, at Hamburgh, between the kings of Prussia and Sweden, by their respective plenipotentiaries.

On the 26th of may, lieutenant colonel de Belgrade, with 300 men, under the orders of colonel Torreck, fell upon three prussian squadrons, and 200 foot, by surprise, near Freyberg, killed many, made near 80 prisoners, dispersed the rest, and took all their baggage. Three days after, another skirmish happened also to the disadvantage of the prussians, when one of their posts, at Schluben, was attacked by M. de Magyary; when 21 prussians were killed, 69 made prisoners, including officers, and 145 horses taken. Two days after, major-general M. de Kleefeld attacked ed colonel Dingelſtedt near Gerinſwalde, and obliged him to retreat to the poſt of Waldheim, with the loſs of 189 men made priſoners, five officers included. The auſtrians had only ſix killed, and forty wounded.

On the 2d of june, the auſtrians being reinforced from Sileſia, attacked the pruſſians on all ſides, but, according to the London Gazette, were repulſed with the loſs only of 200 men; though the auſtrians made the loſs of their enemies much more conſiderable, at the ſame time concealing their own. M. Daun, with an army of 80,000 veterans, took the field on the 15th, and encamped at Kratzlau, in ſuch a manner as to cover Schweidnitz, and obſerve the motions of the king of Pruſſia, at this time in the neighbourhood of Breſlau. The king, notwithſtanding the approach of the enemy, encamped on the 11th, with ſeven battalions only, at Butterlin, within three german miles of the auſtrian army, and five from Breſlau. This month the garriſon of Teſchen, in Upper Sileſia, conſiſting of 200 men, ſurrendered to the pruſſian general Werner. And major-general Grant, commandant of Neiſſe in Sileſia, defeated a body of auſtrians near Otmachau; and made general Draſkowitz and ſeveral officers, together with 400 men, priſoners of war. But on the 6th of july, general Nieuwied made three unſucceſsful attacks upon the auſtrian general Brentano, who guarded the defiles of Adelſbach with 3000 men. The cannonade continued from three in the morning till after eight. His pruſſian majeſty was preſent, and much expoſed during the whole attack; he loſt upwards of 1000 men in killed, wounded, and priſoners. But the next day general Nieuwiedt penetrated to Weiſſe in Bohemia, and made 300 auſtrians priſoners.

About this time the emperor Peter III. was depoſed; he died a few days after, and his wife Catherine II. was declared june 28, O. S. ſovereign and of Ruffia. She thought proper to order her troops in Siberia, Pomerania, and Pruffia to separate on the 22d of july, from thofe of the king of Pruffia, and to return back by the nearest roads to Ruffia. The pruffian irregulars, on the 10th and 11th of july fet fire to, and pillaged the towns of Jaromirz and Konigfgratz in Bohemia. At the latter place large magazines and fmall ones were burnt or deftroyed. A few days after the pruffian general Kleift attacked general Plunket near Einfiedel, took 500 prifoners, and obliged him to retire to Anffig.

The king of Pruffia, on the 21ft of july, attacked the right of marfhal Daun's army, on the heights of Burckerfdorff, which were carried by the pruffians. An attack was then made on the village of Ludwigfdorff and Leuthmaufdorff, from whence the auftrians were likewife driven; and, by thefe fucceffes, their communication with Schweidnitz was entirely cut off. It was refolved the next day to have attacked the poft of Bofdorff, towards the left of marfhal Daun's army, near Tanhaufen, where the head quarter was; but the marfhal retired, with part of his army, near Braunau in Bohemia; and the other part had withdrawn into the county of Glatz. The pruffians took 14 pieces of cannon, and upwards of 1000 prifoners; the lofs of the pruffians did not exceed 300 men. This fuccefsful attack was executed entirely by pruffian troops.

The marfhal's retreat made way for the fiege of Schweidnitz. Twenty-two battalions of infantry were deftined for this fervice, commanded by lieutenant-general Tauenzin, governor of Breflau, who had under him major-general Thaddin, and M. de Fern, as chief engineer. The garrifon confifted of 9000 men, under the command of general Guafco, who had under him M. Janini, and M. de Grimboval, as chief engineer. The pruffian infantry encamped on the heights near Schweidnitz, and the cavalry formed a
chain

chain in the plain of Kautzendorff, near to the army of Wurtemberg, who was posted so as to watch the motions of the enemy in the county of Glatz, and to cover the artillery and military stores arriving from Neiss, in the neighbourhood of which general Werner was arrived, as was the prince of Bevern to that of Cassel. His majesty in person commanded the army that covered the siege.

While the armies were in these situations, M. Laudohn was detached by Daun with a superior force, to attack the prince of Bevern, and dislodge him from the advantageous post he occupied; but the prince defended himself so gallantly, that the king had time to come to his assistance, who, putting the austrians between two fires, soon routed them, and pursued them with a terrible slaughter. In this engagement the prussians are said to have taken two pair of silver kettle drums, seven standards, several colours, besides 1500 prisoners, and a number of cannon.

The same day general Seidlitz came up with the army of the empire, near Averbach, obliged one part to retire to Plaven, and the other to Eybenstock, made upwards of 300 prisoners, and took a quantity of baggage. The prince of Bevern and general Werner abandoned Troppau and Gratz. On the second of august, the generals Seidlitz and Kleist, with a body of 12,000 prussians, attacked the prince of Lowestein, at the head of 8000 austrians, near the village of Guadrop, at a small distance from Toplitz in Bohemia. After a warm dispute, the former were obliged to retire with the loss of 500 men killed, between 3 and 400 prisoners, and 400 deserters. The next day general Kleist renewed the attack, but with no better success; upon which he evacuated Bohemia. This is the account given by the austrians of this affair; but the prussians, with less credibility, reported that their force was inferior to that of the enemy;

that

that they took 400 men prisoners, and that their whole loss in killed, wounded, and missing, did not exceed 200. However, the prussians, on the 2d, 3d, and 4th of the same month, plundered the town of Dux in Bohemia; though with little advantage to themselves, yet the damage the inhabitants received, amounted to 30,000 florins.

The austrians, with a view to relieve Schweidnitz, marched thirty-three battalions, eleven regiments of cavalry, and three of hussars, commanded by Beck, Brentano, Lascy, and O'Donnel, to attack the duke of Bevern, upon the heights of Peile beyond Reichenbach. They begun the attack at 5 o'clock in the afternoon, august 16, but the duke resolutely maintained his ground till the king of prussia, with thirty battalions and eight squadrons, came in person to his assistance. His majesty charged and defeated the five regiments under general O'Donnel, after a warm and obstinate dispute: but night coming on, the austrians abandoned their enterprize. The consequence of this action was variously reported by the two different parties. According to the austrians account, they took 500 prisoners, and 2 pieces of cannon, with the loss only of 17 officers wounded, or prisoners, 131 private men killed, 354 wounded, and 336 missing, in all 1834; besides the loss of 3 standards: but the prussians reported the loss of the enemy to have exceeded 2000 men, and 5 standards.

Nothing material after this happened till the 11th of september, when the prussian general le Grand, commandant of Neisse, was attacked by an inferior body of austrians, under colonel de Lanius. Le Grand having had 121 men killed, and 103 taken prisoners, and lost 2 pieces of cannon in the action, was obliged to make a hasty retreat to Neisse; the austrians had only 7 men killed, and 40 wounded. Two days after, the prussians, commanded by general Schmettau, took Zittau, after having permitted the garrison to to retire to Gubel. But having taken hostages from that town and the neighbouring places, the prussians retired the next day to Gorlitz.

Prince Henry being advantageously situated, with his corps, at Welsdruf, Pretshendorf, Travenstein, and Burkenheim, the austrians and imperialists under general Haddick, made a vigorous attack upon them the latter end of september. The prussians made a brave resistance for three days, and both parties lost a considerable number of men; but in the night between the 29th and 30th, prince Henry thought prudent to make his army repass the Mulda: this they successfully effected, and the next morning drew up in order of battle on the other side of the Mulda. Prince Henry afterwards retired to Freyberg, and general Hulsen towards Katzenhausen.

At length a very important event took place, the surrender of Schweidnitz. This place, after a siege of two months and two days, capitulated * to the king of Prussia on the 9th of october. Lieutenant-general Guasco did his best to obtain more favourable terms for his brave garrison; but, on the 8th of october, a grenade from the besiegers fell upon a magazine of powder, No. 2. and blew up 256 men, officers included; and in the night of the same day a mine took full effect, carried away part of the rampart, made a considerable breach in the covered way, and filled up the ditch with the rubbish; they were therefore now obliged to surrender. The garrison, consisting of 8000 effective men, besides sick and wounded, marched out with the honours of war, laid

---

* This place changed its master four times during the course of the war. It was taken by the empress queen, november 12, 1757, after the trenches had been opened sixteen days. It was retaken april 17, 1758, upon the seventeenth day after the opening of the trenches, by the king of Prussia. General Laudohn retook it by assault, september 30; and october 9, 1762, it was once more recovered, as above, by the king of Prussia, for the fourth time.

down

down their arms, and became prisoners of war; but in consideration of their bravery, were promised the preference in case of an exchange. The garrison had suffered a great loss of men during the siege; they had 32 officers, and 1249 soldiers killed; 53 officers, and 2223 soldiers wounded; and the number of prisoners of every denomination, including the sick and wounded, amounted to 8784 private men, besides 238 officers, in all 12,341. A great quantity of artillery and military stores were found in the place. The loss on the part of the prussians amounted to 2929 private men, besides 86 officers, viz. 25 officers, and 1084 subalterns and private men, killed, or who died afterwards of their wounds, and 61 officers, and 1845 subalterns and private men, wounded. His prussian majesty, after having taken possession of this place, sent a large reinforcement to prince Henry, and returned to his former quarters at Peterswalde.

On the 14th of the same month, general Belling was attacked by general Haddick, and the prince of Stolberg, in the Rathswald, or wood of Raths, who obliged him to quit that post. But a considerable reinforcement arriving from prince Henry, Belling, in his turn, repulsed the enemy; but, before he could repossess himself of his former posts, he was the next day re-attacked by the austrians and imperialists. The action was obstinately maintained by both parties for some time; but the prussians were at length driven from the wood, with the loss of 2000 men made prisoners, eight or nine pieces of cannon, eight colours, and two standards. The regiments of Kleist and Salmouth suffered greatly. The hungarian regiment of Guilay behaved with most extraordinary bravery. The consequence of the prussians losing this battle was, the abandoning of Freyberg.

In the course of the same month, part of the regiment of cavalry under the orders of general Dingelstedt,

genstedt was surprised by the austrian general Zollern at Kirchayn, in Lower Lusatia, who took some horses belonging to the baggage, and 300 prisoners.

On the 29th of the same month, the combined army of austrians, near Freyberg, was attacked by prince Henry of Prussia. The action continued many hours, during which a considerable number were killed and wounded on both sides; for the engagement began at day-break, and lasted till two o'clock in the afternoon, when the prussians proving the victors, the enemy abandoned the field of battle, and the town of Freyberg, to them. Lieutenant-general baron de Rodt, one colonel, one major, 24 captains, 41 lieutenants, 11 ensigns, 159 inferior officers, and 4174 private men were taken prisoners by the prussians, besides taking nine standards and colours, and 27 pieces of cannon.

The night between the 3d and 4th of november, the austrians began to abandon their camp at Fravenstein in Saxony, and were pursued by general Belling. At the same time, the prussian general Kleist made, by the way of Ensiedel, an incursion into Bohemia: in his march he destroyed several magazines, particularly one at Saaze, estimated at 900,000 florins, and ravaged the country to the very gates of Prague.

The king of Prussia now determined to hasten his march into Saxony, to end the campaign; leaving therefore the prince of Bevern to command his army in Silesia, the king himself crossed the Elbe on the 6th of november, with 15 battalions. The siege of Dresden was again resolved; but happily, not only a convention for a cessation of hostilities in Silesia, during the winter, took place on the 15th of december, but also a like cessation for Saxony. But though a temporary peace reigned in these two parts, the armies of the empire being defeated and dispersed, several parties of prussians ravaged the countries of those sovereigns, who had combined against his majesty of

Pruſſia. The pruſſians entered Franconia, and puſhed their detachments far and wide, raiſed heavy contributions, and ſpread diſtreſs wherever they came: many principalities, to avoid being plundered, accepted of a neutrality. A convention was afterwards ſettled between the ſtates of the empire and his pruſſian majeſty, by which the former engaged to withdraw their contingents from the imperial army, and his majeſty to recal his troops from the circles. Thus was a temporary peace reſtored to the empire, which at laſt happily proved permanent; for the negociations for a peace between the empreſs queen and his majeſty of Pruſſia, were ſo ſucceſsfully and rapidly carried on, that on the 15th of february, 1763, peace was ſigned between thoſe two powers, and the elector of Saxony, at Hubertſberg. On the 18th of march following, the ratifications of the definitive treaties with the empreſs queen, and elector of Saxony, arrived at Hubertſberg, and were immediately exchanged; and on the 5th of the ſame month the proclamation of his pruſſian majeſty's peace with the abovementioned powers was publiſhed, with the uſual ſolemnities, at Berlin. Thus, after a great variety of fortune, the brave and illuſtrious king of Pruſſia ſits down in the full and quiet poſſeſſion of all his territories, and Europe once more enjoys peace.

APPENDIX.

List of French and English ships of war and frigates, taken, destroyed, or lost, during the late war.

French line of battle ships.

Taken.	Guns.	Destroyed.	Guns.
Formidable	80	Ocean	84
Foudroyant	80	Soleil Royal	84
Centaur	74	Bein Aimé	74
Temeraire	74	Entreprennant	74
Achille	64	Heros	74
Alcide	64	Prudent	74
Belliqueux	64	Redoutab	74
Lys	64	Thesée	74
Modeste	64	Juste	70
Orphée	64	Superbe	70
Raisonable	64	Capricieux	64
St. Anne	64	Celebre	64
Arc en Ciel	50	Alegon	50
Oriflamme	53	Apollon	50

French frigates.

Taken.	Guns.	Taken.	Guns.
Abenaquis	44	Guirlande	22
Danae	40	Hardie	20
Arethuse	32	Mignonne	20
Bellone	32	Escarboucle	16
Blonde	32	Anemone	14
		Boufonne	

Taken.	Guns.	Taken.	Guns.
Boufonne	32	Epreuve	14
Brune	32	Sardoigne	14
Commette	32		
Diane	32	*Destroyed.*	
Hermione	32	Aquilon	48
Sirene	32	Atalante	36
Vestale	32	Felicite	36
Emeraude	28	Fidelle	36
La Folle	24	Rose	36
Opale	24	Fleur de Lys	32
Galathée	24	Nymphe	30
Terpsichore	24	Pomona	24
Tygre	24	Cleone	16
Zephire	24	Biche	16

English men of war taken and destroyed by the French this whole war.

Taken.	Guns.	Taken.	Guns.
Warwick, retaken	60	Merlin, retaken	14
Greenwich, since lost	50	Stork	14
Winchelsea, retaken	24	*Destroyed.*	
Blandford, restored	20	Bridgewater	20
Hawke, retaken	16	Triton	20

French ships lost by accident.

	Guns.		Guns.
Northumberland	70	Concord	30
Opiniatre	64	Sauvage	30
Leopard	60	Harmonie	26
Aigle	50	Zenobie	26
Greenwich	50	Minerve	24

English

English ships loft this war by accident.

Ramilies	90	Humber	40
Prince George	84	Huffar	28
Invincible, F.	74	Leoftoffe	28
Refolution	74	Lyme	26
Conqueror	70	Tartar's prize, F.	24
Duc d'Aquitaine	64	Biddeford	20
Effex	64	Mermaid	20
Mars, F.	64	Queenborough	20
Raifonable, F.	64	Ferret	16
Sunderland	60	Pheafant, F.	16
Tilbury	60	Peregrine	16
Litchfield	50	Diligence	14
Newcaftle	50	Scorpion	14
Chefterfield	44		

There are fome few articles befides referred to in the courfe of this work, but as it has already much exceeded the length intended, in order to avoid an increafe of expence to the public, the reader is referred for them to the Magazines for the feveral years, if he fhould think it neceffary to fee at length what for brevity fake hath only been abridged.

The definitive treaty of peace between his britannic majefty, the moft chriftian king, and the king of Spain, concluded at Paris the 10th day of february, 1763, to which the king of Portugal acceded on the fame day.

In the name of the moft holy and undivided trinity, Father, Son, and Holy Ghoft. So be it.

BE it known to all thofe to whom it fhall, or may, in any manner, belong.

It has pleafed the moft high to diffufe the fpirit of union and concord among the princes, whofe divifions had spread troubles in the four parts of the world, and to inspire them with the inclination to cause the comforts of peace to succeed to the misfortunes of a long and bloody war, which, having arisen between England and France, during the reign of the most serene and most potent prince, George the second, by the grace of God, King of Great-Britain, of glorious memory, continued under the reign of the most serene and most potent prince, George the third, his successor, and in its progress, communicated itself to Spain and Portugal: consequently, the most serene and most potent prince, George the third, by the grace of God, king of Great-Britain, France, and Ireland, Duke of Brunswick and Lunenbourg, archtreasurer and elector of the holy Roman empire; the most serene and most potent prince, Lewis the fifteenth, by the grace of God, most christian king; and the most serene and potent prince, Charles the third, by the grace of God, king of Spain and of the Indies, after having laid the foundations of peace in the preliminaries, signed at Fontainebleau the 3d of november last; and the most serene and most potent prince, Don Joseph the first, by the grace of God, king of Portugal and of the Algarves, after having acceeded thereto, determined to complete, without delay, this great and important work. For this purpose, the high contracting parties have named and appointed their respective ambassadors extraordinary and ministers plenipotentiary, viz. his sacred majesty the king of Great-Britain, the most illustrious and most excellent lord, John, duke and earl of Bedford, marquis of Tavistock, &c. his minister of state, lieutenant-general of his armies, keeper of his privy-seal, knight of the most noble order of the garter, and his ambassador extraordinary and minister plenipotentiary to his most christian majesty; his sacred majesty the most christian king, the most illustrious and most excellent lord Cæsar Gabriel de Choiseul, duke

duke of Praflin, peer of France, knight of his orders, lieutenant-general of his armies, and of the province of Britanny, councellor in all his councils, and minifter and fecretary of ftate, and of his commands and finances; his facred majefty the catholic king, the moft illuftrious and moft excellent lord, Don Jerome Grimaldi, marquis de Grimaldi, knight of the moft chriftian king's orders, gentleman of his catholic majefty's bed-chamber in employment, and his ambaffador extraordinary to his moft chriftian majefty; his facred majefty the moft faithful king, the moft illuftrious and moft excellent lord, Martin de Mello and Caftro, knight profeffed of the order of Chrift, of his moft faithful majefty's council, and his ambaffador and minifter plenipotentiary to his moft chriftian majefty.

Who, after having duly communicated to each other their full powers, in good form, copies whereof are tranfcribed at the end of the prefent treaty of peace, have agreed upon the articles, the tenor of which is as follows.

Article I. There fhall be a chriftian, univerfal, and perpetual peace, as well by fea as by land, and a fincere and conftant friendfhip fhall be re-eftablifhed between their britannic, moft chriftian, catholic, and moft faithful majefties, and between their heirs and fucceffors, kingdoms, dominions, provinces, countries, fubjects, and vaffals, of what quality or condition foever they be, without exception of places or of perfons: fo that the high contracting parties fhall give the greateft attention to maintain between themfelves and their faid dominions and fubjects, this reciprocal friendfhip and correfpondence, without permitting, on either fide, any kind of hoftilities by fea or by land to be committed, from henceforth, for any caufe, or under any pretence whatfoever, and every thing fhall be carefully avoided which might hereafter prejudice the union happily re-eftablifhed, applying themselves, on the contrary, on every occasion, to procure for each other whatever may contribute to their mutual glory, interests, and advantages, without giving any assistance or protection, directly or indirectly, to those who would cause any prejudice to either of the high contracting parties: there shall be a general oblivion of every thing that may have been done or committed before, or since, the commencement of the war, which is just ended.

II. The treaties of Westphalia of 1648; those of Madrid between the crowns of Great-Britain and Spain, of 1667 and 1670; the treaties of peace of Nimeguen of 1678 and 1679; of Ryswick of 1697; those of peace and of commerce of Utrecht of 1713; that of Baden of 1714; the treaty of the tripple alliance of the Hague of 1717; that of the quadruple alliance of London of 1718; the treaty of peace of Vienna of 1738; the definitive treaty of Aix la Chapelle of 1748; and that of Madrid, between the crowns of Great-Britain and Spain, of 1750; as well as the treaties between the crowns of Spain and Portugal, of the 13th of february 1668; of the 6th of february 1715; and of the 12th of february 1761; and that of the 11th of April 1713, between France and Portugal, with the guaranties of Great-Britain; serve as a basis and foundation to the peace, and to the present treaty: and for this purpose, they are all renewed and confirmed in the best form, as well as all the treaties in general, which subsisted between the high contracting parties before the war, as if they were inserted here word for word, so that they are to be exactly observed for the future in their whole tenor, and religiously executed on all sides, in all their points, which shall not be derogated from by the present treaty, notwithstanding all that may have been stipulated to the contrary by any of the high contracting parties: and all the said parties declare, that they will not suffer any privilege, favour, or indulgence,

gence, to subsist, contrary to the treaties above confirmed, except what shall have been agreed and stipulated by the present treaty.

III. All the prisoners made, on all sides, as well by land as by sea, and the hostages carried away, or given during the war, and to this day, shall be restored without ransom, six weeks at latest, to be computed from the day of the exchange of the ratification of the present treaty, each crown respectively paying the advances, which shall have been made for the subsistence and maintenance of their prisoners, by the sovereign of the country where they shall have been detained, according to the attested receipts and estimates and other authentic vouchers, which shall be furnished on one side and the other: and securities shall be reciprocally given for the payment of the debts which the prisoners shall have contracted in the countries where they have been detained until their entire liberty. And all the ships of war and merchant vessels, which shall have been taken since the expiration of the terms agreed upon for the cessation of hostilities by sea, shall be likewise restored, bona fide, with all their crews and cargoes: and the execution of this article shall be proceeded upon immediately after the exchange of the ratifications of this treaty.

IV. His most christian majesty renounces all pretensions which he has heretofore formed, or might form, to Nova Scotia, or Arcadia, in all its parts, and guaranties the whole of it, with all its dependencies, to the King of Great-Britain: moreover, his most christian majesty cedes, and guaranties to his said britannic majesty, in full right, Canada, with all its dependencies, as well as the island of Cape Breton, and all the other islands and coasts in the gulph and river of St. Laurence, and, in general, every thing that depends on the said countries, lands, islands and coasts, with the sovereignty, property, possession, and all rights acquired by treaty, or otherwise, which

the

the most christian king, and the crown of France, have had, till now, over the said countries, islands, lands, places, coasts, and their inhabitants, so that the most christian king cedes and makes over the whole to the said king, and to the crown of Great-Britain, and that in the most ample manner and form, without restriction, and without any liberty to depart from the said cession and guaranty, under any pretence, or to disturb Great-Britain in the possessions abovementioned. His britannic majesty, on his side, agrees to grant the liberty of the catholic religion to the inhabitants of Canada: he will consequently give the most effectual orders, that his new roman catholic subjects may profess the worship of their religion, according to the rites of the romish church, as far as the laws of Great-Britain permit. His britannic majesty further agrees, that the french inhabitants, or others who had been subjects of the most christian king in Canada, may retire with all safety and freedom wherever they shall think proper, and may sell their estates, provided it be to subjects of his britannic majesty, and bring away their effects, as well as their persons, without being restrained in their emigration, under any pretence whatsoever, except that of debts, or of criminal prosecutions: the term limited for this emigration shall be fixed to the space of eighteen months, to be computed from the day of the exchange of the ratifications of the present treaty.

V. The subjects of France shall have the liberty of fishing and drying on a part of the coasts of the island of Newfoundland, such as is specified in the 13th article of the treaty of Utrecht; which article is renewed and confirmed by the present treaty, (except what relates to the island of Cape Breton, as well as to the other islands and coasts, in the mouth and in the gulph St. Laurence) and his britannic majesty consents to leave the subjects of the most christian king

king the liberty of fishing in the gulph of St. Laurence, on condition that the subjects of France do not exercise the said fishery, but at the distance of three leagues from all the coasts belonging to Great-Britain, as well those of the continent, as those of the islands situated in the said gulph of St. Laurence. And as to what relates to the fishery on the coast of the island of Cape Breton out of the said gulph, the subjects of the most christian king shall not be permitted to exercise the said fishery, but at the distance of 15 leagues from the coasts of the island of Cape Breton; and the fishery on the coasts of Nova Scotia, or Arcadia, and every where else out of the said gulph, shall remain on the foot of former treaties.

VI. The king of Great-Britain cedes the islands of St. Pierre and Miquelon, in full right, to his most christian majesty, to serve as a shelter to the french fishermen: and his said most christian majesty engages not to fortify the said islands, to erect no buildings upon them, but merely for the convenience of the fishery, and to keep upon them a guard of 50 men only for the police.

VII. In order to re-establish peace on solid and durable foundations, and to remove for ever all subject of dispute with regard to the limits of the british and french territories on the continent of America, that, for the future, the confines between the dominions of his britannic majesty, and those of his most christian majesty, in that part of the world, shall be fixed irrevocably by a line drawn along the middle of the river Mississippi, from its source to the river Iberville, and from thence, by a line drawn along the middle of this river, and the lake Maurepas and Pontchartrain, to the sea; and for this purpose, the most christian king cedes, in full right, and guaranties to his britannic majesty, the river and port of the Mobile, and every thing which he possesses, or ought to possess, on the left side of the river Mississippi,

sippi, except the town of New Orleans, and the island
in which it is situated, which shall remain to France;
provided that the river Mississippi shall be equally
free, as well to the subjects of Great Britain, as to
those of France, in its whole breadth and length,
from its source to the sea, and expresly that part which
is between the said island of New Orleans, and the
right bank of that river, as well as the passage both
in and out of its mouth: it is futher stipulated, that
the vessels belonging to the subjects of either nation,
shall not be stopped, visited, or subjected to the payment of any duty whatsoever. The stipulations, inserted in the 4th article, in favour of the inhabitants
of Canada, shall also take place, with regard to the
inhabitants of the countries ceded by this article.

VIII. The king of Great Britain shall restore to
France the islands of Guadaloupe, of Marie Galante,
of Desirade, of Martinico, and of Belleisle; and the
fortresses of these islands shall be restored in the same
condition they were in when they were conquered by
the british arms; provided that his britannic majesty's
subjects, who shall have settled in the said islands,
or those who shall have any commercial affairs to
settle there, or in the other places restored to France
by the present treaty, shall have liberty to sell their
lands and their estates, to settle their affairs, to recover their debts, and to bring away their effects, as
well as their persons, on board vessels, which they
shall be permitted to send to the said islands, and
other places restored as above, and which shall serve
for this use only, without being restrained on account
of their religion, or under any other pretence whatsoever, except that of debts, or of criminal prosecutions: and for this purpose, the term of 18 months
is allowed to his britannic majesty's subjects, to be
computed from the day of the exchange of the ratifications of the present treaty; but as the liberty
granted to his britannic majesty's subjects, to bring
away

away their perfons and their effects, in veffels of their nation, may be liable to abufes, if precautions were not taken to prevent them; it has been exprefsly agreed between his britannic majefty and his moft chriftian majefty, that the number of englifh veffels, which fhall have leave to go to the faid iflands and places reftored France, fhall be limited, as well as the number of tons of each one; that they fhall go in ballaft; fhall fet fail at a fixed time; and fhall make one voyage only; all the effects belonging to the Englifh being to be embarked at the fame time. It has been further agreed, that his moft chriftian majefty fhall caufe the neceffary paffports to be given to the faid veffels; that for the greater fecurity, it fhall be allowed to place two french clerks, or guards, in each of the faid veffels, which fhall be vifited in the landing places and ports of the faid iflands and places reftored to France, and that the merchandife, which fhall be found therein fhall be confifcated.

IX. The moft chriftian king cedes and guaranties to his britannic majefty, in full right, the iflands of Grenada, and of the Grenadines, with the fame ftipulations in favour of the inhabitants of this colony, inferted in the IVth article for thofe of Canada; and the partition of the iflands, called neutral, is agreed and fixed, fo that thofe of St. Vincent, Dominica, and Tobago, fhall remain in full right to Great-Britain, and that of St. Lucia fhall be delivered to France, to enjoy the fame likewife in full right; and the high contracting parties guaranty the partition fo ftipulated.

X. His britannic majefty fhall reftore to France the ifland of Goree in the condition it was in when conquered: and his moft chriftian majefty cedes, in full right, and guaranties to the king of Great Britain, the river Senegal, with the forts and factories of St. Lewis, Podor, and Galam, and with all the rights and dependencies of the faid river Senegal.

XI. In

XI. In the East-Indies, Great Britain shall restore to France, in the condition they are now in, the different factories which that crown possessed, as well on the coast of Coromandel and Orixa, as on that of Malabar, as also in Bengal, at the beginning of the year 1749. And his most christian majesty renounces all pretension to the acquisitions which he had made on the coast of Coromandel and Orixa, since the said beginning of the year 1749. His most christian majesty shall restore, on his side, all that he may have conquered from Great-Britain, in the East-Indies, during the present war; and will expresly cause Nattal and Tapanoully, in the island of Sumatra, to be restored; he engages further, not to erect fortifications, or to keep troops, in any part of the dominions of the Subah of Bengal. And in order to preserve future peace on the coast of Coromandel and Orixa, the english and french shall acknowledge Mahomet Ally Khan for the lawful nabob of the Carnatic, and Salabat Jing for lawful subah of the Decan; and both parties shall renounce all demands and pretensions of satisfaction with which they might charge each other, or their indian allies, for the depredations, or pillage, committed on the one side, or on the other, during the war.

XII. The island of Minorca shall be restored to his britannic majesty, as well as fort St. Philip, in the same condition they were in, when conquered by the arms of the most christian king; and with the artillery which was there, when the said island and the said fort were taken.

XIII. The town and port of Dunkirk shall be put into the state fixed by the last treaty of Aix-la-Chapelle, and by former treaties. The Cunette shall be destroyed immediately after the exchange of the ratifications of the present treaty, as well as the forts and batteries which defend the entrance on the side of the sea; and provision shall be made, at the same time,

time, for the wholesomeness of the air, and for the health of the inhabitants, by some other means, to the satisfaction of the king of Great Britain.

XIV. France shall restore all the countries belonging to the electorate of Hanover, to the Landgrave of Hesse, to the duke of Brunswick, and to the count of la Lippe Buckebourg, which are, or shall be occupied by his most christian majesty's arms: the fortresses of these different countries shall be restored in the same condition they were in when conquered by the french arms: and the pieces of artillery, which shall have been carried elsewhere, shall be replaced by the same number, of the same bore, weight and metal.

XV. In case the stipulations, contained in the XIIIth article of the preliminaries, should not be completed at the time of the signature of the present treaty, as well with regard to to the evacuations to be made by the armies of France of the fortresses of Cleves, Wezel, Gueldres, and of all the countries belonging to the king of Prussia, as with regard to the evacuations to be made by the british and french armies of the countries which they occupy in Westphalia, Lower Saxony, on the Lower Rhine, the Upper Rhine, and in all the empire, and to the retreat of the troops into the dominions of their respective sovereigns; their britannic and most christian majesties promise to proceed, bona fide, with all the dispatch the case will permit of, to the said evacuations, the entire completion whereof they stipulate before the 15th of march next, or sooner if it can be done; and their britannic and most christian majesties further engage, and promise to each other, not to furnish any succours of any kind to their respective allies, who shall continue engaged in the war in Germany.

XVI. The decision of the prizes made, in the time of peace, by the subjects of Great-Britain, on the spaniards, shall be referred to the courts of justice of the admiralty of Great Britain, conformably to the rules established among all nations, so that the validity of the said prizes, between the british and spanish nations, shall be decided and judged, according to the law of nations, and according to the treaties, in the courts of justice of the nation who shall have made the capture.

XVII. His britannic majesty shall cause to be demolished all the fortifications which his subjects shall have erected on the bay of Honduras, and other places of the territory of Spain in that part of the world, four months after the ratification of the present treaty: and his catholic majesty shall not permit his britannic majesty's subjects, or their workmen, to be disturbed, or molested, under any pretence whatsoever, in the said places, in their occupation of cutting, loading, and carrying away logwood. And for this purpose, they may build without hindrance, and occupy without interruption, the houses and magazines which are necessary for them, for their families, and for their effects: and his catholic majesty assures to them, by this article, the full enjoyment of those advantages and powers on the spanish coasts and territories, as above stipulated, immediately after the ratifications of the present treaty.

XVIII. His catholic majesty desists, as well for himself, as for his successors, from all pretensions which he may have formed, in favour of the Guipuscoans, and other his subjects, to the right of fishing in the neighbourhood of the island of Newfoundland.

XIX. The king of Great Britain shall restore to Spain all the territory which he has conquered in the island of Cuba, with the fortress of the Havannah; and its fortress, as well as all the other fortresses of the said island, shall be restored in the same condition they were in when conquered by his britannic majesty's arms; provided that his britannic majesty's subjects, who shall have settled in the said island, restored

stored to Spain by the present treaty, or those who shall have any commercial affairs to settle there, shall have liberty to sell their lands, and their estates, to settle their affairs, to recover their debts, and to bring away their effects, as well as their persons, on board vessels which they shall be permitted to send to the said island, restored as above, and which shall serve for that use only, without being restrained on account of their religion, or under any other pretence whatsoever, except that of debts, or of criminal prosecutions: and for this purpose, the term of eighteen months is allowed to his britannic majesty's subjects, to be computed from the day of the exchange of the ratifications of the present treaty: but as the liberty granted to his britannic majesty's subjects, to bring away their persons and effects, in vessels of their nation, may be liable to abuses, if precautions were not taken to prevent them; it has been expressly agreed between his britannic majesty and his catholic majesty, that the number of english vessels, which shall have leave to go to the island restored to spain, shall be limited, as well as the number of tons of each one; that they shall go in ballast; shall set sail at a fixed time; and shall make one voyage only; all the effects belonging to the english being to be embarked at the same time: it has been further agreed, that his catholic majesty shall cause the necessary passports to be given to the said vesseffels; that, for the greater security, it shall be allowed to place two spanish clerks, or guards, in each of the said vessels, which shall be visited in the landing-places, and ports of the said island restored to Spain, and that the merchandize, which shall be found therein, shall be confiscated.

XX. In consequence of the restitution stipulated in the preceding article, his catholic majesty cedes and guaranties, in full right, to his britannic majesty,

jesty, Florida, with fort St. Augustin, and the bay of Pensacola, as well as all that Spain possesses on the continent of North-America, to the east, or to the south-east, of the river Mississipppi. And in general, every thing that depends on the said countries, and lands, with the sovereignty, property, possession, and all rights, acquired by treaties or otherwise, which the catholic king, and the crown of Spain, have had, till now, over the said countries, lands, places, and their inhabitants; so that the catholic king cedes and makes over the whole to the said king, and to the crown of Great-Britain, and that in the most ample manner and form. His britannic majesty agrees, on his side, to grant to the inhabitants of the countries, above ceded, the liberty of the catholic religion: he will consequently give the most express and the most effectual orders, that his new Roman catholic subjects may profess the worship of their religion, according to the rites of the romish church, as far as the laws of Great-Britain permit: his britannic majesty further agrees, that the spanish inhabitants, or others, who had been subjects of the catholic king in the said countries, may retire, with all safety and freedom, wherever they think proper; and may sell their estates, provided it be to his britannic majesty's subjects, and bring away their effects, as well as their persons, without being restrained in their emigrations, under any pretence whatsoever, except that of debts, or of criminal prosecutions: the term, limited for this emigration, being fixed to the space of eighteen months, to be computed from the day of the exchange of the ratifications of the present treaty. It is moreover stipulated, that his catholic majesty shall have power to cause all the effects, that may belong to him, to be brought away, whether it be artillery, or other things.

XXI.

XXI. The french and spanish troops shall evacuate all the territories, lands, towns, places, and castles, of his most faithful majesty, in Europe, without any reserve, which shall have been conquered by the armies of France and Spain, and shall restore them in the same condition they were in when conquered, with the same artillery and ammunition which were found there: and with regard to the portuguese colonies in America, Africa, or in the East-Indies, if any change shall have happened there, all things shall be restored on the same footing they were in, and conformable to the preceding treaties which subsisted between the courts of France, Spain, and Portugal, before the present war.

XXII. All the papers, letters, documents, and archives, which were found in the countries, territories, towns, and places, that are restored, and those belonging to the countries ceded, shall be, respectively, and *bona fide*, delivered, or furnished at the same time, if possible, that possession is taken, or, at latest, four months after the exchange of the ratifications of the present treaty, in whatever places the said papers or documents may be found.

XXIII. All the countries and territories, which may have been conquered, in whatsoever part of the world, by the arms of their britannic and most faithful majesties, as well as by those of their most christian and catholic majesties, which are not included in the present treaty, either under the title of cessions, or under the title of restitutions, shall be restored without difficulty, and without requiring any compensation.

XXIV. As it is necessary to assign a fixed epoch for the restitutions, and the evacuations, to be made by each of the high contracting parties; it is agreed, that the british and french troops shall complete, before the fifteenth of march next, all that shall remain to be executed of the XIIth and XIIIth articles of the preliminaries, signed the third day of november last, with regard to the evacuation to be made in the empire, or elsewhere. The island of Belleisle shall be evacuated six weeks after the exchange of the ratifications of the present treaty, or sooner if it can be done. Guadaloupe, Desirade, Mariegalante, Martinico, and St. Lucia, three months after the exchange of the ratifications of the present treaty, or sooner if it can be done. Great Britain shall likewise, at the end of three months after the exchange of the ratifications of the present treaty, or sooner if it can be done, enter into possession of the river and port of the Mobile, and of all that is to form the limits of the territory of Great-Britain, on the side of the river Mississippi, as they are specified in the VIIth article. The island of Goree shall be evacuated by Great-Britain, three months after the exchange of the ratifications of the present treaty; and the island of Minorca, by France, at the same epoch, or sooner if it can be done: and according to the conditions of the VIth article, France shall likewise enter into possession of the islands of St. Peter, and of Miquelon, at the end of three months after the exchange of the ratifications of the present treaty. The factories in the East-Indies shall be restored six months after the exchange of the ratifications of the present treaty, or sooner if it can be done. The fortress of the Havannah, with all that has been conquered in the island of Cuba, shall be restored three months after the exchange of the ratifications of the present treaty, or sooner if it can be done: and, at the same time, Great-Britain shall enter into possession of the country ceded by Spain, according to the XXth article. All the places and countries of his most faithful majesty, in Europe, shall be restored immediately after the exchange of the

the ratifications of the present treaty; and the portuguese colonies, which may have been conquered, shall be restored in the space of three months in the West-Indies, and of six months in the East-Indies, after the exchange of the ratifications of the present treaty, or sooner if it can be done. All the fortresses, the restitution whereof is stipulated above, shall be restored, with the artillery and ammunition which were found there at the time of the conquest. In consequence whereof, the necessary orders shall be sent by each of the high contracting parties, with reciprocal passports for the ships that shall carry them, immediately after the exchange of the ratifications of the present treaty.

XXV. His britannic majesty, as elector of Brunswick Lunenbourg, as well for himself, as for his heirs and successors, and all the dominions and possessions of his said majesty in Germany, are included and guarantied by the present treaty of peace.

XXVI. Their sacred britannic, most christian, catholic, and most faithful majesties, promise to observe, sincerely and *bona fide*, all the articles contained and settled in the present treaty; and they will not suffer the same to be infringed, directly or indirectly, by their respective subjects; and the said high contracting parties, generally and reciprocally, guaranty to each other all the stipulations of the present treaty.

XXVII. The solemn ratifications of the present treaty, expedited in good and due form, shall be exchanged in this city of Paris, between the high contracting parties, in the space of a month, or sooner if possible, to be computed from the day of the signature of the present treaty.

In witness whereof, we the underwritten, their ambassadors extraordinary, and ministers plenipotentiary, have signed with our hand, in their name, and in virtue of our full powers, the present definitive treaty, and have caused the seal of our arms to be put thereto.

Done at Paris the tenth of February, 1763.

BEDFORD, C. P. S.
(L. S.)

CHISEUL, DUC DE PRASLIN.
(L. S.)

EL MARQUIS DE GRIMALDI.
(L. S.)

ARTICLE I.

"SOME of the titles made use of by the contracting powers, either in the full powers, and other acts, during the course of the negociation, or in the preamble of the present treaty, not being generally acknowledged; it has been agreed, that no prejudice shall ever result therefrom to any of the said contracting parties, and that the titles taken or omitted, on either side, on occasion of the said negociation, and of the present treaty, shall not be cited, or quoted as a precedent.

" II. It has been agreed and determined, that the french language made use of in all the copies of the present treaty, shall not become an example, which may be alledged, or made a precedent of, or prejudice, in any manner, any of the contracting powers; and that they shall conform themselves, for the future, to what has been observed, and ought to be observed, with regard to, and on the part of powers, who are used, and have a right, to give and to receive
copies

copies of like treaties in another language than french; the present treaty having still the same force and effect, as if the aforesaid custom had been therein observed.

"III. Though the king of Portugal has not signed the present definitive treaty, their britannic, most christian, and catholic majesties, acknowledge, nevertheless, that his most faithful majesty is formally included therein as a contracting party, and as if he had expresly signed the said treaty: consequently their britannic, most christian, and catholic majesties, respectively, and conjointly, promise to his most faithful majesty, in the most express and most binding manner, the execution of all and every the clauses, contained in the said treaty, on his act of accession."

"The present separate articles shall have the same force as if they were inserted in the treaty."

"In witness whereof, we the underwritten ambassadors extraordinary, and ministers plenipotentiary of their britannic, most christian, and catholic majesties, have signed the present separate articles, and have caused the seal of our arms to be put thereto."

Done at Paris the 10th of February, 1763.

BEDFORD, C. P. S.
(L. S.)

CHOISEUL, DUC DE PRASLIN.
(L. S.)

EL MARQUIS DE GRIMALDI.
(L. S.)

His Britannic Majesty's full Power.

GEORGE R.

GEORGE the third, by the grace of God, king of Great-Britain, France, and Ireland, defender of the faith, duke of Brunswick and Lunenburg, arch-treasurer, and prince elector of the Holy Roman Empire, &c. To all and singular to whom these presents shall come, greeting. Whereas, in order to perfect the peace between us and our good brother the most faithful king, on the one part, and our good brothers the most christian and catholic kings, on the other, which has been happily begun by the preliminary articles already signed at Fontainebleau the third of this month, and to bring the same to the desired end, we have thought proper to invest some fit person with full authority, on our part; know ye, that we, having most entire confidence in the fidelity, judgment, skill, and ability in managing affairs of the greatest consequence, of our right trusty and right entirely beloved cousin and councillor, John duke and earl of Bedford, marquess of Tavistock, baron Russel of Cheneys, baron Russel of Thornhaugh, and baron Howland of Streatheam, lieutenant-general of our forces, keeper of our privy-seal, lieutenant and custos rotulorum of the counties of Bedford and Devon, knight of our most noble order of the garter, and our ambassador extraordinary and plenipotentiary to our good brother the most christian king, have nominated, made, constituted, and appointed, as by these presents we do nominate, make, constitute, and appoint him, our true, certain, and undoubted minister, commissary, deputy, procurator, and plenipotentiary, giving to him all and all manner of power, faculty, and authority, as well as

our

our general and special command (yet so as that the general do not derogate from the special, or on the contrary) for us and in our name, to meet and confer, as well singly and separately, as jointly and in a body, with the ambassadors, commissaries, deputies, and plenipotentiaries of the princes whom it may concern, vested with sufficient power and authority for that purpose, and with them to agree upon, treat, consult, and conclude concerning the re-establishing, as soon as may be, a firm and lasting peace, and sincere friendship and concord; and whatever shall be so agreed and concluded, for us and in our name, to sign, and to make a treaty or treaties, on what shall have been so agreed and concluded, and to transact every thing else that may belong to the happy completion of the aforesaid work, in as ample a manner and form, and with the same force and effect, as we ourselves, if we were present, could do and perform; engaging and promising, on our royal word, that we will approve, ratify, and accept in the best manner, whatever shall happen to be transacted and concluded by our said plenipotentiary, and that we will never suffer any person to infringe or act contrary to the same, either in the whole or in part. In witness and confirmation whereof, we have caused our great seal of Great-Britain to be affixed to these presents, signed with our royal hand. Given at our palace at St. James's the 12th day of november, 1762, in the third year of our reign.

His Most Christian Majesty's full power.

LEWIS, by the grace of God, king of France and Navarre, to all who shall see these presents, greeting. Whereas the prelimininaris, signed at Fontainebleau the third of november of the last year, laid the foundation of the peace re-established between

us

us and our most dear and most beloved good brother
and cousin the king of Spain, on the one part, and
our most dear and most beloved good brother the
king of Great-Britain, and our most dear and most
beloved good brother and cousin the king of Portugal, on the other, we have had nothing more at
heart, since that happy epoch, than to consolidate
and strengthen, in the most lasting manner, so salutary and so important a work, by a solemn and
definitive treaty between us and the said powers.
For these causes, and other good considerations us
thereunto moving, we trusting entirely in the capacity and experience, zeal and fidelity for our service,
of our most dear and well-beloved cousin, Cæsar Gabriel de Choiseul, duke of Praslin, peer of France,
knight of our orders, lieutenant-general of our
forces, and of the province of Brittany, councillor
in all our councils, minister and secretary of state,
and of our commands and finances, we have named,
appointed, and deputed him, and by these presents,
signed with our hand, do name, appoint, and de-
pute him, our minister plenipotentiary, giving him
full and absolute power to act in that quality, and
to confer, negociate, treat, and agree, jointly with
the minister plenipotentiary of our most dear and
most beloved good brother the king of Great-Britain, the minister plenipotentiary of our most dear
and most beloved good brother and cousin the king
of Spain, and the minister plenipotentiary of our
most dear and most beloved good brother and cousin the king of Portugal, vested with full powers, in
good form, to agree, conclude, and sign such articles, conditions, conventions, declarations, definitive
treaty, accessions, and other acts whatsoever, that he
shall judge proper for securing and strengthening the
great work of peace, the whole with the same lati-
tude and authority that we ourselves might do, if

we

we were there in person, even though there should be something which might require a more special order than what is contained in these presents, promising, on the faith and word of a king, to approve, keep firm, and stable for ever, to fulfil and execute punctually, all that our said cousin, the duke de Praslin, shall have stipulated, promised, and signed in virtue of the present full power, without ever acting contrary thereto, or permitting any thing contrary thereto, for any cause, or under any pretence whatsoever, as also to cause our letters of ratification to be expedited in good form, and to cause them to be delivered, in order to be exchanged within the time that shall be agreed upon. For such is our pleasure. In witness whereof, we have caused our seal to be put to these presents. Given at Versailles, the 7th day of the month of February, in the year of grace 1763, and of our reign the forty-eighth. Signed Lewis, and on the fold, By the King, the duke de Choiseul. Sealed with the great seal of yellow wax.

His Catholic Majesty's full power.

DON Carlos, by the grace of God, king of Castille, of Leon, of Arragon, of the Two Sicilies, of Jerusalem, of Navarre, of Granada, of Toledo, of Valencia, of Galicia, of Majorca, of Seville, of Sardinia, of Cordova, of Corsica, of Murcia, of Jaen, of the Algarves, of Algecira, of Gibraltar, of the Canary Islands, of the East and West Indies, Islands and Continent, of the Ocean, archduke of Austria, duke of Burgundy, of Brabant and Milan, count of Hapsburg, of Flanders, of Tirol, and Barcelona; lord of Biscay and of Molino, &c. Whereas preliminaries of a solid and lasting peace, between this crown and that of France on the one

part

part, and that of England and Portugal on the other, were concluded and signed in the royal residence of Fontainebleau, the third of november of the present year, and the respective ratifications thereof exchanged on the 22d of the same month, by ministers authorized for that purpose, wherein it is promised, that a definitive treaty should be forthwith entered upon, having established and regulated the chief points upon which it is to turn: and whereas in the same manner as I granted to you, Don Jerome Grimaldi, marquis de Grimaldi, knight of the order of the Holy Ghost, gentleman of my bedchamber with employment, and my ambassador extraordinary to the most christian king, my full power to treat, adjust, and sign the before-mentioned preliminaries, it is necessary to grant the same to you, or to some other, to treat, adjust, and sign the promised definitive treaty of peace as aforesaid: therefore, as you the said Don Jerome Grimaldi, marquis de Grimaldi, are at the convenient place, and as I have every day fresh motives, from your approved fidelity and zeal, capacity and prudence, to entrust to you this, and other like concerns of my crown, I have appointed you my minister plenipotentiary, and granted to you my full power, to the end that, in my name, and representing my person, you may treat, regulate, settle, and sign the said definitive treaty of peace between my crown and that of France on the one part, that of England and that of Portugal on the other, with the ministers who shall be equally and specifically authorised by their respective sovereigns for the same purpose; acknowledging, as I do from this time acknowledge, as accepted and ratified, whatever you shall so treat, conclude, and sign; promising, on my royal word, that I will observe and fulfil the same, will cause it to be observed and fulfilled, as if it had been treated, concluded, and signed by myself. In

witness

witness whereof, I have caused these presents to be dispatched, signed by my hand, sealed with my privy seal, and counter-signed by my underwritten counsellor of state, and first secretary for the department of state and of war. Buen Retiro, the tenth of december, 1762.

(Signed)   I THE KING.
(And lower)   RICHARD WALL.

Declaration of His Most Christian Majesty's plenipotentiary, with regard to the debts due to the canadians.

THE king of Great-Britain having desired, that the payment of the letters of exchange and bills, which had been delivered to the canadians for the necessaries furnished to the french troops, should be secured, his most christian majesty, entirely disposed to render to every one that justice which is legally due to them, has declared, and does declare, that the said bills, and letters of exchange, shall be punctually paid, agreeably to a liquidation made in a convenient time, according to the distance of the places, and to what shall be possible, taking care, however, that the bills and letters of exchange, which the french subjects may have at the time of this declaration, be not confounded with the bills and letters of exchange, which are in the possession of the new subjects of the king of Great-Britain.

In witness whereof, we the underwritten minister of his most christian majesty, duly authorized for this purpose, have signed the present declaration, and caused the seal of our arms to be put thereto.

Done at Paris, the 10th of february, 1763.

     CHOISEUL, DUC DE PRASLIN.
          (L. S.)

Declaration of his britannic majesty's ambassador extraordinary and plenipotentiary, with regard to the limits of Bengal in the East-Indies.

"WE the underwritten ambassador extraordinary and plenipotentiary of the king of Great-Britain, in order to prevent all subject of dispute on account of the limits of the dominions of the subah of Bengal, as well as of the coast of Coromandel and Orixa, declare, in the name and by order of his said britannic majesty, that the said dominions of the subah of Bengal, shall be reputed not to extend farther than Yanaon exclusively, and that Yanaon shall be considered as included in the north part of the coast of Coromandel or Orixa."

" In witness whereof, we the underwritten minister plenipotentiary of his majesty the king of Great-Britain, have signed the present declaration, and have caused the seal of our arms to be put thereto."

" Done at Paris the 10th of february, 1763."

BEDFORD, C. P. S.
(L. S.)

Accession of His Most Faithful Majesty.

In the name of the Most Holy and Undivided Trinity, Father, Son, and Holy Ghost.

So be it.

"BE it known to all those to whom it shall, or may belong; the ambassadors and plenipotentiaries of his britannic majesty, of his most christian majesty, and of his catholic majesty, having concluded and signed at Paris, the 10th of february
of

of this year, a definitive treaty of peace, and separate articles, the tenor of which is as follows.

[Fiat insertio.]

" And the said ambassadors and plenipotentiaries having, in a friendly manner, invited the ambassador and minister plenipotentiary of his most faithful majesty to accede thereto, in the name of his said majesty; the underwritten ministers plenipotentiary, viz. On the part of the most serene and most potent prince, George the third, by the grace of God, king of Great-Britain, France, and Ireland, duke of Brunswick and Lunenbourg, arch-treasurer and elector of the holy roman empire, the most illustrious and most excellent lord, John, duke and earl of Bedford, marquis of Taviftock, &c. minister of state of the king of Great-Britain, lieutenant-general of his forces, keeper of his privy-seal, knight of the most noble order of the garter, and his ambassador extraordinary and plenipotentiary to his most christian majesty; and on the part of the most serene and most potent prince, Don Joseph the first, by the grace of God, king of Portugal and of the Algarves, the most illustrious and most excellent lord, Martin de Mello and Castro, knight professed of the order of Christ, of his most faithful majesty's council, and his ambassador and minister plenipotentiary to his most christian majesty, in virtue of their full powers, which they have communicated to each other, and of which copies shall be added at the end of the present act, have agreed upon what follows, viz. his most faithful majesty, de-desiring most sincerely to concur in the speedy re-establishment of peace, accedes, in virtue of the present act, to the said definitive treaty and separate articles, as they are above transcribed, without any reserve or exception, in the firm confidence that every thing that is promised to his said majesty, will be *bona fide*

fide fulfilled, declaring at the same time, and promising to fulfil, with equal fidelity, all the articles, clauses, and conditions, which concern him. On his side, his britannic majesty accepts the present accession of his most faithful majesty, and promises likewise to fulfil, without any reserve or exception, all the articles, clauses, and conditions, contained in the said definitive treaty and separate articles above inserted. The ratifications of the present treaty shall be exchanged in the space of one month, to be computed from this day, or sooner if it can be done."

"In witness whereof, we, ambassadors and ministers plenipotentiary of his britannic majesty, and of his most faithful majesty, have signed the present act, and have caused the seal of our arms to be put thereto."

"Done at Paris, the 10th of February, 1763."

BEDFORD, C. P. S.
(L. S.)
De MELLO et CASTRO.
(L. S.)

His Most Faithful Majesty's full power.

"DON Joseph, by the grace of God king of Portugal, and of the Algarves, on this side the sea, and on that side in Africa, lord of Guinea, and of the conquests, navigation, commerce of Ethiopia, Arabia, Persia, and India, &c. I make known to those who shall see these my letters patent, that desiring nothing more than to see the flame of war, which has raged so many years in all Europe, extinguished, and to co-operate (as far as depends upon me) towards its being succeeded by a just peace, established upon solid principles: and being informed, that

that great part of the belligerent powers entertain the same pacific difpofitions, I am to nominate a perfon, to affift, in my name, at the affemblies and conferences to be held upon this important bufinefs, who, by his nobility, prudence, and dexterity, is worthy of my confidence: whereas thefe feveral qualities concur in Martin de Mello de Caftro, of my council, and my envoy extraordinary and plenipotentiary to the court of London; and as from the experience I have, that he has always ferved me to my fatisfaction, in every thing I have charged him with, relying, that I fhall, from henceforward, have frefh caufe for the confidence I have placed in him, I nominate and conftitute him my ambaffador and plenipotentiary, in order that he may, as fuch, affift, in my name, at any congrefs, affemblies, or conferences, as well public as private, in which the bufinefs of pacification may be treated: negociating and agreeing with the ambaffadors and plenipotentiaries of the faid belligerent powers, whatever may relate to the faid peace; and concluding what he fhall negociate between me and any belligerent kings and princes, under the conditions he fhall ftipulate in my royal name: therefore, for the above purpofes, I grant him all the full powers and authority, general and fpecial, which may be neceffary; and I promife, upon the faith and word of a king, that I will acknowledge to be firm and valid, and will ratify, within the time agreed upon, whatever fhall be contracted and ftipulated by my faid ambaffador and plenipotentiary, with the aforefaid ambaffadors and minifters of the belligerent kings and princes, who fhall be furnifhed by them with equal powers: in witnefs whereof, I have ordered thefe prefents to be made out, figned by myfelf, fealed with the feal of my arms thereunto affixed, and counter-figned by my fecretary and minifter of ftate for foreign affairs and war. Given at the palace of our lady of Ajuda, the eighteenth day of september, of the year from the birth of our lord Jesus Christ, 1762."

THE KING.

Locus Sigilli pendentis.   Don Lewis da Cunha.

"Letters patent whereby your majesty is pleased to nominate Martin de Mello de Castro, to be your ambassador and plenipotentiary for the negociation and conclusion of peace, in the form above set forth."

"For your majesty's inspection."

Declaration of His Most Faithful Majesty's ambassador and minister plenipotentiary, with regard to the alternating with Great-Britain and France.

"WHEREAS, on the conclusion of the negociation of the definitive treaty, signed at Paris this 10th day of february, a difficulty arose as to the order of signing which might have retarded the conclusion of the said treaty, we the underwritten, ambassador and minister plenipotentiary of his most faithful majesty, declare, that the alternative observed, on the part of the king of Great-Britain, and the most christian king, with the most faithful king, in the act of accession of the court of Portugal, was granted by their britannic and most christian majesties, solely with a view to accelerate the conclusion of the definitive treaty, and, by that means, the more speedily to consolidate so important and so salutary a work; and that this complaisance of their britannic and most christian majesties shall not be made any precedent of for the future; the court of Portugal shall not alledge it as an example in their favour; shall derive therefrom no right, title, or pretension,

sion, for any cause, or under any pretence whatsoever."

" In witness whereof, we, ambassador and minister plenipotentiary of his most faithful majesty, duly authorized for this purpose, have signed the present declaration, and have caused the seal of our arms to be put thereto."

" Done at Paris, the 10th of february, 1763."

MARTIN de MELLO et CASTRO.
(L. S.)

THE END.

www.ingramcontent.com/pod-product-compliance
Lightning Source LLC
Chambersburg PA
CBHW030603300426
44111CB00009B/1090